Kaputt

»»»»»»»»» «««««««««

Curzio Malaparte

Kaputt

TRANSLATED FROM THE ITALIAN BY

CESARE FOLIGNO

NORTHWESTERN UNIVERSITY PRESS

EVANSTON, ILLINOIS

»»»»»»»»»» «««««««««

Northwestern University Press
Evanston, Illinois 60208-4210

This translation of *Kaputt* first published 1946 by E. P. Dutton & Co., Inc.
Published 1982 by The Marlboro Press. Northwestern University Press edition
published 1995. All rights reserved.

Printed in the United States of America

ISBN 0-8101-1341-4

Library of Congress Cataloging-in-Publication Data

Malaparte, Curzio, 1898–1957.
    [Kaputt. English]
    Kaputt / Curzio Malaparte ; translated from the Italian by Cesare
Foligno.
        p.   cm. — (European classics)
    Originally published: New York : Dutton, 1946.
    ISBN 0-8101-1341-4 (pbk. : alk. paper)
    1. Malaparte, Curzio, 1898–1957. 2. World War, 1939–1945
—Personal narratives, Italian. 3. War correspondents—Italy
—Biography. I. Foligno, Cesare, b. 1878 II. Title. III. Series:
European classics (Evanston, Ill.)
D811.M2843   1995
940.54'8145—dc20   95-36162
                                               CIP

The paper used in this publication meets the minimum requirements of the
American National Standard for Information Sciences—Permanence of Paper
for Printed Library Materials, ANSI Z39.48-1984.

CONTENTS

CONTENTS

PART FOUR

THE BIRDS

PART FIVE

THE REINDEER

PART SIX

THE FLIES

The History of a Manuscript

THE MANUSCRIPT of Kaputt *has a tale of its own, and it seems to me that the secret history of the manuscript is the most appropriate preface for the book. I began* Kaputt *in the summer of 1941—at the beginning of the German war against Russia—in the village of Pestchanka in the Ukraine, in the home of a Russian peasant, Roman Suchena. Every morning I sat in the garden under an acacia tree and worked while Suchena, squatting on the ground by the pig sty, sharpened his scythe or chopped beets and cabbages for the pigs. The garden adjoined the House of the Soviets which was occupied at this time by a detachment of Hitler's SS men. Whenever an SS trooper came near the hedge, Suchena gave a warning cough.*

The thatched-roof hut with its mud and straw walls plastered with ox dung was small and clean; its only luxuries were a radio, a gramophone and a small library of the complete works of Pushkin and Gogol. This was the home of an old peasant whom three five-year plans and collective farming had freed from the bonds of misery, ignorance and filth. The son of Roman Suchena, a Communist party member, had been a mechanic on the Voroshilov Collective Farm in Pestchanka. He and his wife had worked on the same collective and had followed the Soviet Army with their tractor. She was a silent and gentle girl; in the evenings, when work in the small field and in the garden was done, she sat under a tree and read Pushkin's Eugene Onegin *from the special State edition published in Kharkov on the centenary of the great poet's death. She reminded me of Croce's two oldest daughters, Elena and Alda, who used to sit under a heavily laden apple tree in the garden of their summer home in Meana and read Herodotus in the original.*

When I had to visit the front, only a couple of miles from Pestchanka, I entrusted the manuscript of Kaputt *to my friend Roman*

Suchena who hid it in a hole in the wall of the pig sty. When the Gestapo came at last to arrest and expel me from the Ukraine because of the sensation caused by my war dispatches in the Corriere della Sera, *Suchena's daughter-in-law sewed the manuscript into the lining of my uniform. I will always be grateful to Suchena and his young daughter-in-law for helping me to save my dangerous manuscript from the hands of the Gestapo.*

I resumed work on Kaputt *during my stay in Poland and while on the Smolensk front, in January and February of 1942. When I left Poland for Finland, I carried the pages of the manuscript hidden in the lining of my sheepskin coat. I finished the book, except for the last chapter, during the two years spent in Finland. In the fall of 1942 I returned to Italy on sick leave after a serious illness I had contracted on the Petsamo front in Lapland. At the Templehof Air Field, near Berlin, all passengers were searched by the Gestapo. Fortunately I had not a single page of* Kaputt *on me. Before leaving Finland I had divided the manuscript into three parts; I gave one part to the Spanish Minister in Helsinki, Count Augustin de Foxa, who was leaving his post to return to the Foreign Ministry in Madrid; I gave another part to the Secretary of the Romanian Legation in Helsinki, Prince Dinu Cantemir, who was leaving to assume a new post with the Romanian Legation in Lisbon; and I gave the third part to the press attaché of the Romanian Legation in the Finnish capital, Titu Michailescu, who was returning to Bucharest. After a long odyssey the three parts of the manuscript finally reached Italy, where I hid them in the wall surrounding the woods of my house on Capri, facing the Faraglioni reefs.*

My friends de Foxa, Cantemir and Michailescu know how deeply I am indebted to them. Some day I hope to return to Berlin to thank my German friends whose names I still dare not mention, for preserving for several months, at the gravest risk to themselves, the chapters of Kaputt *that I wrote in Berlin.*

In 1943 I was in Finland and, as soon as I heard the news of Mussolini's fall, I flew back to Italy with the manuscript of the final chapters concealed in the double soles of my shoes. Two days after my arrival in Rome, on July 31, I was arrested because I had publicly declared that the German offensive against Italy was imminent and had blamed Badoglio for not taking active steps to meet the danger.

I was not even given time to change my shoes, but was sent just as I was, to the prison of Regina Coeli, with which I had become so familiar during the preceding years. The happy fact that I and my manuscript were released from prison is due to the quick intervention of Ambassador Rocco, then Minister of Popular Culture and later Ambassador at Ankara, of General Castellano who met with the Allies to discuss Armistice terms, of Minister Pietromarchi, and of Counselor of the Legation Rulli, then chief of the foreign press section. Once out of prison, I left Rome and sought refuge on Capri where I awaited the arrival of the Allies and where in September, 1943, I finished the last chapter of Kaputt.

Kaputt is a horribly gay and gruesome book. Its gruesome gaiety is the most extraordinary spectacle that I have witnessed in the debacle of Europe in the war years. Among the characters in this book War is of secondary importance. I am tempted to say that it serves only as a pretext, but pretexts inevitably belong to the sphere of Destiny. So in Kaputt, War is Destiny. It does not appear on the scene in any other way. War is not so much a protagonist as a spectator, in the same sense that a landscape is a spectator. War is the objective landscape of this book. The chief character is Kaputt, the gay and gruesome monster. Nothing can convey better than this hard, mysterious German word Kaputt—which literally means, "broken, finished, gone to pieces, gone to ruin," the sense of what we are, of what Europe is—a pile of rubble. But I prefer this Kaputt Europe to the Europe of yesterday—and of twenty or thirty years ago. I prefer starting anew, rather than accepting everything as if it were an immutable heritage. Let us hope that the new era will really be new and that writers will enjoy liberty and respect, because Italian literature needs respect as much as it needs liberty. I say "let us hope" not because I lack faith in liberty and its benefits —I belong to that group of people who have suffered imprisonment

7

and deportation to the Island of Lipari for their freedom of spirit and their contribution to the cause of liberty—but because we all know how difficult it is in Italy and throughout large sections of Europe to be a human being, and how dangerous it is to be a writer.

May the new era be an era of liberty and respect for everyone—including writers! Only through liberty and respect for culture can Europe be saved from the cruel days of which Montesquieu spoke in the Esprit des lois: "Thus, in the days of fables, after the floods and deluges, there came forth from the soil armed men who exterminated each other."—BOOK XXXII, CHAPTER XXIII.

CURZIO MALAPARTE

KAPUTT

PART ONE

THE HORSES

I

Du côté de Guermantes

PRINCE EUGENE OF SWEDEN stopped in the middle of the room.
"Listen," he said.

A sad, yearning wail was swept with the wind through the oaks
of Oakhill, the pines of Valdemarsudden Park, from beyond the
inlet of the sea stretching as far as Nybroplan, in the heart of
Stockholm. It was not the nostalgic sound of the ships' sirens rising
from the sea to the harbor, nor the raucous cry of the seagulls; it
was a feminine voice, doleful and distracted.

"It is the horses of the Tivoli, the amusement park opposite the
Skansen," said Prince Eugene in a low voice.

We went and stood by the large windows overlooking the park,
pressing our foreheads against the windowpanes that were filmed
with the blue mist rising from the sea. Three white horses, followed
by a little girl in a yellow dress, were limping along the path that
slopes down the hill. They passed through a gate to a small beach
cluttered with sloops, canoes and fishermen's boats painted green
and red.

It was a clear September day of almost springlike softness.
Autumn was already reddening the old trees of Oakhill. Large gray
ships with huge Swedish flags—a yellow cross on a blue field—
painted on their bulwarks, steamed along the inlet onto which
juts the headland where stands the Villa Valdemarsudden, the
residence of Prince Eugene, brother of King Gustav V of Sweden.
Flocks of seagulls screeched their laments, like wailing children.
Below, by the docks of Nybroplan and of Strandvägen rocked white
steamers that bear the quaint names of villages and islands and that
ply back and forth between Stockholm and the islands. Beyond the
arsenal a cloud of blue smoke was rising that a darting seagull
pierced from time to time with a flash of white. The wind carried

the sound of the music played by the little orchestras at Belman-nere and Hasselbacken, the shouts of sailors, soldiers, girls and children crowding around acrobats, jugglers and the strolling musicians who hang about the entrance to the Skansen.

Prince Eugene followed the horses with his attentive, affectionate half-closed eyes, his light eyelids traced by green veins. Seen in profile against the tired glow of sunset, his rosy face (the lips rather swollen, greedy, to which his white mustache lent a childlike gentleness, the arched nose, the high forehead crowned with curly white hair, ruffled like that of a newly awakened child) had the medallion-like cast of the Bernadotte. Of the whole Swedish royal family, Prince Eugene is the one who most resembles Napoleon's marshal, the founder of the Swedish dynasty; that clear-cut, sharp, almost hard profile contrasts strangely with the sweetness of his expression, and with the delicate elegance of his mannerisms in talking, smiling and moving his shapely hands, the Bernadotte hands with pale slender fingers. (A few days before I had seen in a shop in Stockholm the designs that King Gustav V embroidered, surrounded by his family and by his most intimate court circle, during the long winter evenings in the Royal Palace designed by Tessin and in the white summer nights in the Castle of Drottningholm—designs with a grace and delicacy of pattern that bring to mind old Venetian, Flemish and French art.)

Prince Eugene does not embroider, he is a painter. His very manner of dressing bespeaks that free and careless Montmartre manner of fifty years ago, when Prince Eugene and Montmartre were both young. He wore a heavy tobacco-colored Harris tweed jacket, of an old-fashioned cut, buttoned high. A knitted tie, twisted like a plait of hair, cast a shadow of a deeper blue on his pale blue shirt with white, faded stripes.

"They go down to the sea every day, at this time," said Prince Eugene in a low voice. In the rosy and sky-blue light of sunset those three white horses, followed by a girl dressed in yellow, were sad and very beautiful. Knee deep in the surf, spreading their manes on their long arched necks, they shook their heads and neighed.

The sun was setting. For many months I had not seen a sunset. After the long northern summer, after the endless unbroken day without dawn or sunset, the sky at last began to fade above the woods, above the sea and the roofs of the city; and something like a shadow (it was perhaps only the reflection of a shadow—the shadow of a shadow) was gathering in the east. Little by little night was being born, a night loving and delicate; and in the west, the sky was blazing above the woods and the lakes, curling itself up within the glow of sunset like an oak leaf in the fragile light of autumn.

Amid the trees of the park, the two statues, Rodin's "Penseur" and the "Niké of Samothrace" wrought in excessively white marble made one think, in an unexpected and peremptory way, of the decadent and Parnassian *fin de siècle* Parisian taste that at Valdemarsudden seemed artificial and unreal against the background of that pale and delicate northern landscape.

In the large room where we stood with our foreheads pressed against the panes of the wide windows—it was the room where Prince Eugene studied and worked—there still lingered a languid and discordant echo of Parisian estheticism as it was in those years around 1888, when Prince Eugene had a studio in Paris (he lived in rue Monceau under the name of Monsieur Oscarson) and was a pupil of Puvis de Chavannes and Bonnet. Some of his early canvases were hung on the walls—landscapes of the Île-de-France, of the Seine, of the Chevreuse valley, of Normandy; portraits of models with their hair flowing over their bare shoulders, pictures by Zorn and by Josephson. Oak branches with russet gold-veined leaves filled amphorae of Marieberg porcelain and vases decorated by Isaac Grünevald in the style of Matisse. A large white majolica stove decorated in relief with two crossed arrows topped by a closed heraldic coronet, occupied a corner of the room. A handsome mimosa plant that Prince Eugene had brought over from a garden in southern France, blossomed in a vase of Orefors crystal. I closed my eyes a moment; it was really the scent of Provence, the scent of Avignon, of Nîmes, of Arles that I was breathing; the scent of the Mediterranean, of Italy and of Capri.

"I wish I could live as Axel Munthe does in Capri," said Prince Eugene. "He seems to live surrounded by flowers and birds, and I sometimes wonder," he added smiling, "whether he truly loves flowers and birds."

"The flowers love him," I said.

13

"And do the birds love him?"

"They mistake him for an old withered tree."

Prince Eugene was smiling, his eyes half closed. As in previous years, Axel Munthe had spent the summer at Drottningholm Castle, as the King's guest, and he had started back for Italy a few days earlier. I was sorry not to have met him in Stockholm. Five or six months before, on the eve of my departure for Finland, at Capri, I had gone up to the Torre di Materita to take leave of Munthe, who was to give me letters to Sven Hedin, Ernst Manker and other friends of his in Stockholm. Axel Munthe was waiting for me under the pines and cypresses of Materita. He stood there stiff, wooden, sulky; an old green cloak over his shoulders, a little hat perched crossways on his ruffled hair, his lively mischievous eyes hidden behind dark glasses, which gave him something of that mysterious and menacing air that belongs to the blind. Munthe held a police dog on a leash, and although the dog looked tame, as soon as Munthe saw me among the trees, he began to shout to me not to come too close. "Keep away! Keep away!" he shouted, wildly gesticulating with one arm, urging the dog not to leap at me, not to tear my flesh, pretending that he was restraining it with great difficulty, that he was scarcely able to hold back the furious thrusts of that wild beast of his that watched my approach quietly wagging its tail in a friendly welcome. I advanced slowly, simulating fear, happy to lend myself to that innocent comedy.

When Axel Munthe is in a good mood, he amuses himself with improvising mischievous jokes at the expense of his friends. And that was perhaps his first good day after some months of raging loneliness. He had gone through a dismal autumn, a prey to his black whims, his irritable melancholy, shut up day after day in his tower, stripped bare and like an old bone gnawed by the sharp teeth of the southwest wind that blows from Ischia, and by the north wind that carries the acrid smell of the Vesuvian sulphur as far as Capri; locked up in his prison damp with brine, amid his faked old pictures, his faked Hellenic marbles, his fifteenth-century Madonnas carved from pieces of Louis XV furniture.

Axel Munthe looked calm that day; after a while, he began talking of the birds of Capri. Every evening toward sunset he comes out of his tower and moves with slow and cautious steps through the park to a spot where the trees thin out and expose the grass to the sky; he stops and waits—stiff, lean, wooden, like an old tree trunk, worn and withered by the sun, by the frost and the storms and with a happy smile hidden amid the hair of his small beard like that of an aged faun; and the birds fly to him in flocks, twittering lovingly; they perch on his shoulders, on his arms, on his hat. They peck at his nose, his lips and his ears. And Munthe remains there, stiff, motionless, talking to his little friends in the sweet Capri dialect, until the sun sets and dives into the blue-green sea; and the birds fly away to their nests all together with a high chirrup of farewell. . . .

"Ah, that rascal Munthe," said Prince Eugene; his voice was loving, trembling a little.

. . . We walked for a while in the park, beneath the pines swollen with wind. Later, Axel Munthe took me to the topmost room of his tower. It must once have been a granary; he uses it now as his bedroom for the black days of loneliness when he shuts himself up as in a prison cell, stopping his ears with cotton in order not to hear a human voice. He sat down on a stool, with a heavy stick between his knees and the dog's leash coiled around his wrist. The dog, crouching at his feet, gazed at me with a frank, sad look. Axel Munthe raised his face; a sudden shadow had overcast his brow. He told me that he could not sleep—that war had killed his sleep; he spent his nights in tortured wakefulness, listening to the call of the wind through the trees, to the distant voice of the sea.

"I hope," he said, "that you have not come to talk about the war."

"I shall not talk to you about the war," I replied.

"Thank you," said Munthe. And suddenly he asked me whether it was true that the Germans were so dreadfully cruel.

"Their cruelty," I replied, "is made of fear; they are ill with fear. They are a sick nation, a *Krankesvolk*."

"Yes, a sick people," said Munthe, tapping the floor with the tip of his cane, and after a long silence he asked me whether it was true that the Germans were thirsting for blood and destruction.

"They are afraid," I replied, "they are afraid of everything and everybody; they kill and destroy out of fear. Not that they fear death; no German, man or woman, young or old, fears death. They are not even afraid of suffering. In a way one may say that they like

15

pain. But they are afraid of all that is living, of all that is living outside of themselves and of all that is different from them. The disease from which they suffer is mysterious. They are afraid above all of the weak, of the defenseless, of the sick, of women and of children. They are afraid of the aged. Their fear has always aroused a profound pity in me. If Europe were to feel sorry for them, perhaps the Germans would be healed of their horrible disease."

"They are bloodthirsty then, it is true then, that they butcher people without mercy?" broke in Munthe tapping his stick impatiently on the floor.

"Yes, it is true," I replied. "They kill the defenseless; they hang Jews on the trees in the village squares, burn them alive in their houses, like rats. They shoot peasants and workers in the yards of the *kolkhoz*—the collective farms—and factories. I have seen them laughing, eating and sleeping in the shade of corpses swinging from the branches of trees."

"It is a *Krankesvolk*," said Munthe removing his dark glasses and wiping the lenses carefully with his handkerchief. He had lowered his eyelids. I could not see his eyes. Later he asked me whether it was true that the Germans kill birds.

"No, it is not true," I replied. "They have no time to bother with birds. They have just time enough to bother with human beings. They butcher Jews, workers, peasants. They set fire to towns and villages with savage fury, but they do not kill birds. Oh, how many beautiful birds there are in Russia! Even more beautiful perhaps than those of Capri."

"More beautiful than those of Capri?" asked Axel Munthe in an irritable voice.

"More beautiful and happier," I replied. "There are countless families of the most beautiful birds in the Ukraine. They fly about in thousands, twittering among the acacia leaves. They rest on the silvery branches of birches, on the ears of wheat, on the golden petals of sunflowers in order to peck the seeds out of the large black centers. They can be heard singing ceaselessly through the rumble of guns, the rattling of machine guns, through the deep hum of aircraft over in the vast Ukrainian plain. They rest on the shoulders of men, on saddles, on the manes of horses, on gun carriages, on rifle barrels, on the Panzers' conning towers, on the boots of the

16

dead. They are not afraid of the dead. They are small, alert, merry birds, some gray, others green; still others red and some yellow. Some are only red or blue on their chests, some only on their necks, some on their tails. Some are white with a blue throat; and I have seen some that are very tiny and proud, all white, spotlessly white. At dawn they begin to sing sweetly in the cornfield, and the Germans raise their heads from a gloomy slumber to listen to their happy song. They fly in thousands over the battlefields on the Dniester, the Dnieper, the Don. They twitter away free and merry, and they are not afraid of the war. They are not afraid of Hitler, of the SS, or of the Gestapo. They do not linger on branches to look down on the slaughter, but they float in the blue singing. They follow from above the armies marching across the limitless plain. The birds of the Ukraine are truly beautiful."

Axel Munthe raised his face, removed his dark glasses, looked at me with his lively, mischievous eyes and smiled. "At least the Germans do not kill birds," he said. "I am really happy that they do not kill birds."

"Dear Munthe," said Prince Eugene, "has truly a tender heart, truly a noble soul."

Suddenly there came a long low neighing from the sea, and Prince Eugene shuddered. He wrapped himself in his wide gray woolen cloak that he had left on the back of his armchair. "Come and see the trees," he said. "At this time the trees are very beautiful."

We went into the park. It was getting cold. The eastern sky looked like filmed silver. The slow death of the light, the return of darkness after the endless summer day, gave me a feeling of peace and of calm. I felt as if the war were over and Europe still alive, "the glory that was . . ." etc., "the grandeur that was . . ." etc. I had spent the summer in Lapland, on the Petsamo front, on the Liza, in the vast Inari forests, in the dead, moonlike, arctic tundra, lit by a merciless sun that never sets; and now those first autumn shadows called me back to warmth, to rest, to a feeling of life serene, untainted by the continuous presence of death. I wrapped myself in the shadow that I had at last found again, as if it were a woolen blanket. The air had the warmth and the scent of a woman.

17

I had reached Stockholm only a few days previously, after a long cure in a Helsinki hospital, and I recaptured in Sweden the sweetness of a serene life that had once been the grace of Europe. After so many months of savage loneliness in the far North among the bear-hunting, reindeer-breeding, salmon-fishing Lapps, the almost forgotten peaceful business of life, such as I had just been admiring in the streets of Stockholm, exhilarated, almost bewildered me. The women above all—the athletic and gentle grace of the clear and transparent Swedish women, blue-eyed, with hair of old gold, and little breasts placed high like two medals for athletic valor—like two memorial medals for the eighty-fifth birthday of King Gustav V—restored my feeling of the dignity of life. The shadows of the first sunsets added feminine gentleness to something secret and mysterious.

Along the streets sunk into a blue light, under a sky of pale silk, in the air illuminated by the white reflections of the house fronts, the women passed as comets of blue gold. Their smiles were warm, their glances absorbed and innocent. The couples embracing on the benches in Humle Garden, under trees already damp with the night, seemed to me ideal replicas of the embracing couple in Josephson's "Festive Scene." The sky above the roofs, the houses along the sea, sailing boats and steamers moored in the Strom and along the Strandvägen were as blue as Marieberg and Rörstrand porcelain, blue as the sea around the islands, as the Mälaren near Drottningholm, as the woods round Saltsjöbaden, as the clouds above the highest housetops of the Valhallavägen; that blue that is discernible in the white of the North, in the snow of the North, in the rivers, the lakes, and the forests of the North; the blue that is in the stuccoes of Swedish ecclesiastical architecture, in the coarse, white-painted Louis XV furniture found in the houses of Norrland and Lapland peasants; that blue about which Anders Öesterling talked to me in his warm voice as we walked between the white wooden columns with golden Doric fluting in the auditorium of the Swedish Academy in the Gamle Stade; the milky blue of the Stockholm sky at dawn, when the ghosts who have wandered all night through the streets (the North is the land of ghosts—trees, houses and animals are ghosts of trees, houses and animals) glide back along the pavements like blue shadows; and I had watched them from my window at the Grand Hotel or from the windows of Strindberg's house, the red brick house at Number Ten Karlaplan where Maioli, First Secretary of the Italian Legation, and the Chilean singer Rosita Serrano now live on different floors. (Rosita Serrano's ten dachshunds rushed up and down the stairs barking, Rosita's famous voice rose husky and sweet above the notes of the guitar, and I saw the same blue ghosts wandering through the square that Strindberg met on the stairs returning home at dawn, or caught sitting in his hall, stretching on his bed, leaning from his window, pale against the pale sky making signs to invisible passers-by.) Through the gurgling of the fountain in the middle of the Karlaplan the leaves of the trees could be heard rustling in the breeze that blew over the morning sea.

We were sitting in the little neoclassical temple at the end of the park, where the rock drops steeply to the sea, and I watched the white Doric columns etched against the background of the blue autumnal landscape. By degrees, something bitter was arising in me, something like a sad anger; bitter words came to my lips, and my effort to choke them back was useless. Thus I began almost unwittingly, to talk about Russian prisoners in the Smolensk camp who fed on the corpses of their mates under the impassive gaze of German officers and soldiers. I felt horror and shame at my own words. I would have liked to apologize to Prince Eugene for that cruelty of mine; and Prince Eugene kept silent, wrapped in his gray cloak, his head bent down over his chest. Suddenly he lifted his face, his lips moved as if in speech, but he kept silent, and I read a pained reproach in his eyes.

I would have liked to read the same cold cruelty in his eyes and on his brow that had hardened the countenance of Obergruppenführer Dietrich when I told him about the Russian prisoners in the Smolensk camp who fed on the corpses of their comrades. Dietrich had burst out laughing. I had met Obergruppenführer Dietrich, the commander of Hitler's bodyguard, in the villa of the Italian Embassy on the shores of the Wannsee near Berlin: I had felt strangely attracted by his pale face, his unbelievably cold eyes, his huge ears and his small fish-mouth. Dietrich burst out laughing: *"Haben sie ihnen geschmeckt?*—Did they enjoy eating them?" he laughed opening wide his small pink-roofed fish-mouth, showing his crowded sharp fishlike teeth. I would have liked to see Prince Eugene's face harden with the same cruel expression that disfigured Dietrich and to hear him also ask me in his tired mellow voice, "Did they enjoy eating them?" But Prince Eugene raised his eyes and gazed at me with a look of pained reproach.

His face was covered with a mask of deep suffering. He knew that I also was suffering and he gazed silently at me with loving pity. I felt that if he had spoken, if he had said one single word, if he had touched my hand, I might have burst into tears. But Prince Eugene gazed silently at me and cruel words rose to my lips; I became suddenly aware that I was telling him about a day when I had gone to the Leningrad front. I motored through a deep forest, near Oranienbaum, with a German officer—a Lieutenant Schultz of Stuttgart, to be exact—he hailed from the valley of the Neckar, Schultz called it "the poet's valley," and he talked to me about Hölderlin, and Hölderlin's madness.

"He was not mad, he was an angel," said Schultz, moving his hand in a slow vague gesture, as if he were drawing invisible wings in the frosty air, and he looked upward as if he followed an angel's flight with his eyes. The forest was deep and thick; the blinding reflection of the snow was mirrored with a slight blue tinge by the tree trunks; the car glided on the frozen track with a mellow rustle, and Schultz said, "Among the trees of the Black Forest Hölderlin flew like a large bird," and I kept silent staring at the deep forest, listening to the rustle of the wheels on the icebound track. Schultz recited Hölderlin's lines:

> On the Rhine where the Neckar's lawns grow
> they think that to abide
> there is no better spot in the world.
> But let me to the Caucasus go.

"Hölderlin was a German angel," I said smiling.
"He was a German angel," said Schultz, and he recited:

> But let me to the Caucasus go.

"Hölderlin also wanted to go to the Caucasus, didn't he?" I said.
"*Ach, so!*" said Schultz.

20

Just then, where the forest was thickest and deepest, and another track crossed our way, I perceived suddenly in front of us looming out of the mist a soldier sunk to his belly in the snow; he stood motionless, his right arm outstretched, pointing the way. When we passed him, Schultz raised his hand to his cap as if to salute him and thank him. Then he said: "There's another one who would like to go to the Caucasus," and he began to laugh throwing himself against the back of the seat.

Farther on, at another crossing of tracks, another soldier loomed in the distance; he also was sunk into the snow, his right arm outstretched.

"They'll die of cold, these poor devils," I said.

Schultz turned to look at me. "There's no danger that they will die of cold," said he and laughed. I asked him why he thought that these poor devils ran no risk of being frozen. "Because, by now, they are used to the cold," replied Schultz, laughing and patting my shoulder. And having stopped the car, he turned to me smiling: "Do you wish to see him close by? You'll be able to ask him whether he is cold."

We climbed out of the car and approached the soldier. He stood there motionless, his right arm outstretched to point the way. He was dead. His eyes were wide open, his mouth half closed. He was a Russian soldier, dead.

"That's our traffic police," said Schultz. "We call them the 'Silent Police.'"

"Are you sure they won't talk?"

"That they won't talk? *Ach, so!* Try to ask him."

"I'd better not. I feel sure he would answer me," I said.

"*Ach,* very amusing!" exclaimed Schultz laughing.

"Yes, very amusing, *nicht wahr?*" Then I added, feigning indifference, "Are they dead or alive when you place them on their posts?"

"Alive, of course!" replied Schultz.

"And then they freeze to death, of course," said I.

"*Nein, nein.* They do not die of the cold! Look here!" and Schultz pointed to a clot of blood, a clot of red ice on the temple of the corpse.

"*Ach, so.* Very amusing."

"Very amusing, isn't it?" said Schultz, and he added still laughing: "Russian prisoners must be put to some use."

. . . "Stop, please," said Prince Eugene softly. He said only: "Stop, please." And I wanted to hear him also tell me in his mellow, tired, rather distant voice, "Of course, Russian prisoners must be put to some use." But he kept silent and I felt a horror and a shame at my own words. Perhaps I was expecting Prince Eugene to place his hand on my arm. I felt humbled, a sad and cruel rancor gnawed at my heart.

The noise of restless hooves beating the damp soil, and of soft neighing reached us from the deeps of the wood of Oakhill. Prince Eugene raised his brow and stood listening for a moment. Then he got up and moved in silence toward the villa. I followed him. We went silently to his study and sat at a small table on which tea was served in the fine Russian transparent, slightly bluish china of Catherine's days; the teapot and the sugar bowl were of old Swedish silver, not as shiny as the Fabergé Russian silver, but slightly dull, with the dark luster that old *tenn* * has in the Baltic countries. The neighing of the horses reached us dimly, mingled with the rustle of the wind through the leaves.

I had gone to Upsala the previous day to visit the famous garden of Linnaeus and the tombs of the old Swedish kings, those large earthen graves similar to the tombs of the Horatii and Curiatii on the Appian way. I asked Prince Eugene whether it was true that the old Swedes sacrificed horses on the tombs of their sovereigns.

"Occasionally they sacrificed the sovereigns on the tombs of the horses," replied Prince Eugene, and he laughed mischievously as if pleased to see me composed once again, without a hint of cruelty in my voice or in my eyes. The wind was blowing through the trees in the park, and I was thinking of the heads of horses hanging from the branches of the Upsala oaks around the graves of their sovereigns. I was thinking of the large equine eyes filled with that same damp light that women's eyes have when pleasure or pity shines in them.

* *Tenn*—Pewter.

"Did it ever occur to you," I said, "that the Swedish landscape is equine in character?"

Prince Eugene smiled and asked. "Do you know Carl Hill's drawings of horses, Carl Hill's *häster?*" And he added, "Carl Hill was mad; he thought trees were green horses."

"Carl Hill," I replied, "painted horses as if they were landscapes. There is something strange in Swedish nature, the same sort of madness that is in the nature of horses. There is also the same gentleness, the same morbid sensitiveness, the same free and abstract fancy. The equine character, the equine madness of the Swedish landscape is revealed not only in the great, solemn, incomparably green trees of the forests but also in the silky gloss of the vistas of water, woods, islands and clouds, in the light and deep airy vistas in which a transparent white lead, warm vermilion, cold blue, damp green and shiny turquoise compose a clear and elusive harmony, as if the colors never rested long on the woods, meadows and waters, but flitted instantly away like butterflies. (If you touch the Swedish landscape it tinges your fingertips just like a butterfly's wing.) It is a landscape as smooth to the touch as a horse's coat. And it possesses the same elusive tones, the same airy lightness and shine, the same changing gloss that is seen on the coat of a horse fleetly prancing along stretches of grass and leaves in the turmoil of the hunt, beneath a gray and pink sky.

"Look at the sun," I said, "when it rises above the blue pine woods, on the light birch groves, on the old silver of the water, on the greeny blue of the meadows; look at the sun," I said, "when it rises on the horizon lighting up the landscape with the liquid splendor of a large, staring equine eye. There is something unreal in Swedish nature, full of fancies and whims, of that tender and lyrical madness that shines from the eye of a horse. The Swedish landscape is a galloping horse. Listen," I said, "to the neighing of the wind through the trees. Listen to the neighing of the wind among the leaves and the grass."

"The Tivoli horses are returning from the sea," said Prince Eugene listening.

"Some time ago," I said, "I went to the steeplechase near the Royal Hussar barracks, to the Stockholm Fatrittklubb, on the last day of the horse show when the best horses of the finest royal regiments were competing. The horses, the trees, the grass of the field, the dead gray walls of the large indoor tennis court, the light dresses of the feminine· spectators, the pale blue uniforms of the officers made up a delicate and tender picture by Degas shaded in light gray, pink and green tones in the silvery air.

"It was on that last day of the horse show that the horse Führer, ridden by Lieutenant Eriksson of the Norrland Royal Artillery in the *löktaren* race, knocked down at the start bars, fences and every kind of hurdle, and the onlookers kept silent in order that the Führer's Germany across the sea might not find a pretext to invade Sweden. It was on that day that, owing to a highly sensitive spirit of neutrality the horse Molotov, ridden by an officer with an English name, and thus an awkward name at the time—Captain Hamilton of the Göta Royal Artillery—had withdrawn from the race at the very last moment, as much because of the dangerous tension that just then existed between Sweden and the U.S.S.R. after the sinking of some Swedish ships in the Baltic, as to avoid a public competition between Führer and Molotov.

"Two or three hundred people seated informally on rough benches that took the place of the customary stands belonged to the select circle of Stockholm and were gathered around the Crown Prince, who sat in the center of a long backless bench; the foreign diplomatic corps cut a gray rent through the green, red, yellow and blue skirts and the pale blue uniforms.

"After a time, all the horses on the field answered to the loud, sweet, mellow and almost amorous whinnying of Rockaway, ridden by H.R.H. Prince Gustavus Adolphus. It seemed a love challenge and Bäckahästen ridden by Rittmaster Ankarcrona, Royal Hussars; Miss Kiddy ridden by Lieutenant Nyholm, Norrland Royal Dragoons, and Babian ridden by Lieutenant Nihlen, Svea Royal Artillery, began frisking on the meadow under the stern eyes of the Crown Prince, while from behind the screen of trees, from the end of the field, and from the stables of the Royal Hussars across the road came the neighing of invisible horses. The horses of the gala royal carriages also began neighing, and for a time only voices of horses could be heard; little by little, the voice of the wind, the hooting of the steamboats, the raucous lament of the seagulls, the rustling of the branches of the trees and the dripping of the invisible soft rain recovered strength and daring, and the neighing abated. But during those few moments, I believed I really heard the voice of Swedish nature in its purity; it was an equine voice, an amorous neighing, a profoundly feminine voice."

Prince Eugene placed his hand on my arm, and smiling said: "I am glad that you—" and he added in an affectionate tone, "don't go back to Italy yet. Stay a little longer in Sweden. You will recover from all your suffering."

Little by little daylight was fading, the color of violets at night slowly filled the room. And little by little an indefinable feeling of shame was taking possession of me. I felt shame and horror for all I had endured in those years of war. Then as always in my journeys to and from Finland, I was stopping for a short time in Sweden—that happy island in the midst of a Europe humiliated and defiled by hunger, by hate and by despair, where I recovered the sense of a serene life, the sense of human dignity. I felt free again, but it was a painful, cruel feeling. I was to start for Italy in a few days. The thought that I would have to leave Sweden, to travel through Germany, to look again at those German faces distorted by hatred and fear and bathed in morbid sweat, filled me with disgust and humiliation. In a few days I was to see Italian faces again—my Italian faces, cowed, white with hunger. I was to see myself in the secret anguish of those faces, in the eyes of the crowd, in the trolleys, in the buses, in the cafés and the streets, beneath the large portraits of Mussolini stuck on the walls and on the shop windows, beneath that swollen and whitish head with its cowardly eyes and lying mouth. And little by little I was overcome by a sensation of pity and revulsion.

Prince Eugene stared at me in silence. He understood what was happening within me, what anguish was obsessing me, and he began to talk gently of Italy, of Rome, of Florence, of Italian friends whom he had not seen for many years; and after a while, he asked me what the Prince of Piedmont was doing.

I would have liked to answer, "He is losing his hair." But I only said, smiling, "He is at Anagni near Rome at the head of the troops defending Sicily."

He smiled, too, but not at my innocent malice; then he asked whether it was long since I had seen the Prince. "I saw him in Rome, shortly before I left Italy," I replied. And I should have liked to tell him that my last meeting with Prince Umberto had left me with a feeling of sorrow and regret. A few years had sufficed to turn that proud and smiling young Prince into a poor, sad and humbled-looking man. Something in his face, in his eyes, revealed a cowed and restless conscience. Even his cordiality, once kindly and sincere, was no longer spontaneous; his smile looked humble and uncertain. I had already perceived this dejection one evening shortly before the war at supper at Zum Kater Hiddigeigei, in Capri, on the narrow glass-covered terrace facing the road. In the next room a crowd of young people led by Countess Ciano danced noisily amid the excitable and sweating throng of a Neapolitan Sunday crowd. The Prince of Piedmont watched with a dull gaze the table at which the Countess Ciano's youthful court was seated, and the small group gathered at the bar around Mona Williams, Noel Coward and Eddi Bismarck. The Prince rose from time to time and with a brief bow asked Elisabetta Moretti or Marita Guglielmi—a daughter of the President of the Senate, or Cyprienne Charles Roux—daughter of the French Ambassador to the Vatican, or Countess Eileen Branca or Countess Lola Caetani to dance. Between the dances he came back to our table and sat down, mopping up the perspiration with his handkerchief. He smiled but his smile was bored, almost frightened. He wore white linen trousers, short and tight fitting, and a blue woolen sweater in the style that Gabriella Robilant had made fashionable that year. He had taken off his jacket and hung it on the back of his chair. I had never seen him dressed so carelessly. I noticed with pained surprise the glaring bare patch on the top of his head. It looked like a kind of large tonsure. He appeared greatly aged. His voice also had aged; it had grown yellow, hoarse, quite throaty.

Softness, lassitude, boredom appeared in his every gesture, in his smile, in the look of his large black eyes; and I felt a gentle pity for that young prince, so faded and downcast, aging so humbly with soft resignation. I thought that we all had prematurely aged in Italy, that the same softness, the same lassitude and boredom slackened the gestures and infected the smiles and the looks of all of us. There was nothing pure, nothing truly young any more in Italy. The wrinkled face of that young prince, his premature baldness and withered skin were almost a mark of vulgar destiny. I felt that a painful and humiliating thought was weighing on his mind, that the humiliation of slavery had corrupted him, that he was a slave, and I could have laughed thinking that he, too, was a slave.

He was no longer that azure prince who walked through the streets of Turin with a warm smile on his proud red lips, that Prince Charming who appeared on the threshold of friendly houses by the side of the Princess of Piedmont at dinners and dances tendered to the young couple by the aristocracy of Turin. They were then a truly charming pair and pleasant to see, the Prince rather bothered by too tight a wedding ring, his Princess rather cross and diffident, her clear gaze resting on the other young women with a jealous suspicion that her silent graciousness could not fully conceal.

The Princess of Piedmont also had looked sad and downcast the last time I had seen her. How different from the first time I had met her at a dance in Turin, all dressed in white, sweet and splendid. It was one of the first dances she attended in Italy after her wedding; she entered, and it seemed as if she penetrated our lives softly like a secret image. How different she was now from the person I used to meet in Florence or at Forte dei Marmi; whom I sometimes surprised in Capri on the rocks or in the grottos of the Marina Piccola toward the Faraglioni. Now there was something humiliated—even in her.

I had become aware of it a few years before on the Côte d'Azur. I was sitting one evening with some friends close to the swimming pool on the terrace of Monte Carlo Beach. On the stage of the open air theater rhythmically rose and fell a wavering fringe of bare legs of a famous troupe of New York chorus girls. It was a warm night, the sea stretched out on the rocks and slumbered. Toward midnight the Princess of Piedmont appeared. With her was a relative of the Royal family, Count Gregorio Calvi di Bergolo, and after a while she sent Calvi to invite us to her table. The Princess was silent. She watched the show with a strangely concentrated gaze; the orchestra played "Stormy Weather" and "Singing in the

Rain." After a while she turned to me and asked when I would return to Turin. I replied that I would never return to Italy, unless
things changed. She gave me a long, silent, sad look.

"Do you remember the other night at Vence?" she asked suddenly.

A few days earlier I had gone up to Vence to carry the greetings
of Roger Cornaz, the French translator of D. H. Lawrence, to two
young American girls who were famous at the time throughout the
Côte d'Azur for certain "sacred dances" they performed. The two
American girls lived alone in a small old house, extremely poor and
apparently happy. The younger one resembled Renée Vivien. They
told me that they were expecting the Princess of Piedmont that
evening. While the younger one concealed behind a dusty curtain
prepared for her dance, and her friend selected records and wound
the gramophone, the Princess of Piedmont entered accompanied by
Gregorio Calvi and several others. At first I did not discern any
change in her, but gradually I became aware that something was
withered, humiliated in her too. The young American who resembled Renée Vivien began dancing in that ill-lit room, low-vaulted
like a grotto, on a tiny wooden stage decorated with cloth and
paper. It was a pitiful dance, deliciously *démodée*, "inspired by a
fragment of Sappho," her friend explained. At first the dancer appeared to be burning with a pure fire, a blue flame shone in her
clear eyes, but after a while she appeared tired, bored. Her friend
stared at her with a loving yet commanding look, while she talked
softly to the Princess of Piedmont about sacred dances, Plato, and
Aphrodite's statues. In the reddish light of two lamps with bell-like
shades of purple satin, the dancer moved slowly about the tiny
stage and raised and lowered first one leg, then the other, to the
husky rhythm of the gramophone, at times lifting her arms and
joining her hands over her head, at times letting them drop to her
sides with a supreme gesture of abandon, until she stopped, bowed
and, saying with childlike simplicity, "I am tired," sat down on a
cushion. Her friend took her in her arms calling her *petite chérie*.
She turned to the Princess of Piedmont saying, "Isn't she wonderful?"

"Do you know what I was thinking the other night while we
watched that young American dancing?" the Princess asked me. "I

was thinking that her gestures were not pure. I do not mean sensuous or lacking in modesty. I mean to say that they were proud. Not pure. I often ask myself why it is so hard to be pure today. Don't you think we ought to be more humble?"

"I believe," I replied, "that you are using the dances of that young American only as an excuse, that perhaps you are thinking of something else."

"Yes, perhaps I am thinking of something else." She was silent for a while and then repeated, "Don't you think we ought to be more humble?"

"We ought to have more dignity, more self-respect," I replied. "But perhaps you are right. Only humility can raise us from the humiliation into which we have sunk."

"Perhaps that is what I meant," said the Princess of Piedmont lowering her head. "We are ill with pride. And pride is not enough to raise us from humiliation. Our actions, our thoughts are not pure." She went on to say that a few months before, when she had Monteverde's *Orpheus* performed in the Royal Palace at Turin for a small audience of friends and connoisseurs, she had been overtaken at the last moment by a feeling of shame. She had felt as if her intention had not been pure. As if she were only making a proud gesture. I said: "I, too, was at the Royal Palace that day and I felt uneasy; I did not know why. Perhaps, now, in Italy, even Monteverde sounds false. But it is a pity that you should waste your feeling of shame on things that do honor to your taste and intelligence. There are many other things that should cause us all to blush; even you."

The Princess of Piedmont looked greatly taken aback at my words and I saw that she blushed slightly. I had already regretted having spoken to her in that way. I feared I had offended her. But after a few moments she said to me in a gentle voice that one morning, perhaps tomorrow, she would go to Vence to visit Lawrence's tomb (*Lady Chatterley's Lover* was much read and talked about in those days), and I spoke of my last visit there. Night had already fallen when I reached Vence. The cemetery was closed; the attendant was asleep and he refused to get up, saying that "cemeteries, at night, are intended for sleep." Pressing my head against the bars of the gate, I endeavored to make out in the silvery moonlight, the simple and humble tomb, and the coarse mosaic of colored pebbles portraying a phoenix, the immortal bird Lawrence wanted to have on his tombstone.

"Do you think Lawrence was a pure man?" asked the Princess of Piedmont.

"He was a free man," I replied.

Later, when she was saying good-by, the Princess said to me in a low voice and a sad tone that surprised me, "Why don't you go back to Italy? Don't take my words as a reproach. It is the advice of a friend."

I returned to Italy two years later. I was arrested, locked up in a cell at *Regina Coeli,* and sentenced to five years' imprisonment without a trial. While in prison, I was thinking that the Princess of Piedmont was already a prey to the deep sadness of the Italian people, that she was humiliated by the general slavery, and I was grateful to her for the sad, almost affectionate tone I had detected in her words.

My last meeting with her occurred some time ago in the station lobby in Naples just after an air raid. The wounded waiting for the ambulances lay on stretchers ranged under the shed. There was anguish in the deathly pale features of the Princess of Piedmont, and not anguish alone, but something deep and secret. She had grown thinner, there were dark circles under her eyes, and there was discernible a white, very faint tattoo of wrinkles on her temples. The pure splendor that had emanated from her when she first came to Turin, a few days after her wedding to Prince Umberto, was quenched by now. Her movements were slower, she had grown more serious, she seemed strangely faded. She recognized me and stopped to greet me, asking from which front I had arrived.

"From Finland," I replied.

She looked at me and said: "You will see, all will end well. Our people are marvelous."

I broke into a laugh and wanted to reply, "The war is already lost. We have all lost the war, you too." But I said nothing. I only said: "Our people are very unhappy," and she moved on among the crowd with her slow, rather uncertain step. . . . This, all this I should have liked to say to Prince Eugene, but I held myself back and smiled, thinking of that young princely couple.

"The Italian people are very fond of them, aren't they?" asked Prince Eugene, and before I could answer, "Yes, the people are very fond of them." (But I would have liked to answer him differently, and did not dare.) He went on saying that he possessed many letters from Umberto—he actually said "from Umberto"—that he was putting them in order because he intended to collect and publish them, and I was unable to gather whether he was talking of King Humbert or of the Prince of Piedmont. He asked me later whether in Italian, Umberto is written with an "*h.*"

"Without the '*h*,'" I replied. And I laughed thinking that the Prince of Piedmont was a slave himself, as we all were—a poor, crowned slave, his chest laden with medals and crosses. I thought that he too was a slave, and I laughed. I was ashamed of my laughter, and still I laughed.

I noticed after a while that Prince Eugene's gaze was slowly turning toward a canvas hanging on the wall of the room. It was the famous picture "Pa balkong"—"From the Balcony"—that he had painted in Paris during his early years, in about 1888. A young woman, Friherrina Celsing, leans from a balcony facing one of the avenues radiating from the Etoile. The brown skirt with its blue and green reflections, the warm blond hair tucked under a little hat such as Manet's and Renoir's women wore, stand out in the canvas against the transparent white lead, the gray-pink of the house fronts, and the damp green of the trees in the avenue. A carriage is passing below the balcony. It is a black cab and, seen from above, the horse looks as if it were made of wood: stiff and lean, it strikes a note of a childish play in that quaint and delicate Parisian street. The horses of the omnibus that is driving down from the Etoile appear to be freshly varnished with the same shiny enamel as that of the horse-chestnut leaves. They look like the wooden horses on a merry-go-round during a provincial fair in that delicate provincial hue of trees, of houses, of sky above the roofs of the avenue. The sky is still that of Verlaine and already that of Proust.

"Paris was very young then," said Prince Eugene approaching the canvas. He was gazing at Friherrina Celsing leaning from the balcony, and he spoke to me softly, almost reluctantly of that young Paris of his, of Puvis de Chavannes, of his painter friends, Zorn,

Wahlberg, Cederström, Arsenius, Wenneberg and of those happy
years. "Paris was very young then. It was the Paris of Madame de
Morienval, Madame de Saint-Euvert, of the Duchess of Luxem-
bourg (and also of Madame de Cambremer and of the young Marquess de Beausergent), and of those Proustian goddesses *la pro-
fondeur du parterre de feux inhumains, horizontaux et splendides*
—whose glances enflamed the depths of the orchestra with inhuman,
horizontal and splendid fires. Of the *blanches déités*—white goddesses, dressed in *fleurs blanches*—white flowers, *duvetées comme
une aile*—downy as a wing, *à la fois plume et corolle*—at the same
time feather and flower, *ainsi que certaines floraisons marines*—do
well as certain marine vegetation, who spoke with the delicious
refinement *d'une sécheresse volue, à la Mérimée ou à la Meilhac,
aux demi-dieux du Jockey Club*—of a studied brittleness, in the
Mérimée or Meilhac manner, to the elect of the Jockey Club, in the
atmosphere of Racine's *Phèdre*. It was the Paris of the Marquess de
Palancy who passed through the transparent shadows of his box
at the theater *comme un poisson derrière la cloison vitrée d'un
aquarium*—like a fish behind the glass enclosure of an aquarium.
And it was also the Paris of the *Place du Tertre,* of the earlier cafés
of Montparnasse, of the *Cloiserie des Lilas,* of Toulouse-Lautrec, of
the *Goulue* and of Jean le Desosse. I should have liked to interrupt
Prince Eugene to ask him whether he had ever seen the Duke de
Guermantes entering a box *et d'un geste commander de se rassoir
aux monstres marins et sacrés flottant au fond de l'antre*—and with
a gesture commanding those sacred marine monsters floating on
the bottom of the grotto to be seated—in order to ask him to talk
about the women, *belles et légères comme Diane*—beautiful and
easy of virtue like Diana, of the smart people who used the *jargon
ambigu*—strange lines—of Swann and Monsieur de Charlus. And I
was just going to ask him the question that had been for some
moments surging to my lips. I was just going to ask him with a
tremor in my voice, "You have no doubt met Madame de Guermantes—" when the Prince turned, and offered his face to the tired
light of sunset. He moved away from the canvas and seemed to
step out of that warm and golden shadow of that *côté de Guermantes* in which he too appeared to conceal himself, emerging from
behind the glass of an aquarium, himself like some *monstre marin*

et sacré—sacred sea monster. Settling in an armchair at the end of the room that was farthest away from the balcony of Friherrina Celsing, he began talking about Paris, as if Paris in his painter's eyes were only a color—the memory and yearning for a color: those pinks, grays, greens, blues all faded. Perhaps for him Paris was only a mute color, a soundless color—his visual recollections, the pictures of his young Parisian years, stripped of any quality of sound, lived by themselves in his memory, moved, were lighted, flew away *comme les monstres ailés de la préhistoire*—like those prehistoric winged monsters. The mute pictures of that young, distant Paris of his crumbled noiselessly before his eyes, but not to a point when the destruction of that happy world of his youth would *ternisse, de la vulgarité d'aucun bruit, la chasteté de silence*—spoil the chastity of silence by the vulgarity of any noise.

Meanwhile, as if to work free of the sad spell of that voice and of the pictures that were called up by it, I raised my eyes and looked across the trees in the park at the Stockholm houses, ash-colored in the tired glow of the sunset. I saw a blue sky slowly darkened by the night, similar to the Paris sky, looking down on the Royal Palace far away and on the churches of the Gamle Stade—that Proustian sky of *papier gros bleu*—blue wrapping paper—which I used to see from the windows of my Paris house in Place Dauphine over the roofs of the rive Gauche, over the spire of the Sainte Chapelle, over the bridges on the Seine, and over the Louvre; and those dull purples, those fiery pinks, those gray-blue hues of the clouds delicately attuned with the shaded black of the slate roofs, were sweetly gripping my heart. I thought then that perhaps Prince Eugene was also a character *du côté de Guermantes. Peut-être un de ces personnages qu'évoque le nom d'Elstir.*—Perhaps one of those types that remind you of Elstir. I was just going to ask him the question that had been surging to my lips for some moments. I was just going to ask him with a tremor in my voice to speak to me of her, of Madame de Guermantes, when Prince Eugene fell silent, and after a long silence during which he seemed to gather the pictures of his youth behind the screen of his lowered lids, as if to protect them, he asked whether I had ever been back to Paris during the war.

I would have preferred not to answer. I felt a sort of painful reluctance; I should not have liked to talk to him of Paris, of my own young Paris, and I shook my head. I kept slowly shaking my head, gazing at him. Then I said, "No, I have not been back to Paris during the war. I do not wish to return to Paris while the war lasts."

The painful and beloved pictures of a younger Paris, more troublous perhaps, more restless and sad were gradually superimposing themselves on the faraway pictures of the Paris of Prince Eugene and Madame de Guermantes. As faces of passers-by loom out of the mist outside the windows of a café, there rose in my memory the faces of Albertine, Odette, and Robert de Saint Loup, the shadows of young men with brows marked with drink, lack of sleep and lust—who may be found behind the shoulders of Swann and M. de Charlus, in the characters of Apollinaire, Matisse, Picasso, Hemingway and Paul Eluard's gray-blue ghosts.

"I have seen German soldiers in every town in Europe," I said. "I do not want to see them in Paris."

Prince Eugene dropped his head on his chest and said in a distant voice: "Alas, Paris!"

Suddenly he raised his face, crossed the room and approached the portrait of Friherrina Celsing. Leaning from the balcony, the young woman looks down on the avenue damp with autumn rain. She looks on the cab-horse and the bus-horses swinging their heads beneath the green trees already parched by the first autumn fire. Prince Eugene placed his hand on the canvas, stroked with his long pale fingers the house fronts, the sky above the roofs and the leaves; he caressed that Paris air, that Paris color, those pink, gray, green and blue hues, all slightly faded—that pure and transparent Paris light. He turned and looked at me with a smile. And I saw that his eyes were wet with tears, that a tear was slowly rolling down his cheek. Prince Eugene brushed away the tear with an impatient movement and said, smiling, "Please don't say anything to Axel Munthe. He is an old rascal. He would tell everybody that he has seen me weep."

II

Horse Kingdom

DAYLIGHT was beginning to lose its youth after the ghostlike endlessness of a pellucid summer day, without dawn or sunset. Already the face of the day was growing wrinkled, and little by little the evening was darkening the first, still-luminous shadows. Trees, rocks, houses and clouds sweeter and more intense in their foreboding of the coming night were slowly melting into the mellow autumnal landscape, as in those landscapes of Elias Martin.

Suddenly I heard the Tivoli horses neighing, and I said to Prince Eugene: "It's the voice of the dead mare of Alexandrovska, in the Ukraine—the voice of the dead mare." . . .

Evening was already falling; occasional rifle shots of the partisans were piercing the vast red flag of sunset fluttering in the dusty wind far away on the horizon. I had arrived within a few miles of Nemirovskoye, near Balta, in the Ukraine. It was the summer of 1941. I meant to push on to Nemirovskoye to spend the night in safety. But it was dark already and I preferred to stop in an abandoned village, lying in one of those valleys that cut the vast plain from north to south, between the Dniester and the Dnieper.

The village was called Alexandrovska. In Russia the villages are all alike, as are their names. There are many villages called Alexandrovska in the Balta region. There is one in the west of Balta, some seventeen miles away. Another, eleven miles to the south. A third one, west of Federimova, on the road to Odessa, where the electric railway passes. And a fourth one, some nine miles north of Federimova. The one where I had stopped to spend the night, lay close to Nemirovskoye, along the Kodima river.

I had left my car, an old Ford, at the roadside, close to a fence surrounding the orchard of a prosperous looking house. Next to the wooden gate was stretched out the dead body of a horse. I lingered a moment looking at the carrion; it was a beautiful mare, a dark bay with a long yellow mane. It lay on its side, its hind legs sunk in a puddle. I pushed the gate open, crossed the orchard and leaned on the house door that opened with a squeak. The house had been abandoned; the floors were littered with scattered papers, straw, newspapers and clothes. The drawers were pulled half open, the cupboards ajar, the beds unmade. It was certainly no peasant's home. Perhaps it belonged to a Jew. In the room I chose, the mattress on the bed had been ripped open. The windowpanes were intact. It was very hot. A thunderstorm, I thought, as I closed the window.

Night had fallen and the large, black, golden-lashed eyes of the sunflowers shone in the faint light. They gazed at me swaying their heads in the wind, already damp with the far-off rain. Romanian cavalrymen walked along the road leading their horses after watering them—fine full-hipped horses with yellow manes. The sand-colored uniforms stained the shadows with yellowish spots; they seemed like large insects entangled in the thick and sticky air of the coming storm. The yellow horses followed them, raising a cloud of dust.

There was still some bread and cheese in my knapsack, and walking up and down the room, I began eating. I had taken off my boots and barefooted I paced the packed-down, earthen floor along which columns of large black ants were marching. I felt the ants crawling over my feet, squeezing between my toes, climbing upward to explore my ankles. I was dead tired; I could not even chew, my jaws were so heavy and my teeth were so tender from fatigue. Finally, I threw myself on the bed and closed my eyes but I could not sleep. Once in a while close by or far away a shot pierced the night. They were shots fired by the partisans concealed amid the wheat and the sunflower forests that cover the vast Ukrainian plain toward Kiev, toward Odessa. And as the night grew thicker, the stench of carrion merged with the smell of grass and sunflowers. I could not sleep. I lay stretched out on the bed with my eyes shut and I could not fall asleep, my bones were too sore from fatigue.

Suddenly the stench of the dead mare penetrated the room; it stopped on the threshold. It looked at me. I felt that the smell was

gazing at me. Half asleep, I thought, it's the dead mare. The air
was as heavy as a woolen blanket, the impending storm crushed
the thatched roofs of the village. It rested its heavy load on the
trees, the wheat and the dust on the road. Now and again the
noise of the river sounded like bare feet shuffling through the grass.
The night was as black, thick and clammy as black honey. It's the
dead mare, I thought.

The squeaking of cart wheels across the fields, of those four-
wheeled Romanian and Ukrainian *carutza*, drawn by little lean,
hairy horses that follow the armies with loads of ammunition,
clothes and arms along the endless Ukrainian tracks—the squeaking
of these cart wheels reached me from across the fields. I thought
the dead mare had dragged itself to the threshold and that it was
gazing at me. I cannot say how I came to believe this. I was dead
tired, drugged with sleep. I could not rid myself of these thoughts.
It was as if the heat and the stench of carrion had filled my room
with black slimy mud into which I was slowly sinking, and my
struggles were growing more and more feeble. I cannot say how I
came to think that the mare was not dead, only wounded, its
wounds festering; that it was already rotting and still alive, like
those prisoners whom Tartars tie to corpses, stomach to stomach,
face to face, mouth to mouth, until the corpse devours the living.
That stench was there at the door, and it was gazing at me.

I felt all of a sudden that it was approaching, getting slowly
closer to my bed. "Off—off with you!" I shouted in Romanian.
"Merge! Merge!" Then it occurred to me that perhaps the mare was
Russian, and I shouted: *"Poshol! Poshol!"* The stench halted. A moment later it began getting closer to my bed again. Then I became
frightened. I clutched the automatic that I had shoved under the
mattress, and sitting up suddenly, I turned on my flashlight. The
room was empty; nothing was on the threshold. I jumped out of
my bed and barefooted approached the door. I looked outside.
The night was empty. I went out into the orchard. The sunflowers
were bending mildly with the wind; the storm weighed down upon
the horizon. It looked like an enormous, painfully breathing black
lung. Swollen and empty like an enormous lung. I saw the sky ex-
pand and contract; I saw it breathe like a huge lung, its network of
veins and bronchial tubes for a moment lighted by the sulphurous

flashes of lightning. I pushed the little wooden gate open and went into the road. The carrion lay there, sideways in the puddle, its head resting on the dusty edge of the road. Its wrinkled belly was swollen. Its wide-open eye shone damp and round. Its dusty yellow mane, smeared and clotted with blood and mud, stood rigidly erect, like the manes on the helmets of ancient warriors. I sat on the roadside, my shoulders resting against the fence. A black bird flew by in slow silent flight. Soon it would rain. Invisible gusts of wind rushed through the sky, dust clouds ran along the road with a long soft hiss; particles of dirt clawed at my face and lashes, and crawled through my hair like ants. Soon it would rain. I went back into the house and stretched out on the bed. My arms and my legs ached. I was dripping with sweat. And suddenly I fell asleep.

And then the carrion stench came in again. It stopped on the threshold. I was not quite awake; my eyes were still shut and I felt that the stench was gazing at me. It was now a soft and greasy stench; a thick, slimy, deep smell, a yellow smell, stained with green. I opened my eyes. It was sunrise. The room was enveloped in a spider web of uncertain whitish light. Things grew slowly out of the shadows, so slowly they became distorted and twisted like things pulled out of the neck of a bottle. A cupboard stood against the wall between the door and the window, the hangers dangled—empty, swaying. The wind made the window curtains flutter; there were heaps of paper, dirty rags, cigarette butts on the earthen floor, and the papers rustled in the wind.

Suddenly the stench came in, and on the threshold stood a young foal. It was lean and hairy. It stank of decay, of carrion. It gazed fixedly at me and snorted. It came close to the bed, stretched its neck and sniffed at me. It stank horribly. As I started to get out of bed, it turned suddenly, knocked its side against the cupboard, and fled, neighing with fright. I drew on my boots and followed it out on the road. The foal was stretched alongside the dead mare. It gazed at me fixedly. "*Asculta!*—Listen here!" I called out to a passing Romanian soldier carrying a pail of water. I told him to take care of the foal.

"It was foaled by the dead mare," said the soldier.

"Yes," I replied, "it was foaled by the dead mare."

The little foal was gazing fixedly at me, rubbing its back against the side of the carcass. The soldier approached and began stroking the foal's neck.

"It must be taken away from its mother. If it stays here, it will end by rotting. It can be your squadron's mascot," I said.

"Yes," said the soldier. "Yes, poor beast. It will bring luck to our squadron." Saying this he took off his trouser belt and looped it around the foal's neck. At first the foal did not want to get up, then it leaped up and backed, neighing and twisting its neck toward the dead mare. The soldier dragged it toward the camp in the woods. I stood watching it for a while; then I pulled open the door of my car and started the motor. I had forgotten my knapsack. I went back to the house, took my sack and kicking the door shut, I climbed into my car and drove off to Nemirovskoye.

In the whitish light of dawn the river had a strange glitter. The sky was overcast; it looked like a winter sky. The wind blew along the river. Thick reddish clouds of dust passed low on the horizon like clouds escaping from a fire. Water birds among the reeds along the banks croaked raucously; flocks of wild ducks rose into flight, beating their wings slowly above the water, through thickets of willows shivering in the biting cold of the morning. And everywhere hung that smell of things rotting, of decomposing matter.

From time to time, I passed long rows of Romanian army carts. The soldiers walked ahead of their horses chattering aloud among themselves and laughing, or they slept stretched out on sacks of bread, ammunition boxes, bundles of spades and hoes. And that odor of rotting things rose from everywhere. Sometimes along the banks of the river and on the sandbars emerging from it, the reeds and willows began to sway as if some wild beast at the approach of men had hidden among them. The soldiers shouting "Mice! Mice!" unslung their rifles and shot into the reeds, out of which women, disheveled girls, men dressed in long coats, and small boys came rushing hither and yon, stumbling, falling and getting up again. They were Jews from the neighboring villages who had escaped and who had taken cover among the reeds and willows.

Farther along on a marshy stretch between the road and the river, a Soviet armored car lay overturned. The gun stuck out of the conning tower, the trap door was open and twisted by the explosion; inside, amid the mud that had filled the car, was a man's arm. It was a carcass of an armored car. It stank of oil and petrol, of burnt paint, of gutted leather and scorched iron. It was a strange odor. A new odor. The new odor of the new war. I felt sorry for that armored car, but sorry in a different way than I had felt at the sight of the dead horse. It was a dead machine. A rotting machine. It had already begun to stink. It was iron carrion, overturned in the mud.

I stopped and went down to the side of the mudhole, close to the armored car. I grasped the arm of the tankman and tried to pull him out. I pulled with all my strength until I felt the arm yielding and saw a head gradually emerging from the mud. It was a mud ball. I wiped the face with my hand. I clawed with my nails at that mass of filth, and a small gray face with black lashes and black eyes appeared under the palm of my hand. It was a Tartar, a Tartar tankman. I began pulling once more to draw him out of the car, but soon gave up; the mud was stronger. I climbed into my car and drove off toward a cloud of smoke that rose from the plain, on the edge of a huge blue forest.

Meanwhile the sun was coming up from the horizon of green, and gradually the hoarse call of the birds was becoming shriller and more lively. The sun seemed to beat down hammer-like on the cast-iron plate of the lagoons. A shiver ran along the water with a kind of metallic vibration and spread to the surface of the pools, just as the sound of a violin spreads like a shiver along the arms of a musician. By the roadside, and here and there in the cornfields, were overturned cars, burned trucks, disemboweled armored cars, abandoned guns, all twisted by explosions. But nowhere a man, nothing living, not even a corpse, not even any carrion. For miles and miles around there was only dead iron. Dead bodies of machines, hundreds upon hundreds of miserable steel carcasses. The stench of putrifying iron rose from the fields and the lagoons. The cockpit of a plane was sticking up from the mud in the middle of a pool. The German cross was clearly discernible: it was a Messerschmitt. The smell of rotting iron won over the smell of men and horses—that smell of old wars; even the smell of grain and the penetrating, sweet scent of sunflowers vanished amid that sour stench of scorched iron, rotting steel, dead machinery. The clouds of dust lifted by the wind from the far ends of the vast plain carried no smell of organic matter with them but a smell of iron filing. And all the time, while I was pushing into the heart of the plain and approached Nemirovskoye, the smell of iron and of petrol grew stronger in the dusty air; even the grass seemed to be permeated with that undefinable, strong and exhilarating smell of gasoline, as if the smell of men and beasts, the smell of trees, of grass and mud was overcome by that odor of gasoline and scorched iron.

I was forced to stop some miles from Nemirovskoye. A German Feldgendarme—a field policeman—with his glittering brass plate like some knightly order hanging on a chain from his neck, commanded me to stop. *"Verboten!*—Prohibited!" It was impossible to go ahead. *"Nein! Nein! Nein!"* I drove along a side road, a kind of cart track; I meant to get as close as possible to Nemirovskoye, so I could see the Russian "bulge" that the Germans had encountered on their way, and were now attacking on all sides. Fields, ditches, villages, the *kolkhoz*—the collective farms—were all full of German troops. And everywhere *verboten.* Everywhere *zurück*—turn back. Toward sunset I made up my mind to go back. It was useless to lose time and to try to get through. Much better to turn back toward Balta and edge northward toward Kiev.

I drove on and stopped after a long stretch in an abandoned village where I ate a little of my dry bread and cheese. Most houses had been destroyed by fire. From the southwest came the roar of guns at my back. Yes, literally at my back. A large hammer and sickle were painted on the front of a house. Entering I saw that it was a Soviet office. A huge portrait of Stalin was pasted on the wall. Some Romanian soldiers had penciled: *"Aiurea!"* under that portrait, which means "Oh, yeah!"

I sat down on a writing desk cluttered with papers: the floor also was covered with papers, rags, books and propaganda pamphlets. And I thought of the dead mare stretched in front of the house where I had spent the night in the village of Alexandrovska; I thought of the poor, lonely carrion lying on the side of the road, in the midst of the crowd of dead machines and steel carcasses. I thought of the poor, lonely stench of the dead mare overcome by the smell of scorched iron, gasoline, rotting steel, of the new smell of this new war of machinery. I thought of the soldiers in *War and*

41

Peace, of the Russian roads along which Russian and French bodies and carcasses of horses were scattered. I thought of the odor of dead men, dead beasts, of the soldiers in *War and Peace* who were left alive by the roadside to the rapacious beaks of the crows. I thought of the Tartar horsemen armed with bows and arrows, the horsemen of the Amur river, whom Napoleon's soldiers called *les Amours*—those tireless fleet, merciless Tartar horsemen, speeding out of the woods and flaying the enemy stragglers, that ancient and noble race of horsemen who were born and lived with horses, fed on horse flesh and mare's milk, dressed in horses' skins, slept under tents made out of horsehides, and were buried in deep graves astride their horses.

I thought of the Tartars in the Red Army, who are the best mechanical workers in the U.S.S.R., the best Storm Troopers among workers, the best *udarniki*—"shock" workers—and *stakhanovtzi* *— the spearheads of the "attacking squads" of the Soviet heavy industry. I thought of the Tartars in the Red Army who are the best drivers of tanks, the best engineers in the armored divisions and in the Flying Corps. I thought of the young Tartars whom three five-year plans have transformed from horsemen into industrial workers, from horse-breeders into *udarniki* in the iron works of Stalingrad, of Kharkov and of Magnitogorsk.

"Aiurea!" meaning "Oh yeah!" was penciled in Romanian beneath Stalin's portrait. Undoubtedly it had been written by some poor Romanian peasant, who had never examined a machine, who had never touched a screw, or loosened a bolt, or taken an engine apart—some poor Romanian peasant whom Marshal Antonescu— the "Red Dog" as his officers call him—had driven into that war of peasants against the huge army of engineering workers of the U.S.S.R.

I reached for Stalin's picture and began to tear off the section of the poster with the word *"Aiurea!"* Just then I heard footsteps in the yard. I went to the door and some Romanian soldiers who were there asked me the time. "Six o'clock," I answered. They said *"Multzumesc"* which means "thanks" and invited me to have a cup of tea with them. I said *"Multzumesc"* and following them through the village, shortly reached a partially wrecked house where five or

* Workers under the "speed-up" plan.

six more soldiers welcomed me warmly, asked me to have a seat, and offered me a cup of tea and a bowl of *ciorba de pui*—the Romanian chicken soup.

I said "*Multzumesc.*" We began to talk and the soldiers told me that they were a liaison post in the village, that their division was some ten miles farther on, to the right. There was not a living soul in that village. The Germans had passed through it ahead of the Romanians.

"The Germans," said one of those soldiers in a deep voice, and all the others laughed.

"The Germans went through here before we did," another soldier repeated as if apologizing. They laughed softly while eating the *ciorba de pui.*

"*Aiurea!*" said I.

"It is quite true," said one of them who was a corporal, "the Germans passed through here ahead of us. It is quite true."

"*Aiurea!*" said I.

"*Domnule*—Sir—*Capitan*," said the corporal, "if you don't believe me, ask the prisoner. We do not destroy villages; we do not harm the peasants. We only have it in for the Jews. It's quite true. You, there, *asculta!*—listen here!" he shouted turning toward the corner of the room. "Isn't it true that the Germans passed through here ahead of us?"

I turned toward the dark corner and saw a man sitting on the floor with his back against the wall. He was dressed in khaki; a yellow service cap sat on his shorn head. He was barefoot. A Tartar. He had a small lean face, the gray, shiny skin was tightly drawn over his prominent cheekbones; his eyes were fixed, black, perhaps veiled with hunger and fatigue. Motionless, he gazed at me with those veiled eyes of his. He did not reply to the corporal's question; he kept gazing at me.

"Where did you capture him?" I inquired.

"He was inside the armored car left in the square. There was something wrong with the motor, and the tank couldn't budge, but it kept on firing. The Germans were in a hurry and went off leaving us to deal with it. There were two men inside. They went on shooting till the very end. One of them was dead. We had to force the trap door open with a jimmy. He refused to surrender. He didn't

43

have a single shot left; he said nothing; he squatted inside and did not want to open. The other one, the gunner, was dead. This one was the driver. We have to take him to the Romanian headquarters at Balta; but now nobody passes through here; the convoys of trucks drive along the main road. It's three days since anyone has passed through here."

"Why did you take off his boots?" I asked.

The soldiers began laughing, looked insolently at me.

"A lovely pair of boots," said the corporal, "you look, *Domnule Capitan,* what boots these pigs of Russians have." He got up, rummaged in a sack and drew out a pair of heelless Tartar boots of soft leather. "They are better clothed than we are," went on the corporal pointing to his down-at-the-heel shoes and to his torn trousers.

"It means they have a better country than yours," I said.

"These pigs have no country," said the corporal, "they are like animals."

"Even animals have a country," I replied, "a far better country than ours. Better than the Romanian country or the German country or the Italian country."

The soldiers gazed fixedly at me; they did not understand; they looked at me and silently chewed bits of chicken swimming in the *ciorba,* and the corporal said uncomfortably, "A pair of boots such as these is worth at least two thousand *lei.*"

The soldiers shook their heads and drew in their lips. "Yes," one of them said, "a pair of boots like these, two thousand *lei* at the very least, if not more," and again they shook their heads and compressed their lips. They were Romanian peasants and Romanian peasants do not know what animals are; they do not know that animals also have a country; they do not know what machines are; that machines also have a country; that boots also have a country; a far better country than ours. They are peasants, and they do not even know what being peasants means; the Bratianu law has given the land to a horse, to a cow, to a sheep. They only know that they are Romanian and Greek Orthodox. They shout "Long Live the King!"; they shout "Long live Marshal Antonescu!"; they shout "Down with the U.S.S.R.!" But they do not know what the King is, what Marshal Antonescu is, what the U.S.S.R. is. They know that a pair of boots such as these are worth two thousand *lei* at least.

They are poor peasants, and they do not know that the U.S.S.R. is a machine; that they are fighting a machine, a thousand machines, a million machines. But a pair of boots like these is worth two thousand *lei* at least, if not more.

"Marshal Antonescu," I said, "has a pair of boots, a hundred pair of boots far better than these."

The soldiers gazed fixedly at me and drew in their lips.

"A hundred pair?" asked the corporal.

"A hundred, a thousand pair," I replied, "far better than these. Haven't you ever seen Marshal Antonescu's boots? They are very beautiful. Of yellow leather, black leather, red leather, white leather; cut in the English style with a rosette below the knee. They are beautiful. Marshal Antonescu's boots are more beautiful than those of Hitler or Mussolini. Hitler's boots are fine enough. I have looked at them closely. I have never spoken to Hitler, but I have looked at his boots from very near. They are spurless. Hitler never wears spurs, he is afraid of horses; but even without spurs, they are fine enough. Also Mussolini's boots are fine, but they are useless. They are not fit for walking or riding. They are only fit for standing in the grandstand, during a parade, and watching soldiers with torn shoes and rusty rifles march by."

The soldiers drawing in their lips gazed fixedly at me.

"After the war," I said, "we shall go and pull off Marshal Antonescu's boots."

"Also *Domnule* Hitler's," said a soldier.

"Also *Domnule* Mussolini's," said another.

"Certainly, also Mussolini's and Hitler's," I said. They all began laughing, and I asked the corporal, "How much do you think Hitler's boots are worth?"

They all ceased laughing, and suddenly, I don't know why, they turned to look at the prisoner who crouched in his corner and gazed at me with his veiled slanting eyes.

"Did you give him something to eat?" I asked the corporal.

"Yes, *Domnule Capitan.*"

"That's not true. You did not give him anything to eat," I said.

The corporal took a bowl from the table, then filled it with *ciorba de pui,* and passed it to the prisoner.

"Give him a spoon," I said, "he cannot eat soup with his hands."

The soldiers gazed at the corporal as he took a spoon from the table, cleaned it by rubbing it with his hands and offered it to the prisoner.

"*Ochen spassibo*—Many thanks," said the prisoner.

"*La dracu!*" exclaimed the corporal, which means "to the devil."

"What are you going to do with the prisoner?" I asked.

"We have to take him to Balta," replied the corporal, "but nobody goes by here; we are off the beaten track; we shall have to walk him there. If no truck passes today, we shall take him to Balta tomorrow, on foot."

"It would be quicker to kill him, don't you think?" I asked the corporal gazing at him. All burst out laughing, watching the corporal.

"No, *Domnule Capitan*," replied the corporal blushing slightly. "I cannot. The orders are to bring at least one prisoner to headquarters when we capture any. No, *Domnule Capitan*."

"If you take him on foot, you'll have to give him his boots back. No one can walk barefoot as far as Balta."

"Oh, he can walk barefoot as far as Bucharest," said the corporal laughing.

"If you like, I'll take him to Balta in my car. Give me a soldier as an escort and I will take him with me."

The corporal looked pleased; the other soldiers also looked pleased.

"You'll go, Grigorescu," said the corporal.

Private Grigorescu strapped on his cartridge belt, took the rifle that was leaning against the wall (they were French cartridge pouches, wide and flat, and the rifle was a French Lebel with its long triangular bayonet), he took his haversack from a nail on the wall, flung it across his shoulder, spat on the ground and said, "Let's go."

The prisoner continued to sit in his corner. He looked at us with his glazed eyes. "*Podiom*—Let's go!" I told the prisoner. The Tartar rose slowly to his feet; he was tall, as tall as I am; his shoulders were rather narrow, his neck thin. He followed me stooping a little, and Private Grigorescu kept behind him with his rifle ready.

A fierce wind was blowing; the sky was gray, as heavy as a cast-iron plate; the wheat's voice rose and fell with the wind, like the voice of a river. From time to time, the forests of sunflowers were heard squeaking in the hoarse dusty gusts.

"*La revedere*—See you again," said the corporal shaking my hand. The soldiers came up one by one, to shake hands. "*La revedere, la revedere, Domnule Capitan, la revedere.*" I started the motor, left the village, and drove along a track full of holes and ploughed in deep furrows (the tracks of the caterpillar tanks were sharply imprinted in the yielding mattress of dust). Private Grigorescu and the prisoner were sitting behind me, and I felt the fixed gaze of the Tartar boring into my back.

The storm was approaching from the end of the vast plain; little by little it covered the breadth of the sky like a huge frog. It was a green cloud, spotted white here and there; the soft frog's belly could be seen throbbing with labored breathing. From time to time a harsh croaking reached us from the edge of the horizon. In the fields, by the roadside, there lay hundreds of burned-out machines, carcasses of lorries, steel carrion stretched out sideways with legs apart, miserable and obscene. And lo! by degrees, I seemed to recognize the road, I had certainly driven through there before, a few days before, perhaps that very morning: there were the river and the pools, their shores thick with reeds and willows. The reflection of the whitish belly of the huge frog, swallowing the sky with raucous croaks, floated on the livid surface of the water. A few drops, slow, hot and heavy, pierced the dust on the road sizzling like a red-hot iron dropped in water. At last I made out some houses through the dusk, and I recognized the houses of Alexandrovska, the abandoned village where I had spent the night.

"We had better stop here," I said to Private Grigorescu. "It's too late to go on; Balta is still far off."

I stopped the car in front of the house where I had slept. The rain had begun, it fell heavily with a subdued thud, raising a thick cloud of yellow dust. The mare's carcass still lay at the edge of the road in front of the wooden gate. Its wide-open eye was filled with a white light. We entered the house. Everything was as I had left it in the morning, in the same motionless, ghostlike disorder. I sat down on the bed, looking at the Private Grigorescu, who removed his cartridge belts and hung his haversack on the door handle. The

47

prisoner was leaning against the wall, his arm hanging by his sides, and he gazed at me with his small, slanting eyes.

I stood in the door; the night was as black as coal. I went into the orchard, pushed the gate open and sat down on the edge of the road close by the mare's carcass. The rain drenched my face, ran down my back. Greedily I took in the scent of wet grass, and little by little the soft, greasy stench of the carrion penetrated that fresh and exhilarating scent, conquered the odor of rotting steel, dissolving iron and putrified metal. I felt as if the ancient law of war—human and animal—was mastering the new law of mechanical war; I felt at home in the odor of the dead horse as if in an old fatherland, a fatherland that I had found again.

Later I went back to the house and stretched out on the bed. I was dead tired; my bones ached; sleep was throbbing in my head as in a pulsing artery.

"We will take turns watching the prisoner," I said to the soldier, "you must be tired too. Wake me in three hours."

"*Nu, nu, Domnule Capitan,*" said the soldier, "I am not tired. I am not sleepy."

The prisoner, whose hands and feet Grigorescu had tied with a knotted rope, sat in a corner of the room against the wall between the window and the cupboard. The thick stench of the carrion stagnated within the room. The yellow light of an oil lamp swayed along the walls; the sunflowers squeaked in the orchard under the rain. The soldier faced the prisoner and squatted on the floor with crossed legs—his rifle with a fixed bayonet rested on his knees.

"*Nopte buna*—Good night," I said closing my eyes.

"*Nopte buna, Domnule Capitan,*" said the soldier.

I was unable to sleep. The storm had broken and raged furiously. The sky split with a roar, sudden light flooded from the clouds and pelted onto the plain; rain fell as hard and heavy as if it were raining stones. And the stench of the mare's carcass, whipped up by the rain, penetrated fat and slimy into the house and stagnated beneath the low ceiling. The prisoner sat motionless, the back of his head leaning against the wall, and gazed at me fixedly. His hands and feet were tied; his hands, small and pale, ash-colored, with the rope knotted tightly round the wrists, hung loosely between his knees.

"Why don't you untie him?" I asked Grigorescu. "Are you afraid that he might get away? You might at least free his feet."

The soldier bent forward and slowly undid the feet of the prisoner who was gazing at me with his stony eyes.

I woke up a few hours later. The soldier, his rifle across his knees, was still sitting on the floor opposite the prisoner. The Tartar, the back of his head resting against the wall, gazed at me.

"You sleep now," I said getting out of bed. "It's my turn now."

"*Nu, nu, Domnule Capitan,* I am not sleepy."

"Go to sleep, I tell you."

Private Grigorescu rose, crossed the room dragging his rifle along the floor, and still clutching the rifle in his hands threw himself on the bed and turned toward the wall. He looked dead. His hair was white with dust, his uniform torn, his shoes worn. Coarse black hair bristled on the skin of his face. He looked dead.

I settled on the floor opposite the prisoner, crossed my legs and shoved my automatic between my knees. The Tartar gazed at me with his veiled, narrow eyes, slanted like a cat's; they looked as if they were made of glass. They had the gaze that dead people's eyes have; the eyelids, curled up under the brows, formed two scarcely visible sepia-colored folds. I leaned forward to untie the prisoner's hands. I studied his hands while my fingers fumbled with the knots on the rope; they were small, smooth, ash-colored, with nails that were almost white. Although they were marked by short deep lines, the skin was so porous that it looked as if it were seen through a microscope. The palms were thinly coated with calluses but were soft, smooth and almost tender to the touch. Hanging limply, they yielded to my hands as if they were dead, but I sensed that they were strong, nimble, tenacious, and at the same time as light and delicate as a surgeon's, a watchmaker's or a skilled precision worker's.

They were the hands of a young recruit of the *Piatiletka,* of an **udarnik** of the third Five-Year Plan, of a young Tartar who had become an engineer, a tank driver. Softened by the incessant thousand-year-long rubbing against the silky coats of horses, against manes, tendons, hocks, muscles of horses; with reins, with the smooth leather of saddles and harness, they had passed within a few years from horse to machine, from flesh to metal tendons, from reins to controls. A few years had been enough to transform young Tartars of the Don and the Volga, of the Kirghiz Steppe and the shores of the Caspian and the Aral seas, from horse-breeders into qualified workers of the U.S.S.R., from horsemen into *stakhanovtzi* of the labor *Sturm Truppen,* from nomads of the steppe into *udarniki* and *spets*—specialists—of the Five-Year Plan. I undid the last knot and offered him a cigarette.

The prisoner's hands hurt, his fingers were numb; he could not take a cigarette from the package. I placed the cigarette between his lips, and lit his and my own.

"Blagodariu—Thanks," the Tartar said and smiled at me. I smiled at him too, and for a long time we continued to smoke in silence. The stench of the carrion filled the room, greasy, soft and sweetish. I inhaled the stench of the dead mare with a strange enjoyment. The prisoner also seemed to breathe with a delicate, sad pleasure. His nostrils quivered, they throbbed strangely. And I became aware only then that all the life in that pale, ashen face in which the untroubled, slanting eyes had the fixed glassy stare of a corpse, had gathered about his nostrils. His old homeland, the homeland he had found again, was in the odor of the dead mare. We looked into each other's eyes, in silence, and inhaled with a delicate and sad enjoyment that sweetish smell. That carrion odor was his homeland, his ageless and living homeland, and now nothing stood between us any longer. We were brothers living in the ageless odor of the dead mare.

. . . Prince Eugene lifted his face, turned his eyes toward the door; his nostrils quivered as if the dead mare's odor stood on the threshold and looked at us. It was the smell of grass and leaves, of sea and woods. Dusk had already set in, but an uncertain light still wandered across the sky. In that spectral light the faraway houses of Nybroplan, the steamers and sailing boats moored along the quays of Strandvägen, the trees of the park, the ghostly shadows of Rodin's "Penseur" and of the "Niké of Samothrace" were reflected, deformed, on the light landscape as in the drawings of Ernst Josephson and of Carl Hill, who were driven by their gloomy madness to see animals, trees, houses and ships reflected by the landscape as in a distorting mirror.

"He had hands like yours," I said.

Prince Eugene glanced at his hands. He seemed slightly ill at ease. His were the white shapely hands of the Bernadotte—pale slender fingers.

And I told him: "The hands of an engineer, of a tank driver, of an *udarnik* of the third *Piatiletka* are no less beautiful than yours. They are the hands of Mozart, Stradivarius, Picasso, Sauerbruch."

Prince Eugene smiled and, blushing a little, said, "I am all the prouder of my hands."

The voice of the wind gradually had grown stronger, shriller, like a long doleful neighing. It was the north wind, and its voice made me shudder. The recollection of the frightful winter I had spent in Karelia, between the Leningrad suburbs and the shores of Lake Ladoga, called up the vision of the silent, white, endless Karelian forests, and I shuddered as if the wind that caused the panes of the large windows to rattle was the merciless, frozen wind of Karelia.

"It is the north wind," said Prince Eugene.

"Yes, it is the Karelian wind," I said. "I recognize its voice."

And there flashed through my memory the horses of Lake Ladoga.

III

Ice Horses

THAT MORNING I went with Svartström to see the horses freed from their prison of ice.

A greenish sun in the pale blue sky shone like an unripe apple. Since the thaw had set in, the icebound surface of Lake Ladoga had begun creaking; it wailed, at times it shrieked shrilly as if in pain. In the deep of night, from the end of the *korsu* * we could hear it suddenly crying out, wailing for hours at a time, until the dawn. It was already spring; the lake exhaled its fetid breath into our faces, that lean smell of rotten wood and wet sawdust that is typical of the thaw. The opposite shore of Lake Ladoga looked like a thin pencil stroke on blotting paper. Now the sky was a cloudless faded blue: it seemed a sky of tissue paper. Yonder, toward Leningrad—a gray cloud of smoke hung over the besieged city—the sky was slightly dirty, slightly crumpled. A green vein cut across the horizon, it seemed at times as if it could be seen throbbing, as if it were full of hot blood.

That morning we went to see the icebound horses being freed. The night before Colonel Merikallio, sniffing the wind, had said, "The horses caught in the ice crust will have to be buried. Spring is beginning."

We went down to the lake through a thick birch wood in which were scattered huge stones of red granite. Suddenly, in front of us lay the vast dark expanse of Lake Ladoga.

The Soviet shore showed vaguely on the horizon behind a silvery mist, veined with pale blue and pink. From time to time the monotonous call of the cuckoo, the sacred bird of Karelia, reached us from the thick of the vast Raikkola forest. Wild beasts howled among the trees, mysterious voices called answered, called again—

* *Korsu*—A snow-buried shanty or dugout.

persistent, mournful sounds, filled with a sweet and cruel entreaty.

Before leaving the *korsu* of Finnish headquarters to descend toward the lake, I had searched for Lieutenant Svartström. I had knocked in vain at the door of his little room in the *korsu* behind the stables. The forest around headquarters looked deserted. And there was everywhere that lean smell, that tepid smell in the cold air. I approached the *korsu* of the horses. A girl in a *lotta* * uniform was preparing a pail of cellulose horse fodder for the Colonel's horse.

"*Haivää päivää*—Good day," I said.

"*Haivää päivää.*"

She was the daughter of Colonel Merikallio, a tall fair girl, a Finn from Oulu in East Bothnia. She had followed her father to the front, as a *lotta* during the first Finnish war, in the winter of 1939. She saw to the headquarters mess, and under her father's eye served at the table, a few hundred yards from the Russian trenches.

Her hands were livid from the cold as she chopped a large sheet of cellulose paste into a pail filled with warm water. The horse was tied to a tree and was twisting its neck toward the pail filled with the cellulose. The winter had been frightful; the terrible cold, hunger, hardships and toil had shrunk the faces of the Finnish people. The hard, bony features of the Kalevala heroes, as painted by Gallen Kallela, were showing again in the pale fleshless faces.

Soldiers, children, women, old people and animals, were all hungry. There was not a shred of hay, or of straw; not an oat to feed the horses; dogs had been slaughtered wholesale; the soldiers' gloves were made of dogs' skins. The people fed on cellulose bread, and horses relished the sweetish taste of that cellulose mash—the taste of cooked paper.

The girl untied the horse, grasped the halter and, carrying the pail in her left hand, moved toward a wooden tub sitting on a bench. She poured the cellulose mash into the tub and the horse began to eat slowly, gazing round from time to time. It looked toward the lake that shone dully through the trees. A cloud of steam rose from the tub, the horse sank his nuzzle into that cloud; then it raised its head, looked toward the lake and neighed.

"What's the trouble?" I asked the girl. "He seems to be restless."

* *Lotta*—A Finnish Wac.

Colonel Merikallio's daughter turned her face to the lake. "It smells the horses," she said.

I smelt the horses, too: it was a warm, greasy odor, mellowed by the resinous scent of the pines and by the lean odor of birches. The cuckoo gave its call at the edge of the forest; a squirrel, his tail erect, scampered up a tree trunk. The girl picked up the pail and went into the horse *korsu*. I could hear her talking to the horses with that slow sweet intonation of the Finnish language; I could hear the dull thud of the horses' hooves on the litter of birch branches, the twinkle of the iron rings, the short impatient neighing.

I made off toward the lake. Svartström was waiting for me at a turn in the path; he was leaning against a tree trunk, his high sheepskin cap tilted back toward the nape of his neck, his legs sunk halfway to his thighs in Lapp reindeer leather boots with upturned points like Persian slippers. His eyes were lowered and he was slightly stooped as he tapped the bowl of his empty pipe on the palm of his hand. When I reached him, he raised his face, looked at me smiling, and said, "*Haivää päivää.*"

"*Haivää päivää*, Svartström."

He was pale, his brow damp with the sweat of fatigue and lack of sleep. As if apologizing, he told me that he had been in the forest the entire night with a ranger patrol.

"Where is Colonel Merikallio?" I inquired.

"He has gone to the lines," he replied. He glanced at me as he tapped the empty pipe in the hollow of his hand, and from time to time he turned toward the lake. I saw his nostrils quivering. He breathed through his nose as woodsmen do, as *sissit*—the Finnish rangers—do: a thin, cautious, suspicious breathing, just a thread of air.

"You really want to go and see them?" asked Svartström. "It would have been better for you to follow the Colonel to the lines. He purposely went to the trenches not to see them."

The wind was charged with the odor of the horses, that greasy, sweet odor.

"I should like to see them for the last time, Svartström, before they take them away."

We walked on toward the lake. The snow was sodden; it was already spring snow; no longer white, but ivory colored, with those

54

green and yellow spots found in old ivory. Here and there where it filmed the red granite rock, it was the color of wine. And where the trees were thinner, it seemed to be covered with a thin coating of ice like a glistening piece of Orefors crystal through which pine needles, colored pebbles, blades of grass, scales of that white skin' that clothes birch trunks could be seen. Twisted tree roots broke through the crystal sheet like frozen serpents; it seemed as if the trees drew sustenance from the ice, that the young leaves of a more tender green took their sap from that dead, glassy matter. Strange sounds ran through the air; it was not the wail of beaten iron, nor the sonorous shudder that bells make in the wind, nor the drawn-out soft note of a stroking finger on glass; it was not even the high, round hum of wild bees swarming in the thick of the woods, but it really was a wail; it seemed the moan of a wounded beast, the call of a lonely and despairing agony that crossed the sky like an invisible flock of doleful birds.

Winter, that terrible winter of 1942, that had been the great scourge, the great plague of the Finnish people, the white plague that had filled the hospitals and churchyards of the whole of Finland, lay now like a huge naked corpse across the lakes and the woods. That huge decomposing body tainted the air with its lean smell of rotten wood, and the first spring breeze was already bringing its tired scents, its tepid odors, its intimate and bestial dog's breath—the very snow seemed to be lukewarm.

For some days the soldiers had been less sad, more lively; their voices were a little louder, and during certain hours of the day a peculiar restlessness was creeping through the lines in the *korsus*, among *lottalas*,* through the trenches and the dugouts scooped into the thick of the wild Raikkola forest. To celebrate the return of spring, which is their sacred season of the year, the men of the North light great fires on the mountains, sing, drink and dance all night. But spring is the insidious disease of the North; it rots and dissolves the life that winter has jealously guarded and protected within its prison of ice, and brings its fatal gifts—love, the joy of living, the yielding to light thoughts and gay feelings, the enjoyment of strife, of idleness, and of sleep, the fever of the senses, the deluding weddings with nature. It is the season in which the eye of

* *Lottalas*—The recreation halls of the *lottas*.

the man of the North is lighted with a turbid flame, and the proud shadow of death that winter sweeps clean and free, sets on his brow.

"We have taken the wrong way, Svartström."

I no longer recognized the path I had so often followed during the winter on my way to the lake to see the horses. It had become narrower, more winding; the forest had grown thicker. As the snow thaws and changes color and the spring chrysalis bursts into flight out of the shining icy cocoon leaving the bare dead slough of winter, the forest regains mastery over the snow and the frost and becomes thick again—entangled, secretive—a green, mysterious and forbidden universe.

Svartström stepped slowly and cautiously; he stopped now and again to listen, detecting in the rhythmical silence of the forest, in that musical silence of nature, the crackling of the branches, the patter of the squirrel in a pine tree, the darting rustle of the hare, the anxious sniffing of the fox, the call of a bird, the whisper of a leaf, and far away—diseased and defiled—the voice of man. The silence around us was no longer the dead silence of winter, frosty and transparent as a block of crystal. It was a living silence, shot through by warm streams of colors, sounds and odors. The silence was like a river that I felt flowing around us; I thought I was being carried down the current of that invisible river, between the banks that were like warm, moist lips.

The mellow heat of the rising sun was pervading the forest. As the sun gradually climbed up along the arch of the horizon raising a slight pink mist from the silvery surface of the lake, there came with the wind a far-off rattling of machine guns, solitary rifle shots, the rapt song of the cuckoo; and at the end of that landscape of sounds, colors and odors, within a break of the forest, there flashed something opaque, something shiny, like the shimmering of an unreal sea—Lake Ladoga, the vast frozen expanse of Lake Ladoga.

At last we stepped out of the forest onto the shore of the lake and saw the horses.

It happened last year in October. The Finnish vanguard, after crossing the Vuoksi wilderness, crossed the threshold of the wild limitless Raikkola forest. It was full of Russian troops. Almost the entire Soviet artillery of the northern sector of the Karelian isthmus had rushed toward Lake Ladoga to escape the stranglehold of the Finnish army. It had hoped to ship the guns and the horses and to bring them to safety across the lake. But the Soviet lighters and tugs were late in arriving; every hour of delay could prove fatal for the frost had set in, gripping and savage; the lake was likely to freeze at any moment, and the Finnish troops, formed of ranger detachments, were gliding through the thick forest and pressing the Russians on all sides, attacking them from the flanks and the rear.

On the third day a huge fire flared in the Raikkola forest. Men, horses and trees clutched within the circle of fire sent out awful cries. The rangers, firing through that wall of smoke and flames, blocked every avenue of escape. Mad with terror, the horses of the Soviet artillery—there were almost a thousand of them—hurled themselves into the furnace and broke through the besieging flames and machine guns. Many perished within the flames, but most of them succeeded in reaching the shores of the lake and threw themselves into the water.

The lake is not deep there, not more than six feet; but a hundred yards from the shore the bottom suddenly drops. Pressed within that narrow space (the lakeshore curves inward there forming a small bay) between the deeper water and the barrier of fire, the horses clustered, shuddering with cold and fear, their heads stretched out above the surface of the water. Those nearer to land were scorched by the flames and reared and struggled to hoist themselves onto the backs of the others, tried to push a way open by biting and kicking. And while still madly struggling, the ice gripped them.

The north wind swooped down during the night. (The north wind blows from the Murmansk Sea, like an angel of doom, crying aloud, and the land suddenly dies.) The cold became frightful. Suddenly, with the peculiar vibrating noise of breaking glass, the water froze. The heat balance was broken, and the sea, the lakes, the rivers froze. In such instances, even sea waves are gripped in mid-air and become rounded ice waves suspended in the void.

On the following day, when the first ranger patrols, their hair singed, their faces blackened by smoke, cautiously stepped over the warm ashes in the charred forest and reached the lakeshore, a horrible and amazing sight met their eyes. The lake looked like a vast sheet of white marble on which rested hundreds upon hundreds of horses' heads. They appeared to have been chopped off cleanly with an ax. Only the heads stuck out of the crust of ice. And they were all facing the shore. The white flame of terror still burnt in their wide-open eyes. Close to the shore a tangle of wildly rearing horses rose from the prison of ice.

Later winter came; the hissing north wind swept the snow away; the surface of the lake was as clean and smooth as an ice-hockey rink. During the dull days of the endless winter, toward noon, when a little faded light rains from the sky, Colonel Merikallio's soldiers used to go down to the lake and sit on the heads of the horses. They were like wooden horses on a merry-go-round. *Tournez, tournez, bons chevaux de bois*—turn, turn, good wooden horses. The scene might have been painted by Bosch. The wind through the black skeletons of the trees played a sweet, childish, sad music; the sheet of ice seemed to turn, as the horses of that macabre merry-go-round tossing their manes would curve to the sad tune of the sweet childish music. The soldiers would shout, *"Hop la! Tournez, tournez, bons chevaux de bois."*

On Sunday mornings the rangers gathered in the Raikkola *lottala*, and after drinking a cup of tea, walked toward the lake. (The rangers—*sissit*—are the wolves of forest warfare. They are mostly young, some are very young; some mere boys. They belong to the solitary and silent Sillampää * breed of heroes. They spend their entire lives in the depths of the forest. They live like trees, rocks and wild animals.) They used to go down to the lake and sit on the heads of the horses. The accordion player would start a *laulu*, the "Vertiossa," which is the song of the lookout. Wrapped in their sheepskin coats, the rangers would sing together the sad *laulu*. Then the player, sitting on the frozen mane, would run his fingers over the keyboard and the rangers would take up the *Reppurin laulu*, the song of the cuckoo, which is the sacred bird of Karelia.

> *Siell mie paimelauluin lauluin*
> *min muamo mieroon suori*
> *Karjalan maill kuldäkäkoset guk-kuup.* . . .

* Sillampää—A Finnish writer.

The cuckoo's call rang sad and loud in the silence of the forest. Guns rumbled on the opposite shore of Lake Ladoga. The crash of the explosions spread from tree to tree like a flutter of wings, a rustle of leaves. And above the living silence that was rendered deeper and more secret by the occasional ping of isolated rifle shots, rose persistent, monotonous and very pure the call of the cuckoo, a call which seemed to become human. *Gook kooup, gook kooup.*

Sometimes, Svartström and I also went down to the lake and sat on the heads of the horses. Leaning his elbow on the hard icy mane, Svartström tapped the empty pipe in the hollow of his hand and gazed fixedly in front of him across the frozen, silvery expanse of the lake. Svartström hails from Viipuri—called Viborg by the Swedes—the Karelian city on the shore of the Gulf of Finland facing Leningrad. His wife is a young Leningrad Russian of French origin, and he has something delicate and gentle in him that men in the North seldom possess, perhaps something French that he has acquired from his wife, his *baby kulta—"kulta"* meaning "golden" in Finnish. He knows a few French words; he can say *oui, charmant,* and *pauvre petite.* He can also say *naturlement* instead of *naturellement.* He can say *amour,* he often says *amour;* and he also says *très beaucoup.* Svartström, by profession, is a poster-designer; and he spends many hours in drawing red and blue flowers with a red and blue pencil, in cutting *baby kulta's* name into the white bark of birches, and in writing the word *amour* in the snow with the tip of his stick.

Svartström never had any tobacco. For a month he had been tapping the bowl of his empty pipe in the hollow of his hand, and I used to say to him, "Tell me the truth, Svartström. I am sure you would even smoke a piece of human flesh." He used to grow pale then and reply, "If this war goes on . . ." And I said: "If this war goes on, we shall all become like beasts, and you too, don't you think so?" And he answered, "I, too, *naturlement.*"

I was fond of him. I became fond of Svartström on the day I saw him grow pale because of that piece of human flesh—we were in the *Kannas,** in front of the Leningrad suburbs—that the rangers had discovered in the haversack of a Russian paratrooper who had hidden in the forest for two months in a hole next to the corpse of

* *Kanna*—an isthmus.

a companion. In the *korsu* that night, Svartström had vomited. He wept saying: "They have shot him, but is it his fault? We shall all become like wild beasts and we shall end by eating each other." He was not drunk. He very seldom drank. It was not drink. It was that piece of human flesh that made him vomit. I became fond of him that day, but from time to time, when I saw him tapping his empty pipe in the hollow of his hand, I used to say to him, "Isn't it a fact, Svartström, that you would be capable of stuffing your pipe with a piece of human flesh?"

One evening, during dinner at the Spanish Legation in Helsinki, the Spanish Minister, Count Augustin de Foxa, started talking about the piece of human flesh the rangers had discovered in the haversack of that Russian paratrooper. We had had an excellent dinner; the old Spanish wines endowed the Oulu salmon and the smoked reindeer tongue with the delicate warm flavors of the sun. All protested, saying that the Russian paratrooper was not a man, that he was a wild beast, but no one vomited, no one; neither Countess Mannerheim, nor Demetra Slörn, nor Prince Cantemir, nor Colonel Slörn—Adjutant to the President of the Republic; not Baron Bengt von Törne, not even Titu Michailescu, nobody vomited.

"A Christian," said Anita Bengenström, "would rather die of starvation than eat human flesh."

Count de Foxa laughed, "Ha, ha, ha! A Catholic wouldn't; a Catholic wouldn't. Catholics like human flesh."

And as everyone protested, the white reflection of the snow broke through the windowpanes; it was like the reflection of a huge silver mirror shining back with silver flashes from dark solid walnut furniture, from the excessively shiny varnish of the oil portraits of Spanish grandees, from the golden Crucifix hanging on the wall covered with heavy red brocade—then Count de Foxa said, "All Catholics eat human flesh, Jesus Christ's flesh, the very holy flesh of Jesus: the Host, the most divine and most human flesh in the world." And he began to recite in a deep voice that poem of Federico Garcia Llorca, the Spanish poet who was shot in 1936 by Franco's men, the famous *Oda al Santisimo Sacramento del Altar*—"Ode to the Most Holy Sacrament at the Altar"—which begins like a love song: *cantaban las mujeres*—the women were singing. . . . When he came to the lines about the "frog," de Foxa raised his voice:

> *Vivo estabas, Dios mio, dentro del ostensorio*
> *punzando por tu Padre con agujas de lumbre.*
> *Latiendo come el pobre corazon de la rana*
> *que los medicos ponen en el frasco de vidrio.*

> *You lived, O my Lord, in the monstrance* °
> *Pricked by your Father with flashes of light.*
> *Palpitating like the poor heart of a frog*
> *Which doctors preserve in glass jars.*

"This is disgusting," said Countess Mannerheim. "The flesh of Jesus which knocks within the *monstrance* like the heart of a frog! Ah, you Catholics are monsters!"

"There is no better flesh in the world," said Count de Foxa in a deep voice.

"Isn't it true, Svartström," I used to say to him, "that you could be capable of smoking a piece of human flesh?"

Svartström smiled, his was a tired, sad smile. He looked at the heads of the horses protruding from the sheet of ice, those dead heads with hard frozen manes, those shiny wide-open eyes filled with terror. He stroked with a light hand those extended muzzles, the bloodless nostrils, the lips twisted with a despairing neighing— a neighing that was buried within the mouth full of frozen foam. Then, as we walked off in silence, we were wont to caress in passing, the manes white with sleet. The wind was softly hissing over the vast sheet of ice.

That morning we went to see the horses being freed from their prison of ice.

A sweet and greasy odor floated in the mild air. It was near the end of April and the sun was already warm. For some days, since

° *Monstrance*—A transparent vessel in which the Host is kept and shown to the congregation.

the thaw had set in, the heads of the horses gripped within the crust of the ice had begun to stink. During certain hours of the day, that odor of carrion was beyond endurance, and Colonel Merikallio had given the order to take the horses out of the water and bury them in the thick of the forest. Squads of soldiers, equipped with saws, axes, crowbars, mattocks and ropes, had gone down to Lake Ladoga with a hundred sledges.

When we reached the shore, the soldiers were already at work. Some fifty carcasses were heaped crossways on the sledges; they were no longer stiff, but limp, swollen; their long manes freed by the thaw were floating. The eyelids hung on their watery swelling eyes. The soldiers broke the ice crust with mattocks and axes and the horses floated upturned on the dirty whitish water filled with air bubbles and spongy snow. The soldiers roped the carcasses and dragged them to the shore. The heads dangled over the sides of the sledges. The artillery horses scattered through the forest and neighed, smelling that sweet and heavy odor, and the horses hitched to the shafts of the sledges answered with long lamenting neighs.

"Pois, pois! giddy-up!" shouted the soldiers brandishing their whips. The sledges glided away on the muddy snow with a dull rustle. And the harness bells made a gay sound in the tepid air, almost a merry lament.

The room, by now, was steeped in shadow. The voice of the wind among the old trees of Oakhill was loud and sad, and I shuddered listening to the doleful neighing of the north wind.

"You are cruel," said Prince Eugene. "I feel sorry for you."

"I am deeply grateful to you," I said and laughed, but I at once felt ashamed of my laughter, and I blushed—"I feel sorry for myself too. I am ashamed of my feeling of self-pity."

"Oh, you are cruel," said Prince Eugene. "I wish I could help you."

"Let me tell you a strange dream," I said. "It is a dream which often troubles my nights. I walk into a square crowded with people who are all looking upward, and I raise my eyes and see a high mountain sheer above the square. A large cross is on the mountaintop. A crucified horse hangs from the cross beam. The executioners, standing on ladders, are hammering the last nails in. The hammers can be heard striking the nails. The crucified horse dangles its head from side to side and neighs softly. The silent crowd weeps. The sacrifice of the Horse-Christ, the tragedy of that animal Golgotha—I wish you would help me to understand the meaning of this dream. Might not the death of the horse signify the death of all that is noble and pure in man? Don't you think that this dream refers to the war?"

"The very war itself is but a dream," said Prince Eugene passing his hand across his brow and his eyes.

"All that is noble, gentle and pure in Europe is dying. The horse is our homeland. You understand what I mean by this. Our homeland, our ancient homeland is dying. And all those obsessing pictures, that persistent obsession of neighing, of the horrible and sad odor of the dead horses lying on their backs along the roads of the war, don't they seem to correspond to the vision of war, to our voice, our odor, to the odor of dead Europe? Don't you also think that this dream means something similar? It is perhaps better not to interpret dreams."

"Enough," said Prince Eugene. Then he leaned toward me and said in a low voice, "Ah, if I could but suffer as you do!"

PART TWO

THE MICE

IV

God Shave the King

"I AM THE KING; *der König*," said Reichsminister Frank, Governor-General of Poland, spreading his arms and gazing upon his guests with proud complacency.

I glanced at him smiling.

"The German King of Poland, *der deutsche König von Polen*," repeated Frank.

I gazed at him smiling.

"Why do you smile? Have you never seen a king before?" asked Frank.

"Indeed I have spoken to many kings. I have dined with many kings in their palaces and castles; but none of them ever told me—'I'm the king!'"

"*Sie sind ein enfant gaté*—you are a spoilt child," graciously broke in Frau Brigitte Frank, *die deutsche Königin von Polen*—the German Queen of Poland.

"You are right," said Frank, "a real king never says 'I am the king'; but I am not a real king, though my Berlin friends call this country 'Frankreich.' I wield the power of life and death over the Polish people, but I am not the king of Poland. I bestow a king's high-minded benevolence upon the Poles, but I am not a real king. The Poles don't deserve to have me as their king; they are an ungrateful people."

"They are not an ungrateful people," I said.

"I should be the happiest man alive. I should truly be like *Gott in Frankreich*, if the Poles were grateful to me for all that I am doing for them. But the more I strive to allay their misfortunes and to deal justly with them, the more they despise all I am doing for their country. They are an ungrateful people."

A murmur of approval came from the guests.

64

"They are a proud and dignified people," I said smiling amiably, "and you are their master. A foreign master."

"A German master. They do not deserve the honor of having a German master."

"True, they do not deserve it. Pity you are not a Pole."

"*Ja, Schade.*—Yes, it's a shame!" announced Frank enjoying his own gay laughter which was noisily echoed by all the guests. Suddenly Frank ceased laughing and placed both hands on his chest, saying, "A Pole! Look at me. How could I be a Pole? Do I by any chance look like a Pole?"

"You are a Roman Catholic, aren't you?"

"Yes," replied Frank, rather surprised, "I am a German from Franconia—"

"And therefore a Roman Catholic," I said.

"Yes, a German Roman Catholic," replied Frank.

"You have then something in common with the Poles. Roman Catholics are all equals; and thus, as a good Catholic, you ought to feel yourself equal to the Poles."

"I am a Roman Catholic," answered Frank, "a good Catholic, but do you think that's enough? My fellow workers are also Roman Catholics; they all hail from old Austria. But do you think it is enough to be a Catholic in order to rule the Poles? You cannot imagine how hard it is to rule a Roman Catholic people."

"I have never tried my hand at it," I said smiling.

"Beware of it! Particularly," added Frank leaning over the table and speaking softly with an air of mystery, "particularly if as in Poland, you come up against the Vatican at every turn. Do you know who is behind every single Pole?"

"A Polish priest?" I replied.

"No," said Frank, "there is the Pope; the Holy Father himself."

"It's bound to be a trifle tedious," I suggested.

"True enough there is Hitler behind me, but it isn't the same thing."

"Oh, no, it's not the same thing," I said.

"Is the Holy Father also behind every Italian?" asked Frank.

"The Italians do not like to have anybody behind their backs," I replied.

"*Ach, so!*" laughed Frank. "*Ach, so!*"

"*Ach!* You are an *enfant terrible*," graciously said the German Queen of Poland.

"I wonder," continued Frank, "how Mussolini manages to agree with the Pope."

"At first," I said, "there also arose serious difficulties between Mussolini and the Pope. They both live in the same city and both claim to be infallible; they were bound to join issue. Later they managed to agree, and things are now proceeding to everyone's satisfaction. When an Italian is born, Mussolini takes him under his wing; he first entrusts the child to a kindergarten, later sends him to school, gets him trained to a trade and enrolls him in the Fascist party. He puts him to work until he is twenty. At that age, he enlists him in the army, keeps him a couple of years in barracks; then he dismisses him and sends him back to work. He marries him off as soon as he becomes of age; and if any children are born, they are dealt with as their father was. When the father, having grown old, has become unfit for work and useless, Mussolini sends him back home, gives him a pension and waits for him to die. Finally when he is dead, he is handed over to the Pope to do what he likes with him."

The German King of Poland raised his arms, blushed, grew purple in the face as if choking with laughter, and all the guests raised their arms, shouting, "*Ach! Wunderbar! Wunderbar!*—Wonderful!" Finally, after taking a long sip of wine, and with a voice still shaking with emotion, Frank said, "Ah! The Italians! The Italians! What political genius! What juridical sense! Pity," he went on, "all Germans are not Roman Catholics. The religious problem in Germany would be far simpler. Catholics would be handed over to the Pope as soon as they died; but to whom could we hand over Protestants?"

"It is a problem," I said, "that Hitler should have solved long ago."

"Do you know Hitler personally?" asked Frank.

"I never was so honored," I replied. "I saw him only once, in Berlin, during Todt's funeral. I was standing on the sidewalk with the crowd."

"What was your impression of him?" asked Frank waiting for my reply with evident curiosity.

"I thought he did not know to whom to hand over Todt's remains." Loud laughter again greeted my words.

"Let me assure you," said Frank, "that Hitler has solved this problem long ago, *nicht wahr?*—isn't that so?" and he glanced laughing at his guests.

Laughing, they all shouted, *"Ja, ja, natürlich."*

"Hitler is a superior man. Don't you think he is a superior man?" As I hesitated, he looked fixedly at me, and added with a kindly smile: "I should like to have your opinion of Hitler."

"He is almost a man," I replied.

"What?"

"Almost a man. I mean, not quite a real man."

"Ach, so," said Frank. "You mean that he is an *Übermensch, nicht wahr?*—Superman, don't you? Yes, Hitler is not quite a real man; he is an *Übermensch.*"

From his end of the table, one of the guests broke in: "Herr Malaparte has written in one of his books that Hitler is a woman."

It was Himmler's man, the chief of the Gestapo of the government of Poland. His voice was cool, sweet, sad—a faraway voice. I raised my eyes, but I lacked the courage to look at him. That cool, sweet, sad voice of his, that faraway voice, had set my heart trembling slightly.

"Just so," I added after a moment of silence, "Hitler is a woman."

"A woman?" exclaimed Frank gazing at me, his eyes filled with confusion and worry.

Everyone remained silent, looking at me.

"If he is not quite a real man," I said, "why should he not be a woman? What harm would there be? Women are deserving of all our respect, love and admiration. You say that Hitler is the father of the German people, *nicht wahr?* Why couldn't he be its mother?"

"Its mother!" exclaimed Frank, *"die Mutter?"*

"Its mother," I said. "It is the mother who conceives children in her womb, begets them in pain, feeds them with her blood and her milk. Hitler is the mother of the new German people; he has conceived it in his womb, has given birth to it in pain and fed it with his blood and his—"

"Hitler is the father, not the mother of the German people," said Frank sternly.

"Anyway, the German people are his child," I said, "there's no doubt about that."

"Yes," said Frank, "there's no doubt about that. All the peoples of New Europe, to begin with the Poles, ought to feel proud to have in Hitler, a just and stern father. But do you know what the Poles think of us? That we are barbarians!"

"And do you feel hurt?" I asked smiling.

"We are a master people, not barbarians; a *Herrenvolk.*"

"Oh, don't say that!"

"Why not?" Frank inquired with amazement.

"Because masters and barbarians are the same thing."

"I beg to differ," said Frank. "We are a *Herrenvolk,* not barbarians. Do you by any chance feel as though you were among barbarians tonight?"

"No," I replied, "I feel as though I were among masters," and I added smiling, "I must admit that when I entered the Wawel tonight I felt as if I had entered a court of the Italian Renaissance."

The face of the German King of Poland lighted up with a smile of triumph. He glanced around, casting a look of proud satisfaction on each of his guests. He was happy, and I had known beforehand that my words would make him happy. Scheffer had laughingly warned me in Berlin before I left for Poland: "Try not to be ironical with Frank. The worthy man does not understand irony. And, if you really cannot help yourself, don't forget to tell him that he is a prince of the Italian Renaissance. He'll overlook any sin of witticism." I had remembered Scheffer's advice just at the right time.

Before me sat Frank, on his high stiff-backed chair in the old Polish royal palace of the Wawel in Cracow, as if he were sitting on the throne of the Jagellos and the Sobieskis. He appeared to be fully persuaded that the great Polish traditions of royalty and chivalry were being revived in him. There was a light of innocent pride on his face, with its pale, swollen cheeks and the hooked nose suggesting a will both vainglorious and uncertain. His black glossy hair was brushed back revealing a high ivory-white forehead. There was something at once childish and senile in him: in his full pouting lips of an angry child, in his prominent eyes with their thick, heavy eyelids that seemed to be too large for his eyes, and in his habit of keeping his eyelids lowered—thus cutting two deep, straight furrows across his temples.

A slight film of sweat covered his face, and by the light of the large Dutch lamps and the silver candlesticks that ranged along the table and were reflected in the Bohemian glass and Saxon china, his face shone as if it were wrapped in a cellophane mask.

"My one ambition," said Frank thrusting himself back against his chair by propping his hands against the edge of the table, "is to elevate the Polish people to the honor of European civilization, and to turn this uncultured people—" He broke off as if a doubt had crossed his mind, and looking hard at me, he added in German: "*Aber . . . Sie sind ein Freund der Polen, nicht wahr?*—But you are a friend of Poland, aren't you?"

"Oh, *nein!*" I replied.

"How's that?" repeated Frank in Italian. "Aren't you a friend of the Poles?"

"I have never made a secret," I replied, "of my sincere friendship for the Polish people."

Frank gazed at me with a look of deep surprise, and after a brief silence he slowly asked me, "And why, then, did you deny it a minute ago?"

I replied politely smiling: "I said 'no' for almost the same reason that a Russian workman in the Ukraine said 'no' to a German officer:

"During the summer of 1941 I was in Pestchanka, a village in the Ukraine, and one morning I went to visit a large *kolkhoz* close by the village; the *kolkhoz* Voroshilov. The Russians had left Pestchanka just two days before. It was the largest and richest *kolkhoz* I had ever seen. Everything was left in perfect order but the cattle sheds and stables were empty; there was not a grain of wheat in the granges, not a blade of hay in the lofts. A horse was limping around the farmyard; it was old, blind and lame. At the end of the yard, under a long shed, were ranged hundreds upon hundreds of agricultural machines, mostly of Soviet manufacture, but many were Hungarian and some were Italian, German, Swedish and American. The retreating Russians had not set fire to the *kolkhoz*, to the ripe crops, or to the forests of sunflowers; nor had they destroyed the agricultural machines. They took tractors, horses and cattle with them, wheat and sunflower seeds. They had not touched the farm machinery, not even threshing machines; they left them undamaged; they merely took the tractors away. A workman in blue jeans was oiling a large threshing machine leaning over the wheels and gears. I stood in the middle of the courtyard and watched the man working. He oiled his machine and kept on with his job as if the war were far off, as if the war had not even touched the village of Pestchanka. After a few days of rain, the sun was shining; the air was mellow; a pale blue sky flecked with feathery white clouds was reflected in the muddy pools.

"After a while, a German SS officer entered the *kolkhoz* followed by several of his men. He stopped in the middle of the yard with legs wide apart, and looked around. Now and again he turned to talk to his men and some of the gold teeth in his pink mouth glistened. He suddenly noticed the workman oiling the machine and called to him.

" *'Du, komm hier!*—You, come here!'

"The workman approached limping. He was lame, too; they had left him behind with the horse. He held a large wrench in his right hand and a brass oil can in his left. In passing close to the blind horse he said something softly and the horse rubbed its nuzzle on the man's shoulder and took a few limping steps after him. Then the workman stopped in front of the officer and took his cap off. His hair was black and crinkly, his face thin and gray, his eyes were dull. He was unmistakably a Jew.

" *'Du bist Jude, nicht wahr?*—You are Jewish, aren't you?' asked the officer.

" *'Nein, ich bin kein Jude*—No, I'm not Jewish,' replied the workman, shaking his head.

" *'Erto? Ti nie evrey? Ti evrey!*—What? You are not Jewish!' repeated the officer in Russian.

" *'Da, ja evrey*—Yes, I am a Jew,' replied the workman in Russian.

"The officer looked at him a long time in silence; then he asked slowly: 'And why did you deny it a moment ago?'

" 'Because you asked me in German,' answered the workman.

" 'Shoot him!' said the officer."

A fat, jolly laugh came from Frank's wide-open mouth. All the guests laughed noisily, leaning back in their chairs.

When his burst of hilarity had quieted down, Frank said, "That officer gave a very honest reply, and he might have answered much worse, *nicht wahr?* But he had no sense of humor. If he had had any, he might have turned the matter into a joke. *J'aime les hommes spirituels*—I like clever people," he added in French with a polite bow, "*et vous avez beaucoup d'esprit*—and you are very clever. Wit, intelligence, art and culture take first place in the German *Burg* of Cracow. I want to bring an Italian Renaissance court to life in the Wawel; I want to turn the Wawel into an island of civilization and courtesy amid a sea of Slavic barbarism. Do you know that I have even managed to form a Polish philharmonic society in Cracow? All the players are Poles, of course. Furtwängler and Karajan will come to Cracow next spring to conduct a series of concerts."

"Ah, Chopin!" he exclaimed, raising his eyes upward and running his fingers along the tablecloth as if it were a keyboard. "Ah, Chopin! White-winged angel! What does it matter that he is a Polish angel? There is room also for Polish angels in the heaven of music. And yet the Poles do not care for Chopin."

"They do not care for Chopin?" I asked, surprised.

"The other day," continued Frank in a sad voice, "during a concert dedicated to Chopin, the Cracow audience failed to applaud. There was not a single handclap, no surge of love for that white angel of music. I gazed upon that immense audience, silent and motionless, and I tried to discover the reason for that frozen silence. I gazed upon thousands and thousands of glistening eyes, those white brows still warmed by the passing caress of Chopin's wing; I gazed upon lips that were still bloodless from the sad, sweet kiss of the white angel, and I tried to find for myself some reason for the dumb, stony and ghostly immobility of that vast audience. Ah! I shall win these people over by the arts, poetry and music! I shall become the Polish Orpheus. Ha, ha, ha, the Polish Orpheus!" He burst into strange laughter; his eyes shut and his head was thrown against the back of the chair. He had grown pale, his breathing became labored, his forehead glistened with little drops of sweat.

71

Then Frau Brigitte Frank, *die deutsche Königin von Polen,* raised her eyes and turned her face toward the door. At this sign the door opened and there appeared on an immense silver tray a savage, hoary wild boar, fiercely lying in ambush on a scented bed of blueberry greens.

It was a boar which Keith, the Chief of Protocol of the Government of Poland had shot with his own gun in the Lublin forests. The angry beast lay in ambush on its bed of greens as on a bed of brambles in the thicket, ready to hurl itself against rash huntsmen and their fierce packs. Twisted white tusks protruded out of piglike jaws; on its shiny fat-soaked back, on its skin, cracked and crackling from the heat of the open fire, there stood out hard black bristles. And there arose in my heart a mysterious feeling of sympathy for that noble Polish boar, that four-legged partisan of the Lublin woods. Deep down in its dark eye sockets there shone something silvery and hidden, as if it were a glance consumed by a great deep fire. It was the same silvery and reddish light that I had seen shining in the eyes of peasants, woodsmen and workmen in the fields along the Vistula, in the woods of the Tatra mountains toward Zakopane, in the factories of Radom and Czestochowa, in the salt pits of Wieliczka.

"*Achtung!*—Attention!" said Frank, and raising his arm he sank a large knife into the boar's back.

Whether because of the leaping flames in the large fireplace, or because of the luscious food, or because of the precious French and Hungarian wines, I felt I was blushing. I was sitting at the table of the German King of Poland, in the great hall of the Wawel, in the ancient, noble, rich, learned, royal city of Cracow, in the midst of the small court of that simple-minded, cruel and vain German copy of an Italian *Signore* of the Renaissance; and I felt myself blushing with melancholy shame. From the very beginning of dinner, Frank had talked about Plato, Marsilius Ficinus, about the Oricellari Gardens (Frank had studied in the Roman University, and speaks Italian perfectly with a slight romantic strain that he inherited from Goethe and Gregorovius. He has spent days and days in the galleries of Florence, Venice, Siena; he knows Perugia, Lucca, Ferrara and Mantua. He loves Schumann, Chopin and Brahms, and plays the piano divinely.) He had talked about Donatello, Politian and Sandro Botticelli, and he half closed his eyes, as if charmed by the music of his own words.

He smiled at Frau Brigitte Frank as gracefully as Celso smiles at Amorrorisca in the work of Agnolo Firenzuola. While talking, he gazed as lovingly on Frau Wächter and Frau Gassner, as Borso d'Este gazed on the bare shoulders and pink foreheads of the young Ferrarese women at Schifanoia. He turned to the Governor of Cracow, the young and refined Wächter—the Viennese Wächter, one of the butchers of Dolfuss—as amiably and seriously as the Magnificent Lorenzo turned to the young Politian amid the merry company in his villa of Ambra. And Keith, Wolsegger, Emil Gassner and Stahl replied to his courteous remarks with the dignified courtesy that Baldassarre Castiglione recommends to polished courtiers in polished courts. Only Himmler's man, at the end of the table, sat silent and listened. Possibly he listened to the heavy tread in the neighboring rooms, where their noble lord was not awaited by hawkers with a hooded hawk on the leather-covered hand, but by the stern SS guards armed with machine guns.

I felt myself blushing as I had after motoring through the lonely snow-covered plains between Cracow and Warsaw, between Lodz and Radom, between Lwow and Lublin—through dimmed towns and squalid villages with inhabitants who were lean and pale, with faces marked by hunger, anxiety, slavery and despair, and whose light dull eyes possessed that innocent look that is the look of the Polish people in distress—where of an evening I entered the *Deutsches Haus* in some misty town where I was to spend the night and was met by raucous voices, gross laughter and the warm odor of food and drinks. I felt transported as if by magic into some expressionist German court conceived by Grosz. Around the richly-stocked tables there turned up again the napes, the paunches, the mouths, the ears that Grosz draws, and those cold staring German eyes, like fish eyes. And now a sad feeling of shame caused me to blush. While I looked in turn at each one of the guests seated at the table of the German King of Poland in the great hall of the Wawel, I remembered the lean, pale throng treading through the roads of Warsaw, Cracow, Czestochowa, Lodz—those faces sweating with hunger and anxiety, people wandering along streets covered with muddy snow—those unhappy houses, and proud palaces, out of which day by day stealthily were smuggled carpets, silver, glass and china—all the ancient tokens of wealth, vanity and glory.

"What did you go to Batorego Street today for?" inquired Frank with a cunning smile.

"To Batorego Street?" I said.

"Yes, I believe it is called Ulica Batorego, isn't it?" repeated Frank turning to Emil Gassner.

"*Ja, Batoregostrasse,*" replied Gassner.

"What did you call on those young ladies for—what's their name?"

"Fräulein Urbanski," replied Gassner.

"Fräulein Urbanski? They are two elderly young ladies, if I am not mistaken, two spinsters. Why did you call on the Misses Urbanski?"

"You know everything," I said, "and you do not know what I did in Batorego Street? I went to bring some bread to the Misses Urbanski."

"Bread?"

"Yes, Italian bread."

"Italian bread? And did you bring it with you from Italy?"

"Precisely! I brought it from Italy with me. I should have liked to bring an armful of roses from Florence for the Misses Urbanski. But it is a long way from Florence to Cracow, and roses fade quickly. So I brought bread."

"Bread?" exclaimed Frank, "and do you think there is a lack of bread in Poland?" And he seemed to embrace by a wide sweeping gesture the silver trays heaped with slices of that soft white Polish bread with its thin crust, smooth and rustling as silk.

An ingenuous smile of surprise lighted his pale swollen face.

"Polish bread is bitter," I said.

"Yes, that's true. Italian roses are sweeter. You ought to have taken an armful of roses from Florence to the Misses Urbanski. It would have been a kindly souvenir of Italy. Particularly as long as those two 'elderly' young ladies were not the only ones you met in that house, *nicht wahr?*"

"Oh, *vous êtes méchant!*—You are naughty!" said Frau Wächter graciously threatening Frank with her finger. A Viennese, Frau Wächter liked to talk French.

"A Princess Lubomirska, wasn't it?" went on Frank laughing. "Lili Lubomirska. Lili. *Ach, so,* Lili!"

Everyone began to laugh and I kept silent.

"Does Lili like Italian bread, too?" asked Frank, and his words provoked general laughter.

I then turned smiling to Frau Wächter: "I am not a man of wit," I said, "and I don't know how to answer. Won't you answer for me?"

"Oh, I know that you are not a man of wit," replied Frau Wächter kindly, "but it is so easy to answer that. Poles and Italians are friends, and friendship's bread is best. Isn't it so?"

"Thank you," I said.

"*Ach, so!*" exclaimed Frank, adding after a moment's silence, "I forgot that you are a great friend of the Polish people. I mean to say of the Polish nobility."

"All Poles are noblemen," I said.

"Quite so," said Frank, "I cannot tell the difference between a Princess Radziwil and a coachman."

"And you are wrong," I said.

All looked at me in wonder, and Frank smiled at me.

But at this juncture the door opened quietly and there appeared on a silver tray the roast goose, lying on its back amid a garland of potatoes roasted in fat. It was a round fat Polish goose with a flourishing bosom, full hips and a strong neck; and I cannot say why there came into my mind that its neck had not been cut in the good old-fashioned way, but that the goose had been shot against a wall by a platoon of SS men. I seemed to hear the harsh voice ordering "Fire!" and the sudden rattle of shots. No doubt the goose had fallen looking proudly into the eyes of the cruel oppressors of Poland. And I shouted "Fire!" as if to realize what that shout meant, that raucous sound, that harsh voice of command, almost as if I expected to hear the sudden rattle of rifles in the great hall of the Wawel.

And everyone started laughing; they threw their heads backward laughing, and Frau Brigitte Frank looked fixedly at me, her eyes glistening with sensuous joy, her face red and slightly perspiring.

"Fire!" shouted Frank in his turn, and the laughter grew in

volume; they fixed their eyes on the goose, cocking their heads on their right shoulders and closing their left eyes, as if they really were taking aim. Then I laughed too, while a crawling sensation of shame overcame me little by little. I felt a sort of hurt shame. I felt on the side of the goose. Oh, yes! I sided with the goose, not with those who were aiming their rifles, nor with those who were shouting "Fire!" nor with all those who were saying *"Gans Kaputt!* —The goose is dead!"

I sided with the goose, and gazing at the goose, I thought of the old Princess Radziwil, dear old Bichette Radziwil, standing in the rain amid the ruins of the station of Warsaw, waiting for the train that was to take her to safety in Italy. It was raining, and Bichette had been standing there two hours on the platform, under the charred beams of the station's roof, that shells of the artillery and Stuka bombs had ploughed.

"Don't you worry about me, my dear. I am an old hen," she was saying to Soro, a young secretary of the Italian Legation. And now and again she shook her head to rid the brim of her felt hat of the raindrops that had gathered on it.

"If I only knew where to find an umbrella," said Soro.

"An umbrella, come, it would be ludicrous at my age!" and she laughed as with her peculiar voice and accent, and with her eloquent glances she entertained the small gathering of relations and friends who had succeeded in obtaining permission from the Gestapo to see her off, and told them amusing little stories, merry little incidents, diverting little annoyances that she had experienced during her Odyssey across the territories occupied by the Russians and the Germans—as if she were prevented by her charity, her pity and her pride from looking deeply into the vast tragedy of Poland. The rain ran down her face streaking the rouge on her cheeks. Her white hair, stained yellow, drooped in sodden strands from under her felt hat. She had been standing two hours in the rain, her shoes sinking in a mess of mud and coal dust that covered the platform; but she was merry, lively, full of zest. She inquired about this one and that, about relatives, friends, the dead, the escaped, the interned—and when anyone answered, "Nothing is known about him," Bichette pleaded, "Now, come!" as if she felt deprived of a pleasant story, of a piece of amusing gossip. "Ah, that's really amusing," she exclaimed when she was told that somebody was alive. And if it so happened that anyone replied "So-and-so is dead, so-and-so is interned," Bichette pouted and exclaimed, "Is it possible?" as if she were saying, "You are making fun of me," and as if they had told her an incredible story.

She asked Soro for the latest Warsaw gossip, and gazing at the German officers and soldiers who passed along the platform, she said, *"Ces pauvres gens"* in an indescribable tone, an ancient tone, as if she disliked to make them uncomfortable by her presence and she felt sorry for them, as if Poland's destruction was a terrible misfortune that had befallen those poor Germans.

After a time a German officer approached carrying a chair and, bowing to Bichette, he silently offered it to her. Bichette drew herself up, and with a most gracious smile, in a delicious tone in which there was no suspicion of contempt, she said: "I thank you; I accept favors only from my friends." The officer was puzzled, he did not at first dare to show that he had understood; then he blushed, set the chair down, bowed and strode off without a word.

"Come, look," said Bichette. "A chair! Can you imagine that!" She gazed at the forsaken chair in the rain and said: "It is amazing how those *pauvres gens*—poor people—feel at home."

And I thought of the old Polish lady standing in the rain, of that solitary and deserted chair in the rain, and I sided with the goose, with Princess Bichette Radziwil and with the chair—both alone in the rain.

"Fire!" shouted Frank again, and the goose fell backward shot against the ruined walls of the station of Warsaw, smiling at the firing platoon. *Ces pauvres gens.*

Everybody laughed. The Queen alone did not laugh. She sat in a rigid, solemn attitude, as if on a throne. She was gowned in a sort of bell-shaped beltless, green velvet dress, edged at the bottom by a wide band of crimson. The long wide sleeves, of an ancient Gothic cut, were joined at the shoulders with billowing folds that seemed to be puffed up by air, and rose above the shoulders in a noble arch, falling over the arms in ever greater abundance as they descended toward the wrists. Over that green bell was thrown a vast lace cape of the same color as the wide crimson band. The

Queen's hair was dressed very simply in a bun at the top of the head. Her forehead was twice girded with a string of pearls as if with a tiara. Fat, thick-set, with wrists aglitter with gold bracelets, with hands bejeweled with rings that fitted her too tightly and sunk deeply into the flesh, she sat in a Gothic pose, weighed down by the velvet bell and the lace cape as if it were a heavy coat of armor.

Her glistening, flushed face was masked with insolent sensuousness. There was, however, something pure, sad and absent-minded shining in her eyes. Her whole face was thrust forward toward the food heaped on precious Meissen plates, toward the scented wine glittering through Bohemian crystal, and on it, around her nostrils quivered an expression of insatiable greed, almost of gluttonous rage. It throbbed on her thick lips, it engraved her cheeks with a network of spidery wrinkles that tightened and expanded around her mouth and her nose to the rhythm of her labored breathing. I felt something between disgust and pity for her. *Perhaps she was hungry!* I should have liked to help her; to get up, bend across the table, thrust a large slice of goose into her mouth with my fingers; gorge her with potatoes. At any moment I feared lest she might flop down, overcome by hunger, within her green bell and rest her head on the dish filled with greasy food. But each time as I gazed into her flushed face, at her swelling bosom pressed under the heavy velvet armor, I was stopped from helping her by her vague, pure gaze, by that virginal, clear and transparent light that shone from her humid eye.

The other guests, as they greedily ate and drank never withdrew their eyes from the Queen's face; they watched her with glistening eyes, as if they also feared lest, conquered by hunger, she would repose her head on the dish heaped with greasy slices of goose and roast potatoes. They lingered occasionally, gazing at her in a tremulous abstraction, the tips of their forks resting on their lips, their glasses hovering in mid-air. The King, too, followed every movement of his Queen with an attentive look, ready to anticipate her every wish, to guess at her more secret promptings, to interpret the most fleeting impression on her face. But the Queen sat stolid and motionless, from time to time letting her pure, abstract look wander over the guests; she gazed at the Governor of Cracow, young Wächter, or at the abbot-like face of Emil Gassner, another Viennese, with his deceitful and ironical smile, who never met any glance, and timidly, almost fearfully, drooped his lashes whenever the virgin eye of the Queen rested on him. More frequently it rested on the head of the German National-Socialist party in the Government of Poland, on athletic Stahl, whose cold sharp Gothic face with its brow, crowned by an invisible oak wreath, thrust forward toward the Queen—that motionless statue of flesh, clamped within her heavy armor of green velvet, who clutched the slender crystal glass in her fat fist and listened with an absent-minded air wrapped in her thoughts, secret, lofty and pure.

Occasionally, I too broke away from the contemplation of the Queen, and allowed my eyes to wander over the guests, lingering on Frau Wächter's smiling countenance, on Frau Gassner's white arms, on the red perspiring forehead of the Chief of Protocol of the Government, Keith, who was talking about boar hunting in the Lublin forests, the fierce hound-packs of Volhynia, and the beasts in Radziwilom woods. I looked on the Staatsekretärs—State Secretaries—Böpple and Bühler, in their tight-fitting gray uniforms with the red armlet and the swastika, their flushed cheeks, perspiring temples and glistening eyes, as they said, and almost shouted, "*Ja, ja!*" from time to time, whenever the King called out "*Nicht wahr?*"

I gazed on Baron Wolsegger, an old silver-headed Tirolese gentleman with a dashing white pointed beard and clear eyes in a flushed face, and tried to recollect where I had seen that proud and gentle face before; traced my memory back from year to year, from place to place, as far as Donaueschingen in Würtemberg, where in the park of the Princes Fürstenberg the source of the Danube gushes into a marble basin encircled by white statues of Diana and her nymphs. I bent over the side of the new-born river, gazed for a long time at the slow, uncertain rise of the gushing water; then I knocked at the castle gate, crossed the great hall, climbed the marble stairs, and finally entered the vast gallery on the walls of which the canvases of Holbein's famous "Way of the Cross" are hung; and there, against the clear wall I saw the portrait of the seventeenth-century adventurer. I smiled at that far-off recollection of the German *condottiere;* I smiled at Baron Wolsegger. Suddenly my gaze rested on Himmler's man.

I felt as if I saw him for the first time at that moment, and I was startled. He was looking at me, too, and our eyes met. That man was in his middle years, not more than forty; his dark hair was already graying at the temples, his nose thin, his lips drawn and pale, his eyes extraordinarily light. They were gray eyes, perhaps blue or white, like those of a fish. A long scar cut across his left cheek. Suddenly something began to worry me: his ears; they were extremely small, bloodless, waxlike, with transparent lobes—the transparency of wax or milk.

There came to mind a tale by Apuleius, in which the ears of one Ambrose had been gnawed by lemurs while he watched a corpse, and they had been replaced by waxen ears. There was something softish, almost naked in the Gestapo man's face. Although his skull was strong and rough hewn, and the bones in his forehead looked solid, well-knit and extremely hard, the face seemed, nevertheless, that it might give way at the touch of a finger, like the head of a new-born babe; it looked like the skull of a lamb. His narrow cheekbones, his long face and slanting eyes were also like a lamb's; there was something at the same time bestial and childish in him. His brow was white and damp, like a sick man's; and even the perspiration oozing out of that soft waxen skin recalled the perspiration that feverish sleeplessness brings to the foreheads of consumptives as, lying on their backs, they await the dawn.

Himmler's man was silent: he gazed at me in silence, and, by degrees, I perceived a strange smile, shy and very sweet, playing on his thin, pale lips. He gazed at me smiling; and I thought at first that he smiled at me, that he really was smiling at me; but I saw suddenly that his eyes were empty: he did not listen to the words of the guests, he did not hear the sound of voices and of laughter, the tinkling of forks and of glasses—he sat transported into the loftiest and purest heaven of cruelty—that "suffering cruelty" which is the true German cruelty—of fear and loneliness. There was no shade of brutality in his face, rather something shy, vague, like a wonderful and moving loneliness. His left eyebrow was raised at an angle that loftily expressed cold contempt and cruel pride. What knit all his features together, all the traits and the tricks of his face, was that suffering cruelty, that wonderful, melancholy loneliness.

After a time it seemed to me that something began to melt in him, something alive and human—a light, a color, perhaps a look, a child's look, was being born deep down in those empty eyes. He seemed to me to be swooping down as gently as an angel from that lofty, remote and very pure heaven of his; he came down like a spider-angel, gliding slowly along a very high, white wall. Like a prisoner escaping along the sheer wall of his jail.

By degrees there spread a consciousness of deep humiliation over his pallid face. He issued from his loneliness as a fish emerges from its watery den. He swam toward me gazing fixedly at me. And all unknowingly I felt drawn, as well as repulsed by his naked face and his white gaze, until I caught myself watching him with a kind of pity, a kind of morbid compassion for the very repulsion and attraction which that pitiful monster inspired in me.

Suddenly Himmler's man, leaning across the table with a shy smile, said softly, "I am also a friend of the Poles; I like them very much."

So shaken was I by those words and by the strangely sweet, sad voice of Himmler's man, that I did not realize that the King, the Queen and all the guests had risen and were looking at me. I also arose and we all followed the Queen. Standing, she looked fatter; she had the appearance of a good German *hausfrau;* even the green hue of her velvet bell seemed faded. She strode forward slowly with good-natured dignity, and she lingered a moment on the threshold of each drawing room as if to fill her eyes gloatingly with the cold, insolent and stupid magnificence of the furnishing inspired by that *Dritte Reich*—Third Reich style, the purest example of which is to be found in the Chancery at Berlin. Then she crossed the threshold and stopping again a few steps farther along, she raised her arm to point out to me the furniture, pictures, carpets, hanging lights, statues of the Heroes of Breker, the Führer's busts, tapestries bespangled with Gothic eagles and swastikas; and she said to me with a gracious smile, "*Schön, nicht wahr?*—Beautiful, isn't it?"

All the vast pile of the Wawel that I had seen twenty years before in its royal bareness, was now crammed full, from the sub-terranean caves to the top of its highest tower with furniture stolen from the palaces of the Polish gentry, reaped during the crafty raids through France, Holland and Belgium by the committees of antiquarians and experts from Munich, Berlin and Vienna who followed on the heels of the German armies through Europe. A glaring light flowed down from the great lamps hanging from the ceiling, and it glittered back from the walls covered with panels of shiny leather onto the portraits of Hitler, Göring, Göbbels, Himmler and of other Nazi leaders; and the marble and bronze busts (they were scattered everywhere along corridors, on landings, in the corners of rooms, on furniture, on marble pedestals and within niches in the walls) representing the German King of Poland in his several attitudes, inspired by the decadent esthetics of Burckhardt, Nietzsche and Stefan George; by the heroic esthetics of Beethoven's *Third Symphony* and of the "Horst Wessel" song, and by the decorative esthetics of the humanist antiquarians of Florence and Munich. There lingered a cloying odor of fresh paint, new leather and newly polished wood in the airless atmosphere.

Finally, we entered a large hall, generously adorned with *Dritte Reich* furniture, French carpets, and leather wall hangings. It was Frank's study. The gap between two large glass doors opening on the outside loggia of the Wawel (the internal loggia faces on the beautiful courtyard designed by Italian artists of the Renaissance) was taken by a vast mahogany table that reflected the flames of the candles fixed on the arms of two heavy candelabra of gilt bronze. The vast table was bare. "Here I think about Poland's future," said Frank opening his arms wide; and I smiled. I was thinking about Germany's future.

At a nod from Frank the two tall glass doors opened and we walked out onto the loggia. "This is the German *Burg*," Frank said pointing with his raised arm to the imposing pile of the Wawel, sharply cut into the blinding reflection of the snow. Around the ancient palace of the Polish kings, the city settled low, shrouded in her winding-sheet of snow under a clear sky faintly lit by a beam from the thin scythe of a new moon. A bluish mist rose from the Vistula. On the horizon, far away in the distance the Tatra mountains appeared delicate and transparent. The barking of the SS dogs guarding Pilsudski's tomb, from time to time broke the deep silence of the night. The cold was so biting it filled my eyes with tears. I closed them a moment. "It seems like a dream, doesn't it?" said Frank.

When we walked back to the study, Frau Brigitte Frank approached me, and placing her hand familiarly upon my arm, she said softly, "Come with me. I want to reveal his secret to you." Through a small door in the wall of the study we entered a small room with walls that were totally bare and whitewashed. There was not a single piece of furniture, no carpets, no pictures, no books, no flowers—nothing, except a magnificent Pleyel piano and a wooden music stool. Frau Brigitte Frank opened the piano, and leaning her knee on the stool, stroked the keyboard with her fat fingers. "Before taking a crucial decision, or when he is very weary or depressed, sometimes in the very midst of an important meeting," said Frau Brigitte Frank, "he shuts himself up in this cell, sits before the piano and seeks rest or inspiration from Schumann, Brahms, Chopin or Beethoven. Do you know what I call this cell? I call it the Eagle's Nest."

I bowed in silence.

"He is an extraordinary man, isn't he?" she added, gazing at me with a look of proud affection. "He is an artist, a great artist, with a pure and delicate soul. Only such an artist as he can rule over Poland."

"Yes," I said, "a great artist; and it is with this piano that he rules the Polish people."

"Oh, you understand so well!" said Frau Brigitte Frank in a voice full of emotion.

Silently we left the Eagle's Nest; and I don't know exactly why, I felt shaken and sad for a long time. We were gathered in Frank's private apartment, and sprawling on the deep Viennese settees and in the large armchairs upholstered with soft doeskin, we began chatting and smoking. Two valets with coarse hair cut short in the Prussian manner, and dressed in blue livery, were passing coffee, liqueurs and sweets; their footsteps were muffled by the thick French carpets spread over the entire floor. Small green-and-gold lacquered Venetian tables were crowded with bottles of old French brandy with famous labels, boxes of Havana cigars, silver trays heaped with candied fruit and those celebrated Polish chocolates of Wedel.

In this homey atmosphere accentuated by the pleasant crackling of the open fire, the talk by degrees grew cordial, almost intimate. And as always happened in Poland when the Germans gathered together, they all ended by talking of the Poles. They spoke of them, as usual, with vicious contempt; but it was strangely blended with an almost morbid, feminine sense of spite, of regret, frustrated love, unconscious envy and jealousy. There rose up in my mind dear old Bichette Radziwil standing in the rain amid the wreckage of the Warsaw station, and the old-fashioned tone in which she said, *"Ces pauvres gens."*

"The Polish workmen," said Frank, "are not Europe's best, but neither are they the worst. They can work very well, if they want to. I think we may count on them, particularly on their discipline."

"They have, however, a very grave fault," said Wächter, "that of mixing patriotism with the technical problems of work and output."

"Those are not technical problems alone," said Baron Wolsegger, "they are also moral problems."

"The modern technique," replied Wächter, "does not allow for the intrusion of extraneous elements into the problems of work and output. And the patriotic feelings of the workers are the most dangerous element interfering with output."

"No doubt," said Frank, "but the patriotic feeling of the workers is very different from that of the aristocracy and of the middle classes."

"The fatherland of the workman is the machine; it is the workshop," said Himmler's man softly.

"That's a communist conception," said Frank. "I think that it is one of Lenin's slogans. But after all, it expresses the truth. The Polish workman is a good patriot; he loves his own country, but he knows that working for us is the best way to save Poland. He knows that if he refused to work for us," he went on gazing at Himmler's man, "if he resisted—"

"We know many things," said Himmler's man, "but the Polish workman does not know them, or would prefer not to know them," he added with a shy smile.

"If you wish to win the war," I said, "you must not destroy the workman's fatherland. You must not destroy the machines, the workshops and the industries. It is a European problem, not only a Polish one. Also in all the other countries of Europe you have occupied, you may destroy the fatherland of the nobles, the fatherland of the middle classes, but you cannot destroy the workman's fatherland. The very meaning of this war or at least a great part of it, seems to me to be found in this."

"The peasants," said Himmler's man.

"If necessary," said Frank, "we shall crush the workmen with the weight of the peasants."

"And you will lose the war," I said.

"Herr Malaparte is right," said Himmler's man, "we would lose the war. It is necessary for the Polish workmen to love us. We must endear ourselves to the Polish people." As he spoke he looked at me and smiled; then he stopped and turned toward the fire.

"The Poles will end by loving us," said Frank, "they are a romantic people. The next Polish romanticism will be their love for the Germans."

"So far," said Baron Wolsegger, "Polish romanticism . . . there is a Viennese saying that well describes our position in respect to the Polish people: *Ich liebe dich, und du schläfst.*"

"Oh yes," said Frau Wächter, " 'I love you, and you sleep'; very funny, isn't it?"

"Yes, very amusing," said Frau Brigitte Frank.

"In the end the Polish people will certainly awaken," said Wächter, "but so far they are asleep."

"I rather think that they pretend to be asleep," said Frank. "At heart they ask for nothing better than to be loved. Every people can be judged by its women."

"Polish women," said Frau Brigitte Frank, "are famous for their beauty and elegance. Do you really find them so pretty?"

"I find them worthy of admiration," I replied, "and not for their looks and their elegance alone."

"I cannot see that they are really so pretty as they are supposed to be," said Frau Brigitte Frank. "Female beauty in Germany is more severe, more genuine and more classical."

"Nevertheless some are very pretty and very smart," said Frau Wächter.

"In the good old days in Vienna," said Baron Wolsegger, "they were considered more elegant even than the Parisian women."

"Ah, the Parisian women!" exclaimed Frank.

"Are there any Parisiennes left?" asked Frau Wächter, gracefully tilting her head.

"I think that the elegance of the Polish women is dreadfully provincial and old-fashioned," said Frau Brigitte Frank, "and it is surely not all the fault of the war. Germany also has been two and a half years at war, and in spite of it, German women are today the most elegant in Europe."

"It appears," said Frau Gassner, "that Polish women do not wash much."

"Oh yes, they are terribly dirty," said Frau Brigitte Frank swinging her velvet bell, that sent forth a long green sound across the room.

"It isn't their fault," said Baron Wolsegger, "they have no soap."

"They will soon be unable to plead any excuse," said Frank, "they have found a way in Germany to make soap out of a substance that costs nothing and is very abundant. I have already placed a large order for Polish ladies so that they may wash. That soap is made out of dung."

"Out of dung?" I shouted.

"Yes, naturally, out of dung," replied Frank.

"And is it a good soap?"

"Excellent," said Frank, "I have tried it for shaving, and I was enchanted with it."

"Does it make a good lather?"

"A wonderful lather. It gives a perfect shave. It is a soap fit for a king."

"God shave the King!" I sang out.

"Only—" added the German King of Poland.

"Only—" I said holding my breath.

"It has one fault: the smell and the color are as they were."

A shout of laughter followed his words. "*Ach, so! Ach, so!* wonderful!" they all shouted. And I discerned a voluptuous tear running down the cheek of Frau Brigitte Frank, the German Queen of Poland.

V

Forbidden Cities

I HAD REACHED Warsaw at night from Radom, having motored through the vast Polish plain buried under the snow. And as I entered the city, its squalid, bomb-riddled suburbs, the Marszalkowska flanked by the skeletons of palaces charred black by fire, the ruins of the railway station, the black disemboweled houses that the livid light of the evening rendered more forbidding, became almost a welcome refuge and relief to my eyes blinded by the dazzling snow.

The streets were deserted, a few passers-by scuttered along the walls; German patrols stood at the corners, their tommy guns cradled in their arms. Saxe Square seemed vast, ghostlike. Raising my eyes to the first floor of the Europeiski Hotel, I looked for the window of the apartment where I had lived for two years in 1919 and 1920, when I was a young attaché with the Royal Italian Legation. Light showed through the window. I halted in the courtyard of the Bruhl Palace, crossed the hall, and set my foot on the first step of the main staircase.

Fischer, the German Governor of Warsaw, had invited me that evening to the dinner he was giving for Governor-General Frank, Frau Brigitte Frank and some of the principal collaborators of the Governor-General. Bruhl Palace, formerly the seat of the Foreign Office of the Polish Republic and now occupied by the German Government of Warsaw, stood unscathed two steps away from the ruins of the Hotel d'Angleterre, the old hotel in which Napoleon had lodged during one of his stays at Warsaw. It had been hit by only one bomb that had crumbled the ceiling of the main staircase and the inner loggia leading to the luxurious private apartments of the former Minister of the Polish Republic, Colonel Beck, and was now occupied by Fischer. I set my foot on the first step and before starting up, raised my eyes.

At the top of the stairway, flanked on both sides by two rows of slender white-stuccoed columns without base or capital, belonging to the lean and offensive modern classicism, there were revealed to me, crudely illuminated by lights ranged along the stairs between one column and the other, like stage footlights, two massive statues of flesh, that weighed down threateningly on me as I slowly went up the pink marble steps. Clothed in gold lamé, with stiff deep pleats resembling the flutings of a column, Frau Fischer rose solemnly, her brow crowned by a lofty castle of blond hair with glints of copper—so queerly arranged that it resembled a Corinthian capital superimposed on a Doric column. From beneath her skirt protruded two enormous feet, two rounded legs with fleshy calves that the shiny gray silk of the stockings made glisten like steel. Her arms did not rest limply at her sides, but were stiffly stretched down as if loaded with a great weight. Next to her stood the imposing mass of Governor Fischer, fat, Herculean, garbed in a tight-fitting black dress suit of Berlin cut, with sleeves that were too short. His head was small and round, his face pink and swollen, his eyes protruding and rimmed with red lids. From time to time, perhaps as a means of overcoming his shyness, he ran his tongue over his lips with a slow and studied deliberation. He stood with legs wide apart, arms stiffly hanging a little away from his sides, his big fists clenched; he looked like the statue of a prize fighter. As I was slowly going up the stairs, owing to a trick of perspective, those two massive figures appeared to me to be leaning backward as statues look in a photograph taken from below: precisely as in a photograph, the hands, the feet, the legs appeared to be enormous, out of proportion to the rest of the bodies—strangely swollen and deformed. With each step there rose in me a vague feeling of fear that overcomes me whenever, from a seat in the first row, I behold a singer step to the front of the stage and hang over me, with wide-open mouth and a raised arm, in order to gargle an aria. Just at that moment the two massive statues of flesh lifted their right arms and said in loud voices: *"Heil Hitler!"* (Suddenly, Governor Fischer and Frau Fischer melted before my eyes into the cold bluish light of the lamps, and in their place there rose before me the two tall, slender shadows of Madame and Colonel Beck. Madame Beck was smiling, bending forward a little to stretch out her hand to me, as if she meant to help me up the last steps, and Colonel Beck, tall and lean, with his small birdlike head, bowed with the dry elegance of an Englishman, almost imperceptibly bending his left knee. They seemed two pale pictures far removed in time and memory; and yet it was only yesterday; they moved with ghostlike grace against the background of the ruins of Warsaw amid which padded its way a starving throng, livid with rage and suffering, raising their arms and screaming. Madame Beck seemed to be unaware of the throng at her shoulders and she smiled, stretching her hand out to me. But Colonel Beck, pale and harassed, every now and then seemed about to turn, twisting his scrawny neck with its birdlike head—the blue glow of the lamps was reflected on his polished skull and on his prominent nose—throwing his shoulders back, he gave the impression of pushing away from himself the ruins of Warsaw, the streets crowded with unkempt people dressed in shabby furs, in worn and faded raincoats, hatless or wearing headgear that was discolored by the rain and snow. Snow was falling; and from time to time, out of the throng slowly filing along the sidewalks, a living glance—a flash of hate and despair— amid the thousands of dull glances, followed a German soldier crossing the road in hobnailed boots. Groups of women turned to exchange tired and hopeless looks in front of the Bristol and Europeiski hotels, in front of the Nowy Swiat cinema and St. Andrew's church, where Chopin's heart is preserved in an urn, in front of the smashed shop windows of Wedel and Fuchs. Swarms of boys running and sliding on the ice stopped to watch the bustle of German officers and soldiers in the courtyard of the Potocki Palace, housing the Kommandatur. Silent clusters of women and men crouching in the snow stretched out their hands toward the heat of the great bonfires in the center of the squares. All turned, staring at the two pale shadows gracefully remote at the top of the marble staircase of the Bruhl Palace. From time to time someone lifted his arms, screaming. Groups of manacled prisoners escorted by SS men passed, and all turned their faces toward Madame Beck who smilingly stretched out her hand to me—toward Colonel Beck, who restlessly twisted his small birdlike head on his scrawny neck, seeming to push away from himself the squalid background of Warsaw ruins, that gray and dirty landscape like a wall stained with blood and riddled with the bullets of firing squads.)

At Governor Fischer's dinner in Colonel Beck's apartments, besides Governor-General Frank and Frau Brigitte Frank, I met again the whole court of the Wawel in Cracow: Frau Wächter, Keith, Emil Gassner, Baron Wolsegger and Himmler's man; in the confusion I scarcely noticed three or four of Fischer's assistants, gray and distracted looking.

"Here we are all together again," said Frank turning to me with a hearty smile. And he added, repeating Luther's famous words: "*Hier stehe ich, ich kann nicht anders*—Here I stand, I cannot do otherwise."

"*Aber ich kann stehts anders. Gott helfe mir!*—But I can do otherwise. God help me!" I replied.

There was loud laughter at my words, and Frau Fischer, frightened at this unaccustomed "*ouverture* of convivial conversation," as Frank called it in the flowery language he always affected at the beginning of a dinner—smiled at me, opened her lips, almost broke into speech, blushed and glanced round at the guests, saying, "Have a good dinner!"

Frau Fischer was a young, buxom woman, stupid and sweet in manner. Judging by the way the men gazed at her, she must have been good-looking; and apart from a vulgar strain, perceptible only to non-Germanic eyes, she certainly must have been a very refined woman. Her hair, golden and smooth with coppery tints that gave evidence of the use of curling irons, was twisted into long curls that dangled on her forehead like Medusa's head, bristling with flexible springy little snakes that the hairdresser had propped up with a rat of human hair of a darker shade. She smiled shyly, resting her fat white arms on the table in a childish attitude, and she kept silent, only answering with a sweet *Ja* whenever someone addressed her. Frau Brigitte Frank and Frau Wächter who, at the beginning of the dinner, had watched her with a persistent and ironical dislike, ended by ignoring her, concentrating all their attention on the food, and on the conversation over which Governor-General Frank presided with his usual conceited eloquence. Frau

Fischer listened silently, staring at him dreamily with her large doll's eyes, and she did not awake from her dream until the roast deer appeared on the table. Governor Fischer recounted how he had killed the deer with a bullet between the eyes; and Frau Fischer said with a sigh: "*So ist das Leben*—Such is life." It was a dinner, as Frank said, dedicated to Diana the Huntress, and he smiled with a gallant bow to Frau Fischer. First pheasants appeared on the table, then hare, and lastly deer; and the talk that had at first turned to Diana and her wild loves, to the chase as sung by Homer and Virgil or as painted by medieval German artists or as toasted by Italian Renaissance poets, switched to hunting in Poland, to the game preserves of Polish noblemen, to Volhynian hound packs, and to the question as to which were better—German, Polish or Hungarian packs. Then little by little, the talk slipped, as it always did, to the subject of Poland, of the Poles and thence, as always, it ended by falling onto the shoulders of the Jews.

In no part of Europe had Germans appeared to me so naked, so exposed as in Poland. In the course of my long war experience, the conviction had grown within me that the German has no fear of the strong man, of the armed man who faces him with courage and stands up to him. The German fears the defenseless, the weak and the sick. The *leitmotiv* of fear, of German cruelty as a result of that fear, had become the principal keynote of my entire war experience. In an attentive observer with a modern and Christian mind, this "fear" arouses horror and pity, and nowhere was I moved to such horror and such pity as in Poland, where the morbid, feminine quality of its nature was revealed to me in its full complexity. That which drives the German to cruelty, to deeds most coldly, methodically and scientifically cruel, is fear. Fear of the oppressed, the defenseless, the weak, the sick; fear of women and of children, fear of the Jews. Although the German strives to hide this mysterious "fear," he is forever driven to talk about it, and always at the least suitable times, particularly at the dinner table where, either because he has been warmed by wine and food, or because company gives him self-confidence, or because he has a subconscious urge to prove to himself that he is not afraid, the German exposes himself—lets himself go in talking about hunger, shooting, slaughter—with a morbid compassion that not only reveals rancor, jealousy, frustrated love and hate, but also a pitiful and wonderful passion for self-abasement.

I listened to the words of the guests with a horror and pity that I strove in vain to conceal; when Frank, noticing my emotion, perhaps with a view to making me share his own morbid feeling of abasement, turned to me and smiling ironically, asked: "Have you been to see the ghetto, my dear Malaparte?"

A few days earlier I had gone to the ghetto in Warsaw. I had crossed the threshold of the "forbidden city" inclosed by the high red-brick wall that the Germans raised in order to inclose as if in a cage those miserable, defenseless wild beasts. SS sentries armed with machine guns were guarding the gate to which was affixed an order signed by Governor Fischer making it a capital offense for any Jew to attempt to leave the ghetto. And as with my first steps through the "forbidden cities" of Cracow, Lublin and Czestochowa, I felt aghast at the frozen silence that weighed upon the streets thronged with squalid, ragged and terrified crowds. I had tried to go to the ghetto alone, free from the escort of the Gestapo agent who followed me everywhere like a shadow, but Governor Fischer's orders were strict, and this time I was again compelled to put up with the company of a Black Guard—a tall, fair young man with a fleshless face and eyes that were clear and cold. His face was handsome, his brow high and pure, darkened by the helmet as if by a hidden shadow. He moved among the Jews like an Angel of Jehovah.

A transparent silence seemed to float without weight in the air, and in that silence the soft crunching of snow under thousands of feet seemed like the grinding of teeth. The throng, stirred to attention by my uniform of an Italian officer, lifted bearded faces and gazed at me with eyes reddened by cold, fever and hunger; tears glistened on the lashes and rolled down into grimy beards. If I happened to jostle someone in the crowd, I apologized; I said *prosze pana*—beg your pardon—and a face would be raised to me in wonder and disbelief. I repeated: *prosze pana;* for I knew that my courtesy was a wonderful thing for them to hear. I knew that after two and a half years of anguish and of bestial slavery, it was the first time that an enemy officer—I was not a German but an Italian officer; yet it was not enough that I was not a German officer, perhap* it was really not enough—had said a kindly *prosze pana* to a poor Jew of the Warsaw ghetto.

From time to time I had to step over a dead body. I walked in the throng without seeing what my feet trod on, and every once in a while I stumbled over a corpse stretched out on the sidewalk between Jewish ritual candelabra. The dead, lying abandoned in the snow, waited for the cart that was to take them away, but the death rate was high and the carts were few; time was too short to take away all the dead, and they lay there for days and days stretched out in the snow between extinguished candelabra. Many lay on the floors in the halls of the houses, on the landings, in the corridors, and on beds in the rooms thronged with pale and silent people. Their beards were sodden with mud and slush. Some had wide-open eyes that followed us with a blank stare as they watched the passing crowds. They were stiff and hard, they looked like wooden statues. Just like the dead Jews in a Chagall canvas. Their beards looked blue in those fleshless faces made livid by frost and death. It was so pure a blue as to recall certain seaweeds. It was a blue so mysterious as to recall the sea, that strange blue of the sea during certain mysterious hours of the day.

The silence in the streets of the forbidden city, that frozen silence, like a shudder, like a slight crunching of teeth, preyed so heavily on me, that there came a moment when I began to talk aloud to myself. Everyone turned to look at me, their eyes filled with deep wonder and fear. Then I began to notice the eyes of the people. Almost every face was bearded; beardless faces were frightful, so greatly had hunger and despair ravished them; the faces of the young were sparsely covered with a curly blackish or reddish down; the skin seemed of wax; the faces of women and children seemed made of paper. In every face there was already the bluish shadow of death. The eyes, in those faces the color of gray paper or white chalk, seemed like weird insects busily rummaging with their hairy little legs in the pits of the sockets and sucking what little light still shone in the hollow of the orbits. When I approached, those loathsome insects became restless, they broke away from their prey for a moment, came out from those sockets as out of a lair, gazing at me in fear. They were eyes of extraordinary alertness, scorched with fever, or else wet and sad. Other eyes glittered with greenish reflections, like scarabs. Others were red, others black, others white, others lightless and opaque—almost clouded by the thin veil of a cataract. The eyes of the women were courageously steady; they held my glance with an insolent contempt; then they turned their gaze to the face of the Black Guard who escorted me, and I saw them darken suddenly with a shadow of fear and revulsion. But the eyes of the children were terrible; I could not look at them. A sky of dirty wadding, a sky of cotton wool stagnated over that black throng clad in long black caftans with black skull caps on their heads.

Jewish policemen stood in pairs at the street crossings with the star of David stamped in red on their yellow armlets; they stood motionless and impassive amid the incessant traffic of sledges pulled by troikas of boys, baby carriages, hand carts loaded with furniture, heaps of rags, old iron, and all sorts of miserable junk. From time to time groups of people gathered at street corners, stamped their feet on the frozen snow and clapped their open hands on their shoulders; they stood close with their arms round one another—ten, twenty, thirty of them, in order to give each other a little warmth. The squalid little Nalewki, Przyrynek, and Zakroczymska street cafés were crowded with old, bearded men, standing pressed together, silent, perhaps like animals giving each other warmth and courage. When we appeared on the threshold those who were near the door drew back in fear; I heard some frightened screams, some groans; then silence fell again, broken only by panting breaths, the silence of animals already resigned to death. All gazed at the Black Guard who followed me. All gazed at his angel's face, a face that all recognized, that all had seen a hundred times shining amid the olive trees near the gates of Jericho, of Sodom, of Jerusalem. The face of an angel announcing God's wrath. Then I smiled, I said, "*Prosze pana*—I beg your pardon," and I was aware that those words to them were a wonderful present. I said *prosze pana* smiling, and all around me I saw smiles of wonder, of joy and of gratitude, coming to life on those faces the color of soiled paper. I said *prosze pana* and I smiled.

Squads of young men went through the streets picking up the dead bodies; they went into the halls, climbed the stairs and found their way into the rooms. They were young gravediggers, mostly, students from Berlin, Munich and Vienna, some deported from Belgium, Holland, France and Romania. Many of them had once been rich and happy; they had lived in beautiful homes; they had grown up amid fine furniture, old pictures, books, musical instruments, valuable silver and delicate china; and now, their clothes in tatters, they laboriously dragged feet wrapped in rags through the slush. They spoke French, Czech, Romanian and the mellow Viennese German; they were cultured young men trained in the best universities of Europe—ragged, hungry, devoured by vermin, still sore from the blows, the insults and the suffering that they had endured in concentration camps and during the awful trek from Vienna, from Berlin, from Munich, from Paris, from Prague, from Bucharest to the ghetto of Warsaw. But there was a wonderful light in their faces, a youthful determination to help one another, to relieve the measureless misery of their people; there was gentle and resolute challenge in their gaze. I lingered to watch them during their work of mercy, and in a low voice I said in French: *"Un jour vous serez libres, vous serez heureux et libres*—Some day you will be free, some day you will be happy and free," and the young gravediggers lifted their faces and looked at me smiling. Then they turned their eyes slowly on the Black Guard who followed me like a shadow; they gazed fixedly upon the cruel-faced and handsome Angel, the death-warning Angel of the Scriptures, and they bent over the dead bodies stretched out on the sidewalks—they bent over, bringing their own happy smiles close to the bluish faces of the dead. They lifted the dead gently as if they were lifting wooden statues, and they placed them on carts drawn by teams of ragged and wan youths; the outlines of the corpses remained in the snow with those horrible and mysterious yellowish stains that corpses leave on everything that comes into contact with them. Packs of bony dogs ran sniffing after these funeral processions; and flocks of ragged boys, their faces marked with hunger, lack of sleep and fear, scoured the snow picking up rags, pieces of paper, empty tins, potato peelings—all that precious refuse that is always left by hunger, poverty and death.

Sometimes I heard within the houses soft singing and monotonous wailing that broke off as soon as I appeared on the threshold. An indescribable stench of filth, wet clothing and dead flesh filled the air in the squalid rooms in which pitiful throngs of old people, women and children lived heaped like prisoners in a crowded jail, some sitting on the floor, some leaning against the walls, some stretched out on bundles of straw and paper. On the beds lay the sick, the dying and the dead. Everyone suddenly became silent, staring at me, staring at the Angel who followed me. A few went on silently chewing some miserable morsel. Others, mostly young people with wan faces, with blank eyes that the lenses of spectacles made larger, were gathered around the window, reading. That too was a means of cheating the debasing expectancy of death. Occasionally, when we appeared, someone would rise from the ground, turn away from the wall or leave a group of his companions and come to meet us slowly, saying softly in German: "Let's go."

As in the ghetto in Czestochowa, a few days before, when I had appeared at the threshold of a house, a young man who had been sitting on the floor near the window came forward; he had a mysteriously happy air as if he had lived for that day in an anguish of waiting, and as if he thought that the moment had come at last, and he welcomed as a liberation that moment that he had hitherto feared. Everyone stared silently at him; not a word came from those lips, not a groan, not a cry, not even when I gently pushed the youth back and smiling told him that I had not come for that reason, that I was not a Gestapo officer, that I was not even a German. I perceived disappointment slowly coloring his face, and that same anguish returning from which my sudden appearance had freed him for a few moments.

Also, in Cracow one day I had gone to the ghetto. When I looked into the door of one of those houses, I saw a lean youth—with a sweaty face and all wrapped up in a filthy shawl—reading a book in a corner of the room. He rose as I entered. When I asked him what he was reading, he showed me the title page; it was a volume of Engels' letters. Meanwhile he was getting ready to leave. He buttoned his shoes, arranged the dirty rags he wore as socks, and rummaged about under the lapels of his coat for the collar of his tattered shirt. He coughed shielding his mouth with his puny hand. He turned to nod his farewell to the people gathered in the room and everybody stared at him, silently; suddenly, when he had already reached the door he turned, removed his shawl and with

96

tender hands arranged it around an old woman seated on a couch; then he came back to me on the landing, and though I smiled and told him to go back I could not make him understand my words.

Later, recollecting that before coming out to me he had taken off his shawl, there came into my mind a picture of the two completely naked Jews I had met one morning in the ghetto. They were walking between two SS guards. One was an old, bearded man; the other was still a boy; he could not have been more than sixteen. When I mentioned that meeting to Wächter, the Governor of Cracow, he gently replied that many Jews when the Gestapo went to fetch them, stripped and distributed their clothing among relatives and friends, no longer having any use for them. They walked naked through the snow on an icy winter morning, slashed by the knives of a frosty thirty degrees below.

I turned to the Black Guard, saying, "Let's go." I walked along the sidewalk in silence beside the Black Guard whose face was beautiful, whose gaze was clear and cruel, whose brow was hooded by the steel helmet; it seemed to me that I walked by the side of Jehovah's Angel, and I expected him to stop at any moment and say to me, "We are there." I thought of Jacob and of his struggle with the Angel. An icy wind was blowing, the color of a dead child's face. Night was falling, the day was dying along the walls like a sick dog.

As we walked down Nalewki Street toward the exit from the "forbidden city," we fell in with a small, silent crowd on the corner of a street. In the middle of the crowd two girls were fighting, silently tearing at each other's hair and clawing each other's faces. When we suddenly appeared the crowd melted away, the two girls separated; one of them picked up something from the ground; it was a raw potato, and she went off drying with the back of her hand the blood that smeared her face. The other stood there looking at us. She was arranging her hair, roughly setting aright her torn and disordered clothes. She was a poor girl, pale, fleshless and hollow-chested; her eyes were filled with hunger, modesty and shame. Suddenly she smiled at me.

I blushed. I had nothing to give her. I wanted to help her, to give her something, but I had only a little money with me, and the mere thought of offering her money filled me with shame. I did not know what to do; I stood there facing her smile, and I did not know what to do or what to say. Suddenly I made up my mind, stretched out my hand and offered her ten *zloti* notes, but the girl grew pale, stopped my hand, and said smiling, "*Dziekuje bardzo—* Many thanks." Slowly pushing away my hand, she gazed into my eyes and smiled; then she turned and smoothing her hair walked away.

At that moment I remembered that I had a cigar in my pocket, a fine Havana cigar given to me by Doctor Egen, Lieutenant-Governor of Radom; I ran, caught up with her and offered her the cigar. The girl gazed uncertainly at me, blushed, took the cigar, and I understood that she was only accepting it to please me. She said nothing, not even thanks; she walked away slowly without turning, holding the cigar in her hand, bringing it close to her face from time to time to inhale its scent, as if I had given her a flower.

"Have you been to see the ghetto, my dear Malaparte?" inquired Frank smiling ironically.

"Yes," I replied coldly.

"It's very interesting, isn't it?"

"Oh, yes, very interesting," I answered.

"I don't like going into the ghetto," said Frau Wächter, "it is very sad."

"Very sad, why?" asked Governor Fischer.

"*So schmutzig*—So dirty," said Frau Brigitte Frank.

"*Ja, so schmutzig*—Yes, so dirty," said Frau Fischer.

"The ghetto of Warsaw is undoubtedly the best in all of Poland, the best organized," said Frank, "a real model. Governor Fischer has a happy touch in matters of this kind."

The Governor of Warsaw blushed with pleasure: "It's a pity," he said with an air of modesty, "that I had so little space. If more space had been available, I might have arranged things much better."

"Oh, yes, it is a pity!" I said.

"Just think!" went on Fischer. "More than one and a half million Jews are now living in the same space where three hundred thousand people lived before the war. It's not my fault if they have to be squeezed."

"Jews like to live like that," said Emil Gassner laughing.

"On the other hand," said Frank, "we cannot force them to live differently."

"It would be contrary to the law of nations," I remarked smiling.

Frank gave me an ironical glance. "Nevertheless," he said, "the Jews complain. They charge us with not respecting their wishes."

"I trust you do not take their protests seriously," I said.

"On the contrary," said Frank, "we all do our best to anticipate their protests."

"*Ja, natürlich*—Yes, of course," said Fischer.

"As for the filth," went on Frank, "it cannot be denied that they live under deplorable conditions. A German would never tolerate living like that, not even as a joke." And he repeated with a loud laughter, "Ha, ha, ha! not even as a joke!"

"It would be an amusing joke," I remarked.

"A German would not be able to live under such conditions," said Wächter.

"The German people are a civilized people," I said.

"*Ja, natürlich*," said Fischer.

"It must be admitted that it is not altogether the fault of the Jews," said Frank. "The space in which they are herded is rather small for a population that size. But, basically, the Jews like to live in filth. Filth is their natural habitat. Perhaps it is because they are all sick, and the sick, as a last resort, tend to take refuge in filth. It is sad that they die like rats."

"They do not appear to appreciate very much the honor of living," I said. "I mean to say the honor of living like rats."

"I don't mean to criticize them in any way," countered Frank, "when I say that they die like rats. It is merely a statement of fact."

"One ought to bear in mind that under the conditions in which they are living it is very difficult to prevent them from dying," said Emil Gassner.

"Much has been done," suggested Baron Wolsegger in a prudent voice, "to lower the death rate in the ghettos, but . . ."

"In the ghetto of Cracow," said Wächter, "I have ordered the relatives of the dead to defray the expenses of the burial. And I have obtained good results."

"I feel sure," I said ironically, "that the death rate dropped overnight."

"You've guessed right; it has dropped," said Wächter laughing. Everyone laughed and looked at me.

"You should deal with them as with rats," I said. "Give them rat poison. It would be simpler."

"It's not worth the trouble to poison them," said Fischer. "They die at an incredible rate. Last month forty-two thousand died in the Warsaw ghetto."

"It's rather a high rate," I said. "If they go on like this in a couple of years the ghetto will be empty."

"It's impossible to foretell as far as Jews are concerned," said Frank. "All the estimates of our experts have proved wrong. The faster they die, the faster their number increases."

"The Jews persist in having children," I said. "It is all the fault of the children."

"*Ach, die kinder!*—Ah, the children!" said Frau Brigitte Frank.

"*Ja, so schmutzig*—Yes, so dirty," said Frau Fischer.

"Ah, did you notice the children in the ghetto?" asked Frank. "They are horrible! They are dirty and diseased; they are covered with scabs and prey for vermin; they would be pitiful if they were not so loathsome. They look like skeletons. The child death rate is very high in the ghettos. What's the children's death rate in the Warsaw ghetto?" he asked turning to Governor Fischer.

"Fifty-four per cent," replied Fischer.

"The Jews are a diseased race, in full decay," said Frank. "They are all degenerates. They do not know how to rear children or how to care for them, as we do in Germany."

"Germany is a country with a high *Kultur*," I said.

"*Ja, natürlich,* in child hygiene Germany leads the world," said Frank. "Did you notice the vast difference between German and Jewish children?" . . . The Jewish children are not children I was thinking as I walked through the streets of the ghettos of Warsaw, Cracow and Czestochowa. German children are clean. Jewish children are *schmutzig*. German children are well fed, well shod, well clad. Jewish children are famished, half naked, they walk barefoot in the snow. German children have teeth. Jewish children are toothless. German children live in clean houses, in heated rooms; they sleep in little white beds. Jewish children live in foul houses, in cold rooms thronged with people; they sleep on rags or papers close to the beds on which the dead and the dying are stretched. German children play: they have dolls, rubber balls, wooden horses, tin soldiers, air guns, trumpets, music boxes, tops; they have all that a child needs for play. Jewish children do not play; they have nothing to play with, they have no toys; moreover, they do not know how to play! No, the ghetto children do not know how to play. They are truly degenerate. Disgusting! Their one amusement is to follow the hearses heaped with dead bodies, and they are unable to weep; they like to go to the fortress wall to see their parents and brothers shot. Their one amusement is to go and see their mothers being shot. A fit amusement for Jewish children. . . .

"It is not an easy matter for the technical departments to cope with such a large number of dead," said Frank. "At least two hundred trucks would be necessary, instead of the few score hand carts. We do not even know where to bury them. It is a serious problem."

"I trust that you bury them," said I.

"Naturally! Do you fancy that we give them to their relatives to eat?" said Frank laughing.

Everyone laughed, "*Ach so, ach so, ach so, ja, ja, ja!*" And of course I broke into laughter too. My idea that they might not bury them was really amusing. I laughed so hard that tears came into my eyes. Frau Brigitte Frank pressed her bosom with both her hands, tilting back her head, and opening her mouth wide: "*Ach so, ach so, wunderbar!*—that's wonderful!"

"*Ja,* so amusing!" said Frau Fischer.

The dinner was drawing to an end; we had come to the ritual that German hunting men call "the honor of the knife." "*Le cortège d' Orphée,*" as Frank put it quoting Apollinaris, when a young roe deer from the Radziwilom forests, spitted on a pole was borne to the table by two men-servants in pale blue liveries in accordance with the old Polish hunting tradition. The appearance of the spitted roe deer, with a little black swastika on a red Nazi flag stuck into its back, had for a while diverted the guests from the subject of ghettos and Jews. They stood solemnly in deference to Frau Fischer, who with a color heightened by emotion, with a smile and a shy bow offered the honor of the knife to Frau Brigitte Frank. Frau Brigitte Frank curtsied graciously as she received from Frau Fischer's hands the hunting knife with its horn handle, its broad blade hidden in a silver sheath. After dedicating the victim to the hosts and to the guests by turning her head right and left, she began the ceremony by unsheathing the knife and sinking its blade into the deer's back.

Slowly, with skill, patience and grace, that drew surprised exclamations and applause from the guests, Frau Brigitte Frank carved the haunches and the breast of the deer into large, thick slices of pink, tender venison. Assisted by Keith, she served the guests with knowing little nods of the head, a rolling of the eye, a pouting of the lips and other gestures of doubt and indecision. Owing to my position, or rather, as Frank put it, by "virtue" of my being a foreigner, I was served first. To my great surprise, Frank was second; the last, to my still greater surprise, was not Fischer but Emil Gassner. The end of the ceremony was greeted with general applause, to which Frau Brigitte Frank replied with a deep curtsy, that, to my mild astonishment, was not lacking in grace. The knife remained stuck in the deer's back, next to the little red flag with the black swastika, and I confess that the sight of that knife and that flag implanted in the back of the noble animal gave me an uncomfortable feeling with which was mixed a subtle sense of horror as the conversation of the guests, little by little drifted back to ghettos and Jews.

Governor Fischer, as a golden rain of gravy dripped from a spoon onto the slices of venison before him, recounted how the Jews of the ghetto were buried: "A layer of corpses and a layer of lime," he said. "A layer of lime and a layer of corpses," as if he were saying, "A layer of venison and a layer of gravy, a layer of gravy and a layer of venison."

"It's the most sanitary system," said Wächter.

"As far as hygiene," said Emil Gassner, "the living Jews are more contagious than the dead."

"*Ich glaube so!*—I should say so!" exclaimed Fischer.

"The dead don't worry me," said Fischer. "It's the children who worry me. Unfortunately there is little that can be done to reduce the children's death rate in the ghettos. I should like, however, to do something to relieve the suffering of those unfortunate children. I should like to train them to love life, I would like to teach them to walk smiling through the ghetto streets."

"Smiling?" I asked. "Do you wish to teach them to smile? To walk smiling? The Jewish children will never learn to smile, not if you teach them with the whip. Neither will they ever learn to walk. Don't you know that the Jewish children do not walk. Jewish children have wings."

"Wings?" exclaimed Frank.

Deep wonder was evident on the faces of the guests. They stared at me in silence, holding their breath.

"Wings!" shouted Frank stretching his mouth wide open with irrepressible laughter; raising both his arms and waving his hands over his head as if they were wings, he chirped, "Cheep, cheep, cheep," in a voice choked with laughter, and all the guests in their turn raised their arms and, waving their hands above their heads, shouted: "*Ach so! ach so!* cheep, cheep, cheep!"

At last the dinner came to an end, and Frau Fischer rose and lead us to her private sitting room that formerly had been Colonel Beck's study. The back of the armchair in which I was reclining barely touched the knees of a white marble statue that was done in the so-called "Munich style," and portrayed a Greek athlete. The light was dim, the carpets thick; an oak fire crackled in the fireplace. The room was hot, and the air smelt of brandy and tobacco. The voices around me sounded raucous, broken by those German fits of laughter that I cannot hear without feeling slightly uncomfortable.

Keith was mixing in crystal glasses a red Burgundy wine, a thick and tepid Volney, with pale Mumm champagne. It was *"Turkisch-blut*—Turkish blood," the traditional drink of German hunting men.

"And so," said Frank, at that point, turning to me as if sincerely concerned, "and so the Jewish children have wings, have they? If you go to Italy and say that, the Italians will believe it. That's how legends about the Jews are born. If one believed British and American newspapers, the Germans would appear to do nothing else in Poland but kill Jews from morning till night. In spite of this, you have been in Poland for over a month, and you cannot say that you have seen a single hair pulled out of a Jewish head. The pogroms are legends, no less than the wings of Jewish children. You may drink without qualms," he added raising the Bohemian glass full of *Turkischblut*, "you may drink without fear, my dear Malaparte, this is not Jewish blood. *Prosit!*"

"*Prosit!*" I said raising my glass; and I began to tell the story of the events that took place in the noble city of Jassy, in Moldavia.

VI

The Rats of Jassy

I PUSHED THE DOOR open and went inside. The house was empty; it evidently had been left in a hurry. The window curtains had been torn down and the shreds were scattered about the rooms. In the vast bedroom beneath a hanging brass lamp stood a large round table with some chairs around it. The goose feathers had been emptied out of the ripped-open mattress, and when I first stepped into the room a white cloud rose from the floor, whirled about me and stuck to my sweaty face. The drawers were open and clothes and papers were strewn over the floor. I switched on the light. At least the electricity was still working. The kitchen was littered with straw and bits of broken crockery. Pots and pans lay overturned every which way in the fireplace. A heap of potatoes molded in a corner. An odor of filth and of decaying food infested the air.

It certainly was not a palace, but in Jassy, Moldavia, during those days toward the end of June 1941—the first days of the German war against Soviet Russia—I could have found nothing better than that little house at the end of a large abandoned orchard at the head of Lapusneanu Street, close to the Jockey Club and to the Corso Restaurant. Later, I learned that it was not an abandoned orchard, but the ancient Orthodox cemetery of Jassy.

I threw open the windows and began cleaning up. I was dead tired, and I did not attempt anything more that evening than to tidy up and sweep the bedroom. *La dracu*—To the devil with— everything else, *la dracu* the war, *la dracu* Jassy, *la dracu* all the Jassy houses. I had set up my cot and hung my Winchester rifle, my Contax camera, my field battery light, and the photo of my poor dog Febo on the wall.

Two rifle shots broke the stillness of the night; the bullets splintered the window and penetrated the ceiling. I switched off the light and peeked outside. A patrol of soldiers was standing in the middle of the cemetery in front of the house; I could not make out whether they were German or Romanian. "*Lumina! lumina!*" they shouted. They were Romanians. "*La dracu!*—To the devil!" I shouted. The reply was another bullet that whistled past my ear. In Bucharest, a few days earlier, shots had been fired from the square into my window at the Athénée Palace Hotel. Soldiers and police had been ordered to shoot at any window through which even a glimmer of light shone. "*Nopte buna!*—Good night!" I shouted.

I felt about in the dark for the gramophone that I had noticed, and at random picked up one of the records that had been thrown haphazardly into a drawer; I felt the needle with my finger, wound the machine, and rested the needle on the edge of the record. It was a Romanian folk song sung by Chiva Pitzigoi. In the darkness Chiva's sweet and husky voice began:

> *Ce-ai in gusa, Marioara*
> *Ce-ai in gusa, Marioara ...*

I threw myself on the bed and closed my eyes, but very soon I got up, went into the kitchen, drew a pail of water, and placed in the cool water a bottle of *zuica* that I had brought with me from Bucharest. I put the pail close to the bed and stretched myself out again on the ripped mattress and closed my eyes. The record ended and the steel needle grated softly. I rose, wound up the gramophone, and set the needle on the edge of the record. The husky, sweet voice of Chiva Pitzigoi started again:

> *Ce-ai in gusa, Marioara ...*

Had I been allowed to switch on the light I would have read. I had brought with me Harold Nicolson's book, *Helen's Tower*, that I had found in Bucharest in my Jewish friend Azafer's bookshop— the one near the Curentual. Rather an oldish book, printed in 1937, it describes the life of Lord Dufferin, Harold Nicolson's uncle. *La dracu* Harold Nicolson and his uncle, Lord Dufferin. *La dracu* everyone. It was very hot; the summer was stifling; for three days a thunderstorm like a ripe tumor had been ready to break over the roofs of the city. Chiva Pitzigoi was singing in her husky voice, full of sweet blood; suddenly, the song broke off, the steel needle began to grate softly. I didn't want to get up from the bed; *la dracu* Marioara and her *"gusa." "Nopte buna, Domniscoara* Chiva." Thus, little by little, I fell asleep and began dreaming. . . .

At first I did not realize that I was dreaming; later I became suddenly aware that it was a dream. Perhaps I really had fallen asleep and had begun dreaming, then having suddenly awakened, as one does when one is very tired, I had gone on dreaming though I was awake. At that moment the door opened and Harold Nicolson came in. He was dressed in gray, in a light blue shirt of Oxford linen, enlivened by a bright blue tie. He threw his hat—a black felt Lock—onto the table and taking a chair a little away from my bed, he sat there and gazed at me, smiling.

Slowly the room assumed a different shape; it began turning into a street, then into a square with some trees. I recognized the Paris sky above the roofs. I saw Place Dauphine, the windows of my house in Place Dauphine. Walking close to the walls so as not to be recognized by the newsdealer on the Pont Neuf, I turned the corner of Quai de l'Horloge and halted before Number Thirty-nine in front of my gate. It was really the gate of my house, the gate of Daniel Halévy's house. I inquired of the concierge, Madame Martig, "Is Monsieur Malaparte at home?" Madame Martig looked at me in silence, without recognizing me; I felt grateful to her for not recognizing me. I felt ashamed to return to Paris in an Italian officer's uniform. I felt ashamed seeing the Germans in the Paris streets. How could she know me again after so many years? "No, Monsieur Malaparte is not in Paris," replied Madame Martig. "I'm a friend of his," I said. "We have no news of him," answered Madame Martig, "perhaps Monsieur Malaparte is still in prison, in Italy; perhaps he is at the front, somewhere in Russia, in Africa, in Finland—who knows? Perhaps dead or a prisoner—who knows?" And I asked whether Madame and Monsieur Halévy were at home. "No, they are not here, they have just left," was Madame Martig's soft-voiced reply. Then I walked slowly up the stairs and turned smiling toward Madame Martig, who perhaps knew me then. She smiled uncertainly; perhaps she had smelled the odor I had brought with me—the odor of dead horses, the odor of the grass on the tombs of the ancient abandoned cemetery of Jassy. I came to a stop in front of Daniel Halévy's door; I searched for the door handle and tried to turn it, as I had that day when I went to bid him good-by before returning to Italy, before leaving for detention and exile on Lipari Island. Jacques Emile Blanche and Colonel De Gaulle; a gloomy foreboding gripped by heart. "Monsieur Halévy is not at home," Madame Martig shouted from the foot of the stairs. I resumed my climb up the narrow wooden steps leading to my garret. I knocked at the door, and after a while heard a step inside. I recognized it, and Malaparte opened the door. He was young, much younger than I am, with a clear countenance, black hair, and eyes that were opaque. He looked silently at me, and I smiled at him; but he did not smile back, he looked at me suspiciously, as if I were a stranger. I entered my own home and looked around. Seated in the library were all my friends, Jean Giraudoux, Luigi Pirandello, Henri Malraux, Bassand-Massenet, Jean Guehenno, Harold Nicolson, Glenway Wescott, Cecil Sprigge and Barbara Harrison. All my friends were there in front of me, sitting silently, some among them were dead, their faces pale, their eyes without light. Perhaps they had been there all those years waiting for me, and they did not recognize me. Perhaps they no longer hoped that I would return to Paris after so many years of detention, exile and war. The screeching of the tugs steaming up the Seine with their train of barges, sounded faint and doleful. I looked out of the window and saw the bridges of Paris, from Saint Michel to the Trocadero. I saw the green foliage along the quays, the front of the Louvre and the trees of Place de la Concorde. My friends gazed silently at me and I sat down among them. I wanted to hear their voices again, I wanted to hear them talk, but they sat motionless and impenetrable; they gazed intently at me, and I felt that they were sorry for me. I wanted to tell them that it was through no fault of mine that I had become cruel; we have all grown cruel; you too, Bassand-Massenet; you too, Guehenno; you too, Jean Giraudoux; and you too, Barbara; isn't that so? And Barbara smiled and nodded as if to tell me that she knew, that she understood. The others smiled, too, and nodded, as if to say that it was not our fault that we had all grown cruel. Then I stood up and walked to the door, and smiling I turned on the threshold to look at them. Slowly I went down the stairs, and Madame Martig said in a low voice, "He has never written us." I wanted to apologize for never having written to her from *Regina Coeli* prison or from Lipari Island. "It was not because of pride, you know, but because he was ashamed." I felt the prisoner's shame, that shame of a hunted man, locked up in a cell, infested with vermin, with sleeplessness, with fever; gnawed by loneliness and by cruelty. "Yes, Madame Martig, gnawed by his own cruelty."

"Perhaps," said Madame Martig in a low voice, "he has forgotten us." Then she went on: "Perhaps he has forgotten you too."

"Oh, no! He has not forgotten us; he is ashamed of his own suffering, he feels ashamed of what we have all become during this war. You know, don't you? that he feels ashamed of his own suffering. You know it, don't you, Madame Martig?"

"Yes," said Madame Martig in a low voice, "we know him well, we know Monsieur Malaparte well." . . .

"Good morning, Childe Harold," I said sitting up in bed.

Harold Nicolson slowly removed his gloves and, stroking his mustache with his short white hand glistening with a thin reddish down, kept his fingers pressed to his lips for a long time. Harold Nicolson's mustache had always made me think of Chelsea Barracks, rather than of a young diplomat of the Foreign Office; it appeared to me to be a typical product of the English public school, of Sandhurst and of the army. Harold Nicolson was gazing at me and smiling as on that day in Paris, when he had come to take me to luncheon at Larue's in the rue Royale, where Mosley was waiting for us. I could no longer remember where I had first met Nicolson. It was Mrs. Strong who first spoke to me about him one morning, at lunch in the house of some friends in Faubourg St. Honoré. A few days later, Mrs. Strong had telephoned me that Nicolson would take me to meet Mosley.

Seated in my library, Nicolson was stroking his mustache with his short white hand glistening with a thin reddish down. From the Seine came the doleful lament of the tugs. It must have been an October morning, misty and warm. The meeting with Mosley was arranged for two o'clock. We started walking along the Seine toward Rue Royale, and when we entered Larue's it was five minutes of two.

We sat at a table, ordered a Martini; half an hour later **Mosley** had not yet made his appearance. From time to time Nicolson rose to telephone Mosley, who lived, as I was told, at the Napoleon Hotel near the Arc de Triomphe. A wonderful address for England's future Mussolini. Around three o'clock Mosley still had not shown up. I suspected him of having calmly remained in bed, and of being asleep. After more waiting—it was half-past three by then—Nicolson issued for the tenth time from the telephone booth and triumphantly announced that Sir Oswald Mosley was about to arrive. And he added laughing, as a sort of apology for him, that Mosley was in the habit of lying in bed the entire morning, that he rose late, never before twelve, and that from twelve until two he fenced a little in his own room; then he left his hotel on foot and arrived late to whatever meeting he had arranged—usually when everyone was tired of waiting for him and about to leave. I asked him whether he knew Talleyrand's saying: "In life it is easy to arrive, but difficult to leave."

"The danger for Mosley," said Nicolson, "is that he may leave before arriving."

When Mosley at last entered Larue's it was almost four o'clock. Nicolson and I had already had some seven or eight Martinis and had begun eating; I do not remember what we were eating or what we were talking about; I only remember that Mosley had a very small head and a soft voice, that he was tall—very tall—thin and lazy looking, rather stooped. He was not in the least sorry about being late, but on the contrary, quite pleased with himself. He said, "One never rushes when the purpose is to be late." He was not apologizing, but just letting us understand that he was not so stupid as not to realize that he was late. A glance exchanged between Nicolson and me was enough to bring us to an agreement, and throughout the luncheon Mosley never suspected that we had agreed to make fun of him. He appeared to be endowed with a rich sense of humor, but like all dictators—Mosley was only an aspiring dictator, but he was certainly of the stuff of which dictators are made! and we all know what that stuff is—he hadn't the least inkling that anyone could make fun of him.

He had brought with him a copy of the English edition of my book, *Coup d'Etat: The Technique of Revolution,* and he wished me to write something on the title-page. No doubt he expected a very fancy dedication from me. To tease and to disappoint him, I wrote only these two sentences from my book: *Like all dictators, Hitler is merely a woman, and dictatorship is the highest form of jealousy.* On reading these words Mosley's face clouded, and looking at me with half-closed eyes he asked, "Was Caesar, in your opinion, also only a woman?" Nicolson did his best not to laugh and winked at me. "He was worse than a woman," I replied. "Caesar was no gentleman."

"Caesar was not a gentleman?" asked Mosley in amazement.

"A foreigner who allows himself to occupy England," I replied, "is certainly no gentleman."

The wines were excellent and Larue's chef—vain, punctilious, and as capricious as a woman or a dictator—by an unbroken stream of exquisite dishes fashioned with proud imagination and sensitive conceit, insisted on honoring the table of those three eccentric foreigners who lunched at such an unusual hour when tea was already steaming in the silver teapots of the Ritz. Mosley's temper was in perfect accord with the temper of the chef and the flavor of the wines. Little by little, he managed to recover his calm and his irony. One by one, the lamps along the rue Royale were lit; the flowersellers of the Madeleine were moving down toward the Concorde with their barrows loaded with withered flowers; and we were still debating the merits of Brie cheese and the best means of seizing power in England.

Nicolson maintained that Englishmen are not sensitive either to force or persuasion, but only to "good manners" and that dictators never have good manners. Mosley countered that good manners, too, were on the downgrade, and that Englishmen, particularly those of "The Upper Ten Thousand," were ripe for dictatorship.

"But how will you get into power?" asked Nicolson.

"By the longest way, of course," replied Mosley.

"Via St. James Park or via Trafalgar Square?" asked Nicolson.

"Via St. James Park, of course," replied Mosley, "my *coup d'état* will be just a walk-over," and he laughed gaily.

"Oh! I see, your revolution will move from Mayfair. And when do you expect to rise to power?" asked Nicolson.

"The date on which the parliamentary regime will reach a crisis in England can already be reckoned with absolute accuracy. I could make an appointment with you in Downing Street today," replied Mosley.

"Right! What day and what time?" asked Nicolson.

"Ah, that's my secret," replied Mosley laughing.

"If the revolution means an appointment, you'll be late in coming into power," said Nicolson.

"So much the better; I shall come into power when it is least expected," replied Mosley.

While we were talking and with relish inhaling the ancient and faraway bouquet of an Armagnac, the Larue dining room was gradually changing, until it became a large room strangely resembling the room where I was lying on the ripped mattress. Harold Nicolson was gazing at me smiling; he was sitting beneath the brass lamp, his elbow on the table near his black Lock hat. After a time, with a glance he called my attention to a corner of the room and, raising my eyes, I beheld Sir Oswald Mosley sitting cross-legged on the floor. I could not understand how Nicolson and Mosley happened to be in Jassy in my bedroom, and I noticed with deep wonder that Mosley had the small rosy face of a child, small hands, very short arms, and extremely long legs—so long, that he was compelled to cross them Turkish fashion to get them into the room.

"I ask myself why you stay in Jassy," said Harold Nicolson to me, "instead of going to fight."

"*La dracu*," I replied. "*La dracu* the war, *la dracu* everybody."

Mosley beat his hands on the floor raising a cloud of goose feathers. His face was plastered with feathers sticking to his sweaty skin, and he laughed, beating his hands on the floor.

Nicolson glanced sternly at Sir Oswald Mosley, "You ought to feel ashamed of these childish tricks of yours. You are no longer a child, Sir Oswald."

"Oh, sorry, sir," said Sir Oswald Mosley lowering his eyes.

"Why don't you go and fight?" went on Nicolson turning to me. "It is every gentleman's duty to fight against these barbarians," and saying this he burst out laughing.

"*La dracu*," I replied, "*la dracu* you too, Childe Harold!"

"Every gentleman's duty," continued Harold Nicolson, "is to go and fight Stalin's armies. Down with the USSR. Ha! Ha! Ha!" and he burst into a loud laugh, as he threw himself back in his chair.

"Down with the USSR!" shouted Sir Oswald Mosley beating his hands on the floor.

Nicolson turned to Mosley. "Don't talk nonsense, Sir Oswald," he said sternly.

Just then the door opened and a tall, massive officer appeared on the threshold followed by three soldiers whose red eyes and faces glistening with sweat I could barely make out in the twilight. The moon peeped over the windowsill; a light breeze blew through the open window. The officer stepped forward, paused at the foot of the bed and with his flashlight fixed a beam of light on my face; I saw that he clutched a pistol in his fist.

"Military police," said the officer. "Have you your pass?"

I burst into laughter and turned to Nicolson. I was just about to say, *la dracu*, when I noticed Nicolson vanishing in a white cloud of goose feathers. A milk-white sky filled the room, and against that misty sky I saw the vague shapes of Nicolson and Mosley floating lazily very slowly upward toward the ceiling like swimmers after a dive rising to the surface from the bottom of the sea amid a spray of air bubbles.

I sat up in bed and became aware that I was awake.

"Have a drink?" I asked the officer.

I filled two glasses with *zuica* and we lifted our glasses saying "*Narok*—Your health."

The cold *zuica* finally brought me to, and imparted a dry and gay tone to my voice. After rummaging through the pockets of my coat hanging at the head of my bed, I passed the document to the officer saying, "Here's the pass. I bet it is forged."

The officer smiled. "It would not surprise me," he said. "Jassy is full of Russian paratroopers." Then he added, "You should not sleep alone in this forsaken house. Only yesterday we found on Usine Road a fellow in bed with his throat cut."

"I'm much obliged for your advice," I answered, "but with this forged document I should be able to sleep safely, don't you think?"

"Of course," said the officer.

112

My pass was signed by Mihai Antonescu, Vice-President of the Council.

"Do you mind seeing if this one is forged too?" I asked, offering another pass signed by Colonel Lupu, Military Commander of Jassy.

"Thanks," said the officer, "your papers are in order."

"Have a drink?"

"I don't mind if I do. There's not a drop of *zuica* left in all Jassy."

"*Narok.*"

"*Narok.*"

The officer, followed by his soldiers went away, and I fell sound asleep again, stretched on my back and clutching the handle of my revolver in a sweating hand.

The sun was already high when I awoke. Birds twittered on the acacia branches and on the stone crosses in the old abandoned churchyard. I dressed and went out to look for something to eat. The streets were cluttered with long columns of German lorries and Panzers; artillery trucks were blocked in front of the Jockey Club building, squads of Romanian soldiers with their large helmets trailing down the napes of their necks, their sand-colored uniforms clotted with mud, moved along treading heavily on the asphalt roads. Groups of idlers lounged at the entrance of the wineshop near the *Cafetaria Fundatia;* and around the doors of the *Coafor* Jonescu and of the *Ceasocornicaria* Goldstein. Mixed with the strong smell of *brenza,* the salty Braila cheese, there hung heavily in the air the odor of *ciorba de pui,* a greasy chicken soup mixed with vinegar. I started off along the Strada Bratianu toward the St. Spiridion Hospital and entered the shop of Kane, the broad and flatheaded Jewish grocer whose ears looked like the handles on an earthenware pot.

"Good morning, *Domnule Capitan,*" said Kane.

He was pleased to see me; he thought I was still at the front along the Prut river with the Romanian troops.

"*La dracu* the Prut," I said to him.

A faint feeling of sickness made me dizzy. I sat down on a bag of sugar and thrusting my fingers between my collar and shirt loosened my tie. A heavy, mixed odor of spices, dried fish, paint, kerosene and soap was stagnating in the shop.

"This silly *razboiou*," said Kane—"This silly war."

The people of Jassy were restless; everyone expected something bad to happen. "One feels in the air that something bad will happen," said Kane. He spoke in a low tone, casting suspicious glances toward the door. Gangs of Romanian soldiers, columns of German lorries and Panzers were moving by. "What do they think they can do with all these weapons, all these guns and armored cars?" Kane seemed to be saying. But he kept silent, moving heavily and slowly about the shop.

"*Domnule* Kane," I said, "I'm down to bedrock."

"I'll always have something nice for you," said Kane.

From a hiding place he fished out three bottles of *zuica*, two one-pound loaves of bread, a little *brenza*, a few boxes of sardines, two pots of jam, a little sugar and a little bag of tea.

"It's Russian tea," said Kane, "real Russian *chai*. It's the last bag. I can't give you any more when you have finished this." He gazed at me shaking his head. "If you need something else in the next few days come back to me; there is always something nice for you in my shop."

He looked sad. He said, "Come back to me" as if he knew that we should never see each other again. There really was something vaguely threatening in the air, and the people were worried. Now and then somebody looked into the shop and said, "Good day, *Domnule* Kane," and Kane shook his head in denial, looked at me and sighed. This silly *razboiou*—This silly war. I stuck the parcels of food into my pockets, tucked the bag of tea under my arm, broke off a bit of bread and began chewing it.

"*La revedere, Domnule* Kane—I'll be seeing you."

"*La revedere, Domnule Capitan,*" said Kane.

We shook hands and smiled. Kane's was the shy, uncertain smile of an uneasy animal. As I was leaving a carriage stopped before the shop. Kane rushed to the door and bowing down to the ground he said, "Good day, *Domna Principessa.*"

It was one of those old-fashioned lordly carriages, black and solemn—a sort of open landau with its hood lowered and fastened down by broad leather straps—that are still to be seen in the Ro-

114

manian countryside. The seats were upholstered in gray material; the spokes of the wheels were painted red. A pair of splendid white Moldavian horses with long manes, their quarters glistening with sweat, were harnessed to the carriage. Sitting on high, wide cushions was a thin lady, no longer young, with the skin of her face withered under a thick coating of white powder. She sat stiffly upright, dressed in pale blue and held in her right hand a red silk parasol with a lace flounce. The brim of her broad Florentine straw hat cast a slight shadow on her lined forehead. There was a proud look in her filmed eyes, but their arrogance had something vague and distant because of her near-sightedness. Her face was motionless, her gaze turned upward, toward a blue silk sky on which white clouds lightly floated, resembling the shadows of clouds mirrored in a lake. She was Princess Sturdza, bearer of a great Moldavian name. Next to her sat Prince Sturdza, proud and remote; he was still a young man, tall, lean, rosy, dressed in white, his brow shaded by the brim of a gray felt hat. He wore a stiff high collar, a gray tie, gray cotton gloves and black buttoned boots.

"Good day, *Domna Principessa*," said Kane bowing down to the ground. I saw the blood rushing to the back of his neck and pulsating in his temples. The Princess did not return the greeting, did not turn her neck that was encircled by a tight lace collar held up by short pieces of whalebone; instead she ordered in a dry and imperious voice, "Hand my tea to Grigori." Grigori, the coachman, was perched on his seat, wrapped in a heavy, faded green silk robe that reached down to the heels of his red leather boots. On his head he wore a little Tartar skull cap of yellow satin embroidered in red and green. He was fat, flabby and pale; he was a member of the Orthodox sect of the *Skoptsi*—the emasculated—whose holy city is Jassy. The *Skoptsi* marry young, and as soon as they have begotten a son, they have themselves castrated. Kane bowed to the eunuch Grigori, mumbled a few words; then darted into the shop, and a few moments later came out again, again bowed to the ground, and in a trembling voice said: "*Domna Principessa*, forgive me, I have nothing left, not a single tea leaf, *Domna Principessa—*"

"Hurry up now, my tea," said Princess Sturdza in a hard voice.

"Excuse me, *Domna Principessa—*"

The Princess turned her head slowly, stared at him without batting an eyelid, and said in a tired voice, "What are these stories? . . . Grigori!"

The eunuch turned and lifted his whip, the long Moldavian whip with a red tassle and a carved handle painted red, blue and green. He dangled it wickedly above Kane's shoulders and brushed his neck with it.

"Excuse me, *Domna Principessa* . . ." said Kane lowering his head.

"Grigori!" said the Princess in a faint voice.

Then, as the eunuch raised his whip, lifting and stretching his arms as if he were holding a flagpole in his fist, and rose to his feet to strike a better blow, Kane turned toward me, stretched out his hand, touched with trembling fingers the bag of tea that I was clutching under my arm, and sweating, pale, imploring, said to me in a low voice, "Excuse me, *Domnule Capitan—*" He grasped the bag that I smilingly held out to him, and he handed it to Grigori with a bow. The eunuch diverted the violent blow to the back of the horses that started, reared and were off; with a sharp tinkling of bells, the carriage disappeared in a cloud of dust. A dab of foam from the bit of one of the horses had fallen onto my shoulder.

"*La dracu, Domna Principessa, la dracu!*" I shouted. But the carriage was already far away, it was already taking the turn at the end of the road, toward the Jockey Club and the *Fundatia*.

"Thank you, *Domnule Capitan*," said Kane in a soft voice, lowering his eyes with shame.

"It's all right, *Domnule* Kane, but to the devil with Princess Sturdza, *la dracu* all these Moldavian nobles."

My friend Kane lifted his eyes, his face crimson with large drops of sweat on his forehead.

"It doesn't matter," I said, "it doesn't matter. *La revedere, Domnule* Kane."

"*La revedere, Domnule Capitan*," answered Kane wiping his brow with the back of his hand.

Walking back toward the churchyard, I passed in front of the druggist on the corner of the Strada Lapusneanu and Strada Bratianu. I entered and went up to the counter.

"Good day, *Domniscoara* Mica."

116

"Good day, *Domnule Capitan*."

Mica smiled as she rested her elbows on the marble counter. Mica was a nice-looking girl, dark, buxom, with a forehead weighed down by a mass of curly black hair, a pointed chin, a large fleshy mouth, and a face covered with a light down that shone with bluish reflections. I had tried to date her before leaving Jassy for the Prut lines. Good Lord, I thought, it's two months since I have had a woman. I had not touched a woman in Bucharest. It was too hot. Good Lord, I scarcely know any longer what women are like.

"*Cum merge a sanatate*—How are you—*Domniscoara* Mica?"

"*Bine, foarte bine*—Well, very well—*Domnule Capitan*."

A fine girl, but as hairy as a goat; she had large, black, glistening eyes and a thin nose in a plump dark face. There must have been some gypsy blood in her veins. She told me that she would like to go for a walk that evening after curfew.

"After curfew, *Domniscoara* Mica?"

"*Da, da*—Yes, yes, *Domnule Capitan*."

Good heavens, what an idea! How was I to take a girl out after curfew, when police and military patrols shouted *stai, stai!* from afar, and shot before there was time to reply? Besides, what an idea to wander around the ruins of houses wrecked by bombs and charred by fire. A house was still burning from the day before in Unirii Square, in front of Prince Gutsa Voda's statue. The Soviet bombers were hammering hard. For three hours the day before they had been flying over Jassy, calmly moving back and forth not more than nine hundred feet above the city. Some planes had grazed the roofs. A Russian bomber on its return trip, on its way to Skuleni, had fallen headlong into a field just outside the city beyond Capou.

The crew was made up of six women. I went to look at them. Some Romanian soldiers were rummaging inside the pilots' cabin; they handled those poor girls with their grubby fingers, dirty with *ciorba, mamaliga* and *brenza*. "Let her alone, you bastard!" I had started shouting to a soldier who was running his fingers through the hair of one of the two pilots, a sturdy blonde with a freckled face. Her eyes were wide open, her mouth half-shut; one of her hands hung by her side, her head rested on the shoulder of her companion in an attitude of modesty and renunciation. They were two brave girls who had carried out their duty and were entitled

117

to respect. Two honest factory girls, weren't they, *Domna Princi-pessa* Sturdza? They wore gray overalls and leather jackets. The soldiers were slowly stripping them, unbuttoning the leather jackets, raising their limp arms, pulling the jackets over their heads. To keep up the head of one of the girls a soldier had caught her under the chin and was clutching her throat as if he had meant to choke her; his broad thumb with a black cracked nail pressed against the half-shut mouth and the thick, bloodless lips. "Bite his finger, you fool!" I shouted as if the girl could hear me. The soldiers looked at me and laughed. Another girl was wedged in between the bomb cradle and a heavy machine gun; in that position it was impossible to remove the jacket from her. A soldier undid her leather helmet, grasped her by the hair and jerked her out, rolling her onto the ground near the remains of the plane.

"*Domnule Capitan,* will you take me for a walk tonight, after curfew?" asked Mica resting her chin on her two open palms.

"Why not, *Domniscoara* Mica? It's nice to be out at night, after curfew. Haven't you ever been in the park at night? There is never anyone."

"Won't they shoot at us, *Domnule Capitan?*"

"Let's hope so; let's hope that they shoot at us, *Domniscoara* Mica."

Mica laughed, leaned across the counter, put her fat hairy face close to mine and bit my lips.

"Come for me at seven, *Domnule Capitan.* I'll wait for you out there, in front of the druggist."

"Right, Mica, at seven. *La revedere, Domniscoara* Mica."

I walked up Strada Lapusneanu, crossed the churchyard, and pushed open the door of my house. I ate a little *brenza,* then I threw myself on the bed. It was hot; the flies hummed incessantly. A bare high-pitched buzz seemed to drop from the sky; a heavy sweet buzz, not unlike the thick scent of carnations, was lazily spreading from the sky dripping with sweat. By heaven, how sleepy I was! The *zuica* was simmering inside me. About five in the afternoon I awoke, went out into the cemetery and sat down on a tombstone buried in the grass. In olden times it had been a churchyard, this garden of mine, an ancient Orthodox cemetery, the oldest in Jassy. Where once a little church stood, in the center of the churchyard was the entrance to a public *adapost,* a shelter into which one descended by a steep little wooden staircase. The mouth of the *adapost* looked like the entrance to an underground mausoleum. Inside the shelter, there was a smell of rotten earth, a thick smell of tombs. On the roof of the *adapost,* which the heaped-up earth lent the shape of a sepulchral mound, rose a pyramid of tombstones placed crossways one on top of the other. From the spot where I was sitting I could read the posthumous praise of *Domnule* Grigorio Soinescu, of *Domna* Sofia Zanfirescu, of *Domna* Maria Pojaescu—carved in the tombstones. It was hot, my lips were parched with thirst, and as I breathed in the dead smell of the earth, I gazed fixedly at the rusty iron railings around a few tombs which had remained unscathed in the shadow of the acacias. I felt dizzy, nausea gripped my stomach. *La dracu* Mica, *la dracu* Mica and all her goat's hair. The flies buzzed wickedly, a damp wind rose from the banks of the Prut.

Now and then from the lower end of town, down toward Usine, Socola and Pacurari, from the railway works of Nicolina, from the buildings scattered along the banks of the Bahlui, from the Tzicau and Tatarasi suburbs, that were once the Tartar quarter, rang out the sharp sound of a rifle shot. Romanian soldiers and policemen are nervous, they shout *stai! stai!* and they fire at people without giving them a chance to raise their arms. And this was still daylight, the curfew had not yet sounded. The wind was swelling the foliage of the trees; the sun charged the air with an odor of honey. Mica was expecting me at seven—in front of the druggist's. And in half an hour I was to go and call for Mica to take her for a walk.

La dracu Domniscoara Mica, *la dracu* the goats, too. A few passers-by slunk cautiously along the walls and brandished their passes in their right hands held high above their heads. There was really something in the air. My friend Kane was right. Something was about to happen. One felt that some misfortune was imminent. One felt it in the air, in one's skin, in one's finger tips.

When I arrived in front of the druggist's shop, it was seven sharp, and Mica was not there. The shop was closed. Mica had closed it early that evening, much earlier than usual. I could have wagered that she was not coming, that she had become frightened at the last moment. *La dracu* all women, they are all alike, they all become frightened, and always at the last moment. *La dracu Dom-niscoara* Mica, *la dracu* the goats, too. I walked slowly up the street toward the cemetery. Groups of German soldiers were passing by dragging their boots along the sidewalk. The owner of the *lustra-geria*, on the corner of Strada Lapusneanu, just in front of the Corso Café-Restaurant, was wielding his last brush strokes on the shoes of his last patron for the day, a Romanian soldier seated high on his brass throne.

The glow of the sunset penetrated to the very back of the dark shop, causing the tins of shoe polish to glisten. From time to time I met a group of manacled Jews who trod along, their heads low, under the guard of Romanian soldiers in their sand-colored uniforms. "Why don't you polish the boots of those unfortunate ones for the last time?" laughed the Romanian soldier seated high on his brass throne. "Can't you see they are barefoot?" replied the owner of the *lustrageria* raising his pale, sweaty face. He was gently panting as he swung his brush with amazing lightness.

The aristocrats of Jassy were looking out of the windows of the Jockey Club—those fat, round-bellied Moldavian gentlemen, sweetly and tamely adipose, their faces smooth and flabby, their gloomy deeply circled eyes shining humid and languid; they looked like figures by Pascin. The houses, the trees and the carriages that stopped in front of the Fundatia Palace also looked as if they had been painted by Pascin. Farther away in the sky, toward Skuleni, toward the Prut sluggishly flowing between its muddy banks thick with reeds—there burst little red and white clouds of flak. The owner of the shoe-shine parlor, while putting on the shutters of his shop, glanced upward at those little clouds in the far-off sky, as if he were watching the approach of a storm.

The Jockey Club, standing where the Hotel d'Angleterre had been, at the crossing of the Strada Brocuraru and Strada Carol, was a fine neoclassical little palace, the one modern building in Jassy that could lay claim to some artistic distinction in its architectural design, its decorations, and even its less conspicuous adornments. Doric columns in bold relief seemed to move in front of its ivory-colored façade. Its side walls were grooved with closely set niches, in which stood stucco Cupids, half-way between ivory and pink in color, with bow and arrows in hand. The shop windows of the

Zanfirescu confectionery and the large windows of the Corso Café-Restaurant—the smartest in the city—ran the length of the ground floor. The entrance to the Jockey Club was at the back of the building, across a loosely cobbled courtyard. Here and there groups of Romanian soldiers in full war equipment, their brows hidden by steel helmets, were stretched out on the cobblestones, sleeping in the sun. Under a glass canopy two large, fat-breasted sphinxes stood guard at the entrance.

The walls of the hallway were wainscoted in dark polished wood; the inner door frames were carved in the French style of Louis Philippe; oil paintings and etchings hung on the walls—Parisian landscapes, Notre Dame, the Île St. Louis, the Trocadero, and portraits of women typical of the French fashion magazines of the period from 1880 to 1900. In the card room, around the tables covered with green felt, the old Moldavian gentlemen played dismal bridge games and wiped their brows with big handkerchiefs on which large coronets were embroidered. A carved-wood gallery, its banister decorated with a neoclassic band of alternating harps and lyres, extended along the wall facing the windows which look out on the Strada Brocuraru. It was the gallery used by the musicians during the gay entertainments given by the nobility of Jassy.

I stopped by a table to watch the game; the players lifted their perspiring faces and nodded their greetings. Stooping slightly, old Prince Cantemir crossed the room and limped through a door in the rear. Swarms of flies like roses whirled about in the air and buzzed persistently at the windows; a warm scent of roses wafted up from the garden and mingled with the odor of the *zuica* and the Turkish tobacco. The gilded youth of Jassy were looking out of the windows facing the street, those fat Moldavian Beau Brummels with swarthy, morose eyes. Before going out I stopped a while to gaze at their vast, round, soft behinds, around which swarms of flies traced delicate circles in the smoky air.

"Buna seara, Domnule Capitan," said Marioara, the little waitress in the Corso Café-Restaurant, when I entered the room thronged with German officers and soldiers; it was a large well-designed room on the ground floor of the Jockey Club. Along its walls ran narrow, horse-hair seats that were broken here and there by wooden partitions, inclosing little booths. Marioara was still a child—thin,

unripe and gentle. She smiled at me tilting her head on her shoulder, as she leaned both her hands on the marble slab of the table.

"Won't you give me a glass of beer, Marioara?"

Marioara moaned as if she were ill, and said, "*Ohi, ohi, ohi, Domnule Capitan, ohi, ohi, ohi.*"

"I am thirsty, Marioara."

"*Ohi, ohi, ohi,* there's no beer, *Domnule Capitan.*"

"You're a naughty child, Marioara."

"*Nu, nu, Domnule Capitan,* there's no beer," said Marioara shaking her head and smiling.

"I will go away, and I shall never come back, Marioara."

"*La revedere, Domnule Capitan,*" said Marioara with a mischievous smile.

"*La revedere,*" I replied moving toward the door.

"*Domnule Capitan?*"

"*La revedere,*" I said without turning.

Marioara was calling me in her childish voice from the door of the Corso Café, "*Domnule Capitan, Domnule Capitan!*"

It is not far from the Corso to the ancient cemetery, not more than fifty steps. Walking between the tombs I heard Marioara's voice calling me, "*Domnule Capitan!*" But I had no intention of going back at once, I wanted to make her wait, to think that I was angry with her for not giving me a glass of beer, well knowing that it was no fault of hers, that there was not a drop of beer to be had in Jassy.

"*Domnule Capitan?*" I was just opening the door of my house, when I felt a hand slightly touch my arm, and heard a voice say: "*Buna seara*—Good evening, *Domnule Capitan.*" It was Kane's voice.

"What do you want, *Domnule* Kane?" In the evening twilight I made out three bearded, black-coated figures behind Kane's back.

"May we come in, *Domnule Capitan?*"

"Of course," I said.

We climbed the steep stairs, entered the house, and I turned on the switch. "*La dracu!*" I exclaimed.

"The current has been cut off," said Kane.

I lighted a candle, closed the windows so the light would not be seen from without, and looked at Kane's three companions. They were three old Jews, with reddish hair covering their faces. Their foreheads were so pale that they shone as if made of silver.

"Be seated," I said pointing at the chairs scattered about the room.

We sat around the table and I looked inquiringly at Kane.

"*Domnule Capitan*," said Kane, "we have come to ask you whether you could—"

"—whether you would help us," broke in one of his companions. He was an old man, incredibly thin and pale with a long, reddish-gray beard. His eyes behind a pair of gold-rimmed spectacles shone with a flickering red light. He was resting his fleshless hands, the color of war, on the table.

"You can help us, *Domnule Capitan*," said Kane, and he added after a brief pause, "you may perhaps be able to tell us what we should do—"

"—to remove the grave danger threatening us," broke in again the same man who had interrupted Kane before.

"What danger?" I asked.

Deep silence followed my words; suddenly another of Kane's companions—his face seemed familiar; I thought I had seen him before, but I could not say where or when—rose slowly to his feet. He was a tall, bony old man with tawny hair and a beard streaked with white; his white eyelids stuck to the lenses of his spectacles; his fixed and blank eyes were like those of a blind man. He gazed at me for a long time without offering a word, then he said in a low voice: "*Domnule Capitan,* a frightful danger is hanging over our heads. Can't you feel the menace hovering over us? The Romanian authorities are preparing a merciless pogrom. The slaughter may begin at any moment. Why don't you help us? What are we to do? Why don't you act, why don't you come to our aid?"

"I cannot do anything," I replied. "I am a foreigner, I am the only Italian officer in all Moldavia. What can I do? Who will listen to me?"

"Warn General von Schobert. Tell him what they are planning to do to us. He can, if he wishes, prevent the massacre. Won't you go to General von Schobert? He will listen to you."

"General von Schobert," I replied, "is a gentleman; he is an old soldier and a good Christian, but he is a German and cares nothing about Jews."

"If he is a good Christian, he will listen to you."

"He will answer that he does not interfere with the internal affairs of Romania. I might go to Colonel Lupu, the Military Commander of Jassy."

"Colonel Lupu?" said Kane. "It is Colonel Lupu himself who is planning the massacre."

"But do something, do something quick!" said the old man softly with a repressed urgency.

"I have lost the ability to act," I replied. "I am an Italian. We are no longer able to act; after twenty years of slavery, we are no longer able to assume responsibility. Like all Italians, I have a broken back. During the last twenty years all our energies have been spent on the effort to survive. We are no longer good for anything. We are only able to applaud. Do you want to go and applaud General von Schobert and Colonel Lupu? If you want, I can go as far as Bucharest and applaud Marshal Antonescu, the 'Red Dog,' if you think that it will help you any. I cannot do anything else. Perhaps you want me to sacrifice myself uselessly for you? Should I have myself shot in Unirii Square defending the Jews of Jassy? If I were capable of it, I would have had myself shot in an Italian square defending the Italians. We no longer dare to act, and we no longer know how; that is the truth," I said, turning away to conceal the color of my face.

"All this is very sad," murmured the old man. Then he leaned across the table and thrust his face toward me, and in a voice that was extraordinarily humble and sweet, in a faraway voice said, "Don't you recognize me?"

I looked closely at the old man. The long reddish beard streaked with silver, those blank fixed eyes, that high pale forehead, and that sweet, sad, faraway voice called back to my mind Dr. Alesi, the director of the *Regina Coeli* prison in Rome. It was his voice above all that made me recognize him again in the flickering candle-light. Doctor Alesi had been the director of the Mantellate, the prison for women, but while I was incarcerated in *Regina Coeli* he temporarily took the place of the regular director who had been ill for several months; and owing to his long habit of dealing with the

124

women of the Mantellate, he had trained his voice to an extraordinary almost feminine sweetness. That very sweet, sad voice—a voice evoking serene days, harmonious curves, green and rosy twilights—coming from an old bearded man as solemn as a patriarch seemed like a window opening onto a springlike countryside. And at that moment there also rose before my eyes the same vista of trees, water and clouds that came to me in my cell in *Regina Coeli*, whenever I heard his sad, sweet, faraway voice in the passage. It was a voice like a landscape; the eye lost itself in the limitless freedom of that view of mountains, valleys, woods and rivers, and the feeling that moved me, the anguish that oppressed me, the despair that sometimes pushed me down onto the straw mattress, or drove me to hammer with my fists the walls of my cell, all were gradually allayed, as if they found some compensation for the humiliation and the suffering of a slave, in the presence of freedom and of the peace of nature. To the prisoners Alesi's voice meant the gift of that marvelous landscape for which all of us yearned and which we tried to imagine beyond our bars; it was the gift of an imaginary landscape penetrated furtively into the narrow cell, between those four white walls—blinding, bare, impervious, inaccessible. Hearing Alesi's voice the prisoners saw opening before their eyes that free, limitless view, lit by a clear, even, mellow light which, falling from above, tinged the valleys with transparent half shadows, pierced the secret of the woods, revealed the mystery of the shining silvery rivers and lakes at the end of the plain and the delicate tremor of the sea. For a moment, for a moment only, each prisoner had the illusion of being free, as if the door of the cell had opened mysteriously and noiselessly, and after a brief moment was slowly closed again as Alesi's voice died away little by little in the crushing silence of the *Regina Coeli* corridors.

"Don't you recognize me?" asked the old Jew of Jassy in a voice that was extraordinarily humble and sweet, in the sad, faraway voice of Alesi. I looked fixedly at him, trembling, my brow sweating with anguish and fear. I wanted to rise and to flee, but Alesi stretched out his arm across the table and held me back.

"Do you remember the day you tried to kill yourself in your cell? It was Cell 46J of the fourth block—do you remember? We were just in time to prevent you from slashing your wrist. Did you think we had not noticed that a piece of glass from the broken tumbler was missing?" and he started laughing, drumming with his fingers on the table to the lilting rhythm of his laughter.

"Why do you revive those memories? You were very good to me then. But I don't know whether I should be thankful that you saved me."

"Was I wrong in saving you?" asked Alesi. And after a long silence he asked me in a low voice, "Why did you want to die?"

"I was afraid," I replied.

"Do you remember that day when you shouted and beat your fists on the door of the cell?"

"I was afraid," I replied.

The old man began to laugh and closed his eyes a little.

"I, too, was afraid; the warders were also afraid. Isn't it true, Picci? Isn't it true, Corda," he added turning around, "that warders were afraid, too?"

I raised my eyes and I saw the faces of Picci and Corda, my two warders at *Regina Coeli*, materializing out of the darkness behind the old man. Their smiles were shy and kindly, and I smiled too; I looked at them with sadness and affection.

"We were also afraid," said Picci and Corda.

Picci and Corda were Sardinians—two short, lean sons of Sardinia, with jet-black hair, slightly slanting eyes and dark faces that expressed centuries of hunger and malaria; framed within the jet-black hair that grew down the temples as far as their eyebrows, the faces resembled Byzantine saints in silver frames.

"We were afraid," repeated Picci and Corda, melting little by little into the darkness.

"We are all cowards, that's true," said the old Jew. "We have all shouted and applauded. But perhaps the others are also afraid. They want to slaughter us because they are afraid of us. They are afraid of us because we are weak and defenseless. They want to slaughter us because they know that we are afraid of them. Ha, ha, ha!" he laughed and he shut his eyes, lowered his head to his chest and gripped the edge of the table with his fleshless waxen hands. We all were silent as if overcome by an unexplainable anguish. "You can help us," said the old man raising his head, "General von Schobert and Colonel Lupu will listen to you. You are not a Jew, you are not one of the poor Jews of Jassy. You are an Italian officer." . . .

I began to laugh without speaking. I felt rather ashamed at that moment. I felt ashamed of being an Italian.

" . . . You are an Italian officer, they will listen to you. Perhaps you can still prevent the massacre."

Thus speaking the old man had risen with a deep bow. The other two old Jews and my friend Kane had also risen and bowed low.

"I have little hope," I said, seeing them to the door.

In silence, one by one, they shook hands with me; they walked out and went down the first steps. I watched them sinking down the steep stairs, disappearing bit by bit—first the legs, then the backs, then the shoulders, their heads last. They disappeared as if they had sunk into a tomb. I threw myself onto the bed and fell asleep almost at once. In the dimness of the room, faintly lit by the flame of the glittering candle, I saw the four Jews sitting around the table. Their garments were torn, their faces bloody. The blood dripped slowly down from their wounded foreheads into their long reddish beards. Kane was also wounded, his forehead was split open, his eyes were clotted with blood. A terrified cry escaped my lips. I found myself sitting up in bed unable to move; an icy sweat dripped down my face, and the frightful sight of those pale bleeding ghosts sitting around my table remained long before my eyes, until the muddy light of dawn, the color of dirty water, crept slowly into the room and, exhausted, I fell into a deep slumber.

I awoke late; it must have been after two in the afternoon. The *lustrageria* at the corner of the Strada Lapusneanu was closed. The windows of the Jockey Club were shut for the sacred hours of the siesta. A group of working men, street cleaners and the coachmen who ply from morning till night in front of the *Fundatia*, were eating in silence, sitting on the tombstones and on the steps of the *adapost*. The greasy smell of *brenza* wafted through my windows followed by swarms of flies.

"Good day, *Domnule Capitan*," said the coachmen and street cleaners raising their eyes and nodding their heads in greeting. By then everybody knew me in Jassy. The workmen also raised their eyes, pointing to their bread and cheese with gestures of invitation.

I shouted, "*Multzumesc*—Thanks!" pointing to my own bread and cheese. But there was something in the air; something was certainly in the air. The sky, overcast with black clouds croaked quietly like a muddy pool. Romanian policemen and soldiers were posting large posters on the walls with Colonel Lupu's proclamation: "All the inhabitants of houses from which shots are fired on the troops and those of the neighboring houses, men and women alike, will be shot on the spot, *fara copii*—except the children."

"*Fara copii*—Except the children." Colonel Lupu, I thought, has already prepared his alibi; fortunately he loves children. It pleased me to think that there was in Jassy at least one decent person who loved children. Squads of policemen remained hidden in doorways of houses and in the orchards. Military patrols walked by clicking their heels hard on the asphalt. "Good day, *Domnule Capitan*," smiled the workmen, the coachmen and the street cleaners sitting on the tombstones. The leaves of the trees were so green against the dark sky they looked as if they had been dyed with a phosphorescent green and rustled in the damp warm wind blowing from the river Prut. Groups of children were running after each other among the mounds and the ancient crosses; it was a lively and gay scene to which the hard leaden sky imparted a feeling of the last moment of a vain and desperate game.

A strange anguish weighed upon the city. A huge, massive and monstrous disaster, oiled, polished, tuned up like a steel machine was going to catch and grind into a pulp the houses, the trees, the streets and the inhabitants of Jassy, *fara copii*. If I had only been able to do something to prevent the pogrom. But General von Schobert's headquarters were at Copou, and I did not feel like walking as far as Copou. The Jews mattered nothing to General von Schobert. An old soldier, a Bavarian gentleman, a good Christian does not get himself involved in certain things. What concern were they of his? What concern were they of mine? I must go to General von Schobert, I told myself; I must at least try; one never knows.

I started off toward Copou on foot. But when I arrived in front of the university, I stopped to examine the statue of the poet, Eminescu. The trees of the avenue were teeming with birds. A little bird had alighted on Eminescu's shoulder. I remembered then that

I had in my pocket an introduction to Senator Sadoveanu. A learned man, Senator Sadoveanu, a happy devotee of the Muses. He might perhaps offer me a glass of iced beer, and he would certainly declaim some of Eminescu's lyrics for me. *La dracu* General von Schobert; *la dracu* the Senator, too. I turned back, crossed the courtyard of the Jockey Club and began to go up the stairs; perhaps it was better for me to go and talk with Colonel Lupu. He would laugh in my face. *"Domnule Capitan,* what do I know about this pogrom of yours? I am no augurer." Nevertheless, if a pogrom was really being engineered, Colonel Lupu would certainly know all about it. In eastern Europe pogroms are always engineered and carried out with official connivance. In the lands across the Danube and the Carpathian mountains chance never plays a part in what takes place; it has no bearing on fortuitous events. He would laugh in my face. *Fara copii. La dracu* Colonel Lupu, *la dracu* the General too.

I went down the stairs and without even turning my head passed the Corso Café-Restaurant and entered the cemetery. I stretched myself on a tomb in the shade of the green transparent leaves of an acacia and watched the black clouds gathering over my head. It was hot; flies were crawling over my face. An ant crept up my arm. After all, what concern of mine was this affair? I had done all that was humanly possible to prevent the massacre; it was no fault of mine if I could do no more. *"La dracu* Mussolini," I said aloud, yawning; *"La dracu* with him, with all his nation of heroes. *We are a nation of heroes . . ."* I began humming. A bunch of bastards is what he has turned us into. I was a fine hero too—no doubt about that. The sky croaked like a swamp.

I was roused toward sunset by the scream of sirens; it was an effort to get up; with a yawn I listened to the hum of the motors, the rattle of anti-aircraft machine guns, the thud of the bombs, and the deep, long, dull crumbling of hit houses. This silly *razboiou.* Laced in their leather jackets, those Russian girls were dropping bombs onto the houses and the gardens of Jassy. Much better if they would stay at home and knit I thought, and I began laughing. As if those girls would have the time and the inclination to stay at home and knit! . . . The sound of a gallop suddenly made me sit up on the tomb. Drawn by a maddened horse, a cart was hurtling down the *Fundatia*, it rushed by in front of the churchyard and smashed against the opposite wall close to the shoe-shine parlor. I saw the horse shatter its head against the wall and, kicking, fall to the ground. The railway station was on fire. Thick clouds of smoke rose above the Nicolina sector. German and Romanian soldiers went by running, cradling their rifles in their arms. A wounded woman was dragging herself along the street. I stretched myself out again on the tomb and closed my eyes.

Suddenly there was silence. A boy went whistling by the churchyard wall. Merry voices could be heard floating on the dusty air. A little later the sirens began screaming again. The hum of the still-distant Russian aircraft spread like a smell in the warm evening. The anti-aircraft batteries of the Copou aviation camp were firing furiously. I must have been feverish; long shudders went through my aching bones. Who knew where Mica was at that moment—hairy as a goat? *Stai, stai!* shouted the patrols through the thickening shadows. Stray rifle shots echoed here and there among the houses and the orchards. Hoarse voices of German soldiers broke through the rumble of the trucks. Laughter, French words, and the clatter of china reached me from the Jockey Club. My God, how I liked Marioara!

Suddenly I became aware that night had already fallen. The Copou batteries were firing at the moon—a yellow, clammy moon, a huge round summer moon that slowly climbed up the cloudy sky. The anti-aircraft guns were barking at the moon. The trees shivered in the damp wind blowing from the river. The dry, angry barking of the flak rose above the hills. Soon the moon became entangled in the branches of the trees, it hung for a moment on a branch, dangled like the head of a man from the gallows, and sank to the bottom of an abyss of black stormy clouds. Blue and green flitting lightning suddenly cut the sky. Within the yawning wounds, as in the fragments of a broken mirror appeared deep perspectives of nocturnal landscapes of a livid and dazzling green.

While I was walking out of the churchyard it began to rain, a slow warm rain that seemed to drop out of a cut vein. The Corso Café-Restaurant was closed. I began hammering against the door with my fist, calling Marioara. At last the door opened slightly and through the crack Marioara's voice began to moan, "Oh, oh, oh,

Domnule Capitan, I cannot open. Curfew has already sounded, *Domnule Capitan,* oh, oh, oh!"

I reached with my hand through the opening of the door and clutched her shoulder in a tight grasp, as sweet as a caress. "Marioara, oh Marioara! Open Marioara! I am hungry, Marioara!"

"Oh, oh, oh, *Domnule Capitan,* I cannot. . . . *Domnule Capitan,* oh, oh, oh!"

Her voice was languid and shy, and as I clutched her small soft-boned shoulder, I felt her shaking all over from head to foot, perhaps because of the strong, sweet caress of my hand, perhaps because of the air scented with rain-sprinkled grass, perhaps because of the languid heat of the summer night, or perhaps because of the moon, that treacherous moon. Perhaps Marioara was thinking about the evening when she had gone with me to the old, abandoned churchyard to watch the sickle of the new moon gently cut the acacia leaves. We were sitting on a tombstone, I held her in my arms and the strong odor of her virginal skin, of her curly hair— that strong and gentle odor of Byzantium that Romanian, Greek and Russian women have, that strong and ancient odor of Byzantium, an odor of roses and of white skin, rose intoxicatingly to my face. Marioara had panted gently, straining herself against me, and I had said "Marioara," I had only said "Marioara" in a soft voice, and Marioara had gazed at me through her black lashes, her lashes of black wool.

"Oh, oh, *Domnule Capitan,* I cannot open! *Domnule Capitan,* oh!" and she looked at me with only one eye through the crack of the door. Then she said, "Wait a moment, *Domnule Capitan,*" and she gently closed the door. I heard her walking away, I heard the patter of her bare feet. She came back after a few minutes bringing a little bread and a few slices of meat. "Oh, thank you, Marioara," I said slipping a few hundred *lei* notes into her bosom. Marioara looked at me with only one eye through the crack of the door, and I felt the hot heavy drops of rain beating on the nape of my neck and running down my back. "Oh, Marioara," I said caressing her shoulder, and she bent her head and pressed her cheek against my hand. I was trying to force the door open with my knee when Marioara leaned with all her weight on the door,

"Oh, *Domnule Capitan*, oh," and she smiled at me through her long lashes of black wool.

"Thank you, Marioara," I said caressing her face.

"*La revedere, Domnule Capitan*," replied Marioara softly and she stood watching me with one eye through the crack of the door as I walked off in the rain.

Seated on the doorstep of my house I munched very slowly and listened to the rain talking in a soft murmur over the delicate acacia leaves. A dog whined uneasily behind the hedge of an orchard at the end of the churchyard. Marioara was still a child—she was only sixteen. I gazed at the black sky, at the yellow reflection of the moon through the gloomy veil of the clouds. Marioara was still a child. And I listened to the heavy tread of patrols, to the rumble of German trucks driving up toward Copou and toward the Prut. Suddenly through the lukewarm spiderweb of the rain the wailing hoot of the sirens sounded once again.

At first it was a far-off hum, very high up in the sky, a hum of bees that little by little came nearer, and became a high, mysterious language of the black sky. It was a mysterious voice, a sweet and secret language, a voice like a memory, like bees humming in a wood. Suddenly I heard Marioara's voice calling me from amid the tombs. "*Domnule Capitan*," she said. "*Oh, Domnule Capitan!*"

She had run away from the Corso; she was afraid of being alone; she wanted me to take her home; she lived on Usine Road, near the power station. But she did not dare to cross the town; the patrols fired on the passers-by; they shouted *stai! stai!* and fired at once without giving anyone time to raise one's arms.

"Oh, take me home, *Domnule Capitan!*" I saw her black eyes shining in the darkness, now bright, now dim in the warm darkness as on the verge of a night remote from me, as on the verge of a black forbidden night.

People wandered silently by amid the mounds and crosses, groups of people who sought shelter in the *adapost* that had been excavated in the center of the churchyard. Those shadows of men, women and half-naked children went down beneath the ground silently, like the spirits of the dead, going back to the bottom of their dark hell. I already knew all of them, they were always the same; they went by every evening on their way to the *adapost—*

the owner of the *lustrageria* across the road, the two old people whom I always saw sitting at the foot of the Unirii monument between the Jockey Club and the *Fundatia,* the coachman whose stable was at the back wall of the churchyard, the woman who sold papers on the corner of the *Fundatia,* the porter of the *desfacere de vinuri* with his wife and five children, the *tutun* seller, the tobacconist whose shop was near the post office.

"*Buna seara, Domnule Capitan,*" they said in passing.

"*Buna seara,*" I replied.

Marioara did not want to go down into the *adapost;* she wanted to go home, she was afraid and wanted to go home. On other nights she slept on a settee in a room of the Corso Café-Restaurant, but that evening she wanted to go home; she was all atremble.

"They will fire at us, Marioara," I said.

"*Nu, nu,* the soldiers cannot fire at an officer."

"Who can tell? It is dark. They will fire at us, Marioara."

"*Nu, nu,*" replied Marioara, "Romanian soldiers will not fire at an Italian officer, will they?"

"No, they will not fire at an Italian captain, they are afraid. Come along, Marioara. Colonel Lupu also is afraid of an Italian officer."

We walked close to one another, along the walls, in the warm rain. Marioara's bosom was heaving gently against my arm, the light breathing of a child. We went down toward Usine Road, among the ghosts of disemboweled houses. From hovels made of wood or straw and mud came voices, laughter, weeping of children, raucous triumphal songs of gramophones. Sharp rifle shots pierced the night down there beyond the station. Through the amplifier of an old gramophone, placed on the sill of a dark window, a sad raucous voice sang:

Voi, voi, voi, mandrelor voi . . .

From time to time we hid behind a tree trunk, behind the wall of an orchard and held our breath until the tread of a patrol had faded away in the distance. "There, my home is there," said Marioara. Before us the massive red-brick building of the central power station loomed out of the darkness like a silo. From the tracks around the railroad station came the mournful whistling of engines.

"Nu, nu, Domnule Capitan, nu, nu," said Marioara.

But I crushed her in my arms, caressed her curly hair, the thick hard eyebrows, the thin little mouth.

"Nu, Domnule Capitan, nu, nu," said Marioara trying to push me away, her hands pressing against my chest.

Suddenly the storm burst like a mine on the roofs of the town. Charred shreds of clouds, trees, houses, streets, men and horses were hurled into the air and whirled about in the wind. A stream of lukewarm blood gushed forth from the clouds torn open by red, green and blue thunderbolts. Romanian soldiers went by in groups shouting *"Parasiutist! Parasiutist!"* They ran firing their rifles aimed into the air; a confused din reached us faintly from the lower city through the high, faraway hum of the Russian planes.

We backed against the fence surrounding Marioara's house, and at that moment two soldiers who came running from the turn in the road fired at us without stopping. We heard distinctly the thud of the bullets against the fence. A sunflower, bending its head, peered at us with its round, polyphemic, impersonal eye, the long yellow lashes half-curled over the great black pupil. I crushed Marioara in my arms, and she leaned back, her eyes turned to the sky. Suddenly she said in a low voice: "Oh, *frumos! frumos!*—Oh, beautiful! beautiful!" I lifted my eyes to the sky and a shout of wonder escaped my lips.

There were men up there, walking on the roof of the storm. Small, awkward, round-bellied, they walked along the edges of the clouds, holding up with one hand a huge white umbrella that swayed in the gusty wind. They were perhaps the old professors of the Jassy university with their gray top hats and pea-green frockcoats, who were returning home along the avenue from the *Fundatia*. They strolled very slowly in the rain, in the livid flashes of lightning, and they talked among themselves. It was funny to see them up there. They moved their legs in an odd way, like scissors opening and closing, cutting the clouds, making a way for themselves through the spiderweb of rain hanging over the town. *"Nopte buna, Domnule Professor,"* they said to one another inclining their heads and raising their gray top hats with finger and thumb, *"Nopte buna!"* Or perhaps they were the proud, handsome ladies of Jassy returning from their promenade in the park, shading their delicate faces under pale blue or pink silk parasols trimmed with white lace; and they were followed at a distance by their old black, solemn carriages, with eunuch coachmen brandishing their whips with the long red tassels above the glistening croups of the fine horses with long yellow manes. Perhaps they were the old noblemen of the Jockey Club, the fat Moldavian noblemen, with side whiskers trimmed Paris fashion, Saville Row clothes, and small ties that were drawn through the narrow openings in their high stiff collars so they could breathe a little fresh air after the endless bridge games in the smoky rooms of the Jockey Club with its smell of roses and tobacco. They swayed from their hips, clipping their scissors, their extended right arms grasping the long handles of their huge white umbrellas, their tall, gray top hats slightly tilted over their ears as those of certain *vieux beaux* of Daumier, or of Caran d'Ache.

"They are the Jassy noblemen escaping," I said. "They are afraid of the war and they are looking for safety in the Athénée Palace in Bucharest."

"Oh no, they are not escaping; down there are the houses of the gypsy women; they are going to make love to the gypsies," replied Marioara gazing at the floating men.

The clouds looked like the foliage of the large green trees that rise among the little tables of the Pavillon d'Armenonville against a background of green, blue and pink trees in a Manet picture of the Porte Dauphine. They really were Manet's greens, pinks, blues and grays in the delicate landscape of lawns and leaves that appeared and disappeared within the gashes between the clouds, whenever a thunderbolt destroyed the tall purple castles of the storm.

"It is truly like a feast," I said, "a gay feast in a beautiful park in springtime."

Marioara gazed at the *demi-dieux* of the Jockey Club—the white demi-gods of Jassy. Jassy is *du côté de Guermantes,* a provincial *côté de Guermantes* belonging to that ideal province that is the true Parisian country of Proust, and in Moldavia everyone knows Proust by heart. She gazed at the gray top hats, the monocles, the white carnations in the buttonholes of the blue coats, the silken lace-edged parasols, the arms covered with lace gloves to the elbows, the little hats decked with birds and flowers, the brittle little feet peeking from under the pleated skirts. "Oh! how I should like to go to that party. I wish I, too, could go in a fine silk dress!" said Marioara touching with slender fingers her poor faded cotton frock stained with *ciorba de pui.*

"Oh, look, look how they run away! Look how the rain is chasing them, Marioara! The party is over, Marioara."

"La revedere, Domnule Capitan," said Marioara, pushing open the little gate leading into her orchard. Marioara's home was a single-story, wooden hovel with a roof of red tiles. The windows were shut, a glimmer of light showed through the slats of the blinds.

"Marioara!" called a woman's voice from inside the house.

"Oh, *la revedere, Domnule Capitan,"* said Marioara.

"La revedere, Marioara," I said, holding her to me.

Marioara yielded to my arms and gazed up at the sky at the fiery tracks of the tracer bullets streaking the black glass of the night; they looked like coral necklaces hanging on invisible feminine necks, flowers thrown into a velvety black abyss, phosphorescent fish darting about a nocturnal sea; they were evanescent shapes of red lips melting into the shade of silk parasols; they were roses blossoming in a secret recess of a garden on a moonless night just before dawn. The *vieux beaux* of the Jockey Club and the old university professors sheltered from the rain under their huge white umbrellas, went home after the party as the last skyrockets were being fired.

Later, the display ended. Suddenly the rain ceased; the moon appeared through a rent in the clouds; it looked like a landscape painted by Chagall: A Jewish Chagall sky, crowded with Jewish angels, with Jewish clouds, with Jewish horses and dogs dangling in their flight over the town. Jewish fiddlers sat on the roofs of the houses or floated in a pale sky above the streets, where old Jews lay dead in the gutter between the lighted ritual candelabra. Jewish lovers were stretched out in mid-air on the edge of a cloud as green as a meadow. And under that Jewish Chagall sky, in that Chagall landscape illuminated by a round transparent moon, from the Nicolina, Socola, and Pacurari districts, rose a confused din, a rattle of machine guns and the dull thud of hand grenades.

"Oh, they are killing the Jews!" said Marioara holding her breath.

The din could also be heard from the center of the town, from the elevation around Unirii Square and the church of the Three Hierarchs. Above that confused roar of people pursued through the streets, could be heard German words shouted in terrible, strident voices, and the *stai! stai!* of Romanian soldiers and policemen. Suddenly a rifle shot whizzed by our ears. From the end of the road came the clamor of German, Romanian and Jewish voices; a crowd of people in flight ran by; they were women, men, boys and girls pursued by a group of policemen firing on the run. Behind the others came a staggering soldier with his face covered with blood, shouting, *"Parasiutist! Parasiutist!—*Paratrooper! Paratrooper!" and aiming his rifle at the sky. He fell to his knees a few steps away from us and hit his head against the fence. He lay stretched out with his face in the mud, under the slow rain of the Soviet paratroopers who dropped one by one from the sky, with lightly poised feet, and hung in their huge white umbrellas from the roofs of the houses.

"Oh, oh!" shouted Marioara, as I lifted her from the ground, ran across the orchard and pushed the door open with my elbow.

"La revedere, Marioara," I said letting her slide slowly through my arms until she touched the threshold.

"Nu, nu, Domnule Capitan, nu, nu!" shouted Marioara clinging to my breast. *"Nu, nu, Domnule Capitan,* oh!" and she buried her teeth in my hand, biting it savagely, whining like a dog.

"Oh, Marioara," I said softly, touching her hair with my lips, and I hit her in the face with my free hand to make her release my other hand. Then I pushed her gently into her dark house, crossed the orchard and walked away along the deserted street, turning now and then to look back at the fence, the sunflower standing above the pointed pickets, the little house with its red-tiled roof splotched with moonlight.

When I reached the top of the hill, I turned around. The town was ablaze. Thick clouds of smoke hung over the lower sections along the banks of the river. The houses and the trees, close to the burning buildings stood out clearly and looked bigger than they were, like enlarged photographs. I could even discern the cracks in the walls, the branches and the leaves. There was something dead about the scene, and at the same time, something too precise, as in a photograph; I would have believed that I was facing a ghostly photographic backdrop, if it had not been for the confused din rising everywhere, the wailing hoot of sirens, the long whistling of steam engines and the rattling of machine guns that imparted a vivid and immediate reality to that terrible sight. Up and down the narrow twisting streets leading toward the center of town, I heard all about me desperate barking, banging of doors, shattering of glass and of china, smothered screams, imploring voices calling *mama! mama!*, horrible beseeching cries of *nu, nu, nu!* and occasionally from behind a fence or from an orchard, or through the half-closed blinds from inside a house a flash, the sharp report of a shot, the whizzing of a bullet and the strident, frightful German voices. In Unirii Square a group of SS men kneeling by the Prince Gutsa Voda monument fired their tommy guns toward the little square where the statue of Prince Ghiha in Moldavian costume stands with his great quilted coat and his brow covered by a tall fur cap. By the light of the fires a black, gesticulating throng, mostly women, could be seen huddled at the foot of the monument. From time to time someone rose, darted this way or that across the square and fell under the bullets of the SS men. Hordes of Jews pursued by soldiers and maddened civilians armed with knives and crowbars fled along the streets; groups of policemen smashed in house doors with their rifle butts; windows opened suddenly and screaming disheveled women in nightgowns appeared with their arms raised in the air; some threw themselves from windows and their faces hit the asphalt with a dull thud. Squads of soldiers hurled hand grenades through the little windows level with the street into the cellars where many people had vainly sought safety; some soldiers dropped to their knees to look at the results of the explosions within the cellars and turned laughing faces to their companions. Where the slaughter had been heaviest the feet slipped in blood; everywhere the hysterical and ferocious toil of the pogrom filled the houses and streets with shots, with weeping, with terrible screams and cruel laughter.

When I finally reached the Italian Consulate on the green road that runs back of the wall surrounding the old abandoned churchyard, Consul Sartori was sitting on the doorstep smoking a cigarette.

He looked tired and bored. He smoked peacefully with an air of Neapolitan indifference. But I know my Neapolitans and I knew that he was suffering. The sound of smothered sobbing reached us from the inside room.

"This outbreak was all we needed!" said Sartori. "I have saved half a dozen of the poor devils; some are wounded. Would you help me, Malaparte? I am no good as a nurse."

I went into the office of the Consulate. Stretched out on the sofas or seated on the floor in the corners were several women, a few bearded old men, five or six boys and three young men who looked like students; a little girl was crying under Sartori's writing desk. A woman sat, her forehead split by a blow with a rifle butt; a student moaned from a gunshot wound in his shoulder. I heated some water and, assisted by Sartori, began washing the wounds and bandaging them with strips of linen cut from a sheet. "What a bore!" said Sartori. "This business is just what we needed, and especially tonight when I have a slight headache."

While I was bandaging her, the woman with the wound in her forehead turned to Sartori and addressing him as *Monsieur le Marquis,* thanked him in French for saving her life. Sartori looked at her with a bored air and he said, "Why do you call me *Marquis?* I am *Signor* Sartori." I liked that fat, placid fellow who renounced that evening a title to which he had no claim but which, nevertheless, flattered him. In moments of danger the Neapolitans can face the most painful sacrifices. "Do you mind handing me another bandage, dear Marquis?" I said, wishing to compensate him for his sacrifice.

Later, we sat on the threshold; Sartori on a chair and I on the doorstep. The garden surrounding the Consulate was thick with acacias and pine trees. Alarmed by the glare of the fires, the birds, beating their wings, moved in silence among the branches. "They are afraid. They will not sing," said Sartori, his eyes fixed on the foliage of the trees. Then pointing to a dark stain on the wall of the villa, quite close to the door, he went on, "Look at that wall. It is stained with blood. One of those poor devils took refuge in here. Policemen came and almost killed him with their rifle butts there, against that wall. Then they took him away with them. He was the owner of this villa—a gentleman." He lit another cigarette and slowly turned to me. "I was alone," he said, "what could I do? I protested. I said that I would write to Mussolini. They laughed in my face."

"They laughed in Mussolini's face, not yours."

"Don't make fun of me, Malaparte. I even grew angry, and when I grow angry . . ." he said with his placid air. He went on smoking, then he added, "Ever since yesterday I have been asking Colonel Lupu for a detachment of police to protect the Consulate. He replied that there was no need for it."

"You may thank the Lord! It is better to have nothing to do with Colonel Lupu's men. Colonel Lupu is a murderer."

"Oh, yes, he is a murderer. What a pity—such a handsome man." I began to laugh and turned my face away so Sartori would not see me. Just then, out in the road, we heard desperate screams, several pistol shots and then the horrible, unbearable, dull, soft thud of the rifle butts on heads.

"Now they are really beginning to rile me," said Sartori. He rose with his apathetic Neapolitan air, in a leisurely way crossed the garden, opened the gate, and said, "Come in here, come in here."

I went out into the middle of the road and was pushing a crowd of people, stupefied with terror, toward the gate. A policeman caught me by the arm, and I kicked him with all my might in the belly.

"That's right," said Sartori calmly, "that ill-mannered fellow deserved it." Sartori was angry, he was using strong language. "Ill-mannered" was a very strong term for him.

We sat on the threshold all through the night and smoked. From time to time we stepped out into the road and pushed flocks of ragged and bleeding people into the Consulate. We gathered about a hundred of them.

"These poor people ought to have something to eat and drink," I said to Sartori when we went back to our vigil after attending to a new batch of wounded.

Sartori looked at me with the eyes of a dog. "I had some food, but the police broke into the Consulate and stole everything. It can't be helped."

"*O' vero*—really?" I asked him in Neapolitan.

"*O' vero*," replied Sartori with a sigh.

140

I liked to be with Sartori during moments like this: I felt safe with that tranquil Neapolitan who was shaking within with fear, horror and pity, but showed no outward sign of it.

"Sartori," I said, "we are fighting for civilization against barbarism."

"*O' vero?*" asked Sartori.

"*O' vero,*" I replied.

The dawn was already breaking in the cloudless sky. The smoke from the fires hovered over the trees and the roofs. It was rather cold.

"Sartori," I said, "when Mussolini hears that they have violated the Consulate of Jassy he'll turn into a mad bull."

"Don't make fun of me, Malaparte," said Sartori. "Mussolini barks but never bites. He will dismiss me for sheltering these poor Jews."

"*O' vero?*"

"*O' vero,* Malaparte."

A little later Sartori rose and invited me to rest inside.

"You are tired, Malaparte. All is over by now. The dead are dead. There is nothing more to do."

"I am not tired, Sartori. You go and lie down on your bed. I'll remain here and stand guard."

"Take at least an hour's rest, for goodness' sake," said Sartori settling himself again in his chair.

As I crossed the churchyard in the uncertain light, I made out two Romanian soldiers sitting on a tombstone. They had some pieces of bread and were eating it in silence.

"Good morning, *Domnule Capitan*," they said.

"Good morning," I replied.

A dead woman lay between two tombstones. A dog whined behind the hedge.

I threw myself onto the bed and closed my eyes. I felt abased. All was over by now. The dead were dead. There was nothing more to do. *La dracu,* I thought. It was ghastly not to be able to do something.

I fell asleep, and through the open window I saw the sky that the dawn was already lighting being licked by the livid reflection of the fires, and in the center of the sky a man was walking about holding a huge white umbrella in his outstretched hand and gazing downward.

"Good rest to you," said the flying man with a nod and a smile. "Thanks. A pleasant stroll to you," I replied.

A couple of hours later I awoke. It was a brilliant morning; the air, cleansed and freshened by the storm of the previous night, glistened on everything like a transparent varnish. I went to the window and looked down Lapusneanu Street. Scattered about in the street were human forms lying in awkward positions. The gutters were strewn with dead bodies, heaped one upon another. Several hundred corpses were dumped in the center of the churchyard. Packs of dogs wandered about sniffing the dead in the frightened, cowed way dogs have when they are seeking their masters; they seemed full of respect and pity; they moved about amid those poor dead bodies with delicacy, as if they feared to step on those bloody faces and those rigid hands. Squads of Jews, watched over by policemen and soldiers armed with tommy guns, were at work moving the dead bodies to one side, clearing the middle of the road and piling the corpses up along the walls so they would not block traffic. German and Romanian trucks loaded with corpses kept going by. A dead child was sitting up on the sidewalk near the *lustrageria* with his back against the wall and his head drooped on one shoulder. I drew back, closed the window and sat on the bed and began to dress very slowly. From time to time I had to lie flat on my back to fight down spasms of nausea. Suddenly, I thought I heard sounds of merry voices, of people laughing, calling and gaily answering each other. I forced myself to go back to the window. The road was crowded with people—squads of soldiers and policemen, groups of men and women, and bands of gypsies with their hair in long ringlets were gaily and noisily chattering with one another, as they despoiled the corpses, lifting them, rolling them over, turning them on their sides to draw off their coats, their trousers and their underclothes; feet were rammed against dead bellies to help pull off the shoes; people came running to share in the loot; others made off with arms piled high with clothing. It was a gay bustle, a merry occasion, a feast and a marketplace all in one. The dead twisted into cruel postures were left naked.

I rushed downstairs and ran across the churchyard striding over the tombs so as not to tread on the corpses scattered about in the grass and at the gate. I flew at a group of policemen busily stripping dead bodies and hurled myself screaming against them. "Dirty cowards," I shouted, "get away, you lousy bastards!" One of them looked at me in amazement, picked up some suits and two or three pairs of shoes from a pile of clothing on the ground and pushed them toward me saying, "Don't get angry, *Domnule Capitan,* there's enough for everybody."

And at that very moment, from Unirii Square turning up the Strada Lapusneanu, appeared Princess Sturdza's landau with harness bells merrily tinkling. Grigori, the very solemn eunuch, sitting on the box in his green robe, dangled his whip over the backs of the fine, white-coated Moldavian horses that trotted proudly, holding their heads high and shaking their long manes.

Sitting stiffly upright on the high, broad wide cushions, the Princess gazed upward as she held in her right hand a red silk parasol trimmed with a fringe of lace. Beside her, proud and remote, sat Prince Sturdza clothed all in white, his face shaded by the brim of a gray felt hat, his left hand clutching a little book in a red leather binding that he held close to his chest.

"Good morning, *Domna Principessa,*" called the despoilers of the dead, interrupting their messy task and bowing deeply.

Princess Sturdza, dressed in pale blue, a large hat of Florentine straw tilted over one ear, turned right and left, curtly nodding her head, while the Prince lifted his gray felt hat with a quick motion of his hand as he smiled and acknowledged the greetings with slight bows.

"Good morning, *Domna Principessa.*"

With a merry tinkling of harness bells the carriage drove on between the piles of naked corpses, flanked by two rows of humbly bowing people who clutched their cruel booty in their hands. It was swept away at a sharp trot by the fine, white horses that were urged on by the eunuch Grigori, who looked bloated and solemn on the box as he lightly dangled over them the long red tassel of his whip.

VII

Cricket in Poland

"How MANY JEWS were killed in Jassy that night?" Frank asked me in an ironical voice as he stretched out his feet toward the fire and laughed softly.

The others were also softly laughing and looking as if they felt sorry for me. The fire crackled in the fireplace, and the frozen snow was tapping with white fingers on the windowpanes. At intervals a high wind, the icy north wind, blew in gusts. It moaned in the ruins of the near-by Hotel d'Angleterre making the sleet whirl in the vast Saxe Square. I rose, went over to the window and looked down on the moonlit square. Faint shadows of soldiers moved along the sidewalk before the Europeiski Hotel. Where twenty years ago the Sobor had stood—the Orthodox Cathedral of Warsaw that the Poles had demolished in obedience to a monk's gloomy prophecy—the snow was now spread in its stainless white sheet. I turned to Frank and I, too, began to laugh softly.

"The official report issued by the Vice-President of the Council, Mihai Antonescu," I replied, "admitted that there were five hundred. But the official count by Colonel Lupu was seven thousand slaughtered Jews."

"Quite a respectable figure," said Frank, "but it was not a decent way to do it; it is not necessary to do it that way."

"No, that's not the way to do it," said Fischer, the Governor of Warsaw, shaking his head in disapproval.

"Not a civilized way," Wächter, the Governor of Cracow and one of Dolfuss' murderers, said in a disgusted tone.

"The Romanians are not a civilized people," said Frank contemptuously.

"*Ja, es hat kein Kultur*—Yes, they have no culture," said Fischer shaking his head.

"Though my heart is not as soft as yours," said Frank, "I share and I understand your horror at the Jassy massacres. As a man, a German, and as Governor-General of Poland I disapprove of pogroms."

"Very kind of you," I answered with a bow.

"Germany is a country that has a higher civilization and abominates barbaric methods," said Frank gazing around him with an expression of sincere indignation.

"*Natürlich,*" the others chorused.

"Germany," said Wächter, "is called upon to carry out a great civilizing mission in the East."

"The term 'pogrom' is not a German word," said Frank.

"Naturally, it is a Jewish word," and I smiled.

"I don't know whether it is a Jewish word," said Frank, "but I know that it never has been and never will be a part of the German vocabulary."

"Pogroms are a Slavic specialty," said Wächter.

"In all things, we Germans are guided by reason and method and not by bestial instincts; we always act scientifically. When necessary, but only when absolutely necessary," repeated Frank stressing each syllable and glaring at me as if to imprint his words on my brow. "We use surgeons as our models, never butchers. Have you perchance ever seen a massacre of Jews in the streets of a German city?" he went on. "You never have, have you? You might have witnessed some demonstrations by students, some harmless rowdy boyish pranks. Yet, within a short time, not a single Jew will be left in Germany."

"All a matter of method and organization," said Fischer.

"To kill Jews is not the German method," continued Frank. "A futile labor, a useless waste of time and of strength. We deport them to Poland and shut them up in ghettos. There they are free to do what they like. Within the Polish ghettos, they live as in a free republic."

"Long live the free republic of the Polish ghettos," I said, raising the glass of Mumm that Frau Fischer had graciously offered me. I was slightly giddy and I felt amiably disposed.

"*Vivat!*" they all repeated in a chorus and raised their glasses of champagne. Laughing they drank and looked at me.

"*Mein lieber* Malaparte," pursued Frank resting his hand on my shoulder with cordial familiarity, "the German people are the victim of an abominable slander. We are not a race of murderers. When you go back to Italy I hope you will tell them what you have seen in Poland. Your duty, as an honest and impartial man, is to tell the truth. You will be able to say with a clear conscience that the Germans in Poland are a great, peaceful and active family. Look around you; you are in an unpretentious, simple, honest German home. That's what Poland is—an honest German home. Just look—" and so saying he made a sweeping gesture with his hand. I turned and looked around me. Frau Fischer had taken from a drawer a cardboard box from which she took a big ball of wool. With a slight bow to Frau Brigitte Frank, as if she were asking her permission, she put on a pair of steel-rimmed spectacles and calmly began plying her needles. Frau Brigitte Frank meanwhile opened a skein of wool and having hung it on Frau Wächter's wrists, began to roll it up into a ball, moving her hands with graceful lightness and speed. Frau Wächter, sitting upright, bosom high, with knees close together and arms bent, was helping to smoothly unwind the thread from the skein by a delicate motion of her wrists. The three ladies were smiling; they were a picture of gentle homeyness. Governor-General Frank rested his glance, glowing with affection and pride, on the three smiling women busy with their work. Meanwhile Keith and Emil Gassner were slicing the cake and pouring coffee into large china cups. From the slight exhilaration of the wine, the homey scene and the rather dull tone of that provincial German interior—the click of the knitting needles, the crackling of the flames in the fireplace, the smothered crunching of teeth chewing the cake, the soft rattle of the china cups—a subtle uneasiness slowly seeped into my consciousness. Frank's hand on my shoulder, though it was not heavy, oppressed me. Little by little, disentangling and considering each feeling that Frank aroused in me and attempting to understand and to define the meaning, the pretexts and the reason for his every word and gesture, and trying to piece together a moral portrait of him out of the scraps that I had picked up about his character in the past few days, I became convinced that he was not to be judged summarily.

The uneasiness that I felt within me in his presence was born precisely because of the complexity of his character—a peculiar mixture of cruel intelligence, refinement, vulgarity, brutal cynicism and polished sensitiveness. There had to be a deep zone of darkness within him that I was still unable to explore—a dark region, an inaccessible hell from which dull, fleeting glows flashed unexpectedly, lighting his forbidding face—that disturbing and fascinating mysterious face.

The opinion I had formed of Frank long ago was, unquestionably, negative. I knew enough of him to detest him, but I felt honorbound not to stop there. Of all the elements that I was conscious of in Frank, some a result of the experience of others and some of my own, something, I could not say what, was lacking—something the very nature of which was not known to me but which I expected would suddenly be revealed to me at any moment.

I hoped to catch a gesture, a word, an involuntary action that might reveal to me Frank's real face, his inner face, that would suddenly break away from the dark, deep region of his mind where, I instinctively felt, the roots of his cruel intelligence and fine musical sensitiveness were anchored in a morbid and, in a certain sense, criminal subsoil of character.

"This is Poland—an honest German home," repeated Frank embracing in a single glance that middle-class scene of domestic simplicity.

"Why don't you, too, take up some kind of feminine work?" I asked. "Your dignity as Governor-General would not be impaired. King Gustav V of Sweden also takes pleasure in feminine accomplishments. In the evenings, among his close relatives and friends, King Gustav V does embroidery."

"*Ach, so?*" exclaimed the ladies with incredulous and amused wonder.

"What else can a neutral sovereign do?" laughed Frank. "Do you think that the King of Sweden would have time for embroidery if he were Governor-General of Poland?"

"No doubt the Polish people would be much happier if their Governor-General embroidered," I replied.

"Ah, that is one of your obsessions!" said Frank laughing. "A few days ago you had me believe that Hitler is a woman, and today you would persuade me to take up feminine work. Do you really think that Poland can be ruled by a set of knitting or embroidery needles? *Vous êtes très malin, mon cher* Malaparte—You are very malicious, my dear Malaparte."

"In a way, it can be said that you *are* embroidering," I went on. "Your political work in Poland is a piece of embroidery."

"I am not like the King of Sweden who takes up schoolgirls' hobbies," said Frank proudly. "New Europe is my tapestry." He crossed the room with slow, regal steps, opened a door and disappeared.

I moved to an armchair by the window from where by turning my head I could see at a glance all of huge Saxe Square and the roofless houses behind the Europeiski Hotel and the wreckage of the palace that stood beside the Bristol Hotel at the corner of the street leading to the Vistula.

That landscape of the several backgrounds against which I had enacted my youthful experiences was perhaps the closest to my heart; and at that moment I could not look at it from that room in the Bruhl Palace amid that company without feeling moved to a sad humiliation. After a lapse of over twenty years, that landscape was rising before my eyes again with the wornout realness of an old faded photograph. The Warsaw days and nights welled up from the distant shore of the past, of 1919 and 1920, with the same features and the same feelings as before. . . .

In the quiet rooms smelling of incense and vodka, in the little house where Canoness Walewska lived with her nieces on the lane leading from Theater Square where the bells of the hundred churches of the Stara Miasto could be heard ringing in the clear, icy air on a winter night—smiles rippled on the red lips of the girls while the old dowagers, gathered before the Canoness' fireplace, chatted softly in mischievous secrecy. In the Malinowa Hall of the Bristol, Uhlan officers tapped their feet to mazurka rhythms as they moved toward a row of lovely girls dressed in white, their eyes aglow with a chaste fire. Old Princess Czartoriska, her skinny neck encircled seven times by a huge pearl necklace that reached to her lap, sat silently in front of the old Marchioness Wielopolska in her mansion on Aleja Ujazdwska and looked at the windowpanes reflecting the trees of the avenue. The reflection of the lime trees

spread through the warm room and touched with green the frail
Persian rugs, the Louis XV furniture, the portraits and the landscapes of the French and Italian schools painted in the style of the
Trianon and of Schönbrunn, the old Swedish silver and the Russian
enamels of Catherine the Great's day. Countess Adam Rzewuska,
the golden-voiced Boronat, stood by the piano in the white drawing
room of the Royal Italian Legation in the Potocki Palace of the
Krakowskie Przedmiesce and sang gay Warszawianka songs of the
days of Stanislas Augustus, and the sad Ukrainian songs belonging
to the age of Ataman Chmielnicki and of the Cossack rebellion. I
sat next to Yedwiga Rzewuska and she looked at me in silence,
pale and remote. . . . The swift sleigh parties under the moon as
far as Wilanow. . . . The long evenings spent in the Misliwski Club
amid the mellow perfume of Tokay wine while we listened to old
Polish noblemen talk about hunting, horses and dogs, women and
travels, duels and loves; listened to the "troika" of the Misliwski
Club—Count Henry Potocki, Count Zamoiski, and Count Tarnowski
—debate the merits of wines, tailors and ballet girls; talk in old
voices about St. Petersburg and Vienna, London and Paris. The
long summer afternoons in the cool dimness of his residence with
the Nuncio, Monsignor Achilles Ratti who later became Pope Pius
XI, and with his secretary, Monsignor Pellegrinetti who later became a Cardinal. . . . In the dusty stifling heat of sunset along the
banks of the Vistula, Soviet machine guns were rattling and the
horses of the Third Uhlans clattered under the palace windows as
they marched toward Praha to meet Budenny's Red Cossacks. The
crowd thronged on the pavement of the Nowy Swiat singing:

> *Ulani, Ulani, malowanie dzieci*
> *Niejedna panienka, zawami poleci . . .*

The athletic Princess Woroniecka, patroness of the Third Uhlans,
marching at the head of the regiment and holding a sheaf of red
roses in her arms.

> *Niejedna panienka i niejedna wdowi*
> *Za ami ulani poleciec gotowi . . .*

My quarrel with Lieutenant Potulicki and the three-day cele-
bration that marked our reconciliation. The pistol shot fired one

night at Princess W——'s by Marilski at Dzierjinski across a room thronged with couples dancing to "The Broken Doll," the first fox-trot that had reached Poland in 1919. Dzierjinski stretched out on the floor in a pool of blood with his throat punctured. And Princess W—— telling the musicians: *"Jouez donc, ce n'est rien—* Play, it is nothing." And Marilski, pale and smiling, clutching the pistol in his hand surrounded by the young women excited by the frenzy of the dance and by the sight of blood. Then a month later Dzierjinski, his face still pale and his throat bandaged, arm in arm with Marilski in the Europeiski bar.

At the dances in the British Legation, Princess Olga Radziwill, with blond curly hair cut short like a boy's, yielding laughingly to the arms of Cavendish Bentinck, a young secretary of the British Legation who resembled Rupert Brooke and brought to mind the young Apollo of Mrs. Cornford's famous epigram, "Magnificently unprepared for the young littleness of life"; Isabella Radziwill, tall, with long, silky black hair and eyes like a clear night sky, standing by the window with a young English general, blind in one eye like Nelson and like Nelson with only one arm, who spoke to her in a low voice with sweet and loving laughter. He was certainly a ghost, a gentle ghost of a far-off Warsaw night, that British General Carton de Wiart, blind in one eye and one-armed, who commanded the British forces that landed in Norway in the spring of 1940. I, too, was certainly a ghost, a dull ghost of a remote age—perhaps of a happy age, perhaps of a dead age, perhaps of a very happy age. . . .

I was a shadow, uneasy and saddened, standing by that window, gazing on that landscape of my youthful years. Out of the depths of my memory rose the gentle shadows of that far-off age, and I laughed sweetly. I closed my eyes and looked again at those pale phantoms. I was listening to those voices that were dear to me and had scarcely been faded by time, when the sound of sweet music reached my ear—the first notes of a Chopin "Prelude." In the next room through the half-open door, I saw Frank seated at Madame Beck's piano, his face bowed low on his chest. His forehead was pale and damp with sweat. An expression of deep suffering humbled his proud face. His breath was labored; he was biting his underlip. His eyes were closed; his eyelids were trembling. He is a sick man, I thought. And that thought irritated me.

Everyone around listened in silence and held their breath. Those notes of the "Prelude," so pure and light, floated in the warm air like propaganda leaflets dropped from a plane. On each note was printed "Long live Poland!" in large crimson letters. From the window I saw the snowflakes slowly falling in the vast Saxe Square, and on each snowflake was written "Long live Poland!" in large crimson letters.

I had read the same words, printed in the same large crimson letters twenty years earlier, in October 1919, on the pure, light notes of Chopin that escaped from the white, fragile, precious hands of the Polish Premier Ignace Paderewski, as he sat at the piano in the large, red hall of the Royal Palace in Warsaw. Those were the days of Poland's resurrection; the Polish aristocracy and the members of the diplomatic corps often assembled in the evening around the Premier's piano. Chopin's gentle ghost passed smiling among us, and a shiver ran along the arms and bare shoulders of the young women. The deathless angelic voice of Chopin, like the distant voice of a spring storm, conquered the frightful shriek of revolt and slaughter. The pure light notes floated in the murky air above the livid and fleshless throngs until the last notes gradually faded away. Paderewski slowly lifted his great white head from the keyboard and revealed a face bathed in tears.

Now in the Bruhl Palace, only a few steps away from the ruins of the Royal Palace, in the warm, smoky air of the middle-class German interior, Chopin's pure, seditious notes broke into flight from the white, delicate hands of Frank—from the German hands of the Governor-General of Poland; a feeling of shame and rebellion brought a flush to my face.

"Oh, he plays like an angel!" whispered Frau Brigitte Frank. At that moment the music ceased and Frank appeared on the threshold. Frau Brigitte jumped up and tossing aside her ball of wool, went up to him and kissed his hands. Frank, full of humility and religious fervor, let her kiss his hands with an austere expression of priestly dignity as if he were at that moment descending from an altar after having performed a mysterious ritual; I almost expected to see Frau Brigitte kneel in worship. Instead, she grasped Frank's hands and raising them, turned toward us. "Look!" she said in a tri-umphant voice, "look at the way hands of angels are made!"

I looked at Frank's hands. They were small, delicate and very white. I was surprised and relieved not to see a single drop of blood on them.

For some days I had no occasion to see either Governor-General Frank or Governor Fischer of Warsaw whose time was taken up with Himmler who had suddenly arrived from Berlin to study the delicate situation that was developing in Poland—it was then the be-ginning of February 1942—since the German defeats in Russia. The personal relations between Himmler and Frank were notoriously bad: Himmler despised Frank's "theatricals" and his "intellectual polish"; Frank charged Himmler with "base cruelty." Great changes among the highest Nazi officials in Poland were mentioned; even Frank's position seemed in jeopardy. But when Himmler left War-saw and returned to Berlin, Frank appeared to have won the day. The "great changes" had boiled down to the substitution of a close relative of Himmler—the Stadthauptmann of Czestochowa—for Wächter as Governor of Cracow, and the appointment of Wächter as Governor of Lwow.

Meanwhile Wächter went back to Cracow with Gassner and Baron Wolsegger. Frau Wächter remained behind to keep Frau Brigitte Frank company during the few days that the Governor-General still had to spend in Warsaw. And I, while waiting for per-mission to leave for the Smolensk front, had taken advantage of Himmler's presence—while the Gestapo was being diverted from its usual work to the crushing responsibility of protecting Himmler's sacred life—to secretly distribute letters, parcels of food and money that Polish refugees in Italy had asked me to give to their relatives and friends in Warsaw. The delivery of clandestine correspondence, even a single letter from abroad to Polish citizens, was punishable by death. I had to be, therefore, extremely cautious to escape the watchfulness of the Gestapo, so that I would not endanger other lives; and thanks to my caution and the providential complicity of a German officer—a highly cultured and generous-minded young man whom I had met in Florence years before and to whom I was bound by a close friendship—I succeeded in performing the delicate task that I had so lightly undertaken. The game was dangerous and I had been playing it in a sporting spirit with entire honesty—for I have never failed, even against the Germans, to play cricket according to the rules—and I was fortified by the feeling that I was performing a task affirming man's solidarity and in the best tradition of Christian mercy, as well as by a desire to hoodwink Himmler, Frank and all their police machinery. I had enjoyed the game and I had won; had I lost, I would have cheerfully paid the penalty. But I had won only because the Germans, forever undervaluing their opponents had not imagined that I would play according to the rules of the game.

Two days after Himmler's departure I met Frank again—at a luncheon he gave for Max Schmeling, the prize fighter—in his official residence at the Belvedere, that until Marshal Pilsudski's death had been his residence. That morning as I slowly strolled to the court of honor of the Belvedere along the avenue that leads through the charming eighteenth-century park landscaped with a rather sad and autumnal listlessness by some late pupil of Lenôtre, it seemed to me that the German flags, the German sentries, the German steps, voices and gestures imparted something that was hard and cold and dead to the old noble trees of the park, to the musical gentleness of that architecture that had been devised for the pompous leisure of Stanislas Augustus, to the silence of the fountains gripped in their prison of ice. More than twenty years earlier when I had strolled under the limes of the Aleja Ujazdowska or through the Avenue Laziencki I had discerned at a distance through the branches, the white walls of the Belvedere, and had felt that the marble stairways, the statues of Apollo and of Diana, the white stucco of the building were made of a delicate living material, almost I should say—of rosy flesh. Now on the contrary, when I entered the Belvedere, everything seemed cold, hard and dead. As I crossed the great halls filled with a clear frosty light, halls that once had resounded with the violins and harpsichords of Lulli and Rameau and with Chopin's lofty, pure melancholy, I heard German voices and laughter. I stopped on the threshold, uncertain whether to go in; then Frank's voice called to me and he met me himself with that proud cordiality of his that always surprised and deeply perturbed me.

"I shall knock him out in the first round; you will be the referee, Schmeling," said Frank clutching a hunting knife in his hand.

That day I was not the guest of honor at the table of the Governor-General of Poland in the Belvedere Palace of Warsaw. The guest of honor was Max Schmeling, the famous prize fighter. I was grateful that his presence drew the attention of the guests from me. It allowed me to yield to the sweet sadness of past memories, to recall that far-off New Year's day of 1920 when I had entered that room for the first time to take part in the traditional homage paid by the diplomatic corps to Marshal Pilsudski, the head of the state. The old Marshal had stood motionless in the center of the room and leaned on the hilt of his ancient saber curved like a scimitar, its leather sheath wrought with silver. His pale face was streaked with thick livid veins that resembled scars; his long mustaches dropped in the Sobieski fashion and his wide forehead bristled with hard, close-cropped hair. Over twenty years had passed and the old Marshal still stood before me, in the same spot where a deer just taken off a spit now smoked in the center of the table, while Frank laughingly probed its choice flesh with the broad blade of his hunting knife.

Max Schmeling sat on Frau Brigitte Frank's right. He was self-contained as he looked over the guests one by one, with shy and yet steady upward glances from his lowered head. He was a little above average height, smoothly shaped, round-shouldered and almost elegant in manner. It was difficult to imagine that beneath his well-cut, gray flannel suit, probably Vienna or New York tailored, lurked that great strength. His voice was deep and melodious, and he spoke slowly, smiling—whether out of shyness or because of the instinctive feeling of self-reliance that is characteristic of athletes I wasn't sure. The look in his black eyes was deep and calm. His face was serious and gentle. He leaned forward, his forearms resting on the table, and gazed fixedly in front of him as if crouching expectantly in the ring. He listened attentively, yet suspiciously to the conversation, and now and again his faintly amused glances fell on Frank in an ironical but respectful manner.

In his presence, Frank acted a part that was new to me: the role of an intellectual who, when accidentally placed face to face with an athlete, preens himself, shows off his finest feathers and, while pretending to bend his head in deep reverence before the statue of

Hercules and to extol its muscular torso, bulging biceps and huge hard fists, actually burns incense at Minerva's shrine, thus proclaiming the indisputable superiority of intellect and culture over brute force by an exaggerated courtesy of manners and profuse praise condescendingly bestowed on athletic proficiency and by a few loftily dropped words. Far from seeming hurt or annoyed, Schmeling made no effort to conceal his amused surprise as well as his candid curiosity, as if he were faced with a human species unknown to him. Diffidence was apparent in his firm gaze, ironical smile, and the caution with which he answered Frank's questions and the sulky stubborn way in which he belittled the fame his name was surrounded with and everything else that was alien to his own athletic experience.

Frank asked Schmeling about Crete and the serious wound he had received in the dangerous and heroic operation in which he had taken part as a paratrooper. Turning to me, Frank added that British prisoners in Crete had shouted, "Hello, Max!" as Schmeling was carried past them on a stretcher, and waved their fists in the air.

"I was on a stretcher, but I was not wounded," said Schmeling. "The rumor that I had been hit in the knee was false; Goebbels had it sent out as propaganda. It was even said that I was dead. The truth was much simpler: I was suffering with cramps in my stomach." Then he added, "I want to be frank. I suffered with colic."

"Even for a heroic soldier, there is nothing debasing about suffering with colic," remarked Frank.

"I never thought there was anything debasing in colic," said Schmeling smiling ironically. "I had caught cold, my colic certainly was not due to fear. But when the word 'colic' is mentioned in connection with war, everyone thinks of fear."

"Nobody can associate you with fear," said Frank. Then he looked at me and added, "Schmeling behaved like a hero in Crete. He does not want to hear about it but he is a real hero."

"I am no hero at all," said Schmeling smiling, though I perceived that he was slightly annoyed. "I had not even the chance to fight. A hundred and fifty feet in the air I jumped from the plane, and I remained lying among the bushes with those awful pains in my belly. When I read about my wound, I denied the rumor at once in an interview with a journalist from a neutral country. I told him that I had simply suffered with cramps in my stomach. Goebbels has never forgiven me for that denial. He has even threatened to summon me before a military court as a defeatist. If Germany were to lose the war, Goebbels would have me shot."

"Germany will not lose the war," said Frank severely.

"*Natürlich*," said Schmeling. "German *Kultur* is not suffering with colic."

We all laughed discreetly, and Frank deigned to curl his lips into an indulgent smile.

"German *Kultur*," said the Governor-General austerely, "has sacrificed in this war many of its most noble representatives in the country."

"War is the most noble sport," said Schmeling.

I inquired whether he had come to Warsaw to take part in a boxing match.

"I am here," replied Schmeling, "to organize and direct a series of matches between representatives of the Wehrmacht and the SS. This will be the first great sporting event to take place in Poland."

I added that it almost amounted to a political event.

"Almost," Schmeling agreed with a smile.

Frank caught the allusion and an expression of deep complacency spread over his face. He had just come out victorious in a contest with the head of the SS, and he was unable to refrain from hinting at the causes for his disagreement with Himmler.

"I am not ranged on the side of violence, and certainly Himmler will not bring me around to the idea that a policy of order and justice can be upheld in Poland only by a methodical employment of violence."

"Himmler lacks a sense of humor," I remarked.

"Germany," replied Frank, "is the only country in the world where a sense of humor is not essential to a statesman. But in Poland it is a different matter."

I looked at him and smiled. "The Polish people," I said, "ought to be grateful for your sense of humor."

"Undoubtedly they would feel grateful to me," said Frank, "if Himmler had not seen fit to back my policy of justice and order with violence." He began telling me of the current Warsaw rumors concerning the hundred and fifty Polish intellectuals whom Himmler, before leaving Poland, had ordered shot without Frank's knowledge and despite his objections. Frank was obviously anxious to clear himself in my eyes of the responsibility for that slaughter. Frank told me that he had learned about it from Himmler himself after the shooting as he climbed into the plane that was to take him to Berlin. "Naturally, I made the most vigorous protests," said Frank, "but it was too late."

"Himmler," I said, "probably laughed. Your protests must have appeared ludicrous to a humorless man like Himmler. At any rate you also were laughing gaily on taking leave of Himmler at the airport. The news must have put you in a good humor."

Frank fixed me with a glance filled with surprise and uneasiness. "How do you happen to know that I was laughing?" he asked. "It's true, I was laughing, too."

"All of Warsaw knows it," I replied, "and everyone is talking about it."

"*Ach, so! Wunderbar!*" exclaimed Frank raising his eyes to heaven.

I also raised my eyes to heaven and laughed, and at the same time I could not repress a gesture of wonder and horror. From the ceiling where once had been painted the "Triumph of Venus," a fresco by some eighteenth-century Italian pupil of the great Venetian masters, now hung a mauve-colored wistaria arbor wrought with the precision and realism of that florid style that began with the "modernists" of 1900 and passed through the decorative schools of Vienna and Munich and finally achieved its extreme and highest expression in the official style of the Third Reich. Horrible to say, that wistaria arbor looked real. The slim trunks climbed up the walls like snakes bending and entwining their long twisted tendrils above our heads. The sinuous branches, hung with leaves and clusters of flowers about which fluttered tiny birds, fat multi-colored butterflies and huge hairy bluebottles, made a lattice-work across a blue sky as clean and smooth as the sky in a cupola painted by Fortuny. My eyes glided slowly down the trunks of the wistaria and descended from branch to branch along the walls until it rested on the rich furniture stiffly and symmetrically ranged along the walls. It was dark, massive Dutch furniture over which hung on the walls blue Delft dishes showing landscapes and seascapes, and red souvenir dishes of the Dutch East India Company depicting pagodas and sea birds. Over a tall, solemn "Old Bavaria" cupboard hung a few Flemish-school still-lifes portraying huge silver trays laden with fish and fruit, and dining tables buried beneath a wonderful variety of game that was being sniffed at by setters, pointers and hunting dogs. The curtains on the large windows were typical Saxon provincial—made of an ugly light rayon with a birds-and-flowers design.

Schmeling's eyes met mine and he smiled. I was surprised that a prize fighter, with his hard narrow forehead, a gentle brute, could appreciate the grotesque and horrible in that wistaria arbor, that furniture, those pictures, those curtains, that drawing room where nothing was left of what used to be the pride of the Belvedere with its Viennese stuccos, Italian frescoes, French furniture and huge Venetian hanging lights. Only the shape of the doors and windows, and the architectural proportions testified to its former harmony and seventeenth-century grace.

Frau Brigitte Frank, who for some time, had been following my wandering glances and my lingering, surprised eyes, no doubt imagined that I was struck with admiration for so much art and leaned toward me to say with a proud smile that she herself had supervised the work of the German decorators—as a matter of fact, she used the grand word "artists" instead of "decorators"—who were responsible for that wonderful transformation of the old Belvedere. The wistaria arbor, of which she seemed particularly proud, was the work of a distinguished Berlin woman artist; but she made it clear that the original idea of that arbor was her own. For political reasons, she had first thought of having recourse to the brush of some Polish painter, but then she had given up that idea. "It must be conceded," she said, "that the Poles lack the religious sense of art that is a German heritage."

That hint at the religious sense of art gave Frank the chance to discourse at length on Polish art, the religious spirit of the Poles and on what he was pleased to call Polish idolatry.

"They may be given to idolatry," said Schmeling, "but I have noticed that the Poles have a childish and unspoiled conception of God." He went on to tell that on the previous night, while he was watching the training of some Wehrmacht boxers, a little, old Pole who was sprinkling the ring with sawdust had said to him, "If our Lord had possessed a couple of fists like yours, He would never have died on the cross."

Frank laughingly remarked that had Jesus Christ possessed a pair of fists like Schmeling's, real German fists, the world would be a better place.

"In a certain sense," I said, "a Jesus endowed with a couple of real German fists would not be unlike Himmler."

"*Ach, wunderbar!*" shouted Frank, and everybody joined in the laughter. "Leaving fists aside," went on Frank when the hilarity subsided, "if Jesus Christ had been a German, the world would be ruled by honor."

"I would rather it were ruled by pity," I replied.

Frank broke into hearty laughter. "Yours is really an obsession! Would you have us believe that Jesus Christ was a woman too?"

"The women would feel greatly flattered," said Frau Wächter with a gracious smile.

"The Poles," said Governor Fischer, "are convinced that Jesus Christ is always on their side, even in political matters, and that He prefers them to any other people, even to the Germans. Their religion and their politics are built upon this childish idea."

"Luckily for Him," said Frank with fat laughter, "Jesus Christ has too much sense to get embroiled in the *polnische Wirtschaft*. He would only make trouble for Himself."

"Aren't you ashamed to blaspheme so?" exclaimed Frau Wächter in her sweet Viennese accent as she threatened Frank with her raised finger.

"I promise you I won't do it again," replied Frank assuming the air of a naughty child. Then he added laughing, "If I were certain that Jesus Christ had a couple of fists such as Schmeling's, I would assuredly be more cautious in talking about Him."

"If Jesus Christ were a prize fighter," said Frau Wächter, "He would have knocked you out a long time ago."

We all began to laugh, and Frank gallantly bowed to Frau Wächter and asked her by what blow she fancied Jesus Christ would have knocked him out.

"Herr Schmeling," replied Frau Wächter, "is much better able to tell you."

159

"The answer is not difficult," said Schmeling studying Frank's face carefully as if to determine the right place to strike. "Any blow would knock you out. Your head is frail."

"My head is frail?" shouted Frank blushing. Trying to appear unconcerned he stroked his face with his hand, but he was visibly annoyed. We all laughed with relish and Frau Wächter kept dabbing her eyes that had filled with tears of laughter. Only Frau Brigitte came to Frank's rescue and, turning to me, she added, "The Governor-General is very friendly to the Polish clergy; he is the true protector of religion in Poland."

"Ah, is that so?" I exclaimed pretending to be deeply surprised and pleased.

"The Polish clergy," said Frank, joyfully seizing upon the opportunity to change the subject, "did not care for me in the beginning. I had serious grounds for dissatisfaction with the priests. But after the recent turn of events in Russia, the clergy came over to my side. Do you know why? They fear that Russia will beat Germany. Ha, ha, ha! *Sehr amusant*—very amusing—*nicht wahr?*"

"*Ja, sehr amusant*," I replied.

"There is now perfect understanding between me and the Polish clergy. Nevertheless, I have not altered and shall not alter in the slightest the fundamental lines of my religious policy in Poland. To be respected in a country such as this, one must be consistent; I am, and I shall remain, consistent with myself. Polish aristocracy? I ignore it and have no contact with it. I never enter the houses of Polish noblemen and none of them enter mine. I have allowed them to gamble and to dance freely in their palaces. They gamble, run into debt and dance without perceiving the ruin that faces them. They open their eyes now and again, perceive that they have caused their own ruin, shed tears over the misfortunes of their country and charge me in French of being a cruel tyrant and an enemy of Poland; then they begin laughing, gambling and dancing again.

"The middle classes? The greatest part of the rich middle class escaped abroad in 1939, in the wake of the Republican government. Their property is administered by German officials. Those of the middle class who have stayed, have been mortally hit by the impossibility of practicing their liberal professions and are trying to survive by desperate means, entrenching themselves in an irreducible opposition that is composed of ludicrous chatter and ineffective plots that I weave and undo behind their backs at my leisure. All Poles are born conspirators, especially the intellectuals. Conspiring is their principal passion. Only one thing comforts them in Poland's ruin—the chance to be able at last to give vent to their dominant passion. But I have a long arm and know how to make use of it. Himmler, whose arm is short, dreams only of shootings and concentration camps. Doesn't he really grasp that the Poles fear neither death nor imprisonment? The secondary schools and the universities were hotbeds of political intrigue. I have closed them. What is the use of high schools and universities in a country that has no *Kultur?*

"And now we come to labor. The peasants grow rich on the black market, and I allow them to grow rich. Why? Because the black market is bleeding the middle classes and starving industrial labor, making a coalition of peasants and workers impossible. The workmen toil in silence under the leadership of their own technicians. When the Republic crumbled to pieces the technicians did not flee; they have not left their machinery and labor; they have remained at their places. The technicians and the workmen are our enemies too, but they are enemies who deserve respect. They do not conspire; they work. Maybe their behavior is part of a general plan to fight us. Leaflets containing communist propaganda printed in Russia and smuggled into Poland are passed around in the mines, the factories and the shipyards. Those leaflets urge the Polish workmen and technicians to abstain from acts of sabotage and from lowering the average output, to work in perfect discipline, so as not to give the Gestapo any cause for reprisals against labor. Obviously, if labor succeeds in not having its back broken by Himmler and is not scattered about in graveyards and concentration camps, after the war it will be the only class capable of seizing power. Always assuming of course that Germany loses the war. And if Germany wins the war, she will be forced to lean on the only class that will be on its feet, that is to say on labor. The Polish middle class accuse me of being the source of those leaflets. That is a piece of slander. Those leaflets are not of my making, but I allow them to be circulated. Our main concern is to make the Polish industrial output meet the requirements of war. Why should we refrain from utilizing communist propaganda to achieve our objectives when that propaganda, in order to save the working classes from destruction, urges workers not to damage our war production? German and Russian interests in all of Europe are irreconcilable; there is a single point on which they meet and agree: that is maintaining the full efficiency of the laboring classes until the day when Germany will crush Russia, or Russia will crush Germany.

"And now we come to the Jews. Inside the ghettos they enjoy the most complete freedom. I persecute no one. I allow noblemen to go to ruin gambling and to amuse themselves with dancing. I allow the middle class to conspire, the peasants to grow rich, workers and technicians to work. Very often I even close an eye."

"A person closes an eye," I put in, "when he is aiming a rifle."

"That may be. But please do not interrupt me," went on Frank after a momentary hesitation. "The real fatherland of the Polish people, its real *Rzepospolita Polska,* is the Catholic religion. That is the only fatherland left to this unhappy people. I respect and protect it. At first, there were many grounds for dissension between me and the clergy. Now matters have changed. After the latest war developments in Russia, the Polish clergy has changed its position with regard to German policy in Poland. It does not help us, but neither does it fight us. The German army has fallen before the walls of Moscow; Hitler did not succeed, or, rather, has not yet succeeded in crushing Russia. The Polish clergy fears the Russians more than it fears the Germans, the Communists more than the Nazis. They may well be right. As you see I speak very frankly to you; and I am also sincere when I tell you that I bow before the Polish Christ. You might object that I bow before Him because He is defenseless. But I would bow before the Polish Christ even if He were armed with a tommy gun, because I am prompted by German interests and by my own conscience as a German Catholic. There is only one charge that the Polish clergy can make against me—I have forbidden pilgrimages to the shrine of the Black Madonna of Czestochowa. But I was within my rights. It would have been extremely dangerous to the safety of the German occupation of Poland to tolerate a crowd of hundreds of thousands of fanatics gathering from time to time around that shrine. Every year almost two million faithful visited the Czestochowa shrine. I have forbidden the pilgrimages, and I have forbidden the public exhibition of the Black

Madonna. For any other charge I am answerable only to my Führer and to my own conscience."

Suddenly he stopped and looked around. He had spoken with a sad, resentful eloquence without pausing for a breath. We were silent as we gazed at him. Frau Brigitte was gently weeping and smiling; Frau Wächter and Frau Fischer were moved and did not take their eyes from the sweating face of the Governor-General. I felt oppressed by the silence and discreetly coughed. Frank, who was patting his forehead with a handkerchief, turned and after staring at me for a long time, smiled and asked: "You have been to Czestochowa, *nicht wahr?*"

I had been to Czestochowa a few days earlier to visit the famous shrine as the guest of the Paulite monks. Father Mendera had led me to the underground crypt where the effigy of the Black Madonna is preserved, the most venerated effigy in all of Poland. The image is encased in a silver frame of Byzantine design and is called the Black Madonna because the face was darkened by smoke and flames during a siege. The Stadthauptmann of Czestochowa, who, as a near-relative of Himmler, was especially feared, despised and obeyed by the monks, had made an exception in allowing me to see the effigy of the Black Madonna. This was the first time, since the beginning of the German occupation of Poland that the sacred icon had appeared before the eyes of the faithful, and the monks were filled with joy and amazement at the unhoped-for event.

We crossed the church and went down into the crypt followed by a group of peasants who while they were kneeling in the church, had seen us walk by. The two Nazi inspectors of the Stadthauptmann of Czestochowa, Günter Laxy and Fritz Griehschammer, and the two SS men who accompanied me stopped at the door. Günter Laxy made a sign to Father Mendera who looked at me uneasily and said in Italian, "The peasants." I replied loudly in German, "The peasants stay here." The prior of the shrine, a small, lean man with a creased and wrinkled face, came in at that moment; he wept and smiled, and now and again he blew his nose into a large green handkerchief.

Gold, silver, precious marbles gleamed softly in the dimness of the chapel. The peasants, kneeling in front of the altar, fixed their eyes on the silver door that conceals and guards the ancient image of the Czestochowa Madonna. From time to time we could hear the clattering of the rifles of the SS men who stood guarding the door.

Suddenly the walls of the underground chapel were shaken by a deep rumble of drums and by the sound of silver trumpets blaring Palestrina's triumphal notes. The sliding door was raised little by little and the Black Madonna studded with pearls and precious stones that flashed in the red candlelight appeared holding the Child in her arms. Prostrated, their faces pressed to the ground, the peasants wept. I could hear their repressed sobs, their foreheads beating against the marble floor. They called the Virgin softly by name, "Mary, Mary," as if she were a member of their family—their mother, their sister, their daughter, their wife. No, not as if they had been calling their mother—they would not have said "Mary," they would have said "Mamma." The Madonna was the Mother of Jesus; she was not their mother, she was the Mother of Jesus and only of Jesus. But she was their sister, wife, daughter; and they called her softly, "Mary, Mary," as if they feared being overheard by the two SS guards standing motionless by the door. The menacing deep rumble of the drums, the frightful blare of the long silver trumpets made the walls of the shrine shake; it seemed as if the marble vault were about to collapse. The peasants called "Mary, Mary," as if they called to a dead person, as if they meant to rouse a sister, a wife, or a daughter from her death sleep; they cried out "Mary, Mary, Mary!" At that moment the prior and Father Mendera turned slowly around. The peasants fell suddenly silent and also turned around slowly and looked at Günter Laxy and Fritz Griehschammer, and at the two SS men armed with rifles, their brows hidden by their steel helmets, who stood motionless at the door. They looked at them and wept, silently wept. Deeper rumbled the drums in the stones, shriller blared the trumpets beneath the marble vault, as the sliding door slowly descended and the Black Madonna disappeared in a gleam of jewels and gold. The peasants turned toward me, their faces streaming with tears, and smiled.

It was the same smile that I had seen blossoming suddenly on the lips of the miners in the depths of the Wieliczka salt mines near Cracow. Within the dark caves hewn out of blocks of rock salt a throng of pale faces, worn by hunger and anxiety, had suddenly appeared to me like a throng of ghosts in the smoky light of the torches. Before me rose a little baroque church which had been hewn out of salt with pickaxes and chisels by the Wieliczka miners about the end of the seventeenth century. The statues of Jesus Christ, the Virgin and the saints had been sculptured out of salt too. And the miners, kneeling before the altar built with blocks of rock salt and crowding at the door of the church with their leather caps in their hands, looked like statues of salt too. They gazed at me and smiled through silent tears.

"In the Czestochowa shrine," went on Frank without giving me time to answer, "you heard the rumble of the drums and the blare of the silver trumpets and you believed that you heard the voice of Poland. No, Poland is dumb. The limitless, frosty silence of Poland is louder than our voices, our shouts, the shots of our rifles. It is useless to fight against the Polish people. It is like fighting a corpse. And yet one feels that it is alive, that blood throbs in its brain, that hatred is pulsating in its breast, that it is stronger than you are. It is like fighting a living corpse. Yes, a living corpse. Ha, ha, ha! *Mein lieber* Schmeling, have you ever fought a living corpse?"

"No, never," replied Schmeling in a tone of deep amazement as he stared at Frank.

"And what about you, *lieber* Malaparte?"

"I have never fought against a corpse," I answered, "but I have been present at a fight between living and dead men."

"Is that possible?" exclaimed Frank. "Where?"

Everyone gazed at me attentively.

"At Poduloea," I replied.

"At Poduloea? Where is Poduloea?"

Poduloea is in Romania on the Bessarabian frontier—a village only a score of miles beyond Jassy in Moldavia. I cannot listen to an engine whistling in full daylight without thinking of Poduloea—a dusty village in a dusty valley beneath a blue sky loaded with white clouds of dust. It is a narrow valley, shut in by light, low, treeless hills with only a few scattered acacia groves, some vineyards and lean wheat fields.

A hot wind was blowing, a wind that was as rough as a cat's

tongue. The wheat had already been harvested, the stubble fields gleamed yellow in a slimy, heavy sun. Clouds of dust rose from the valley. It was the end of June 1941, a few days after the great Jassy pogrom. I was motoring to Poduloea with Sartori, the Italian Consul in Jassy whom everybody called "Marquis," and with Lino Pellegrini, "a stupid Fascist" who had come from Italy with his young wife to spend his honeymoon in Jassy and who was sending home to Mussolini's papers articles steeped with enthusiasm for Marshal Antonescu, the "Red Dog," and for all the bloody bastards who were driving the Romanian people to ruin. He was the best looking young fellow who had ever walked under the Moldavian sun. Everywhere between the Transylvanian Alps and the mouth of the Danube women were crazy about him; they leaned out of the windows, they came to the shop doors to see him go by, and they said, sighing, "Ah, *frumoso! frumoso!*—Beautiful, beautiful!" But he was a "stupid Fascist." Moreover it goes without saying that I was somewhat jealous of him, and would have preferred it if he were not so good-looking and less of a Fascist. In my heart I looked down on him until the day I saw him face the Jassy Chief of Police and shout in his face, "Rotten murderer!" He had come to spend his honeymoon in Jassy, under the bombs dropped by the Soviet planes, and he spent his nights with his wife hidden in an *adapost*, the underground shelter that had been dug amid the tombs of the old abandoned graveyard. Now, the three of us were driving to Poduloea to look for the owner of the villa inhabited by the Italian Consulate. He was a Jewish lawyer, an honest man, whom the police had injured severely in the garden of the Consulate by hitting with their rifle butts. Then they had carried him away more dead than alive, probably to finish him elsewhere, so they would not leave on the grounds the evidence that they had murdered a Jew within the precincts of the Italian Consulate.

The day was hot, the car moved slowly along the road pitted with deep holes. A victim of my usual hay fever, I was sneezing continuously. Clouds of furiously buzzing flies followed us. Sartori drove away the flies with his handkerchief. His face streaming with perspiration he said, "What a bore to be looking for a corpse in this heat, with all the thousands of corpses that are lying about in Moldavia! It is like looking for a needle in a haystack!"

"For goodness' sake, don't talk about hay, Sartori!" I said sneezing.

"Ah, Jesus, Jesus!" said Sartori, "I forgot that you have hay fever," and he gazed with eyes full of pity at my congested face, purple nose, red and swollen eyelids.

"You like searching for corpses, Sartori," I said to him. "Confess that you like it. You are a Neapolitan and Neapolitans like dead bodies, funerals, weeping, mourning and cemeteries. You like burying the dead. Isn't it a fact that you like corpses?"

"Don't make fun of me, Malaparte. I could really do without searching for corpses in this heat. But I have given my word to the poor chap's wife and daughter, and a promise is a debt. Those poor women still hope that he may be alive. Do you think it possible, Malaparte, that he is still alive?"

"How could he be alive, if unprotesting you allowed him to be murdered under your very eyes? I realize now why you are as fat as a butcher. Is this the fine way in which things are being done in the Royal Italian Consulate of Jassy?"

"After what you said, if Mussolini were a just man, Malaparte, he would make me an ambassador."

"He will appoint you to the Ministry of Foreign Affairs. I bet you have hidden the corpse under your bed. Be honest, Sartori, you like sleeping with a corpse under your bed."

"Ah, Jesus, Jesus!" sighed Sartori dabbing his face.

We had been looking for the corpse for three days. The night before we had finally gone to see the Chief of Police to try to find out whether by any chance that poor wretch, having been spared at the last moment by his murderers, had been cast into a prison. The Chief of Police had received us kindly; his face was yellow and flabby, his eyes black and hairy with yellow reflections in the shadow of his thick eyebrows. I was surprised to notice that hair was growing along the inside edge of his eyelids; they were not lashes; it was actually a thick fine down of grayish color.

"Have you tried the St. Spiridion Hospital? He may be there," said the Chief of Police after a while, half-closing his eyes.

"No, he is not at the hospital," replied Sartori in his quiet voice.

"Are you quite sure," went on the Chief of Police gazing at Sartori with a narrow sector of his eye flashing black and green through the grayish down, "quite sure that it happened on the Consulate grounds? And that it was done by my men?"

"Would you at least help me trace the corpse?" asked Sartori smiling.

"It would appear," said the Chief of Police, lighting a cigarette, "that some pistol shots were fired from the windows of the Italian Consulate on a police patrol passing along the street."

"I can see that it will not be difficult for me to trace the corpse with your assistance," said Sartori smiling.

"I have no time to bother with corpses," said the Chief of Police with a gentle smile. "I am far too busy with the living."

"Luckily," remarked Sartori, "the living are rapidly growing fewer in number, and you will be able to have some rest."

"I really need it," replied the Chief of Police raising his eyes to the sky.

"Why can't we agree and share the task?" asked Sartori in his placid voice. "While you are busy tracing and arresting the murderers—who certainly are still alive, I shall undertake to find the dead body. What do you say to that?"

"If you fail to bring me the corpse of this gentleman and cannot prove that he has been killed, how can I trace the murderers?"

"I see your point," said Sartori smiling. "I'll bring you the corpse. I'll bring it here, into your office, along with the other seven thousand corpses and you will help me to find it in the pile. Is it agreed?" He spoke slowly, smiling, with imperturbable indifference, but I know my Neapolitans. I know what some Neapolitans are, and I knew that Sartori was quivering with wrath and indignation at that moment.

"Agreed," replied the Chief of Police.

Then Pellegrini, the "stupid Fascist" stood up and, clenching his fists, said to the Chief of Police: "You are a low-down murderer and a cowardly bastard."

I looked at him in amazement. It was the first time that I looked at him without envy. He looked most handsome—tall, athletic; his face was pale, his nostrils quivered and his eyes flashed. His angry movement made his wavy black hair drop in long curls on his forehead. I looked at him with the deepest respect. He was a stupid Fascist, but during the night of the great Jassy pogrom he had several times risked his life to save a handful of unfortunate Jews, and now, when a nod from the Chief of Police would have sufficed to have him murdered on a street corner that very night, he was risking his skin for the sake of the corpse of a Jew. I promised myself that, if Mussolini were to be sent home one of these days, I would take up Pellegrini's defense against anyone who wished to make him pay for his "stupid Fascism." A Fascist who risks his skin to pull doomed Jews out of their murderer's hands, a man who risks his skin for the sake of a corpse, deserves the respect of all free and civilized men.

The Chief of Police also stood up and fixed him with those hairy eyes of his. He willingly would have shot him in the stomach; he would have fired at Sartori, at Pellegrini and at me, but he did not dare. We were not wretched Romanians, we were not three wretched Jews from Jassy. He feared that Mussolini would avenge us. Ha, ha, ha! He feared that Mussolini would avenge us. He did not know that had he killed me, Mussolini would not even have protested. Mussolini had no intention of being bothered. Didn't he know that Mussolini was afraid of everyone—even of *him?* And I laughed thinking about the Chief of Police in Jassy being afraid of Mussolini.

"What are you laughing at?" suddenly asked the Chief of Police, turning abruptly to me.

"What does this gentleman want?" I asked Pellegrini. "Does he wish to know what I am laughing at? I am laughing at him. Can't I laugh at him?"

"It certainly is not forbidden to laugh at him," said Pellegrini, "but I realize why it would not make him very happy."

"It certainly does not make him happy."

"Do you mean it? Are you laughing at him?" asked Sartori in his placid voice. "I beg your pardon, Malaparte, but it seems to me you are wrong. He is a perfect gentleman and should be treated as he deserves."

Quietly we rose and went out. But we had no sooner crossed the threshold when Sartori stopped us and said, "We have overlooked saying good-by to him. Shall we go back?"

"No," I replied, "instead let's go to the Commandant."

The Commandant offered us cigarettes, listened to us kindly and then said, "He may have gone to Poduloea."

"To Poduloea?" asked Sartori. "Why?"

A couple of days after the slaughter, a train loaded with Jews had started for Poduloea, a village some twenty miles beyond Jassy, where the Chief of Police had decided to establish a concentration camp. That train had left three days before and should have been there long ago.

"Let's drive to Poduloea," said Sartori.

So the next morning we started for Poduloea in a car. We stopped to ask for news of the train at a small station lost in the dusty countryside. Several soldiers, sitting in the shade of an abandoned car on a siding told us that the train, made up of about ten cattle cars, had passed through there two days before and had spent a whole night in the station. The unfortunate people packed into the sealed cars had shrieked and moaned begging the soldiers to remove the wooden boards nailed over the windows. About two hundred Jews had been piled into each car, and those wretched people were unable to breathe. The train had started at dawn for Poduloea.

"You may be able to overtake it before it reaches Poduloea," said the soldiers.

The railway track ran along the valley, parallel with the road. We had nearly reached Poduloea when we heard a long whistle from across the dusty countryside. We looked at each other and paled as though we recognized it.

"What heat!" moaned Sartori wiping his forehead.

And I noticed that he at once regretted and felt ashamed because he had said "What heat!" He thought of those people piled into cattle cars, two hundred in each car, without water and without air. That distant whistle through the still glow of the sun had a ghostly sound in that dusty, deserted countryside. After a while we saw the train. It had stopped at a signal and was whistling for a right-of-way. Then it moved on slowly and we kept beside it, following along the road. We looked at the cattle cars and at the wooden boards nailed over the windows. The train had taken three days to go twenty miles. It had to give precedence to military convoys; besides, there was no hurry. Had it reached Poduloea even after three months it still would have been on time.

Meanwhile we had reached Poduloea where the train had stopped on a shunting track just outside the station. The heat was stifling. It was about noon; the railway officials had gone to eat. The engineer, the fireman and the military guards had jumped down from the train and were stretched out on the ground in the shade of the cars.

"Open the cars at once," I ordered the soldiers.

"We cannot, *Domnule Capitan.*"

"Open the cars at once!" I shouted.

"We cannot. The cars are sealed," said the engineer. "The stationmaster would have to be advised."

The stationmaster was at his meal. At first he refused to interrupt his dinner; later, learning that Sartori was the Italian Consul and that I was an Italian *Domnule Capitan,* he rose and trotted along behind us with a pair of heavy pincers in his hand. The soldiers went to work at once trying to open the sliding door of the first car. The wood and iron door would not yield; it seemed as if ten, a hundred hands held it from the inside, as if the prisoners strained every sinew to prevent it from opening. At last the stationmaster shouted, "You there, inside, help us push too!" No one answered. Then all together, we tried to force it. Sartori stood facing the car, his face raised and wiped his sweat with a handkerchief. Suddenly the door yielded and the car was opened.

A throng of prisoners hurled itself at Sartori, knocking him down and falling on top of him. The dead were fleeing from the train. They dropped in masses—with dull thuds, like concrete statues. Buried under the corpses, crushed by their huge, cold weight, Sartori struggled and wriggled trying to free himself from under that dead burden, from under that frozen mountain; finally he disappeared beneath the pile of corpses, as if it were an avalanche of stones. The dead are wrathful, stubborn, ferocious. The dead are stupid—vain and capricious as children and women. *The dead are crazy.* Woe to the living if a dead man hates him. Woe to him if the dead fall in love with him. Woe to the living being if he insults a dead one, touches his self-love or wounds his honor. The dead are jealous and vengeful. They fear no one, they fear nothing—neither blows, nor wounds, nor enemies in overwhelming numbers. They even have no fear of death. They fight tooth and nail, silently, without yielding a step; they never loosen their hold, they never flee.

They fight to the end with a stubborn, cold courage, laughing and sneering, pale and dumb—those mad eyes of theirs wide open and squinting. When finally, they are vanquished, when they resign themselves to defeat and humiliation, when they lie beaten, they exhale a sweet, greasy odor and slowly decompose. Some, attempting to crush him, hurled themselves with all their weight upon Sartori, others dropped on him coldly, rigidly, sluggishly; others butted their heads into his chest, or hit him with their knees and their elbows. Sartori grasped their hair, clutched at their clothing, caught hold of their arms, tried to push them back by gripping their throats or hitting their faces with clenched fists. It was a furious silent struggle. We all ran to his aid and vainly tried to free him from under the oppressive mound of the dead. Finally, after great effort, we succeeded in reaching him and drew him from the pile. Sartori stood up, his suit was in tatters, his eyes swollen, and there was blood on his cheek. He was very pale and perfectly calm. He only said, "See if there is anyone living among them. My cheek has been bitten."

The soldiers climbed into the car and began throwing out the corpses one by one. There were a hundred and seventy-nine of them—all suffocated, all had swollen heads and bluish faces. Meanwhile a squad of German soldiers and a little crowd of local inhabitants and peasants had come up and helped open the cars, throw out the corpses, and range them along the railway embankment. Next came a group of Poduloea Jews, led by their rabbi. They had learned that the Italian Consul was present and this had bolstered their courage. They looked pale but they were calm and did not weep. They spoke with steady voices. All had friends or relatives in Jassy, and each feared for their lives. They were clothed in black and wore odd, hard felt hats. The rabbi and five or six others who said they were on the managing board of the Agricultural Bank of Poduloea, bowed to Sartori.

"It is hot," said the rabbi wiping the sweat with the palm of his hand.

"Yes, it is very hot," replied Sartori pressing a handkerchief to his forehead.

The flies buzzed furiously. The dead, ranged along the railway embankment, numbered about two thousand. Two thousand corpses

stretched out under the sun are a great many—too many. Clutched
between his mother's knees a few months' old baby was still alive.
It had fainted, but it still breathed. One of its arms was broken.
The mother had managed to hold it for three days with its mouth
glued to the door jamb; she had fought savagely not to be wrenched
away by the crowd of the dying; she had been crushed dead by the
merciless pressure. The baby had been buried under the dead
mother, clutched between her knees, sucking that thin thread of air
with its lips. "It's alive," said Sartori in an odd voice. "It's alive, it's
alive!" I was moved as I looked at Sartori, at that fat placid Neapolitan who had at last shed his indifference, not because of all those
dead, but because of a living child, because of a child that was still
alive.

A few hours later, toward sunset, the soldiers working in one end
of a cattle car threw on the embankment a corpse with its head
wrapped in a bloody handkerchief. It was the owner of the house
occupied by the Italian Consulate in Jassy. Sartori looked at him in
silence for a long time. He touched his forehead, then he turned to
the rabbi and said, "He was an honest man."

Suddenly we heard the sounds of a quarrel. A crowd of peasants
and gypsies who had gathered from all over were stripping the
corpses. Sartori made a gesture of protest, but the rabbi put a hand
on his arm. "It can't be helped," he said, "it is the custom." Then
with a sad smile he added in a low voice, "They will come tomorrow to sell us the clothing stolen from the dead and we shall have
to buy it. What else can we do?"

Sartori kept silent and watched those wretched corpses being
stripped. The dead seemed to defend themselves with all their
strength against the violence of those who were stripping them;
men and women dripping with perspiration, screaming and cursing,
were doggedly trying to raise stubborn arms, bend stiff elbows and
knees, in order to draw off the jackets, trousers and underclothing.
The women were most stubborn in their relentless defense. I never
would have thought that it would be so difficult to take a slip off a
dead girl. Perhaps it was modesty still alive in them that gave the
women the strength to defend themselves; sometimes they raised
themselves on their elbows, brought their white faces near to the
grim sweaty faces of those who profaned them and gazed at them

173

with staring eyes until they finally fell with a dull thud naked onto the ground.

"We must go; it is getting late," said Sartori and, turning to the rabbi, asked him to write out a death certificate for the honest man. The rabbi bowed and we all started walking toward the village. The heat was stifling in the office of the manager of the Agricultural Bank. The rabbi sent for the books of the synagogue, wrote out the death certificate and handed the document to Sartori, who folded it with care and put it in his wallet. A train whistled in the distance. A bluebottle buzzed around the inkstand.

"I regret very much that I have to go," said Sartori, "but I must be back in Jassy before night."

"Please wait a moment," one of the board of the Agricultural Bank said in Italian. He was a short, fat Jew with a Napoleon III goatee. He opened a little cupboard, took out a bottle of vermouth, and filled several small glasses. He said that the vermouth was from Turin—real Cinzano, and he began telling me in Italian that he had been in Venice, Florence and Rome several times and that his two sons had studied medicine in Italy at the University of Padua.

"I should like to meet them," said Sartori kindly.

"Oh, they are dead. They died in Jassy the other day." He sighed and added, "I should like to return to Padua so much to see again the university where my two boys had studied."

We sat for a long time in silence in that room filled with flies. Then Sartori rose and we all filed out. While we were getting into the car, the Jew with the Napoleon III goatee placed his hands on Sartori's arm and humbly said in a low voice: "To think that I know the entire *Divine Comedy* by heart!" and he began declaiming:

Nel mezzo del cammin di nostra vita . . .

The car moved off and the group of black-coated Jews disappeared in a cloud of dust.

"The Romanians are not a civilized people," said Frank with contempt in his voice.

"*Ja,* they have no *Kultur,*" said Fischer, shaking his head.

"You are mistaken," I replied. "Romanians are a generous and kindly people. I am very fond of the Romanians. Among all the Latin races the Romanians alone have given evidence of a noble sense of duty in this war and a great generosity in shedding their blood for their Christ and their king. They are a simple people—a people of primitive, kindly peasants. They cannot be blamed if the upper classes, the families and the men who should be an example to them, have rotten souls, rotten minds and rotten bones. The Romanian people are not responsible for the slaughter of Jews. In Romania pogroms are organized and inspired by order or with the connivance of the authorities. The people are not at fault if corpses of Jews, quartered and hung on hooks like beef, have been on display for days in many Bucharest butcher shops for the entertainment of the Iron Guards."

"I understand and I share your feeling of revulsion," said Frank. "Thanks to heaven and, a little to me, you have not had and never will have any occasion to witness such horrors in Poland. No, *mein lieber* Malaparte, in Poland—in German Poland—you will certainly have no occasion or excuse to give vent to your lofty feeling of indignation and pity."

"I should certainly not tell you what Sartori, Pellegrini and I had said to the Jassy Chief of Police, if I had thought differently about you. It would not be prudent. You would have me locked up in a concentration camp, *nicht wahr?*"

"And Mussolini would not even file a protest," laughed Frank.

"No, he would not even file a protest. Mussolini does not wish to be bothered."

"You are aware," said Frank, emphatically, "that I am a just and straightforward man and that I do not lack a sense of humor. If you have something just and straightforward to tell me, you may come to me freely, without any fear. We are in Warsaw, not in Jassy, and I am not the Jassy Chief of Police. Have you by any chance forgotten our agreement? Don't you remember what I told you when you arrived in Poland?"

"You warned me that you would have me watched closely by the Gestapo, but that I would be entitled to think and act as a free man. You have assured me that I may open my mind to you freely and that you would do the same with me, that we would play the game fairly and according to rules."

175

"This agreement is still in force," said Frank. "Didn't I play cricket? To show you how honest I am with you, I will tell you that Himmler does not trust you. I defended you. I told him that you are not only an honest man but also a free man, that in Italy you have suffered imprisonment and persecution for your books, for the freedom of your mind, for your rashness as an *enfant terrible* and not for any lack of honesty on your part. To show him that the opinion I had formed of you was right, I reminded him that in passing through Sweden, as you often do when you go to the Finnish front, it would be easy for you to stay in that neutral country as a political refugee and that no one could stop you, but that you have not done so because you are a war correspondent wearing an Italian officer's uniform which puts you on your honor not to desert. I have also added that your books are published in England, France and America, and that in consequence you are a writer who deserves attention; and it is advisable for us to provide you with evidence that German Poland is as free as Sweden. To be completely frank with you I must add that, to be on the safe side, I have advised Himmler to have you searched when you leave Polish territory. Perhaps I should have warned you in advance that I intended to make this suggestion to Himmler, or else refrained from making it. At any rate I warn you now. And this is also cricket, *nicht wahr?*"

"It is almost cricket," I answered smiling, "but you would have done better if you had advised Himmler to have me searched when I entered Poland. To give you proof of my frankness, I want to tell you how I have spent my time while Himmler was in Warsaw." I told him about the letters, the parcels of food and the money that Polish refugees in Italy had begged me to deliver to their relatives and friends in Warsaw.

"*Ach, so! Ach, so!*" shouted Frank laughing, "and right under Himmler's nose! *Ach, wunderbar!* Right under Himmler's nose!"

"*Wunderbar! Ach, wunderbar!*" they all shouted with noisy laughter.

"I trust you consider this cricket?"

"Yes, that's cricket!" shouted Frank. "Good for you, Malaparte!" and he raised his glass saying "*Prosit!*"

"*Prosit!*" I said raising my glass.

"*Prosit!*" echoed the others.

We drank the German way, all in one gulp.

Finally we rose from the table and Frau Brigitte Frank led us to a neighboring room—a round room lighted by two large, French windows opening on the park—that once had been Marshal Pilsudski's bedroom. Little gray birds hopped about on the branches of the trees; at the crossroad the statues of Apollo and Diana were mantled with snow, and here and there German sentries walked about with rifles cradled in their arms. The reflection of the snow melted softly into the walls, furniture and thick carpets.

"It was in this room," said Frank, "precisely in the armchair in which Schmeling is now sitting, that Marshal Pilsudski died. I gave orders that nothing should be disturbed. I wanted everything to remain unchanged. I only had the bed removed." And he added in a gentle voice, "Marshal Pilsudski's memory deserves our respect, *nicht wahr?*"

He had died gazing in that armchair between the two large French windows at the trees in the park. The large niche in the wall facing the French windows where once Pilsudski's bed stood, was now occupied by a settee on which Frau Fischer and Governor-General Frank were seated. Standing by the armchair in which he had died and in which prize fighter Max Schmeling was now sitting, the old Marshal, his face streaked with bluish veins that resembled scars, his great mustaches drooping in the Sobieski manner, his brow bristling with short, black, closely cropped hair, was waiting for Schmeling to rise and give up his seat to him. Frank was right. Marshal Pilsudski's memory deserved our respect.

Frank was loudly discussing sports and champions with Schmeling.

The air was hot and smelled of tobacco and brandy. I was gradually overcome by torpor; I heard the voices of Frank and of Frau Wächter; I saw Schmeling and Governor Fischer lifting their brandy glasses to their lips, Frau Fischer turned smilingly to Frau Brigitte, and I seemed to be wrapped in a warm mist that was slowly erasing the voices and the faces. I was tired of those faces and voices. I could not bear to remain in Poland any longer. I was to start in a few days for the Smolensk front; that was cricket too—*nicht wahr?*

At that moment I imagined that Frank turned to me and invited me to spend several days in the Tatra mountains at Zakopane, the famous Polish winter resort. "Just before the war in 1914, Lenin spent several months in Zakopane," Frank said, at once laughing. I replied, or I thought I replied, that I could not, that I was due on the Smolensk front and then I found myself saying: "Why not? I could spend five or six days in Zakopane with pleasure." Suddenly Frank rose, we all rose, and Frank suggested that we take a walk through the ghetto.

We left the Belvedere. I was in the first car with Frau Fischer, Frau Wächter and Governor-General Frank. In the second car were Frau Brigitte Frank, Governor Fischer and Max Schmeling. The other guests followed in two more cars. We drove along the Aleja Ujazdowska, turned into the Svientocziska and the Marsalkowska and at the entrance to the "forbidden city," in front of the gate in the high red-brick wall that the Germans had built around the ghetto, we stopped and got out.

"See this wall?" said Frank to me. "Does it look to you like the terrible concrete wall bristling with machine guns that the British and American papers write about?" And he added, smiling, "The wretched Jews all have weak chests. At any rate this wall protects them against the wind."

In Frank's arrogant voice there was something that I seemed to recognize, something turbid—a sad and debased cruelty.

"The atrocious immorality of this wall," I replied, "doesn't lie in the fact that it prevents the Jews from leaving the ghetto but in the fact that it does *not* prevent them from entering it."

"And still," said Frank laughing, "although leaving the ghetto is punishable by death, the Jews go in and out as they please."

"Over the wall?"

"Oh, no," replied Frank, "they get out through rat holes, that they dig by night under the wall and that they cover up by day with a little earth and leaves. They crawl through those holes and go into the city to purchase food and clothing. The black market in the ghetto is carried on mainly through such holes. From time to time one of the rats is caught in a trap; they are children not over eight or nine years old. They risk their lives in a true sporting spirit. That is cricket too, *nicht wahr?*"

"They risk their lives?" I shouted.

"Basically," replied Frank, "they risk nothing else."

"And you call that cricket?"

"Certainly. Every game has its set of rules."

"In Cracow," said Frau Wächter, "my husband has built a wall of an Eastern design with elegant curves and graceful battlements. The Cracow Jews certainly have nothing to complain about. An elegant wall in the Jewish style."

They all laughed as they stamped their feet on the frozen snow.

"*Ruhe*—Silence!" called a soldier who was kneeling concealed behind a mound of snow a few feet away from us with his rifle against his shoulder. Another soldier, kneeling behind him, peered over the shoulder of his companion who suddenly fired. The bullet hit the wall just at the edge of a hole. "Missed!" remarked the soldier gaily, slipping another cartridge into the barrel.

Frank walked over to the two soldiers and asked them what they were firing at.

"At a rat," they replied laughing loudly.

"At a rat? *Ach, so!*" said Frank kneeling and looking over the men's shoulders.

We also came closer, and the ladies laughed and squealed lifting their skirts up to their knees as women do when they hear anything about mice.

"Where is it? Where is the rat?" asked Frau Brigitte Frank.

"It is in the trap," said Frank laughing.

"*Achtung!* Look out!" said the soldier aiming. A black tuft of tangled hair popped out of the hole dug under the wall; then two hands appeared and rested on the snow.

It was a child.

Another shot and again the bullet missed its mark by a few inches. The child's head disappeared.

"Hand me the rifle," said Frank in an impatient voice. "You don't know how to handle it." He grabbed the rifle out of the soldier's hands and took aim.

It snowed silently.

179

PART THREE

THE DOGS

VIII

The Winter Night

AMONG THE MINK, ermine and squirrel skins, among the skins of blue, silver and platinum foxes, a horrible and pitiful dog skin was displayed in the shop window of the Tartar furrier. It was a fine black and white setter with long silky hair, its eye sockets empty, its ears flattened, its muzzle crushed. A price tag was propped against one of its ears, "An English thoroughbred setter skin, six hundred Finnish marks." We stopped in front of the window. A subtle feeling of horror overcame me.

"Haven't you ever seen gloves made of dog skin? Colonel Lukander, that Finnish colonel whom we met on the Leningrad front had a pair," said Count Augustin de Foxa, the Spanish Minister in Helsinki. "I would like to buy a pair to take to Madrid. I would tell everybody that they were made of dog skin. Gloves of spaniel's skin are smooth and soft, and gloves of pointer's skin are coarser. For rainy days I would like a pair of rough terrier gloves. Up here the women wear caps and muffs made out of dog skin," de Foxa laughed, looking slyly at me. "Dog skin is becoming to feminine beauty," he added.

"Dogs are generous," I said.

It was the end of March 1942. We were walking along a street toward the Esplanade and, having turned into the Esplanade near the Savoy, we went down toward the square that faced the harbor where the neoclassical building occupied by the Swedish Legation stood and, close to it, designed in the style of Engel, was the palace of the President of the Finnish republic. The icy cold felt as though we were walking on the edge of a razor. A little way beyond the Tartar furrier's window, on the corner, we passed an undertaking establishment. The coffins—some painted white, some glistening black with huge silver nails, some mahogany color—

were attractively displayed inside. In the window gleamed a single silver coffin for a child.

"I love this," said de Foxa stopping to look at the coffins.

Like all good Spaniards, de Foxa is cruel and funereal. He feels respect only for the soul. Flesh, blood, the suffering of miserable human bodies, their infirmities and wounds—leave him indifferent. He enjoys talking about death, a passing of a funeral procession gladdens him like a feast, he lingers to look at coffins displayed in shop windows; he relishes talking about sores, tumors and monsters. But he is afraid of ghosts; one subject he never talks about is ghosts. He is an intelligent, highly cultured and witty man. Perhaps he is too witty to be truly intelligent. He knows Italy well. He knows most of my friends in Florence and Rome, and I even suspect that at one time we were in love with the same woman without knowing about one another.

He spent some years in Italy as a Secretary of the Spanish Embassy at the Quirinal, until he was expelled for making some witty remarks at the expense of Countess Edda Ciano on the golf links of Acquasanta and in his reports to Serrano Suñer. "Just think, I had been living three years in Rome," he said to me one day, "and I did not know that Countess Edda Ciano was Mussolini's daughter."

While we walked down the Esplanade, Augustin de Foxa told me that one evening in Madrid he and several of his friends had been to see the tombs opened in the ancient cemetery of St. Sebastian. It happened in 1934 when Spain was a republic. In accordance with the needs for new city-planning in Madrid, the Republican government had decided to have the ancient cemetery demolished. When de Foxa and his friends, among whom were several young Madrid authors—Cesare Gonzalo Ruano, Carlos Miralles, Agostin Vignola and Luis Escobar—reached the cemetery, night had fallen and many tombs had already been opened and emptied. The dead could be seen lying in the opened coffins: matadors in their gala attire, generals in full uniform, priests, boys, well-to-do civilians, girls, noblewomen, children. One young woman had been buried with a bottle of perfume clutched in her hand. To her, the poet Luis Escobar later dedicated a poem: "To a very beautiful woman who was called Maria Concepcion Elola." Later Agostin Vignola wrote an ode to a poor sailor who had died by chance in Madrid and had been buried far away from his sea in that gloomy churchyard. De Foxa and his friends, slightly drunk, knelt before the coffin of the sailor and intoned prayers for the dead. On the breast of the corpse, Carlos Miralles placed a sheet of paper on which he had drawn in pencil a boat, a fish and a few sea waves. They all crossed themselves, saying: "In the name of the North, of the South, of the East and of the West."

On the tomb of a student, named Novillo, there was an inscription half effaced by the passage of time, "God has interrupted his studies to teach him the truth."

In a coffin studded with rich silver nails lay the mummified corpse of a young French nobleman, Count de la Martinière, who with a group of French Legitimists had emigrated to Spain in 1830 after the fall of Charles X. Cesare Gonzalo Ruano bowed before Count de la Martinière and said, "I greet you, as an honest French nobleman, loyal and faithful to your legitimate sovereign, and in the presence of your spirit I raise a cry that can no longer come from your lips, a cry that will make your bones tremble, 'Long live the King!'"

A Republican civilian guard, who was in the churchyard, caught Cesare Gonzalo Ruano by the arm and dragged him to prison.

De Foxa, gesticulating as was his custom, talked in a loud voice. "Augustin," I said, "speak softly—the ghosts are listening to you."

"Ghosts?" whispered de Foxa, turning pale and gazing around. The houses, the trees, the statues, the benches in the Esplanade garden seemed to shimmer in the ghostly, cold light that the reflection of snow spread in the evenings of the North. A few drunken soldiers were arguing with a girl on the corner of the Mikonkatu. A policeman walked back and forth on the sidewalk before the Hotel Kämp. Above Mannerheim Street, above the roofs the sky was spread white, uncreased, without a tremor, like the sky in an old, faded photograph. The huge iron letters of the Klubbi cigarette advertisement on the roof of Uosisuoma Palace stood out black against the white sky like the skeleton of a huge insect. The glass tower of the Stockmann Palace and the skyscraper of the Torni Hotel swayed in the livid air.

Nothing will ever remind me so much of the Finnish winter as Linguaphone records. Whenever I see among the advertisements of a newspaper, "Learn foreign languages by the Linguaphone method," whenever I chance to read those two magic words, *Linguaphone Institute,* I think of the Finnish winter, the ghostly forests and the frozen lakes of Finland.

Whenever I happen to hear the Linguaphone records mentioned, I close my eyes and see my friend Jaakko Leppo, thickset and fat, laced in the uniform of a Finnish captain; I see his round, pale face with high cheekbones, his small suspicious eyes, those slanting eyes of his, full of a cold gray light. I see my friend Jaakko Leppo, a glass in his hand, sitting in front of a gramophone in the library of his house in Helsinki and clustered around him, also with glasses in their hands, Liisi Leppo, Madame and Minister P——, Count Augustin de Foxa, Titu Michailescu, Mario Orano, all listening to the raucous voice of the gramophone. I see Jaakko Leppo now and again raising his glass full of brandy, saying, *"Maljanne—*Your health!" . . .

It was two in the morning, and we had just finished our second or third supper. Sitting in the library in front of the huge window-pane carved in the ghostly sky, we were watching Helsinki slowly sinking into the snow. From that white and silent derelict protruded the columns of the Palace of Parliament emerging like the masts of a ship—the smooth front of the Post Office—and, farther away against the background of the trees on the Esplanade and in Brunnsparken—the towers of glass and concrete of the Stockmann and the Torni skyscrapers.

The thermometer hanging outside the window was down to forty-nine degrees below zero. "Forty-nine degrees below zero is Finland's Parthenon," said de Foxa. From time to time Jaakko Leppo raised his glass full of brandy and said, *Maljanne.* I was just back from the Leningrad front. For a fortnight I had done nothing but say *Maljanne* everywhere, in the depths of the Karelian forests, in the *korsus* hewn in the ice, in the trenches, in the *lottalas,* on the tracks of the *Kannas* * each time my sled met another sled—everywhere; I did nothing for a fortnight but raise my glass and say *Maljanne.*

* *Kanna*—An isthmus.

On the Viipuri train I had spent an entire night saying *Maljanne* with the superintendent of railways of the Viipuri district, who had come to call on Jaakko Leppo in our compartment. He was a thick-set, Herculean man, with a pale, swollen face. He removed his heavy sheepskin coat and emerged in a dress suit. Below his spotless white tie the neck of a bottle protruded between his starched shirt and his vest. He had been to his son's wedding. The nuptial feast had lasted for three days, and he was going back to Viipuri, to his engines, his trains and his office, which had been excavated from the wreckage of the station that Soviet mines had destroyed.

"It's odd," he said to me, "today I have drunk a great deal and I am not even tipsy." In my opinion he was very drunk on very little liquor. After a while he drew the bottle from his bosom, a couple of glasses from his pocket, filled them with brandy to the brim, and said "*Maljanne.*"

I said "*Maljanne,*" and we spent the night saying *Maljanne* and gazing at each other in silence. Now and again he began talking to me in Latin—the only language in which we could understand each other—and pointing at the black, hard, ghostly, endless forest that runs along the railway, he said: "*Semper domestica silva,*" and he added, "*Maljanne.*" Then he roused Jaako Leppo with: "*Somno vinoque sepultum,*" from his couch and placing a glass in his hand, he said "*Maljanne.*" Jaakko Leppo said "*Maljanne,*" emptied the glass in one gulp without opening his eyes and fell asleep again. Thus we sat until we reached Viipuri and separated saying "*Vale!*—Farewell!" to one another amid the ruins of the station.

For a fortnight I had done nothing but say *Maljanne* in every *korsu* and every *lottala* in the *Kannas* and Eastern Karelia. I had said *Maljanne* in Viipuri with Lieutenant Svartström and the other officers of his company. I had said *Maljanne* in Terioki, Alexandrovska, in Taippala, in Raikkola, on the shores of Lake Ladoga with the officers of Colonel Merikallio's rangers; I had said *Maljanne* in the trenches in front of Leningrad with the artillery officers of Colonel Lukander. I had said *Maljanne* in the *tepidarium* of the *sauna*, the Finnish national bath; after running out of the *calidarium* where the heat rises to seventy-six degrees Centigrade—and rolling naked in the snow on the edge of the forest in a cold of forty-four degrees below zero. I had said *Maljanne* in the house of the Russian painter Repin in the suburbs of Leningrad, and while gazing at the great painter's tomb amid the trees in the garden I could see yonder, at the end of the road, the first houses of Leningrad beneath the huge clouds of smoke hovering above the city.

Until the uneasy hour when the Finns grow sad, they gaze into each other's faces with a challenging air, bite their underlips and drink in silence without saying *Maljanne,* as if trying to repress a deep wrath within their breasts. I meant to slip away unnoticed, and so did de Foxa, but Minister P—— had caught him by the arm and was saying, "My dear Minister, you know Mr. Ivalo, don't you?" Ivalo was the Permanent Under-Secretary at the Foreign Office.

"He is among my dearest friends," replied de Foxa in a conciliatory tone. "He is a man of uncommon intelligence, and Madame Ivalo is a most gracious lady."

"I did not ask you whether you knew Madame Ivalo," said Minister P——, fixing de Foxa with his small, suspicious eyes. "I wanted to know whether you knew Mr. Ivalo."

"Yes, I know him very well," replied de Foxa, his eyes beseeching me not to desert him.

"Do you know what he has told me about Spain and Finland? I met him tonight in the Kämp Bar. He was with Minister Hakkarainen. You are acquainted with Minister Hakkarainen, are you not?"

"Minister Hakkarainen is a charming man," replied de Foxa, his eyes meantime searching for Titu Michailescu.

"Do you know, Ivalo asked me whether I knew the difference between Spain and Finland?"

"It can be found on the thermometer," prudently replied de Foxa.

"Why on the thermometer? No, it cannot be found on the thermometer," said Minister P—— irritably. "The difference is that Spain is a sympathizer but not a belligerent, while Finland is a belligerent but not a sympathizer."

"Ha, ha, ha, very funny indeed," said de Foxa laughing.

"Why are you laughing?" asked Minister P—— in a suspicious voice.

Jaakko Leppo was sitting motionless on the piano stool, like a Tartar in his saddle, staring at de Foxa with his narrow, slanting eyes, consumed by dark jealousy. He was furious because Minister P—— had not told him what he had told the Minister of Spain.

Then struck the dangerous hour when the Finns sulk with lowered heads, drink on their own without saying *Maljanne* as if they were alone and drinking in secret, and when they talk aloud in Finnish to themselves. Mario Orano had disappeared. He had escaped on tiptoe without being noticed by anyone, although I had kept my eyes on him and had closely followed his every move. But Orano had been living in Finland for two or three years, and he had mastered the difficult art of slipping away mysteriously from a Finnish house just as the dangerous hour is about to strike. I would also have liked to slip away quietly, but every time I managed to get to the door, I felt something cold piercing my back and, turning, I met the gloomy eyes of Jaakko Leppo who was sitting on the piano stool like a Tartar in his saddle.

"Let's go," I said to de Foxa clutching his arm, but just then, Minister P—— approached de Foxa and in a strange voice asked, "Is it true, my dear Minister, that you have told Mrs. McClintock that she wears feathers, I don't remember where?" De Foxa fenced and said that it wasn't true, but Minister P—— paled and said, "What's that? You deny it?"

I said to de Foxa: "Don't deny it! For heaven's sake, don't deny it!"

And Minister P—— persisted, becoming paler and paler, "Do you deny it? Confess that you dare not repeat what you said to Mrs. McClintock."

I said to de Foxa: "For heaven's sake, repeat to him what you said to Helen McClintock."

De Foxa began to recount that one night he had been a guest at the house of the United States Minister, Mr. Arthur Schoenfeld, along with Helen McClintock and Robert Mills McClintock, Secretary of the United States Legation; M. Hubert Guerin, Minister of Vichy France, and Madame Guerin had joined them later. Madame Guerin had happened to ask Helen McClintock if her ancestry was as Spanish as her looks and her accent seemed to suggest. Helen McClintock, who is a Spaniard from Chile, forgetting that the Spanish Minister was present, had replied, "Unfortunately, yes."

"Ha, ha! That's very amusing, isn't it?" shouted Minister P——
slapping de Foxa on the back.

"Wait, the story is not finished," I said impatiently.

De Foxa went on to say that he had replied to Mrs. McClintock,
"My dear Helen, when one is from South America, one is not
Spanish. One wears feathers on the head."

"Ha, ha, ha! Very amusing!" shouted Minister P—— and, turning
to Madame P——, he said, "Did you understand, dear? In South
America, Spaniards wear feathers on their heads!"

I whispered to de Foxa, "Let's go, for heaven's sake!"

But the pathetic hour had struck when Finns become sentimental,
begin to sigh deeply into their empty glasses and gaze at one
another with tearful eyes. Just as de Foxa and I approached Liisi
Leppo who was languidly sprawling in an armchair, to beseech her
in pleading tones to excuse us, Jaakko Leppo rose and said loudly,
"I want you to listen to some records." He added proudly, "I have
a gramophone."

He went to the gramophone, chose a record out of a leather al-
bum, placed the needle and gazed round with a severe look. We
all waited in silence.

"This is a Chinese record," he said.

It was a Linguaphone record. A nasal voice gave us a long lesson
in Chinese pronunciation, to which we listened in complete silence.

Then Jaakko Leppo changed the record, wound up the machine
and announced, "This record is in Hindustani."

A lesson in Hindustani pronunciation followed to which we listened in deep silence.

Then came several lessons in Turkish grammar, then a string
of lessons in Arabic pronunciation and, finally, five lessons in Jap-
anese grammar and pronunciation. We all kept silent as we listened.
"Finally," announced Jaakko Leppo, turning the handle of the
gramophone, "I shall let you listen to a wonderful record."

This was a lesson in French pronunciation; a teacher of the Linguaphone Institute declaimed Lamartine's "Le Lac" in a nasal voice.
We all listened keeping absolutely silent. When the nasal voice
stopped, Jaakko Leppo gazed around with emotion and said, "My
wife has learnt this record by heart. Do you mind, dear?"

Liisi Leppo rose, slowly crossed the room, took a position by the gramophone, threw back her head, raised her arms and keeping her eyes on the ceiling, recited Lamartine's "Le Lac"—all of Lamartine's "Le Lac"—with the same enunciation, in the same nasal voice as the Linguaphone Institute teacher.

"It's wonderful, isn't it?" said Jaakko Leppo in a voice filled with emotion.

It was five in the morning. I cannot remember what else happened before de Foxa and I found ourselves in the street. It was deathly cold. The night was clear, the snow shone gently with a delicate silver glitter. When we reached my hotel, de Foxa shook my hand and said, "*Maljanne.*"

I replied, "*Maljanne.*"

The Swedish Minister, Westmann, was waiting for us in his library, sitting in front of the window. The silvery reflection of snow in the night melted into the dimness of the library—a warm dimness the color of leather, through which the book-bindings sent slight golden ripples. The light was turned on suddenly, outlining the tall, slim figure of Minister Westmann, clean and sharp as an engraved design on old Swedish silver. His movements that had been frozen in the air by the silent outburst of light, slowly melted and faded away, and his small head, his straight, lean shoulders for a moment struck my eyes with the cold immobility of the marble busts of Swedish sovereigns that were ranged along the high oaken bookshelves. His silver hair warmed the dead glow of the marble, and an ironical smile—the restless shadow of a smile, crept over his grave and gentle face.

In the warm dining room the light of two large, silver candelabra standing in the center of the table, delicate and warm, melted into the reflection of the ice-bound sea and of the snow-covered square, breaking on the frosty windowpanes with a harsh violence. Although the pink glow of the candles tinged the white Flemish linen of the tablecloth with a flesh color, and, by veiling the cold bareness of Marieberg and Rörstrand china, warmed the icy splendor of Orefors glass and the glitter of old Copenhagen silver, something ghostly lingered in the air and something ironical as well, if one can speak of irony in connection with ghosts and ghostly things.

As if the subtle witchcraft of the northern night, penetrating the room with the gloomy reflection of the nocturnal snow, held us tied in its charm, something ghostly appeared in our faces, in the restless, wandering glances, in the very words we were uttering.

De Foxa sat by the window mirroring in his face the maze of blue veins that streaks the white flesh of nocturnal snow. Perhaps to overcome in himself the spell of the northern night, he spoke about the sun in Spain, about the colors, the smells, the sounds, the flavoring of Spain, about Andalusian sunlit days and starry nights, about the clean thin wind of the Castilian highlands, about the blue sky falling like a stone after the death of the bull. Westmann, his eyes half closed, listened to him as if he could sniff the scents of the Spanish soil through the glitter of the snow. as if he could hear the sounds and fleshy voices of Spanish streets and Spanish houses coming from beyond the ice-bound sea, as if he could gaze on the landscapes, the portraits, the still-life pictures flooded with warm deep color, the street scenes, the arena and family scenes, the dances, the processions, the idyls, the funerals, the triumphs that de Foxa was re-creating in his resonant voice.

Westmann spent several years in Madrid as the Swedish Minister, and had been appointed Minister in Helsinki only a few months before to conduct important diplomatic negotiations. He was to go back to Madrid and resume his post as Swedish Minister to Spain as soon as he had completed his temporary mission in Finland. He loved Spain with a repressed violence that was sensuous as well as romantic. He listened that evening to de Foxa with a mixture of modesty, jealousy and rancor, as an unhappy lover listens to a lucky rival talking about the woman he loves. "I am the husband, I am not your rival. Spain is my wife and you are her lover," said de Foxa to him. "Alas!" sighed Westmann in reply. But in his feeling for Spain there was that indefinite tinge of sensuous passion and hidden repugnance that always goes with the Northerner's love for Mediterranean lands—the same sensuous repugnance that is portrayed in the faces of the onlookers in the old *Triumphs of Death,* where the sight of the green corpses, exhumed and lying in the sun like dead lizards amid fleshy, strongly scented flowers, has aroused in them a reverent horror and a sensuous enjoyment that at the same time attracts and repulses them.

189

"Spain," said de Foxa, "is a sensuous and funereal land, but not a land of ghosts. The home of the ghosts is the North. In the streets of Spanish towns you meet corpses, but not ghosts." He talked about that odor of death that pervades all of Spanish art and literature, about certain deathlike landscapes of Goya, about El Greco's living corpses, about the putrefying countenances of Spanish kings and grandees that Velasquez painted in the background of his proud golden architecture, about the velvet and purple cloth in the green and gilded dimness of royal palaces, churches and convents.

"Even in Spain," said Westmann, "it is not unusual to meet ghosts. I like Spanish ghosts very much. They are very nice and well behaved."

"They are not ghosts," said de Foxa, "they are corpses. They are not bodiless figures, they are made of flesh and blood. They eat, drink, love, laugh as if they were alive. But they are dead bodies. They do not walk at night as ghosts do, but in the middle of the day, in full sunshine. Spain is so alive because of those corpses that can be met in the streets, that sit in cafés, that kneel down to pray in dark churches, that move slowly and silently with their black eyes shining in their green faces, through the merry bustle of the towns and villages on feast and market days, among the living people who laugh, love, drink and sing. The ones you call ghosts are not Spanish; they are alien. They come from afar, no one knows from where, and only if you summon them by name or call them forth with a magic word."

"Do you believe in magic words?" asked Westmann smiling.

"Every good Spaniard believes in magic words."

"Do you know any?" asked Westmann.

"I know many, but one above all others is endowed with the supernatural power of evoking ghosts."

"Please say it, even if you only whisper it."

"I dare not. I am afraid," said de Foxa becoming slightly pale. "It is the most frightful and dangerous word in the Castilian language. No true Spaniard dares to utter it. Let a corpse be brought here and placed on this table, and I will not bat an eye. But don't call a ghost; don't open a door to him. I would die of fright."

"Tell us at least what the word means," said Westmann.

"It is one of the many names given to snakes."

"Snakes have gentle names," said Westmann. "In Shakespeare's play, Antony calls Cleopatra by the sweet name of a snake."

"Ah!" shouted de Foxa growing white in the face.

"What is the matter? Is that the word that you dare not utter? Yet it has the sweetness of honey on Antony's lips. Cleopatra never had a gentler name. Wait—" went on Westmann with complacent cruelty, "I think I can recall precisely the word that Shakespeare puts in Antony's mouth—"

"Be silent, please!" shouted de Foxa.

"If my memory does not fail me," pursued Westmann with a cruel smile, "Antony calls Cleopatra—"

"For God's sake, be silent!" shouted de Foxa. "Don't speak that word aloud. It is a terrible word that must be spoken thus in a low voice . . ." and scarcely moving his lips, he whispered, *"Culebra!"*

"Ah, 'adder!'" said Westmann laughing. "And that's enough to frighten you? It is a word like any other, and to me is nothing terrible or mysterious. If I am not wrong," he added raising his eyes to the ceiling as if searching his memory, "the word that Shakespeare used is 'snake,' and it does not sound so sweet as the Spanish word *culebra. O mi culebra del antiquo Nilo.*—O my snake of the ancient Nile."

"Please, don't repeat it," said de Foxa. "It is an ill-omened word. One of us, or someone who is near to us will die tonight."

At that moment the door flew open and a glorious salmon from Lake Inari was placed on the table; its rosy color, tender and lively, flashed through the deep cracks in its skin, covered with silvery scales of delicate green and bluish hues, resembling as de Foxa said, the silks in which the statues of the Blessed Virgin are clothed in the churches of Spanish villages. The salmon's head rested on a pillow of herbs fine as women's hair—those transparent weeds that grow in the rivers and lakes of Finland. It looked like the head of a sleeping fish in a still-life painting by Bracque. The taste of that salmon was like a faraway memory of waters, woods and clouds. To me it was like a memory of Lake Inari on a summer night lighted by the pale Arctic sun, tender and childish under a green sky. The rosy color shining through the silvery scales of the salmon was the very color of clouds when the evening sun rests on the edge of the horizon, like an orange on a window sill, and a gentle wind rustles through the leaves of the trees, over the clear water and the grassy shores, as it glides lightly above the rivers, lakes and vast forests of Lapland. It was the same rosy color, tender and lively, that shines through the silvery scales covering Lake Inari when the sun, in the depths of the Arctic night, wanders over a green sky streaked with slender blue veins.

"It is a pity," said de Foxa laughing, "that the USSR flags are not salmon pink in color!"

"Thank God," I replied, "that the USSR flags are red and not salmon pink. Who knows what would happen to poor Europe if the USSR flags had the same pink color as that of a salmon and of the *dessous de femme.*"

"Everything fades in Europe," remarked Westmann. "Very likely, we are moving toward a Middle Age, salmon pink in color."

"I often ask myself," said de Foxa, "what the function of the intellectuals will be in a new medieval period. I bet they would take advantage of the opportunity to try again to save European civilization."

"Intellectuals are incorrigible," said Westmann.

"Even the old Monte Cassino abbot," I said, "sometimes asks himself the same question." I told them that Count Gavronski, the Polish diplomat who is married to Luciana Frassati, the daughter of Senator Frassati, formerly Italian Ambassador in Berlin, a refugee in Rome since Poland had been occupied by the Germans, from time to time spends a few weeks in the guest house of the Monte Cassino Abbey. Old Archbishop Dom Gregory Diamare, the abbot, talking one day to Gavronski about the barbarism into which Europe was in danger of sinking through war, said that during the darkest Middle Ages the monks of Monte Cassino had saved Western civilization by copying the ancient and precious Greek and Latin manuscripts by hand. "What should we do today to save European culture?" concluded the venerable abbot. "Have the same manuscripts copied on typewriters by your monks," replied Gavronski.

After the clear Moselle wine that smelled of hay in the rain—the Moselle's delicate, clear rosy hue, glistening among the silvery scales of the salmon, imparted a taste of the Lake Inari countryside under the nocturnal sun—the red wine of Burgundy with its bloodlike reflections sparkled in our glasses. A side of Karelian pork on a large silver tray in the center of the table filled the room with the warm smell of the oven. After the transparent glitter of the Moselle wine and of the rose-tinted salmon bringing thoughts of the silvery current of the Juutuanjoki and of the pink clouds in the green sky of Lapland, the red Burgundy and the pork of Karelia, just taken from the oven and scented with pine wood, brought to us the memory of a land warmed by the sun.

No wine is so earthy as the red wine of Burgundy that in the warm glow of the candlelight and in the white reflection of the snow was the color of soil, the crimson and gold hue of the Côte d'Or hills at sunset. The bouquet was strong, scented with grass and leaves like a summer evening in Burgundy. No wine is so congenial with the evening dusk or so partial to the night as the wine of Nuits Saint Georges. Even its name, deep and flashing like a summer evening, belongs to the night. It shines bloodlike on the threshold of the night as the glow of sunset on the crystal edge of the horizon. It kindles glints of red and blue in the crimson-colored earth, in the grass and in the leaves still warm with the taste and the aroma of the dying day. Wild beasts, when night steals on them, burrow deep into the earth; the wild boar crashes into the thicket amid a hurried crackling of twigs; the short-flighted pheasant swims silently into the shadows that are already floating above the woods and the glades; the nimble hare glides along the first moonbeam as if drawn by a taut silver string. That is the hour for Burgundy wine. At that hour, during the winter nights, in that room alight with the ebony reflection of snow, the deep odor of the Nuits Saint Georges brought forth memories of summer evenings in Burgundy, of nights asleep on the soil still warm with the sun.

De Foxa and I looked at each other smiling as a warm flush rose in our faces. We looked smiling at one another as if those unexpected memories of the soil were freeing us from the sad spell of the northern night. We were lost in that desert of snow and ice, in that watery land of a hundred thousand lakes, in that sweet stern Finland where the smell of the sea penetrates the inmost depths of the most remote forests of Karelia and Lapland, where the glitter of water may be traced in the blue and gray eyes of man and beast and in the slow and distracted manner, not unlike the movements of swimmers, with which people walk along streets ablaze with the white fire of the snow, or wander in the summer night through parks, raising their eyes to the blue-green, watery glow over the roofs in the endless day without dawn or sunset of the white northern summer. The unexpected memories of the soil made us feel earthy deep down within our bones, and we looked at one another smiling, as if we had escaped from a shipwreck.

"*Skoll!*" said de Foxa, deeply moved, and raised his glass, breaking the rigid Swedish convention that reserves for the host the right to invite his guests to drink with the traditional word of good health.

"I never say *skoll,* when I raise my glass," remarked Westmann mischievously, as if to excuse the gaucherie de Foxa had committed. "There is a character in one of Arthur Reid's plays who says: 'London is full of people, who have just come back from Sweden, drinking *skoll* and saying *snap* at each other.' I too drink *skoll* and say *snap.*"

"*Snap* it shall be!" said de Foxa whom the Burgundy wine had made gay and almost childishly intoxicated.

"*Snap!*" said Westmann smiling, and I followed his example and said, "*Snap!*"

"How comfortable it is to belong to a neutral country, isn't it?" said de Foxa turning to Westmann. "One may drink without wishing for victories or defeats. *Snap* for the peace of Europe."

"*Skoll!*" said Westmann.

"Why? Why do you say *skoll?*" asked de Foxa.

"I like to make mistakes occasionally," replied Westmann with an ironical smile.

"I enjoy saying *snap,*" said de Foxa raising his glass—"*Snap* for Germany and *snap* for England!"

"*Snap* for Germany," said Westmann with an amiable solemnity, "and *skoll* for England."

"You are right," said de Foxa, "*skoll* for England!"

I too raised my glass and said *snap* for Germany and *skoll* for England.

"Instead of saying *snap,* you should say *skoll* for Germany," said de Foxa to me. "Germany is Italy's ally."

"Personally," I replied, "I am not Germany's ally. The war Italy is waging is Mussolini's personal war and I am not Mussolini. No Italian is Mussolini. *Snap* for Mussolini and Hitler!"

"*Snap* for Mussolini and Hitler!" repeated de Foxa.

"And *snap* for France," I said.

De Foxa hesitated for an instant then said, "*Snap* for France, too!" and burst into laughter. Turning to Westmann he went on, "Do you know the story of Malaparte's cricket match in Poland against Governor-General Frank?" He told him about my agreement with Frank and about my revelation to him that during Himmler's stay in Warsaw, I had distributed letters and money that Polish refugees in Italy had asked me to deliver to their relatives and friends in Poland.

"And Frank did not betray you?" asked Westmann.

"No," I replied, "he did not."

"Your encounter with Frank is truly extraordinary," said Westmann. "He might have handed you over to the Gestapo. I must admit that he behaved surprisingly well toward you."

"I was certain that he would not betray me," I said. "What may appear reckless about my frankness was merely a wise precaution. By showing that I considered him a gentleman, I made Frank my accomplice. Nevertheless, later he tried to avenge himself for my frankness by making me pay dearly for his forced complicity. I told him that a few weeks after I had left Warsaw, Frank lodged violent protests with the Italian government about some articles of mine about Poland, charging me with adopting the Polish viewpoint. Frank not only demanded that I publicly refute what I had written, but that I also send him a written apology. By then I was safely in Finland, and of course, my answer to him was *snap!*"

"In your place," said de Foxa, "I would have said *merde.*"

"That's a word that sometimes is very difficult to pronounce," remarked Westmann smiling.

"Do you consider me incapable of answering a German in the way Cambronne answered an Englishman at Waterloo?" said de Foxa with dignity and, turning to me, added, "Would you invite me to supper at the Royal, if I reply *merde* to a German?"

"For God's sake, Augustin, don't forget that you are the Minister of Spain."

"Excellent! I shall reply *merde,* in the name of Spain."

"For goodness' sake, Augustin, can't you see that this one word may drag the Spanish people into a war."

"The Spanish people have waged war for much less."

"Wait at least until Hitler gets to Waterloo," said Westmann. "Unfortunately, so far he has only reached Austerlitz."

"No, I cannot wait, I shall be the Cambronne of Austerlitz."

Luckily just then there was placed on the table a tray laden with those soft pastries of a most delicate flavor, that even the Sisters of the Sacred Heart call by the Voltairian name, *pets de nonne.**

"Do these *pets de nonne* remind you of anything?" asked Westmann of de Foxa.

"They remind me of Spain," replied de Foxa in a grave voice. "Spain is full of convents and of *pets de nonne.* As a Roman Catholic and a Spaniard I appreciate the delicate way in which you have reminded me of my country."

"I was in no way alluding to Spain or to the Catholic religion," said Westmann with a kindly laugh. "These convent delicacies remind me of my childhood. Do they remind you of your childhood? All children love them. At home, in Sweden, where there are no convents, we still have *pets de nonne.* Don't they make you feel young?"

"Your way of rejuvenating your guests is charming," said de Foxa. "This excellent food makes me think of the immortal youth of Spain. As a man I am, unfortunately, no longer a child; but as a Spaniard I am young and immortal. Too bad that one can be young and decayed at the same time. The Latin peoples are decayed." He became silent and lowered his head onto his chest, but suddenly he raised it again and said in a proud voice: "But it is a noble decay. Do you know what one of our friends at the United States Legation told me the other day? We were talking about war, about France, Italy and Spain, and I was telling him that the Latin peoples are decayed. 'They may well be decayed,' he said to me, 'but it is a fine odor.'"

"Yes, it is a fine odor," said Westmann.

* *Pets de nonne*—Nun's fritters or apple-fritters.

"I thank you with all my heart for the love you have for Spain," said de Foxa, leaning across the table—across the icy glitter of the glasses—and smiling at Westmann. "But which Spain do you love: the Spain of God or of man?"

"Naturally, the Spain of man," replied Westmann.

Count de Foxa looked at Westmann with deep disappointment. "You too?" he said. "The men from the North only care for what is human in Spain, and yet all that is young and immortal in Spain belongs to God. One has to be a Roman Catholic to understand and love Spain, real Spain, the Spain that belongs to God, because God is a Catholic and a Spaniard."

"I am Protestant," said Westmann, "and I would be very much surprised if God were a Catholic, but I am prepared to believe that He is a Spaniard."

"If God exists, He is Spaniard. This is not blasphemy—it is a profession of faith."

"In a few months, when I go back to my post of Swedish Minister in Madrid," said Westmann with his slightly ironical grace, "I promise you, my dear de Foxa, to take a little more interest in the Spain of God and a little less in the Spain of man."

"I hope," said de Foxa, "that the Spanish God will interest you more than the golf links in Puerto de Hierre." He told us how a young English diplomat, at the end of the Civil War, as soon as the British Embassy to Franco's government moved to Madrid, made it his concern to inquire first of all whether it was true that the fifth hole of the Puerto de Hierre links had been damaged by a Fascist shell.

"And was it true?" Westmann asked in an uneasy voice.

"No, thank the Lord. The fifth hole was undamaged," replied de Foxa. "Luckily it was a piece of biased news issued by an anti-Fascist agency."

"That's a relief," exclaimed Westmann with a sigh. "I confess that you made me hold my breath. In modern civilization a golf hole is unfortunately as important as a Gothic cathedral."

"Let us beseech the Lord that at least golf holes may be spared in this war," said de Foxa.

Actually de Foxa cared nothing for golf holes or for Gothic cathedrals. He was a devout Catholic, but in the Spanish way—that is to say he considered religious problems as his personal problems and maintained toward the Church and even toward the problems of Catholic conscience, a freedom of mind—the famous Spanish insolence—that has nothing in common with the Voltairian freedom of mind. His attitude toward all other problems, political, social or artistic, was the same. He was a Falangist, but in the same way that a Spaniard is a communist or an anarchist—namely, in a Catholic way. De Foxa described it as "having his back to the wall." Every Spaniard is a free man, but he has his back against a wall— the high, smooth, impassable Catholic wall, the theological wall, the wall of old Spain, the very wall against which the firing squads —anarchist, Republican, communist, monarchist or fascist—execute their enemies, the wall in front of which *autos-da-fé* are staged and theological dialogues of *autos-sacramentales* are heard.

The fact that he represented Franco's Spain in Finland—Hubert Guerin, the Minister of Pétain's France, called de Foxa "The Minister of Vichy Spain"—did not prevent him from laughing with contempt at Franco and his revolution. De Foxa had belonged to that youthful generation of Spaniards who had tried to build a feudal and Catholic foundation for communism, or, as he put it, "to create a theology for Leninism," to reconcile the old Catholic and traditional Spain with the young Europe of the workers. Now he laughed at the generous delusions of his generation and at the failure of that tragic and ludicrous attempt.

At times, when he spoke about the Spanish Civil War, I thought that the voluntary prompting of his conscience induced him to resist his own reasoning and to acknowledge the legitimacy and the truth of the political, moral and intellectual position of Franco's opponents—as on the evening when he spoke about Azana, the President of the Spanish Republic, and about his "secret diary" in which, day by day, and hour by hour, Azana had recorded and commented on the most minute and, apparently, the most trivial details of the revolution and of the Civil War—the color of the sky at a certain hour on a certain day, the musical note of a fountain, the rustling of the wind among the leaves of trees, the echo of a rifle firing in a neighboring street, the paleness, the arrogance, the pity, the fear, the cynicism, the treachery, the hypocrisy and the selfishness of bishops, generals, politicians, courtiers, gentlemen, syndicalist leaders, grandees, anarchists, and others who called on him to offer advice, to make requests and offers of deals, to sell themselves and to betray. Naturally Azana's "secret diary" had not been published, but neither had it been destroyed. De Foxa had read it and he described it as an extraordinary document in which Azana appears peculiarly detached from the events and people, a solitary man living in a pure and abstract atmosphere. At other times de Foxa appeared to be strangely uncertain about the simplest aspects of a problem that he seemed to have settled long before in the irrevocable depth of his Catholic conscience—as on that day in Beli Ostrov in front of Leningrad.

A few days earlier, on Good Friday, I had been with de Foxa in a Beli Ostrov trench before Leningrad. About five hundred yards away, behind the barbed-wire entanglements, behind the twin lines of Soviet trenches and casemates, two Russian soldiers were openly walking through the snow, along the edge of a wood, carrying a pine log on their shoulders. They walked in step swinging their arms with a certain air of defiance. They were tall Siberians, with their large gray Astrakhan fur caps on their heads, sand-colored coats that reached the heels of their boots, and rifles slung over their shoulders. They seemed to be magnified into giants by the dazzling reflection of the snow struck by the sun. Colonel Lukander turned to de Foxa and said, "Would you like, Minister, to have a couple of shells fired at those two men?" De Foxa, clumsily wrapped in a white ski costume, gazed at Colonel Lukander from beneath the peak of his hood. "It's Good Friday," he replied. "Why should I on this particular day burden my conscience with those two men? If you really wish to please me, don't open fire." Colonel Lukander looked very surprised. "We are here to wage war," he said. "You are right," replied de Foxa, "but I am a mere tourist." His tone, as well as his gestures were unusually brusque and they made me wonder. His face was extremely pale and large drops of sweat stood out on his brow. What made him shudder was not the thought that those two men would be offered up as a sacrifice in his honor, but the thought that they would be killed on Good Friday.

Colonel Lukander, not fully understanding de Foxa's emotional French, or else intending to honor him, or else mistaking his refusal for a conventional gesture of politeness, gave orders to fire a couple of shells at the two Russian soldiers. The shells burst a few steps away without hurting them. When de Foxa saw the two Soviet soldiers resuming their march without dropping the pine log and swinging their arms as if nothing had happened he smiled, and sighing with relief said in a regretful tone: "Pity that it is Good Friday! I would have gladly seen those two fine fellows blown to pieces." Then with his arm stretched out over the parapet, he pointed at the huge dome of Saint Isaac's Orthodox cathedral in Leningrad that seemed to swing above the gray roofs of the besieged city and added: "Look at that dome, how very Catholic it is, isn't it?"

Facing the ironical and smiling Westmann with his lean, light features, sat the fleshy and florid de Foxa with his full red face, resembling the Catholic devil who, in the *autos-sacramentales*, sits on the steps of the church before the silver-garbed angel. His witty impishness was occasionally weighted down with something sensuous, maybe by that persistent assertion of pride that hinders and often restrains spontaneous reactions, deep urges, and a free and easy play of the intellect in the Latins and particularly in the Spaniards. I discerned a teasing suspicion in de Foxa, a fear of revealing himself, of stripping bare some secret part of himself, of exposing himself, of being vulnerable to a sudden wound. I listened in silence. The ghostly reflection of the snow, where the pink fire of the candlelight faded away, and the cold glow of the glass, the china and the silver endowed the words, the smiles and the glances with something peremptory and abstract, with a feeling that a trap was always set and always evaded.

"The workers are not Christians," said de Foxa.

"Why not? They, too, are *naturaliter* Christians," replied Westmann.

"Tertullian's definition is not applicable to the Marxists," said de Foxa, "and workers are *naturaliter* Marxists. They do not believe in Heaven or Hell."

Westmann stared at de Foxa with eyes full of mischief: "And what about you? Do you believe in them?" he asked.

"Not I," replied de Foxa.

Suddenly, there appeared on the table a large chocolate cake, a large monk-like cake, round like a wheel, ornamented with a flowery embroidery of sugar and pistachios, so green and springlike against chocolate, the color of a monk's habit. De Foxa began to talk of Don Juan, Lope de Vega, Cervantes, of Calderon de la Barca, Goya, Federico Garcia Llorca. Westmann spoke of the Sisters of the Sacred Heart, the sweets they make, their embroideries, their prayers in French in that honeyed French, rather old-fashioned in tone, that is a direct descendant of the *Princesse de Clèves* rather than of Pascal. "Of the *Liaisons dangereuses*," de Foxa added, "rather than Lamennais." De Foxa spoke of the younger generation in Spain; of their sporting interests, their Catholicism, their religious fervor; of the Blessed Virgin, the saints and of sport and of their Christian ideal—not the ideal of St. Louis with a lily, nor of St. Ignatius with a stick, but of a young syndicalist or communist worker from the Madrid or Barcelona suburbs in a cyclist's or a football player's sweater. He told us that during the Civil War in Spain, the football players were mostly Reds, and the bull-fight fans were Francoists almost to a man. The spectators of the *corridas* were Fascists; those of the soccer matches all Marxist.

"As a good Catholic and a good Spaniard," said de Foxa, "I am ready to accept Marx and Lenin if, instead of having to share their theological, social and political views, I may worship them as saints."

"Nothing prevents you from worshipping them as saints," countered Westmann, "you certainly would kneel before the King of Spain. Why shouldn't one be a communist by divine right?"

"That's precisely the idea behind Franco's Spain," replied de Foxa laughing.

The night was well advanced when we rose from the table. While we sat in the deep leather armchairs in the library in front of the large windows overlooking the harbor, we followed the flight of the seagulls around the ships gripped by a floor of ice. The reflection of the snow struck against the windowpanes with the cold and soft wing of a sea bird. I watched Westmann as he moved lightly and noiselessly in that ghostly light, like a transparent shadow. His eyes were of an extremely light blue, like the white glass eyes of ancient statues; his silvery hair outlined his forehead like the frame on a Byzantine icon. His nose was straight and thin, his lips narrow, pale and rather weary, his hands small with long slender fingers, burnished by a life-long contact with the leather of reins and saddles, with the coats of thoroughbred horses and dogs, with precious materials and china, with pitchers of old Baltic *tenn*, with Lillehammer and Dunhill pipes. What horizons of white snow, deserted water and limitless forests are in these blue eyes of a man of the North! What serene boredom in that clear, almost white gaze—the noble and ancient boredom of the modern world, already aware of its death! What loneliness on that pale brow!

There was something transparent about him. His hands, caressing the bottles of Port and whisky and the clear crystal glasses, seemed to melt into the air, they appeared so light and fleeting in the ghostly reflection of the snow. He was like a shadow, a gentle ghost flitting through the room. His fingers followed gently the curves of the furniture, of glasses, bottles and backs of leather arm-chairs. The scent of Port and whisky mingled with the warm aroma of English tobacco, with the old weary smell of leather and with the lean smell of the sea.

Suddenly there came from the square a panting and mournful voice. We stepped out on the porch. At first the square seemed deserted to us. The frozen plain of the sea was stretched out before us. Through the diaphanous whiteness of the snow were vaguely outlined the islet with the Yacht Club, the other islands, and further away, the Suomenlinna fortress, stiffly gripped by the icy edge of the horizon. The eyes rested with a feeling of repose on Observatory Hill and on the trees in Brunnsparken, their leafless branches covered with a glistening shell of snow. The harsh moan that came from the square became a smothered howl, a cry of pain in which the stag's moan gradually turned into the neighing of a dying horse. "Ah, cursed *culebra!*" exclaimed de Foxá with superstitious terror. But by degrees, as our eyes grew accustomed to the dazzling reflection of the snow, we made out or we thought we made out, a dark blot on the wharf in the port, a vague shape that at our appearance, sent forth a piercing scream that subsided into a panting silence.

It was an elk. A superb animal with huge antlers rising like bare branches of a tree in winter from its broad, round forehead covered with short, thick reddish hair. Its eyes were large and dark; moist, deep eyes in which something glistened—the glitter of tears. It was wounded. It had broken a thigh, probably in falling into a crevice in the marble floor that covered the sea. Perhaps it had wandered from Esthonia, across the desert of ice of the Gulf of Finland, or from the Aaland Islands, or perhaps from the shores of the Gulf of Bothnia or from Karelia. Attracted by the odor of houses and by the warm odor of man it had dragged itself as far as the wharf of the harbor. Now, it was lying panting in the snow and gazing at us with its deep, moist eyes.

When we went near it, the elk tried to rise, but it fell back on its knees with a moan. It was as large as a huge horse; its eyes were tame and mild. Sniffing the air as if it recognized a familiar scent, it dragged itself over the snow across the square toward the palace of the President of the republic, went through the open gate of the parade ground, and stretched itself out at the bottom of the steps, between the two motionless sentries who stood with their large steel helmets and their rifles held at attention on either side of the door.

The President of the Finnish republic, Ristu Ryti, was certainly asleep at that hour. A president of a republic sleeps far more lightly than a king, and President Ristu Ryti, awakened by the moans of the wounded elk, wanted to know what that unusual and peculiar noise was. Soon afterward Colonel Slörn, the President's senior aide-de-camp, appeared on the threshold of the palace.

"Good evening, Minister," said Colonel Slörn, surprised at seeing Westmann, the Minister of Sweden.

Then he recognized Count de Foxa, the Minister of Spain. "Good evening, Minister," said Colonel Slörn, more than ever surprised.

Then he saw me. "You too?" he asked looking at me with amazement. Turning to Westmann he added, "I trust this is not an official call?" and he hastened to go and warn the President of the republic that the Ministers of Sweden and Spain along with a wounded elk were at the gate of the palace. "Along with a wounded elk? What can they possibly want of me?" asked President Ristu Ryti with great surprise. It was one o'clock in the morning. But in Finland the care of animals is not only a moral obligation fulfilled by an entire people in a generous spirit, it is a law of the land; very soon President Ristu Ryti, wrapped in a heavy wolf coat and with a high fur cap on his head appeared on the threshold. He greeted us cordially; then he approached the wounded elk, bent over to examine its broken leg and began talking to it in a low voice, stroking its neck with his gloved hand.

"I bet you," said de Foxa to me, "that the President's gloves are made of dog skin."

"Why don't you ask him?"

"Right you are," replied de Foxa, and going up to the President of the republic, he made a slight bow and said, "Mav I ask whether your gloves are dog skin?"

President Ristu Ryti, who speaks no French, looked at him with surprise and embarrassment and silently appealed to his aide-de-camp for assistance who, just as surprised and embarrassed, softly translated for him the odd question asked by the Minister of Spain. The President of the republic seemed amazed and pretended he had not understood. Perhaps he could not fully grasp what the Spanish Minister wanted to know and was trying to understand the real meaning of the strange question, as well as detect any secret political significance it might have.

While President Ristu Ryti knelt on the snow by the side of the elk and looked with embarrassment at de Foxa, now and then glancing at his gloves, there chanced to drive through the square on their way to Brunnsparken, the Helsinki diplomatic quarter, the Minister of Brazil, Paulo de Souzas Dantas, the Secretary of the Danish Legation, Count Adam de Meltke-Huitfeldt, and the Secretary to the Vichy France Legation, Pierre d'Huart. One by one, the entire diplomatic corps gathered round the wounded elk and the President of the republic. The line of cars was continuously growing longer. The unusual sight of a large group of people and of the cars with diplomatic licenses standing in the middle of the night in front of the palace of the President of the republic attracted the attention of the foreign diplomats who were crossing the square on their way to Brunnsparken. They stopped, alighted from their cars and joined the group of people whom they greeted in voices full of curiosity and uneasiness.

While Colonel Slörn was calling a veterinary colonel at the cavalry barracks, the group was joined by the Minister of Romania,

Noti Constantinidu with one of the secretaries of the Legation, Titu Michailescu; the Minister of Croatia, Ferdinand Bosnjakovi with a secretary to the Legation, Marijan Andrasevic and the Minister of Germany, Wipert von Blücher.

"Ah, those Blüchers!" said de Foxa softly. "They are always on time." Then turning to the German Minister, he said, "Good evening" and raised his arm in the Hitler salute that is also the salute of the Spanish Falange.

"What is this? You, too, are lifting your paw?" asked the Secretary to the Vichy French Legation, Pierre d'Huart in a low voice.

"Don't you think it is better to raise one hand, than to have to raise both?" de Foxa asked him with a smile.

Pierre d'Huart gracefully acknowledged the thrust and replied, "I'm not surprised. Once upon a time men worked with their hands, and greeted one another with their hats; now, they greet with their hands, and work with their hats—*on travaille du chapeau*," he said in French.

De Foxa laughed and replied: "Well said, d'Huart! I bow before your wit." Then he turned to me and asked me in a low voice: "What the devil does *travailler du chapeau* mean?"

"It means that you have a bee in your bonnet," I replied.

"One can never finish learning the French language," said de Foxa.

Stretched out on the snow between the two sentries, surrounded by a little group of diplomats that had been augmented by several soldiers, two rather drunken girls, some sailors from the port and two policemen with their rifles behind their shoulders, the wounded elk was moaning gently, snorting from time to time and turning its huge head to lick its broken thigh. A blood stain slowly widened on the snow. Just as the elk turned its head, a branch of its huge antlers caught in a fold of President Ristu Ryti's fur coat. Such is an elk's strength, that his sudden movement upset the President of the republic who certainly would have fallen flat on the snow if the German Minister, von Blücher, had not steadied him with his hand. "Ha! ha! ha!" laughed the foreign diplomats in a chorus, as if that innocent gesture of the German Minister had a symbolic political meaning.

"*Perkele!*" exclaimed one of the girls, seeing the President of the republic stagger. *Perkele* means "devil" in Finnish, but it is a word that is as shocking in Finland, as "bloody" was in England in Queen Victoria's day. Everybody laughed at the girl, while some of those who were nearest rushed to disengage the fur coat from the antlers of the elk. At that very moment, Minister Rafael Hakkarainen, Chief of the Protocol in the Foreign Office, appeared out of breath just in time to hear the forbidden word *perkele* on the lips of the merry girl. Minister Hakkarainen shuddered deep in the marrow of his bones within the warm nest of his priceless, marten fur coat.

It was an oddly attractive scene—the snow-covered square, the livid and ghostly houses, the steamers gripped in the crust of ice and that group of people in rich furs and tall fur caps, gathered around a wounded elk stretched out between two sentries in front of the gate of a palace. It was a scene that would have charmed one of those Swedish or French painters who, like Schjölderbrand and Viscount de Beaumont at the end of the eighteenth and the beginning of the nineteenth centuries, pushed on into the hyperborean regions with their pencils and drawings. The veterinary colonel and the military nurses who had meanwhile turned up in an ambulance, fussed around the elk, which followed their movements with its mild, moist eyes. After many tries, in which everyone—the President of the republic, the foreign ministers, and the two gay girls—lent a hand, the elk was placed on a litter, and the litter borne on the shoulders and was hoisted into the ambulance that moved off slowly and disappeared at the end of the Esplanade in a white dazzle of snow.

The foreign diplomats lingered a few moments jesting with one another, lighting cigarettes, and stamping their feet on the ice. The cold was devastating.

"Good night, gentlemen, and many thanks," said the President of the republic raising his fur cap and bowing.

"Good night, Mr. President," replied the foreign diplomats removing their fur caps and bowing respectfully.

The little throng broke up exchanging loud farewells. The cars drove away with a faint humming of motors toward Brunnsparken, while the soldiers, the girls, the sailors and the policemen scattered about the square, laughing and shouting at one another. Westmann, de Foxa and I walked back toward the Swedish Legation. Now and then we turned to look at the two motionless sentries guarding the gate of the President of the republic, in front of the bloodstain that was slowly disappearing in the windswept sleet.

Once again we were sitting in the library before the fire, drinking and smoking in silence.

At intervals we could hear a dog barking: a sound of sad, almost human purity, that lent a warm, full-blooded feeling to the clear night, and to the cloudless sky bleached by the white glare of the snow. It was the only living and familiar voice in the frozen silence of that ghostly night, and it made my heart race. Now and then we could hear in the wind the squeaking of the ice-bound sea. The birch logs crackled on the fire, the crimson reflection of the flames flitted up the walls, around the gilded backs of the books, and around the marble busts of the Swedish sovereigns ranged on the high, oaken bookshelves: and I thought of those ancient Karelian icons in which Hell is pictured not by living and beneficial flames, but by blocks of ice that imprison the damned. The barking of the dog reached us faintly, perhaps from aboard a sailing ship gripped by ice near the Suomenlinna Island.

Then I told them about the Ukrainian dogs, the "red dogs" of the Dnieper.

IX

Red Dogs

It had been raining for days and days and the sea of Ukrainian mud slowly spread beyond the horizon. It was the high tide of autumn in the Ukraine. The deep black mud was everywhere swelling like dough when yeast begins to work. The heavy smell of mud was borne by the wind from the end of the vast plain and mingled with the odor of uncut grain left to rot in the furrows, and with the sweetish stale odor of sunflowers. One by one the seeds dropped out of the black pupils of the sunflowers, one by one fell the long yellow eyelashes from around the large, round eyes, blank and void like the eyes of the blind.

The German soldiers returning from the front line, when they reached the village squares, dropped their rifles on the ground in silence. They were coated from head to foot in black mud, their beards were long, their hollow eyes looked like the eyes of the sunflowers, blank and dull. The officers gazed at the soldiers and at the rifles lying on the ground, and kept silent. By then the lightning war, the *Blitzkrieg*, was over, the *Dreizigjährigerblitzkrieg*, the thirty-year lightning war, had begun. The winning war was over, the losing war had begun. I saw the white stain of fear growing in the dull eyes of German officers and soldiers. I saw it spreading little by little, gnawing at the pupils, singeing the roots of the eyelashes and making the eyelashes drop one by one, like the long yellow eyelashes of the sunflowers. When Germans become afraid, when that mysterious German fear begins to creep into their bones, they always arouse a special horror and pity. Their appearance is miserable, their cruelty sad, their courage silent and hopeless. That is when the Germans become wicked. I repented being a Christian. I felt ashamed of being a Christian.

The Russian prisoners, moving from the front to the rear, were

208

no longer the same we had seen during the first months of the Russian war. They were no longer the men of June, July and August, whom the German soldiers escorted on foot toward the rear in a blistering sun, on foot for days and days through the red and black dust of the Ukrainian plains. During the first months of the war, the village women looked out of the doors of the houses, laughing and weeping with joy, and they hastened to bring drink and food to the prisoners. "*Oh bednii, oh bednii*—Poor fellow!" they shouted. They also brought food and drink for the German guards who sat in the center of the little square, on the benches around the white statues of Lenin and Stalin that lay overturned in the mud, and smoked and talked gaily among themselves with their tommy guns between their knees. During an hour's halt in a village, the Russian prisoners were almost free, they were permitted to come and go, even to enter houses, or to wash themselves at the fountain. At a whistle from the German corporal they all ran to take their places, the column moved out of the village and, singing, disappeared into the green and yellow sea of the vast plain. Women, old men and children, laughing and weeping, followed the column a long way. After a while, they stopped and stood waving good-by and throwing kisses to the prisoners who went off into the blistering sunshine, turning back from time to time to shout, "*Do svidanya, daragaya!*—See you soon, my dear!" The German guards, their tommy guns slung behind their shoulders, walked chattering and laughing among themselves between the hedges. The sunflowers peeped over the hedges to see them go by, following them a long way with their black round eyes, until the column disappeared into the dust.

By then the winning war was over, the losing war had begun, the *Dreizigjährigerblitzkrieg*, and the columns of Russian prisoners became steadily fewer: the German soldiers escorting them no longer walked with their tommy guns slung behind their shoulders, chattering and laughing among themselves, instead they closed in on the flanks of a column, howling in raucous voices and fixing the prisoners with the black, glistening eyes of their tommy guns. The prisoners, pale and lean, dragged their feet through the mud, they were hungry and sleepy. In the villages, women, old men and children looked at them with tearful eyes, murmuring "*Nichevo,*

nichevo!" They had nothing left, not a bit of bread, not a glass of milk; the Germans had taken everything, stolen everything, *nichevo, nichevo.* "It doesn't matter, *daragaya,* it doesn't matter, my dear." "*Vsyo ravno*—it makes no difference—*vsyo ravno,*" replied the prisoners in the rain. The columns went through the villages without halting, to that hopeless cadence, *vsyo ravno, vsyo ravno, vsyo ravno,* and sinking into the sea of mud in the vast plain.

Then began the first "lessons in the open," the first reading exercises in the yards of the *kolkhoz*—the collective farm. Only once, in a *kolkhoz* of a village near Nemirovskoye, I chanced to be present at one of those lessons. After that I always refused to assist with these reading exercises. "*Warum nicht?*—Why not?" the German officers of General von Schobert asked me. "Why don't you want to watch the lessons in the open? It is a very interesting experiment, *sehr interessant.*"

The prisoners were lined up in the yard of the *kolkhoz.* Along the walls of the yard and under the large sheds were piled haphazardly, hundreds of agricultural machines—reapers, cultivators, mechanical ploughs, threshing machines. It rained and the prisoners were soaked to their skins. They had been standing there, in silence, leaning against each other; they were big, fair boys, with close-cropped heads and light eyes in their broad faces. Their hands were flat and thick with squat, arched, calloused thumbs. Almost all were peasants. The workmen, mostly engineers and mechanics from the *kolkhoz,* could be distinguished among them by their height and their hands; they were taller, leaner and lighter skinned; their hands were bony, with long fingers, and smooth finger-tips glazed from gripping hammers, planes, wrenches, screwdrivers and controls. They could be distinguished by their stern faces and glazed eyes.

Finally, a German N.C.O., a Feldwebel,* came into the yard followed by an interpreter. The Feldwebel was short and fat, the type I playfully called "Fettwebel." Standing with his legs wide apart he faced the prisoners and began talking to them in the good-natured way of a head of a family. He said that a reading test was to be held, and each would have to read aloud a passage from

* Feldwebel—A sergeant-major.

a newspaper. Those who passed the examination well would be drafted as clerks into the offices of the prisoners' camps; the others, those who failed, would be sent to work on the land or be employed as laborers and dockworkers.

The interpreter was a Sonderführer,* short and thin, not more than thirty years old, his face covered with little red pimples. He had been born in Russia in the *Deutschvolk* colony of Melitopol and spoke Russian with an odd German accent. The first time I met him, I said jokingly that Melitopol means the city of honey. "Yes," he replied in a harsh voice and with a sullen look, "there is a lot of honey in that district, but I am not concerned with bees; I am a schoolmaster." The Sonderführer translated the brief and good-natured speech of the "Fettwebel" word for word, and he added in a tone of a schoolmaster upbraiding his pupils, that they had to be careful with the pronunciation, and read with attention and ease, because if they failed to pass the examination, they would have reasons to regret it. Later when I recalled his words, I felt a shiver creeping down my spine.

The prisoners listened in silence, and when the Sonderführer stopped they all began talking among themselves and laughing. Many of them seemed to feel humiliated. They gazed around like whipped dogs and glanced from time to time at their horny peasant hands, but many others laughed contentedly; they felt certain of passing, and of being sent into some office as clerks. "*Eh, Pyotr! eh Ivanushka!*" they shouted to their companions, and slapped each other roughly on the backs with the simple-minded gaiety of the Russian peasant. The workmen among them were silent, turning their stern faces toward the administration building of the *kolkhoz*, where the German headquarters were. From time to time they looked at the Feldwebel, but they never deigned to glance at the Sonderführer. Their eyes were deep and glazed.

"*Ruhe!*—Silence!" suddenly shouted the Feldwebel.

A group of officers was already approaching, led by an old colonel, tall and thin, a little stooped, with gray mustaches clipped short, he walked slightly dragging one of his legs. The colonel glanced absent-mindedly at the prisoners and began speaking rapidly in a monotonous voice, swallowing half of his words, as if he

* Sonderführer—A civilian technician or advisor attached to the army.

were in a hurry to finish his sentences. At the end of each sentence, he made a long pause, but his eyes remained fixed on the ground. He said that those who would pass the examination and so on, and so on. . . . The Sonderführer translated the colonel's brief speech word for word. Then, on his own account he added that the Moscow government had spent millions on Soviet schools, that he knew this because he had been a schoolmaster among the *Deutschvolk* of Melitopol before the war, and that all those who failed in the examination were to be set to work as laborers and dockworkers; it was their fault if they had learned nothing in school. The Sonderführer seemed very anxious that all of them should read fluently and with a good pronunciation.

"How many are there?" the colonel asked the Feldwebel as he scratched his chin with a gloved hand.

"One hundred and eighteen," replied the Feldwebel.

The colonel gave a sign to one of the officers who was clutching a bundle of newspapers under his arm and the examination began.

Five prisoners took a step forward. Each of them stretched out a hand, took a paper that the officer held out to him—they were old issues of *Izvestia* and *Pravda* found in the office of the *kolkhoz*—and began reading aloud. The colonel raised his left arm to look at his wristwatch. He kept his arm breast-high and his eyes fixed on the watch. It was raining and the newspapers were soaked; they drooped in the hands of the five prisoners whose faces were either red or extremely pale and sweating as they stumbled over the words, halted, stammered, blundered the accents and skipped lines. They could all read with difficulty, except one very young man who read with assurance, from time to time raising his eyes from the paper. The Sonderführer listened to the reading with an ironical smile in which I seemed to sense a vengefulness—as interpreter, he was the sole judge. He stared at the readers, shifting his eyes from one to the other with a deliberate and nasty slowness. "Stop!" said the colonel.

The five prisoners raised their eyes from the papers and waited. At a nod from the judge, the Feldwebel shouted, "Those who have failed will go and stand on the left; those who have been promoted, over there, to the right." The first four failures at a sign from the judge went dejectedly to cluster on the left, and a youthful ripple of laughter ran along the ranks of the prisoners, a gay, mischievous, peasant laughter. The Sonderführer also laughed. *"Oh, bednii*—Oh poor fellows!" the prisoners called to those who had failed. "You will be sent to work on the roads, *Oh bednii,* you'll carry stones on your backs," and they laughed. The one who had passed, all alone on the other side, laughed more than the others, chaffing his unlucky comrades. They all laughed except the prisoners who looked like workmen; they stared at the colonel's face and were silent.

Then came the turn of the next five. They also struggled to read well, without stumbling over the words, without placing the wrong accents, but only two could read fluently; the other three, red with shame or pale with anxiety, clutched the papers tightly in their hands, and from time to time licked their parched lips. "Stop!" said the colonel. The five prisoners raised their faces, wiping the sweat with the papers. "You three, over there, to the left; you two, to the right!" shouted the Feldwebel at a nod from the Sonderführer. The prisoners continued chaffing the ones who had failed saying, *"Oh, bednii Ivan!"* or *"Oh, bednii Pyotr!"* and patted their shoulders as if to say, "You will be hauling stones!" They all laughed.

Again, one of the five prisoners in the third batch read excellently, fluently, pronouncing each syllable, and from time to time he raised his eyes to look at the colonel. The newspaper he was reading was an old issue of *Pravda,* dated June 24, 1941, and the page read: "The Germans have invaded Russia! Comrade soldiers, the Soviet people will win the war and will crush the invaders!" The words rang out under the rain, and the colonel laughed, the Sonderführer, the Feldwebel, the officers laughed, everybody laughed; and the prisoners also laughed, looking with envy and admiration at their companion who could read like a schoolmaster. "Well done!" said the Sonderführer and his face shone. He seemed proud of the prisoner who could read so well: he was happy and proud as if the prisoner had been his pupil. "You, to the right, over there," said the Feldwebel in a good-natured voice giving him a kindly push with his hand. The colonel glanced at the Feldwebel, started to say something, but checked himself, and I noticed that he was blushing.

The group assembled on the right laughed contentedly; those who had passed looked at their less fortunate companions with a bantering air; they pointed their fingers at their own breasts saying "Clerks!" Making grimaces, they pointed at those who had failed and said, "Stones on the back!" Only the prisoners who looked like workmen and who, one by one, went to swell the ranks of those sent to the left, kept silent and gazed at the colonel who, chancing to meet their eyes, blushed and shouted with a gesture of impatience, "*Schnell!*—Quick!"

The examination lasted for about an hour. When the last batch of three prisoners completed the two minutes of reading, the colonel turned to the Feldwebel and said, "Count them!" The Feldwebel began counting from a distance, pointing at each man with his finger, "*Ein, zwei, drei . . .*" On the left were eighty-seven, on the right were thirty-one who had passed successfully. Then, at the colonel's bidding, the Sonderführer began to speak. He seemed like a schoolmaster dissatisfied with his pupils. He said that he was disappointed, that he was sorry to have flunked so many, that he would have preferred to pass them all. At any rate, he added, those who had not succeeded in getting through the examination would have no reason to complain, provided they worked and displayed a greater skill than they had displayed at school. While he spoke, the group of the successful prisoners gazed at their less fortunate comrades with a compassionate air, and the younger ones dug their elbows into each other's ribs and giggled. When the Sonderführer had finished speaking, the colonel turned to the Feldwebel and said: "*Alles in Ordnung. Weg!*" and he walked off toward his headquarters followed by the other officers who looked back occasionally and exchanged whispers.

"You'll stay here until tomorrow, and tomorrow you will start for the labor camp," said the Feldwebel to the group on the left. Then he turned toward the group on the right who had passed and harshly ordered them to fall in line. As soon as the prisoners formed a close line touching one another's elbows—they looked pleased, and laughed, glancing at their companions as if making fun of them—he counted them again quickly, said "Thirty-one," and made a sign with his hand to a squad of SS men waiting at the end of the courtyard. He ordered, "Right about, turn!" The prisoners turned right about, marched forward stamping their feet hard in the mud and, when they came face to face with the wall surrounding the yard, the Feldwebel commanded "Halt!" Then turning to the SS men who had lined up behind the prisoners and had already raised their tommy guns, he cleared his throat, spat on the ground and shouted, "Fire!"

When he heard the rattle of the guns, the colonel who was within a few steps of the office, stopped, turned abruptly; the other officers stopped and also turned. The colonel passed his hand over his face as if wiping away sweat and, followed by his officers, entered the building.

"*Ach, so*," said the Melitopol Sonderführer walking past me. "Russia must be cleared of all this learned rabble. The peasants and workers who can read and write too well are dangerous. They are all communists."

"*Natürlich*," I replied, "but in Germany everyone, whether they are peasants or workers, can read and write well."

"The German people are a people of high *Kultur*."

"Naturally," I replied. "The German people have a high *Kultur*."

"*Nicht wahr?*" said the Sonderführer laughing, and walked toward headquarters.

I was left alone in the center of the yard facing the prisoners who could not read well, and my whole body was shaking.

Then, as their mysterious fear grew, as that mysterious white stain spread over their eyes, they began killing prisoners whose feet were blistered and who could no longer walk. They began setting fire to the villages that were unable to hand over a fixed number of loads of wheat and flour, a certain number of loads of corn and barley and of heads of horses and cattle to the requisitioning platoons.

When only a few Jews remained, they began hanging the peasants. They strung them by their necks or by their feet to the branches of trees in the little village squares, around the bare pedestals where the white statues of Lenin and Stalin had stood only a few days before. They hung them side by side with the rain-washed corpses of the Jews that had been dangling for days under the black sky, side by side with the dogs of the Jews that had been strung up on the same trees with their masters. "Ah, the Jewish dogs—*die jüdische Hunde!*" said the German soldiers as they passed along.

In the evening, when we halted in the villages for the night—we were by then in the heart of the ancient Cossack land of the Dnieper—and fires were lighted to dry the soaked clothes on our backs, the soldiers cursed softly between their teeth and greeted one another scornfully saying, "*Ein Liter!*—One liter!" They did not say "*Heil* Hitler!" They said "*Ein Liter!*" and they laughed as they stretched toward the fire their swollen feet, covered with the little white blisters.

Those were the first Cossack villages we saw on our slow, laborious and endless march east. Old bearded Cossacks sat in the doors of their houses, watched the columns of German transports go by and occasionally glanced upward at the sky gently arching above the huge plain. That wonderful Ukrainian sky, light and delicate, supported by lofty Doric columns of spotless white clouds rising on the skyline from the far end of the crimson autumn steppes.

"*Berlin raucht Juno,*" said the soldiers, and laughingly threw the last empty packages of Juno cigarettes at the old Cossacks sitting in the doorways of their houses. Tobacco was becoming scarce and the soldiers cursed. "*Berlin raucht Juno!*—Berlin smokes Junos!" they scornfully shouted. I thought of buses and trams in Berlin bearing the inscription *Berlin raucht Juno,* of U-bahn * stairways with the words *Berlin raucht Juno* painted in red on every step. I thought of the clumsy, leering, badly washed Berlin crowd with their ashen-colored faces glistening with grease and sweat, of the disheveled women, with red eyes, swollen hands and string-darned stockings, of the old people and of children with hard, spiteful faces. In the midst of that leering and frightened crowd I saw again the soldiers on leave from the Russian front—those silent, lean, stern soldiers, almost all bald, even the youngest among them. I watched that mysterious stain widening in their eyes, and I thought about the *Herrenvolk* and about the useless, hopeless heroism of the *Herrenvolk.* "*Aus dem Kraftquell Milch,*" said the soldiers scornfully throwing the last empty cans of Milei milk-egg at the old Cossacks sitting in the doors of their houses. *Aus dem Kraftquell Milch* was

* *Untergrundbahn*—Subway.

216

written on the empty cans thrown into the mud, and a shiver ran down my back as I thought about the *Herrenvolk* and about the *Herrenvolk's* mysterious fear.

At night I sometimes left the bivouac or the house in which I had found shelter and, taking my blankets with me went and lay down in a corn field, close to the camp or to the village. There, stretched out among the rain-sodden stalks, I waited for the dawn and listened drowsily to the noises of passing transports, troops of Romanian cavalry, columns of armored cars. I listened to harsh, brutal German voices and the merry high-pitched Romanian voices calling, *"Inainte, baiatsi, inainte!*—Forward, boys, forward!" Herds of starving vagrant dogs came close to me and sniffed, wagging their tails —those small Ukrainian mongrels, with yellowish hair, red eyes and bandy legs. Some of the dogs often huddled beside me licking my face, and whenever a step sounded on the neighboring path or the wheat rattled in a strong gust of wind, the dog would growl softly and I would say: "Down, Dmitri!" I felt as if I were talking to a man, to a Russian. I said: "Shut up, Ivan!" and I felt as if I were talking to one of those prisoners who had tried so hard to read well, who had passed their examination and now lay in the mud, their faces gnawed by lime—over there by the wall encircling the yard of the *kolkhoz* in the village near Nemirovskoye.

One night I spent in a sunflower field. It was really a sunflower forest—a real forest. Bending on their tall hairy stalks, their large, round black eyes with long yellow lashes misty with sleep, the sunflowers slept with drooping heads. It was a clear night, the sky steeped in stars shone with blue and green reflections, like the hollow of a huge sea shell. I slept hard and I was awakened at dawn by a gentle, soft crackling. It sounded like the rustle of people walking barefoot through grass. I listened holding my breath. The faint coughing of motors came to me from the near-by encampment—faint voices calling to one another in the wood by the brook. A dog was barking in the distance. Down on the skyline the sun was breaking through the black shell of the night, rising warm and red over the plain glistening with dew. That rustle spread and became louder every minute. It was by now like the crackling of a brushwood fire. Now it was like the subdued creaking of a vast army marching cautiously through a field of stubble. Lying on the ground, I held my breath, watching the sunflowers slowly raising their yellow eyelids and gradually opening their eyes.

The sunflowers were raising their heads and gently twisting on their stalks, turning their large black eyes to the rising sun. It was a slow, even, vast movement. The entire sunflower forest was turning to gaze at the young glory of the sun. I, too, raised my face to the east and watched the sun rising little by little amid the rosy vapors of the dawn, above the bluish clouds of smoke from the far-off fires on the plain.

Then the rain ceased and, after a few days of strong, cold winds, the frost suddenly set in. Not snow, just a sudden, fierce autumnal frost. During the night the mud hardened, the pools of water were covered with glistening glass as thin as human skin. The air turned limpid; the sky, blue-gray in color, looked cracked like a broken mirror.

The German march toward the east became more rapid; the bark of the guns, the rattle of rifles and machine guns sounded sharply and clearly, unbroken by echoes. The heavy armored cars of General von Schobert that had crawled laboriously during the rainy days, like clumsy toads, through the slippery, sticky mud of the plain between the Bug and the Dnieper, began roaring again over the frost-hardened ruts. The bluish smoke from the exhausts etched faint clouds that melted away at once over the trees and yet left something of their mysterious presence in the air.

This was the most dangerous moment of the great Russian crisis during the autumn of 1941. The army of Marshal Budenny, the Russian Murat, was slowly retiring toward the Don, leaving as a rear guard, units of Cossack cavalry and groups of those small armored cars that the Germans called *Panzerpferde*—armored horses. The *Panzerpferde* were nimble little cars, mostly driven by young Tartar workmen, *stakhanovtzi* and *udarniki* from the Soviet steelworks of the Don and the Volga. They used the tactics of Tartar cavalry; they turned up suddenly to worry the flanks, they disappeared into the bushes and thickets, hid in the folds of the soil and turned up suddenly again in the rear, drawing wide curves across the stubble fields and the meadows. They used light cavalry tactics, of which even Murat would have been proud. They circled the plain like horses in a riding school.

But even the *Panzerpferde* became less frequent. I asked myself where Budenny was, where the whiskered Budenny with his huge army of Cossack and Tartar cavalry was hiding. At Yambol, soon after we had crossed the Dniester, the peasants said, "Eh, Budenny is waiting for you behind the Bug." When we had crossed the Bug, the peasants said, "Eh, he is waiting for you behind the Dnieper." Now with a very knowing air they said, "Eh, Budenny is waiting for you behind the Don." Thus the Germans penetrated ever farther into the Ukrainian plain, like a knife, and the wound was already hurting—it was festering and turning into a sore. During the evenings in the villages where the column halted for the night, I listened to the raucous voices of the gramophones. Invariably, there was always a gramophone and a pile of records in the offices of the Soviet, or of the *kolkhoz*, or in the local *Univermag* shop. They were recordings of the usual factory, *kolkhoz* and *rabochii* club songs, and among them there was always the "Budenny March." I listened to the "Budenny March" and wondered, What the devil is Budenny doing? Where has the whiskered Budenny buried himself?

One day the Germans began to hunt for dogs. I supposed at first that because of numerous cases of rabies, General von Schobert had ordered the extermination of all dogs. Later I realized that there was some other reason behind it. As soon as the Germans entered a village, even before they looked for the Jews, they began a hunt for the dogs. Squads of SS men and of *Panzerjäger* ran through the streets firing their tommy guns and throwing hand grenades at those poor mongrels with yellow hair, red shiny eyes and bandy legs. They were routed out of the orchards and hedges and pursued relentlessly through the fields. The poor brutes fled to the woods, crouched in the ditches, in the hollows, behind orchard fences, or else they sought refuge in the houses, huddling in the corners, in the beds of the peasants, behind the ovens, under the benches. The German soldiers entered the houses, drove the dogs out of their hiding places and slew them with rifle butts.

The armored-car men were most fierce in these hunts; the *Panzer-jäger* seemed to have a personal grudge against the poor brutes. I asked the armored-car men, "Why?" The faces of the *Panzerjäger* darkened. "Ask the dogs," they replied, and turned their backs on me.

The old Cossacks sitting in the doors of their houses laughed in their beards and slapped their knees. "Ah, poor dogs," they said, "Ah, *bednii sobachki!*" and they laughed maliciously, as if they felt sorry not for the poor brutes, but for the poor Germans. Old women peered over the orchard fences, the girls who went down to the river balancing two pails on a yoke over their shoulders, the children who mercifully went to bury the murdered dogs in the fields—they all smiled in a way that was both sad and malicious. At night through the fields and the woods one heard scattered barking, whining howls, the dogs scraping and scratching in the orchards and under the houses in search of food, and German sentries shouting, "Who goes there?" in strange voices. One sensed that they were afraid of something terrifying and mysterious—that they were afraid of the dogs.

One morning I was at an artillery observation post, watching the attack of a Panzer division at close quarters. The detachments of heavy armored cars sheltered in the woods, waited for the order to attack. The morning was cold and clear, and I looked at the fields glistening with frost and at the sunflower forests yellow and black in the rising sun. The sun was like the sun described in the Third Book of Xenophon's *Anabasis;* it rose from the rosy vapors on the skyline in front of us. It was really like a young god of the ancients, nude and rosy in the vast blue-green ocean of the sky; it rose lighting up the Doric columns of the *Piatiletka,* the columns of glass, concrete and steel, the Parthenon of the U.S.S.R. heavy industry. Suddenly, I saw the column of armored cars stealing out of the forest and spreading fanlike on the plain.

A few minutes after the beginning of the attack, General von Schobert arrived at the observation post. He searched the battlefield through his field glasses and smiled. The armored cars and the attacking parties marching in the furrows of the caterpillars seemed to be cut with a burin on the huge copper plate of the plain stretching to the southeast of Kiev; there was something of Dürer in that vast scene drawn with harsh precision, in those soldiers monstrously wrapped in camouflage nets, resembling ancient gladiators and ranged like allegorical figures along the margins of the print, in that open and vague perspective of trees, cars, guns, motors, men and horses variously placed and poised in the foreground along the slope descending from the observation post toward the Dnieper, farther away, and deepening and opening as the view became more distant; it also was in the men squatting behind the armored cars with their tommy guns cradled in their arms and in the Panzers scattered here and there among the high grass and the clusters of sunflowers. There was something of Dürer in the purely Gothic care for detail that at once caught the eye, as if the artist's burin had lingered for a moment and the hand had cut a deeper groove in the copper plate on the gaping jaws of a dead horse, on a wounded man crawling through the undergrowth, or over there, on a soldier leaning against a tree trunk, his hand held open above his forehead to shade his eyes against the glare of the sun. The raucous voices, the neighing, the occasional, sharp rifle shots, the harsh creaking of caterpillars seemed also to have been engraved by Dürer on the clear cold air of that autumn morning.

General von Schobert was smiling. The shadow of death was already hovering over him—an extremely light shadow like a spiderweb; and no doubt he felt that shadow weighing on his brow. No doubt he knew that a few days later he would fall in the Kiev suburbs, that his death would have something of the whimsical Viennese grace that appeared in the rather frivolous elegance of his manner. No doubt he knew that he would die a few days later landing in his small plane, a "Stork" on the airport of newly occupied Kiev; that the wheels of his "Stork" gliding over the grass of the landing field would touch off a mine, and he would disappear among a cluster of red flowers in a sudden explosion, and only his blue linen handkerchief with his white embroidered initials would drop intact on the grass of the airport. General von Schobert was one of those old Bavarian noblemen to whom Vienna is but a loving nickname for Munich. There was something ancient and youthful, something old-fashioned in his sharp profile, in his ironical and sad smile, a kind of strange fanciful melancholy in his voice, when at Baltsiu in Bessarabia he said to me, "Alas, we are waging war against the white race," or in his voice when in Soroca, on the

Dniester he said to me, *"Wir siegen unsere Toten*—We conquer our own dead."* He meant that the last, the final laurels of the German victories would spell the death of the German people, that the German nation and all its victories, will win death as the only reward. That morning he watched the column of armored cars spreading out fanlike on the Kiev plain; on the margin of that Dürer engraving—*Wir siegen unsere Toten* was written in black letters.

The armored cars, supported by the attacking units, had already penetrated deeply into the deserted plain. After the first rifle shots a heavy silence had fallen on the rolling ground covered with stubble and grass withered by the first autumn frost; the Russians apparently had abandoned the battlefield, fleeing beyond the river; several flights of large birds took wing from the acacia groves, clouds of little gray birds that resembled sparrows rose and twittered over the meadows, their wings throwing off dull flashes in the flame of the rising sun; from a far-off pool two wild ducks took to the air, paddling with their slow wings. Suddenly a few black dots darted out of a forest in the distance, then more and still more; they moved quickly, disappeared in the bushes, turned up nearer and rushed rapidly toward the German Panzers. *"Die Hunde! Die Hunde!*—The dogs! The dogs!"* cried the soldiers around us in terrified voices. A gay and ferocious barking came to us on the wind, the baying of hounds on the track of a fox.

Under the sudden onslaught of the dogs the Panzers began to rush about zigzagging and firing wildly. The attacking units back of the armored cars stopped, hesitated and scattered; they fled here and there across the plain as if in the throes of panic. The rattle of the machine guns was clear and light, like the tinkling of glass. The baying of the pack bit into the roar of the motors. Now and again came a faint voice smothered by the wind and in the widespread rustle of grass. *"Die Hunde! Die Hunde!"* Suddenly we heard the dull thud of an explosion; then another, and another. We saw two, three, five Panzers blow up, the steel plates flashing within a tall fountain of earth.

"Ah, the dogs!" said General von Schobert passing a hand over his face. They were "anti-armored-car dogs" that had been trained by the Russians to look for food under the armored cars. Kept without food for a day or two, they were brought to the front line whenever an attack was impending. As soon as the German Panzers appeared out of the woods and spread out fanlike on the plain, the Russian soldiers shouted *"Pashol! Pashol!*—Off! Off!" and unleashed the famished pack. The dogs carrying cradles on their backs loaded with high explosives and with steel contact rods like the aerials of a radar set-up, ran quickly and hungrily to meet the armored cars, in search of food under the German Panzers. *"Die Hunde! Die Hunde!"* shouted the soldiers around us. General von Schobert, deathly pale, a sad smile on his bloodless lips, passed a hand over his face, then looked at me and said in a voice that was already dead, "Why? Why? Even the dogs!"

The German soldiers became daily more ferocious. The hunt for the dogs continued with a merciless rage, while the old Cossacks laughed and slapped their knees. *"Ah, bednii sobachki!*—Ah, poor dogs!" they said.

One night barking was heard over the black plain, and the anxious scratching around the fences of the orchards. "Who goes there?" shouted the German sentries in strange voices. The boys awakened, jumped out of their beds, opened the doors with extreme caution and called softly into the dark: *"Idi syuda! Idi syuda!* —Come here! Come here!"

One morning I said to the Sonderführer of Melitopol: "When you have killed them all, when there are no more dogs in Russia, Russian boys will squeeze themselves under your armored cars."

"Ach, they are all of a breed," he replied. "All sons of dogs!" and he walked away spitting on the ground with great contempt.

"I like Russian dogs," said Westmann. "They should be fathers of brave Russian boys."

X

Summer Night

AFTER THE ENDLESS winter night, after the cold clear spring, summer had come at last. The cool, frail, rainy Finnish summer had the smell and taste of green apples. The season for *krapu* was approaching and the first sweet crayfish of the Finnish rivers, the summer delicacy of the North, were already reddening the dishes. And the sun never set.

"Alas, that a Spaniard like myself should be doomed to travel as far as Finland to find the sun of Charles V!" said Count de Foxá gazing at the night sun blossoming on the windowsill of the horizon like a pot of geraniums. In the transparent night the girls of Helsinki strolled about in their green, red and yellow dresses, their faces white with powder, their hair molded by curling tongs and scented with Teo's Eau de Cologne, their foreheads shaded by paper hats bedecked with paper flowers bought at Stockmann's. They walked along the Esplanade in creaking paper shoes.

A thin smell of the sea came up from the end of the Esplanade. The faint shadows of the trees rested lightly on the smooth pale fronts of the buildings; they were extremely pale green shadows, as if the trees were made of glass; young, convalescent soldiers with bandaged heads, with arms in slings, with feet swollen by dressings, sat on the benches listening to the music played by the small orchestra of the Café Royal and watched the blue-paper sky being crumpled by the sea breeze along the edges of the roofs. The shop windows reflected the cold, metallic, ghostly light of the "white night" of the North on which the twittering of the birds seemed to cast a warm shadow. Winter was far away now; it was no more than a memory; but something of the winter seemed still to be floating in the air, perhaps it was the white light resembling the reflection of snow, perhaps a recollection of dead snow that lingered in the tepid summer sky.

Country parties at Krankulla had begun in the villa of the Italian Minister, Vincenzo Cicconardi who was seated before the fire with his old dog, Rex, curled up at his feet and his mad valet standing stiffly, with wide-open eyes behind his chair. Cicconardi spoke Neapolitan with a strong Berlin accent—it was his idea of speaking German—to the German Minister von Blücher. He twisted his mouth overshadowed by a huge Bourbon nose, and joined his hands as if he were praying. I like Cicconardi because of the clash between his Neapolitan indifference and irony, and the aspiration for power and glory that the odd shape and the exaggerated size of his skull, his forehead, his jaws and his nose seemed to express. Facing him, von Blücher, long, thin, stoop shouldered, his gray hair cropped very closely, his pale bluish face creased by thin wrinkles, listened, and monotonously repeated, *"Ja, ja, ja!"* From time to time Cicconardi glanced through the window at his guests who were walking through the wood in the rain and at the violet hat of Madame Blücher that clashed with the green of the foliage as a Renoir purple might clash with one of Manet's green landscapes.

Suppers at Fiskatorp, by the lakeside had begun; suppers with the Romanian Minister, Noti Constantinidu and Madame Colette Constantinidu, with Count de Foxa, with Dinu Cantemir, Titu Michailescu, also the evening parties at the Spanish, Croatian and Hungarian legations. The long afternoons around the tables of the open-air café at the end of the Esplanade or at the Kämp Bar with Minister Rafael Hakkarainen and the musician Bengt von Törne had begun; also the strolls along the Esplanade sidewalks under the green trees thronged with birds; also the long hours on the veranda of the Swedish Yachting Club, on the little island anchored in the middle of the harbor, where people watched the waves gliding like white lizards over the green water. The delightful week ends in the *stugas* * on the lakeshores or on the seashores of the Barösund, in those villas that the French, ever boastful, call *châteaux,* and the Finns, ever modest, more simply call *stugas.* They are old country houses built of wood and stucco on neoclassical lines inspired by

* *Stuga*—Swedish word for cottage.

Engels—the Doric order of the portico covered by a slight green mold. The happy days in the villa the architect Saarinen, who designed the Parliament House in Helsinki, has built for himself on the islet of Bockholm in the middle of the Barösund—there at sunrise we went picking mushrooms among the silver birches and red pines, or else fishing between the islands of Svartö and Strömsö. At night one heard the sirens of the ships mooing plaintively through the mist and the seagulls shrieking harshly with childish voices.

The light days and the white nights of the Finnish summer had begun, and the hours in the front and communication trenches before Leningrad seemed endless. Under the night sun the vast gray city cast metallic reflections on the green background of woods, meadows and marshes. At times Leningrad seemed like a city of aluminum so deadened was its glow and so mellow; at times a city of steel, so cold and cruel its glow; at other times the glow was so vivid and deep that the city seemed as if it was made of silver. On certain nights, gazing at it from the low hills of Beli Ostrov or from the edge of the Terioki woods, it really looked to me like a silver city etched on the delicate skyline by the burin of Fabergé, the last great silversmith of the St. Petersburg Court. The hours seemed endless to me in the front and communication trenches along the sea, facing the fortress of Kronstadt that rises from the waters of the Gulf of Finland among the Totlebens, the artificial steel and concrete islets that encircle it.

I could not sleep at night, and I roamed about the trenches with Svartström, lingering now and then by a loophole to look at the Leningrad parks and trees on the Vasilii Ostrov, beloved by Eugene Onegin and by Dostoevski's characters, or to gaze at the domes of the Kronstadt churches, at the red, green and blue lights of the aerials, the gray roofs of the arsenal or at the flashing glint of the Soviet fleet moored in the harbor in front of us, almost within arm's reach. It really seemed to me that by stretching my hand out toward the parapets of the Beli Ostrov and Terioki trenches, I could touch the Leningrad houses, topped by the dome of St. Isaac's, and the bastions of the Kronstadt fort, so transparent was the air during those white summer nights.

In the Raikkola forest along the shore of Lake Ladoga, I spent long hours in the front line *korsus* listening to the Finnish officers talking about Colonel Merikallio's death—my friend Merikallio who, before dying, had asked his daughter to convey his last greetings to de Foxa, Michailescu and me. Or else I went to a *lottala* in the depth of the forest to drink raspberry sirup with the pale and silent *sissit*—the rangers with their sharp knives hanging from their belts, under the distant and attentive eyes of the young *lottas* dressed in gray linen, their sad faces resting lightly on white collars. Toward evening I walked down with Svartström to Lake Ladoga and we spent long hours sitting on the shore of a small bay where, during the winter, the heads of the horses gripped by the ice had emerged above the glistening crust of ice, and where a little of their jaded odor still lingered in the damp air of the night.

After I left the front and returned to Helsinki, de Foxa would say to me: "Tonight we will go to have a drink in the cemetery." One night, after leaving Titu Michailescu's house we walked to the old Swedish churchyard that has remained unscathed though it was in the heart of Helsinki between the Boulevardi and the Georgkatu. We sat on a bench that stood by the tomb of a certain Sierk. De Foxa drew a bottle of Bordsbrännvin from his pocket and, while we drank, we argued the relative merits of several Finnish brandies—whether Bordsbrännvin, Pommeransbrännvin, Erikois-brännvin or Rajamaribrännvin was best. In that romantic churchyard the tombstones stand in the grass like the backs of armchairs; they really seem to be old armchairs ranged on a stage with a wood for a backdrop. Under the large trees shadowy soldiers sat motionless and dismal on the benches. The high trees with their tender green foliage, the blue reflection of the sea trembling on their leaves, rustled sweetly.

Toward dawn de Foxa glanced around suspiciously and asked me softly, "Have you heard the talk about the ghost of Kalevala Street?" He was afraid of ghosts and insisted that the time for them in Finland was the summer. "I would like to see a ghost, a real ghost," he said in a low voice and he shook with fear, glancing suspiciously around. As we came out of the churchyard and passed the Kalevala monument, de Foxa closed his eyes and turned his head away so he would not see the ghostly statues of the Kalevala heroes.

One evening we went to see the ghost that appeared every night, punctually at the same time, on the threshold of a house at the end of Kalevala Street. It was not so much his childish fear of apparitions that drew my friend de Foxa to that squalid street, as his morbid curiosity to see a ghost not in nocturnal darkness, the traditional setting for ghosts, but in the full glare of the sun, in the dazzling light of a Finnish summer night. For some days all the Helsinki papers had been talking about the ghost of Kalevala Street. Every evening close to midnight, the elevator in a house at the harbor end of the street started suddenly by itself, went up to the top floor, halted and, after a brief pause, came quickly and noiselessly down again; the door of the elevator was opened with a gentle sound; then the handle on the outside door turned a little and a woman stood on the threshold—a pale, silent woman who gazed for a long time at the small crowd gathered on the opposite sidewalk; she withdrew quietly closing the door very slowly; shortly afterward the sound of the elevator door was heard followed by a noise of the elevator as it went quickly and quietly up the steel shaft.

De Foxa walked cautiously, taking hold of my arm from time to time. Our figures seemed ghostlike in the reflection of the shop windows; our faces had the white glitter of wax. A few minutes before midnight we stood opposite the ghost's house in the weird glare of the nocturnal sun. It was a new house, built on the most modern lines and glistened with light paint, glass and chromium steel. The roof bristled with radio aerials. On the jamb—it was one of those doors that can be opened from the inside of each flat by pressing a button—was an aluminum plate with a double row of black, metal bell-buttons and, in a double column a list of names of the tenants. Beneath the aluminum plate gaped the mouth of a speaking tube with its nickel-plated lips by means of which every tenant could speak with his visitors before admitting them. To the right of the door was the window of an Elanto department store in which canned fish was displayed—two very green fishes standing out on a pink label evoked an abstract world of symbols and ghostly signs; a combined barber shop and beauty parlor was on the left with the inscription *Parturi-Kampaamo* painted in yellow on a pale blue background; a waxen female bust, two or three empty bottles and two celluloid combs glistened in the window.

Kalevala Street is narrow and the front of the house when seen from below, appeared to be off balance, as if it were suspended dangerously over the little throng that had gathered on the opposite sidewalk. It was a most modern house, built with great lavishness. The radio aerials bristling on the roof, the bare, smooth, white front in which the countless glass sockets of windows mirrored a clear night sky, with a frosty aluminum glint, made an ideal setting not for one of those lugubrious nocturnal ghosts, horrible and pitiful with livid and fleshless faces, that, wrapped in chilly shrouds, exhale a tainted odor of tombs in the ancient streets of Europe, but for a most up-to-date ghost such as would be evoked by Corbousier architecture, Bracque and Salvador Dali paintings and Hindemith and Honegger music—for one of those streamlined, nickel-plated ghosts that appear on the funereal threshold of the Empire State Building, on the lofty pediment of Rockefeller Center, on the deck of a luxury liner or in the cold bluish light of a central power station.

A small crowd waited silently before the ghost's house—people belonging to the working and middle classes, several sailors, two soldiers and a group of girls in Lottasvärd uniforms. Now and again a streetcar passed along a near-by street and made the walls shake and the windowpanes tinkle. A bicycle dashed around the corner, rushed by us, and for a few moments the rustle of tires on the damp asphalt lingered in the air. Something invisible seemed to pass before our eyes. De Foxa was extremely pale. He stared at the house with a greedy look, pressing my arm, and I felt him trembling with fear and impatience.

Suddenly we heard the elevator start—a slight, prolonged hum; then came the sound of the elevator door opening and shutting up on the top floor—the hum of the descending cage. All at once the door of the house opened and a woman stood on the threshold. A tiny, middle-aged woman dressed in gray, with a black felt hat —it may have been made of black paper—balanced on her blond hair streaked with silver. Her very light eyes made two dull blotches on the pale lean face with its high cheekbones. Her hands were concealed in a pair of green gloves. Her arms hung at her sides, and those green hands against the grayness of the skirt seemed like two withered leaves. She stopped on the threshold, gazing at each of the inquisitive onlookers gathered on the opposite sidewalk. Her eyelids were white, her stare lifeless. Then she turned her eyes to the sky and slowly raised one of her hands; she rested it against her forehead to screen her eyes from the sharp glare of the light. She scrutinized the sky for several moments, lowered her head, let her hand drop by her side and fixed her glance on the crowd that watched her with a cold, almost evil attention. Then the woman withdrew and closed the door. We heard the elevator start with a slight, prolonged hum. Holding our breath, we kept on listening for the sound of the elevator door up there, on the top floor. The hum ascended, growing more distant, and faded away. It seemed as if the elevator had melted into the air, or that it had pierced the roof and risen to the sky. The crowd raised their eyes peering into the clear sky. De Foxa pressed my arm hard; I felt that he was shaking from head to foot. "Let's go," I said to him. We moved off on tiptoe, gliding through the stupefied crowd absorbed in watching a small white cloud high up above the roofs. We walked the length of Kalevala Street and entered the ancient Swedish churchyard, where we sat on the bench next to Sierk's tomb.

"It was not a ghost," said de Foxa after a long silence. "We, ourselves, were the ghosts. Did you notice how she looked at us? She was afraid of us."

"It was a modern ghost," I replied, "a northern ghost."

"Yes indeed," said de Foxa laughing, "modern ghosts go up and down in elevators." He laughed nervously to disguise his childish fear. Then we left the churchyard; we walked down the Boulevardi and crossed Mannerheim Street back of the Swedish Theater. Men and women were stretched on the grass under the trees of the Esplanade and were offering their faces to the white, nocturnal light. During the "white nights" of summertime the people of the North are a prey to a queer restlessness, to a kind of cold fever. They spend the nights walking by the sea, or they stretch out on the grass in the public gardens, or they sit on the benches by the harbor. Later they walk home skirting the walls, their faces turned upward. They sleep only a few hours lying naked on their beds, bathed in the cold glare that penetrates through the wide-open windows. They lie naked in the nocturnal sun as if under a sun lamp. Through their open windows they can see moving through the glassy air, the ghosts of houses, of trees and of the sailing boats rocking in the harbor.

We had gathered in the dining room of the Spanish Legation around the massive mahogany table supported by four huge legs resembling elephant feet and laden with glass and old Spanish silver. The tapestries of red brocade hanging on the walls, the dark squat furniture carved with figures of dancing children, with festoons of fruit and game and with heavy-breasted caryatids—that Spanish interior so sensuous and so funereal, contrasted oddly with the white dazzle of the nocturnal light coming through the open window. The men in evening dress and the bejeweled women in low-cut dresses around that massive table with elephant feet sticking out between silk skirts and black trousers, in the gloomy red glow of brocade and in the dull glint of the silver, had a funereal appearance under the constant stare of the portraits of Spanish kings and grandees hung on the walls with thick cords of twisted silk. A golden Crucifix hung over the sideboard, and Christ's feet touched the necks of champagne bottles sunk in buckets of ice. They looked like paintings by Lucas Cranach; the flesh seemed livid and worn, the eyes circled with blue, the brows pale and hot; a greenish, cadaverous hue spread over every face. The guests sat with staring, wide-open eyes. The breath of the nocturnal day dimmed the windowpanes.

Midnight was approaching and the sunset glow was reddening the treetops in Brunnsparken. It was cold. I looked at the bare shoulders of Anita Bengenström, the daughter of the Finnish Minister in Paris, and I remembered that I was leaving next day with de Foxa and Michailescu for Lapland, north of the Arctic Circle. Summer was already far advanced. We would reach Lapland too late for the best salmon fishing. The Turkish Minister, Agah Aksel, remarked with a laugh that being late is one of the many pleasures of a diplomatic life. He told us that when Paul Morand was appointed Secretary of the French Embassy in London, Ambassador Cambon, who knew Paul Morand's reputation for laziness, at once said to him: "My dear fellow, come to the office whenever you please, but not later." Agah Aksel sat facing the window; his face was copper-colored, his white hair encased his brow like the silver frame of an icon. He was short and stocky and moved cautiously. He always seemed to be looking around with suspicion. *"C'est un jeune Turc qui adore le Konia,"* said de Foxá about him. "Ah, you are a young Turk then?" asked Anita Bengenström. "Alas, I was much more of a Turk when I was younger," replied Agah Aksel.

The Minister of Romania, Noti Constantinidu, who had spent his best years in Italy and wanted to end his days in Rome in Panama Street, spoke about the Roman summer, the voices of the fountains in the deserted squares, the fiery heat at noon and, while he talked, he shivered in the dazzling light of the northern night and gazed at his white hands that seemed like discarded wax hands lying on the tablecloth of pale blue satin. Constantinidu had returned the day before from Mikkeli, Marshal Mannerheim's headquarters, where he had gone to convey a high decoration bestowed on the Marshal by young King Michael of Romania.

"Since I last saw you," Constantinidu had said to the Marshal, "you have lost twenty years; the summer has brought you the gift of youth."

"Summer?" Mannerheim had replied. "There are ten months of winter in Finland and two without summer." The conversation lingered on Marshal Mannerheim, on the clash between his "decadent" tastes and his regal manner and appearance, on the immense prestige he enjoyed among the people and in the army, on the hardships that the war was thrusting on the Finnish people during that terrible first winter of war. Countess Mannerheim remarked that in Finland the cold does not blow down from the North, but breaks in from the East. "Although Lapland is beyond the Arctic Circle," she added, "the cold is much less bitter there than in the Volga region."

"That's a new angle on the everlasting Eastern question," said de Foxá.

"Do you think there still is an Eastern question for Europe?" asked the Minister of Turkey. "I share Philip Guedalla's opinion— for the Western people the entire Eastern question has by now been reduced to finding out what the Turks think of the Western question."

De Foxá mentioned that in the morning he had met the United

States Minister, Arthur Schoenfeld, who was extremely vexed with Philip Guedalla because of his last book, *Men of War,* published in London, a copy of which he had found at Stockmann's bookshop. The English author in his chapter on the Turks made the statement that the barbarian invasions in ancient days had always come to Europe from the East simply because they could not come from anywhere else before America had been discovered.

"The barbarian invasions have always come to Turkey from the West," said Agah Aksel, "as far back as the days of Homer."

"Did the Turks already exist in Homeric days?" asked Colette Constantinidu.

"There are Turkish carpets," replied Agah Aksel, "that are much older than the *Iliad.*"

A few days previously we had visited Dinu Cantemir, who lived in Brunnsparken, opposite the British Legation, in the beautiful house of the Linders, to admire his collection of china and oriental carpets. While Dinu Cantemir's hand was drawing in the air for me the genealogical tree of his finest specimens of Dresden and while Bengt von Törne, standing under the portrait of a famous Linder beauty, spoke to Mircea Berindey and Titu Michailescu about the paintings of Gallen Kallela, the Ministers of Turkey and of Romania, kneeling in the middle of the room, wrangled about two small, sixteenth-century Turkish ritual carpets that Cantemir had spread on the floor. In one of them two squares and two diamond-shaped oblongs were alternately woven in rose, violet and green; in the other there were four squares in pink, blue and gold of a clearly Persian inspiration. The Minister of Turkey extolled the supremely beautiful combination of the tints in the one carpet— the most difficult design he had ever seen; the Minister of Romania praised the almost feminine delicacy of the shades resembling an old Persian miniature in the other carpet.

"Not at all, my dear fellow," said Constantinidu raising his voice.

"I stake my word of honor that you are wrong," replied Agah Aksel in an angry tone. They were both kneeling, gesticulating and waving their arms as if they were worshiping in the Turkish manner. Continuing the argument, they finally sat down opposite one another, their legs crossed, on the two carpets. Agah Aksel said, "People have never been fair to the Turks."

Aksel continued, "Some day there will only be a few carpets left of the great Turkish civilization. We are a heroic and unfortunate people. All our misfortunes arise from our centuries-old tolerance. If we had been less tolerant, we might, perhaps, have subdued all of Christendom."

I asked him what the word "tolerance" meant in Turkish.

"We have always been generous toward the conquered people," replied Agah Aksel.

"I cannot understand," said de Foxa, "why the Turks did not become Christians. It would have simplified things."

"You are right," replied Agah Aksel, "if we had become Christians, we still would be in Budapest and, perhaps, in Vienna today."

"The Nazis are in Vienna today," said Constantinidu.

"If they will become Christians, they will stay there," said Agah Aksel.

"The greatest problem of modern days is still the religious problem," said Bengt von Törne. *"On ne peut pas tuer le dieu*—God cannot be killed." And he told us what had occurred a little time ago in Turku, the Finnish city on the Gulf of Bothnia. A Soviet parachutist who had dropped near the city was captured and locked up in the Turku prison. He was about thirty years old, a workman in a factory in Kharkov and a fervid communist. Being of a thoughtful turn of mind, he seemed not only interested in but also well informed about many subjects, particularly ethics. He was obviously better read than most *udarniki* or *stakhanovtzi*. In his cell the prisoner read extensively, choosing books on religious subjects that the governor of the prison, who was interested in so strange and complex a human specimen, allowed him to take out of his private library. Naturally, the prisoner was a materialist and an atheist.

After a time he was given work as a mechanic in the prison factory. One day he asked to have a talk with a clergyman. A young Lutheran pastor, highly esteemed for his learning and piety, and famous as a preacher, went to the prison and was taken into the cell of the Soviet paratrooper. For nearly two hours the two men were locked up together alone in the cell. At the end of this long talk, when the pastor rose to leave, the prisoner placed his hands on the pastor's shoulders and, after a moment of hesitation, embraced him. Later, these details were printed in the Turku papers.

A few weeks went by, and the prisoner, who for days had appeared to be tortured by secret and painful thoughts, asked again to be allowed to see the pastor, who went to the prison and, as on the previous occasion, was locked up with the communist in his cell. About half an hour went by, when a jailer walking outside heard a shriek and a call for help. He unlocked the cell and saw the prisoner standing against the wall and the pastor lying at his feet in a pool of blood. Before he died, the pastor revealed that at the end of their conversation the prisoner had embraced him and, while his arms were around him, had stabbed him in the back with a sharp iron file. In the course of the trial the murderer declared during his examination that he had killed the pastor because his communist and atheist mind was troubled by the weight of the clergyman's reasonings. He was sentenced to death and shot.

"He had tried," concluded Bengt von Törne, "to kill God in the pastor."

The story of that murder, which appeared in all the Finnish papers, had deeply stirred public opinion. Lieutenant Gummerus, the son of a former Minister of Finland in Rome told me that the commander of the firing squad, a Turku officer who was a friend of his, had been greatly impressed by the murderer's serenity.

"He had made peace with his conscience," said de Foxá.

"But this is horrible!" exclaimed Countess Mannerheim. "How can anyone conceive of the idea of killing God?"

"The entire modern world is trying to kill God," said Agah Aksel. "God's very existence is in peril in the modern consciousness."

"Is it true of the Moslem consciousness?" asked Cantemir.

"Yes, unfortunately, also in the Moslem consciousness. Not because we are near to communist Russia, but because the murder of God is in the air; it is an element of modern civilization."

"The modern state," said Constantinidu, "deludes itself into thinking that it can protect God's life simply with police measures."

"It's not only God's life. The modern state deludes itself that it can protect its own existence," said de Foxá. "Take Spain as an example. The only way to turn out Franco is to kill God, and the attempts on God's life in the streets of Madrid and Barcelona are too numerous to count. Never a day goes by that someone does not fire a pistol at Him." He told us that the day before he had found a very recent Spanish book in Stockmann's bookshop and, opening it on the first page, he had read the first line: "God, that lunatic of genius . . ."

"What is significant about the Turku murder," said Bengt von Törne, "is not so much that a Russian communist has killed a clergyman, but that Karl Marx is trying to kill God. It is a typically Marxist crime."

"We must have the courage to admit that the modern world is more willing to accept *Das Kapital* than the Gospels," said Constantinidu.

"This applies to the Koran also," said Agah Aksel. "It is surprising to see how easily the Mohammedan youth accepts communism. The Mohammedan youth in the eastern republics of the USSR gives up Mohammed for Marx without resistance. What will the Islamic world be without the Koran?"

"The Catholic Church," said de Foxa, "has given evidence of being able to exist without the Gospels."

"Some day there may be communism without Marx. At any rate that's what many Englishmen hope for," said Cantemir. "For many Englishmen the ideal is the Marx *Kapital* in a 'blue book' version."

"The English," said Agah Aksel, "have no reasons to fear communism. For them the problem is to win the class war on the same field where they won the battle of Waterloo—on the playing-field of Eton."

Countess Mannerheim mentioned that a few days previously when the German Minister von Blücher in talking with some colleagues had appeared to be very concerned about the communist threat to Great Britain, Count Adam de Moltke-Hieutfeldt, Secretary of the Danish Legation, had answered, "Don't worry, Britons never will be Slavs."

"Englishmen," said de Foxa, "have the great gift of stripping every problem of all superfluous elements and of laying bare even the most serious and complex problems. We shall see communism," he added, "strolling naked through the streets of Great Britain, just as Lady Godiva rode through the streets of Coventry."

It was about two in the morning. The cold was intense and the metallic light entering through the wide-open window turned the faces of the guests so livid that I begged de Foxa to have the window closed and the lights turned on. We all looked like corpses; nothing looks more like a dead body than a man dressed for the evening in full daylight, or a made-up, bare-shouldered young woman whose jewels glitter in the sun. We sat around the rich table like the dead attending a funeral banquet in Hades. The servants closed the windows and turned on the lights, and something warm, intimate and secret entered the room. The wine sparkled in the glasses, our faces were suffused with the color of blood, eyes shone merrily, and our voices once again became warm and deep, like the voices of living people. Suddenly we heard the long wail of the alert, followed at once by the barrage of anti-aircraft guns. The mellow beelike hum of the Soviet planes came from over the sea.

"This may seem funny," said Constantinidu in a calm voice, "but I am frightened."

"I'm frightened, too," said de Foxa, "and it is not in the least funny."

No one stirred. We heard the deep dull crashes of the explosions; the walls shook. A glass in front of Colette Constantinidu cracked with a faint tinkle. At a sign from de Foxa a servant again opened the window. We could see the Soviet planes, maybe a hundred of them, flying low above the roofs of the city like large insects with transparent wings.

"The strangest thing about these luminous nights of the North," said Mircea Berindey in his tired Romanian accent, "is that nocturnal gestures, thoughts, sentiments, objects that are born only in the secrecy of darkness, and that the night jealously guards and protects in its dark bosom, can be seen in full daylight." Turning toward Madame Slörn, he added, "Look, this is a nocturnal face."

Pale, her lips faintly trembling, her white eyelids quivering, Madame Slörn smiled, lowering her head. Madame Slörn was born in Greece, her face is diaphanous, her eyes black, her brow lofty and pure, and there is an antique gentleness in her smile and her gestures. She has owl's eyes, the eyes of Pallas, with white delicate quivering eyelids.

"I like being afraid," said Madame Slörn.

From time to time a deep silence blended with the rumble of guns, the crash of bombs and the hum of engines. During those sudden streaks of silence we could hear the birds singing.

"The railway station is in flames," said Agah Aksel who sat facing the window.

The Elanto stores were also on fire. It was cold. The ladies had wrapped themselves in their furs; the icy nocturnal sun shone through the trees of the park. Far away, toward Soumenlinna, a dog was barking.

PART FOUR

THE BIRDS

XI

The Glass Eye

PRINCESS LOUISE VON PREUSSE, a grandniece of Kaiser Wilhelm II—Prince Joachim Hohenzollern, her father, now dead for some years, had been a younger brother of the Crown Prince—and Ilse were to meet me that evening at the Potsdam station. "We shall bicycle over from Litzensee," Ilse had phoned.

It was a damp, warm spring evening. When I got off the Berlin train a light drizzle was scattering silvery dust into the air. The houses at the end of the square looked as though they were made of aluminum. Officers and soldiers stood in groups on the sidewalks before the station.

As I was gazing at a propaganda poster of the *Leibesstandart* Adolf Hitler stuck up on the wall of the station—on the poster two SS men armed with tommy guns, their faces clean shaven and clear-cut, their foreheads concealed under large steel helmets, a cold cruel glint in their gray eyes, stood out sharply against a landscape of blazing houses, charred trees and guns sunk in mud up to the wheel hubs—I felt a hand touch my arm. "Good evening," said Ilse. Her cheeks were flushed by the long bicycle ride, her hair was ruffled by the wind. "Louise is waiting for us outside," she said. "She is watching the bicycles." Then she smiled and added, "She is very sad, poor child. Be nice to her."

Louise had rested the two bicycles against a lamp post and was waiting for us with her hand on a handlebar. "How are you?" she inquired in that peculiar Potsdam French, self-conscious and shy. She looked up at me, smiling, her head cocked slightly on one shoulder. She asked me if I had a pin. Was I without a pin, too? "You cannot find a single pin in all of Germany," she said laughing. There was a little tear in her skirt, and she seemed to be very concerned about it. She wore a small green felt Tirolean hat pulled down over the nape of her neck and a tobacco-colored tweed skirt; a leather jerkin of mannish cut encased her bosom, revealing the shortness of her waist and the softness of her hips. Her socks were very short and her legs bare. She was pleased to see me again. Why couldn't I go back with them to Litzensee? She could certainly find a bicycle for me, and I would spend the night at the castle. I could not do it; I was to start next morning for Riga and Helsinki. Couldn't I postpone my departure? Litzensee was very beautiful, it was not really a castle, but an old country house surrounded by gorgeous woods; whole families of deer and fallow-deer lived in the Litzensee forests; nature was very lovely and very young there.

We walked toward the center of town; I was walking beside Louise who was leaning on her bicycle. The rain had stopped; it was a warm, clear, moonless night. I felt as if I were walking by the side of a girl through the suburbs of my hometown; as if I had gone back to my boyhood in Prato; in the evening when the girls left the factories, I would wait for Bianca on the sidewalk of the Fabbricone, beyond the Serraglio Gate, and walk home with her, leaning on my bicycle. The street was muddy and Louise seemed as heedless of the mud as the working girls had been. She stepped into puddles just like the factory girls in my hometown, just like Bianca. The first stars, pale and remote, peeped through the misty sky. On the branches of the trees the birds made sweet and merry music, and the voice of the river swayed at the end of the street like a curtain in the wind. We stopped on the bridge and leaned over to look at the water. A boat with two soldiers was gliding under the arches, sweeping down the stream. Louise, leaning on the marble parapet, watched the stream flowing gently between the grassy banks. She leaned over the parapet, raising herself on tiptoe just as Bianca used to do on the Mercatale Bridge to watch the stream of the Bisenzio gliding along the tall red wall that encircles the town. I used to buy a bag of lupine or pumpkin seeds and Bianca amused herself by spitting the shells into the river.

"If we were in Italy," I said, "I would buy a pennyworth of marrons or lupine seeds for you. But you cannot get a single marron in Germany. Do you like lupines, Louise, and salted pumpkin seeds?"

"When I was in Florence I bought a bag of marrons every day on the corner of Tornabuoni Street. But it all seems like a fairy story now."

"Why don't you come and spend your honeymoon in Italy, Louise?"

"Oh, you have already heard that I am getting married? Who told you?"

"Agatha Ratibor told me the other day. Come to Capri, to my house, Louise. I shall be far away in Finland, and the house will be yours. At Capri the moon is truly as sweet as honey."

"I cannot. My passport has been withdrawn. We cannot leave Germany. We live at Litzensee as if we were in exile."

Life was not particularly easy for the princes of the Imperial house. They were not allowed to move outside a radius of a few miles of their home. Louise laughed. They had to have a special permit to go to Berlin.

The trees were mirrored in the river, the air was sweet, illuminated by a faint veil of silvery mist. We had walked a long way from the bridge, when a young officer stopped and saluted. He was a tall blond young man, with an open smiling face.

"Oh, Hans!" said Louise blushing.

He was Hans Reinhold. He stood at attention in front of Louise, his arms stiffly at his sides, and he smiled at Louise. And little by little, as if drawn by a magic power transcending his will, his face turned toward a platoon of soldiers who marched in step, beating their heels hard on the pavement. They were his soldiers; they had been relieved from guard duty and were going back to the barracks.

"Why don't you come with us, Hans?" Louise asked softly.

"I have not finished playing at soldiers. I'm on duty tonight," said Hans. His glance was now gliding past Louise's face, following the soldiers who moved away beating their heels hard on the asphalt of the street.

"So long, Hans," said Louise.

"So long, Louise," said Hans. He raised his hand to his cap, saluted Louise in the stiff Potsdam manner and then turned to Ilse and me. He said, "So long, Ilse," and after a slight bow to me, overtook his platoon at a run and disappeared at the end of the avenue.

Louise walked in silence. I could only hear the slight swish of the bicycle tires on the damp asphalt, the hum of motors on a distant road and the tread of feet on the pavement. Ilse was also silent, shaking her small blond head from time to time. Now and again, a human voice broke through that silence, through that continuous harmony of faint sounds that make up the silence of a street in a provincial town in the evening, but it was a human voice attuned to that harmony of sounds, just a human voice, nothing but a pure, solitary human voice.

"Hans is to go to the front next month," said Louise. "We shall just have enough time to marry." Then she added after a momentary hesitation, "This war . . ." and she was silent again.

"This war frightens you," I said.

"No, that is not it. No, but there is something about this war . . ."

"What?" I asked.

"Nothing. I meant . . . oh, it is useless!"

We came to a restaurant not far from the bridge and went inside. The larger room was full of people, so we took a table at the end of a smaller side room where a few soldiers sat silently around a table and two girls, mere children, were having supper with an old lady, perhaps their governess. Their long blond hair was braided down their shoulders, and they had starched white collars turned back on their gray school-girl dresses. Louise seemed embarrassed; she gazed around as if searching for someone and now and again she raised her eyes to me, smiling sadly. Suddenly she said: "I cannot bear it any longer." There was a shade of cold severity in her simple grace, that cold severity so peculiar to Potsdam, to its baroque architecture, its neoclassical pretensions, the white stuccos of its churches, its palaces, its barracks, its colleges, its houses—a severity both courtly and middle class, supported by the thick green dampness of the trees.

With Louise I felt as free and unaffected as with a factory girl. Louise's charm was in her simplicity, the simplicity of a girl of the people, and in her shy sadness that seemed to be the result of a joyless existence, of everlasting daily toil—the gloom of a hard drab life. There was in her no trace of downcast pride or heartfelt renunciation, no trace of false humility, vainglorious shamefulness or sudden resentment in which ordinary people see indications of fallen greatness—only a sad simplicity, unconscious patience, a slightly filmed glow, an ancient and noble innocence, a dark patient power that is at the root of pride. I felt as free and unaffected with her as with one of those factory girls that one sees in the evenings in the U-Bahn coaches or in the misty streets of Berlin suburbs near the factories when they come out in groups and walk downcast and sad, followed at a distance by the dull silent crowd of bare-legged, almost nude and disheveled girls whom the Germans had brought back as prisoners from their white-slave raids in Poland, the Ukraine and Ruthenia.

Louise had delicate hands with pale transparent nails. A network of blue veins flowed from her slender wrists into the lines of her hands. She was resting one of her hands on the tablecloth, as she looked at the sporting prints that decorated the walls of the room—the most famous thoroughbreds of the Vienna Hochschule drawn by Vernet and Adam, some prancing, others galloping through landscapes of blue trees and green waters. I gazed at Louise's typical Hohenzollern hand. I could recognize the hands of the Hohenzollerns, famous for their shortness, their provincial refinement, rather plump, with an out-thrust thumb, a tiny little finger with the middle finger scarcely exceeding the other fingers in length. But Louise's hand was red and roughened by scouring powder and covered with a mesh of fine wrinkles, cracked and chafed, like the hands of the Polish and Ukrainian factory women whom I had seen munching bits of brown bread close to the wall of a factory the day I had gone to the Ruhleben suburbs—like the hands of the "white slaves" from the east, of the Russian engineering women workers who in the evenings throng the sidewalks of the industrial quarters of Pankow and Spandau.

"Could you bring me some soap from Italy or Sweden?" asked Louise trying to conceal her hand. "I have to do my own laundry, my stockings and my underwear. A little kitchen soap." And she added after an embarrassed silence, "I would prefer working in a factory. I cannot bear this lower middle-class life any longer."

"Your turn will come soon," I said. "They will send you to work in a factory."

"Oh no, they will have nothing to do with a Hohenzollern. We are pariahs in Germany. They will have nothing to do with us," she added with a spark of contempt. "They will have nothing to do with an Imperial Highness."

At that moment two soldiers, their eyes covered by black bandages entered the room. A nurse was with them to help them find their way. They sat at a near-by table, motionless and silent. The nurse turned now and again to look at us. Finally she whispered something softly to the two blind soldiers who turned their faces in our direction.

"How young they are!" said Louise in a low voice. "They look like mere boys."

"They have been lucky," I said. "The war has not devoured them. The war does not eat corpses—it only eats living soldiers. It gnaws the legs, the arms, the eyes of living soldiers, mostly while they sleep, just as rats do. But men are more civilized; they never eat living men. Heaven knows why, they prefer to eat corpses. Perhaps it is because it must be very hard to eat a living man even though he is asleep. I saw Russian prisoners at Smolensk eating the corpses of their comrades who had died of hunger and cold. The German soldiers stook by looking at them in the most respectful and kindly way. The Germans are full of human feeling, aren't they? But it was no fault of theirs, they had nothing to give the prisoners to eat, and so they stood by looking at them and shaking their heads and saying, '*Arme Leute*—Poor fellows.' The Germans are a sentimental people, the most sentimental and the most civilized people in the world. The German people will not eat corpses; they eat living men."

"Please, don't be cruel, don't talk about such horrors," said Louise resting her hand on my arm. I felt her shivering, and I was overcome by a rush of angry pity.

"The cold was frightful," I went on, "and I was sick. I felt ashamed of appearing so weak before the Germans. The German officers and men looked at me with contempt, as one looks at a puny woman. And I blushed. I meant to apologize for that moment of weakness but my retching prevented me from apologizing to the Germans."

Louise was silent. I felt her hand trembling on my arm. She had closed her eyes; she seemed to have stopped breathing. Keeping her eyes closed and trembling, she said, "I sometimes wonder whether my family is partly responsible for all that is happening now. Do you think we Hohenzollerns are partly responsible?"

"Who is not partly responsible? I am no Hohenzollern—and yet I sometimes think that I, too, am partly responsible for what is now taking place in Europe."

"I sometimes wonder whether, being a German woman, I am bound to love the German people. A Hohenzollern should love the German people, don't you think?"

"You don't have to love them. But the Germans are very nice."

"Oh, yes—they are very nice," said Ilse smiling.

"Do you want me to tell you the story of the glass eye?"

"I cannot bear to listen to these harrowing stories," said Louise.

"It is not a harrowing story. It is a German story, a sentimental story."

"Talk softly," said Louise. "The two blind soldiers might hear you. Can you imagine anything in the world gentler than the blind?"

"Perhaps there is something even gentler in the world—namely, men who have glass eyes. But last winter in Poland I saw men who were gentler than the blind, gentler than men with glass eyes. I was in Warsaw, in the Europeiski Café. I was just back from the Smolensk front, and I was terribly weary, a feeling of nausea prevented me from sleeping. I would awake at night with a cruel pain in my stomach; I felt as if I had swallowed an animal and the animal was gnawing at my insides. I felt just as if I had eaten a piece of a live man—and I would lay by the hour gazing into the darkness with wide-open eyes. This night I was in the Europeiski Café. The orchestra was playing old Polish songs and Viennese *Lieder*. Several German soldiers were sitting with two nurses at a near-by table. The café was crowded with the usual people, splendid and miserable, full of the dignity and chivalrous sadness that is ever present at Polish meeting places during these years of slavery and destitution. Worn looking men and women sat at the tables silently listening to the music or whispering softly among themselves. They wore crumpled clothing, washed-out linen and down-at-the-heel shoes. There was that gentleness in their manner that makes the Polish nation like a misty mirror in which the most common actions are reflected with an old world grace and nobility.

"The ladies were marvelous in their simplicity, full of grandeur and pride that veiled the pallor of hunger in their faces. They smiled wanly, and yet there was no trace of sweetness, resignation or pity. There was nothing humble in the wan smiles on those pain-stricken lips. Their eyes, deep and clear, were stormy; they resembled wounded or caged birds. They resembled those seagulls that fly wearily by, forecasting a storm—white against the black sea sky, mingling their shrieks with the noise of wind and waves. The German soldiers sat at the neighboring table, their eyes staring, their faces motionless. In the center of their staring eyes, I could see their pupils oddly expanding and contracting. I noticed that they did not flicker their eyelids. But they were not blind; some were reading the papers, others watched the musicians, the people coming and going, the waiters fussing around the tables, and, through the misty panes of the large windows, the vast Pilsudski Square deserted in the snow.

"Suddenly I was struck with horror and realized that they had no eyelids. I had already seen soldiers with lidless eyes, on the platform of the Minsk station a few days previously on my way from Smolensk. The ghastly cold of that winter had the strangest consequences. Thousands and thousands of soldiers had lost their limbs; thousands and thousands had their ears, their noses, their fingers and their sexual organs ripped off by the frost. Many had lost their hair. Soldiers were known to have become bald over night; others had lost their hair in patches as if infected with ring-worm. Many had lost their eyelids. Singed by the cold, the eyelid drops off like a piece of dead skin. I was struck with horror watching the eyes of those poor soldiers in the Europeiski Café in Warsaw, those pupils that expanded and contracted in the center of the fixed wide-open eyes, straining in vain to screen them from the pain of light. I thought that those poor fellows slept with eyes wide open in the dark, that night was their only eyelid; that their future was lunacy; that only lunacy could slightly shade their lidless eyes."

"Oh, stop!" Louise almost shouted. She gazed at me, her eyes staring and strangely white. "Say no more," she whispered. She closed her eyes and breathed deeply.

"Let me tell you the story of the glass eye."

"You have no right to make me suffer," said Louise.

"It is merely a Christian story, Louise. Aren't you a princess of the Imperial German House, a Hohenzollern? Aren't you what is described as a well-bred young lady? Why shouldn't I tell you Christian stories?"

"You have no right," said Louise in a sharp voice.

"Let me at least tell you a nursery story," I said.

"Oh, please, keep still!" begged Louise. "Can't you see that I am shaking? You are frightening me."

"It is a story about Neapolitan children and British aviators," I went on. "A gentle story. Even in war there is a certain gentleness."

"What is most horrible in war," said Ilse, "is precisely what is gentle in it. I cannot bear to see smiling monsters."

"I was in Naples at the beginning of the war, when the first bombings began. I went to have supper one evening with a friend of mine who lives at the Vomero. The Vomero is a high cliff that dominates the city from which the Posillipo hills branch off descending to the sea. It is an enchanting place and, up to a few years ago, it was a countryside with scattered little houses and villas lost among the greenery. Each house had its orchard, a few vines, a few olive trees and terraced embankments on which blossomed eggplants, tomatoes, cabbages, peas, scented basil, rose and rosemary. The roses and tomatoes of the Vomero for beauty and fame are not inferior to the ancient roses of Paostum or to the tomatoes of Pompeii. Now the orchards have been turned into gardens. But in between the huge glass-and-concrete buildings a few ancient villas and humble farmhouses survive, and here and there the greenness of a lonely orchard fades sweetly into the vast pale blueness of the gulf; across the water, Capri stands out from the sea in a silvery mist; on the right is Ischia with its high Epomaeo; on the left the Sorrento shore can be seen in the transparent mirrors of the sea and sky, and still farther to the left is Vesuvius, that gentle idol, a kind of great Buddha looking down from the windowsill of the gulf. If one strolls through the lanes of the Vomero where it changes its name and is wedded to the Posillipo hills, between the trees and houses one can see the solemn and most ancient pine tree that shades Virgil's tomb. That is where my friend had his little rustic house and little orchard.

"While we waited for supper, we sat in the orchard under a vine arbor, smoking and talking quietly. The sun had already set and the light was being gradually extinguished. The place, the landscape, the time, the season were the same as those of which Sannazaro had sung; the breeze was Sannazaro's breeze in which the smell of the sea and the scent of the orchards melt into the delicate eastern wind. When night began to rise from the sea with its large bunches of violets already damp with nocturnal dew—at night the sea puts on its windowsills large bunches of violets that scent the air, filling the rooms with the pleasing breath of the sea—my friend said, 'The night will be clear. They will certainly come. I must put the presents for the British flyers in the orchard.' I did not understand, and I was puzzled as I watched my friend enter the house and come out carrying a doll, a little wooden horse, a trumpet and two little bags of sweets which he, without saying a word and perhaps mischievously enjoying my bewilderment, went about carefully placing here and there among the rose bushes and lettuce clumps, on the pebbles of the narrow path and on the edge of a bowl in which a family of goldfish softly flashed.

" 'What are you doing?' I asked.

"He gazed at me with a serious expression and smiled. He told me that his two children, who were already in bed, had been overcome with a terrific fear during the first bombings, that the health of the youngest one had been seriously affected—and that he had evolved a means of changing the fearful bombings of Naples into an entertainment for his children. As soon as the alarm hooted through the night, my friend and his wife jumped out of bed and, gathering the two little ones in their arms, began shouting merrily: 'What fun! What fun! The British planes are coming to throw their presents to you!' They went down into their cellar that offered scant and ineffectual shelter and, huddling there, they passed the hours of terror and death laughing and shouting, 'What fun!' until the boys fell happily asleep dreaming about the presents from the British flyers. From time to time, as the crash of the bombs and the crumbling of buildings came nearer, the little ones awoke, and the father said: 'Now, now, they are throwing down your presents!' The two boys clapped their hands with joy, shouting: 'I want a doll! I want a sword! Daddy, do you think that the British will bring me a little boat?' Toward dawn, when the hum of the motors moved off fading slowly into a sky that was already clear, the father and mother led the children by their hands into the garden, saying, 'Look for them, look! They must have dropped them on the grass.' The two boys searched among the rose bushes, wet with dew, among the lettuce plants and the tomato stalks, and they found a doll here, a little wooden horse there and, farther off, a bag of candy. The two children were no longer afraid of bombings, instead they waited anxiously for them and welcomed them joyfully. Some mornings, searching through the grass, they found little spring-propelled airplanes—undoubtedly poor British airplanes that those nasty Germans had brought down with their guns while they bombarded Naples to make Neapolitan children happy."

"Oh, how lovely!" burst out Louise clapping her hands.

"Now I shall tell you," I said, "the story of Siegfried and the cat. Those two Neapolitan children would not appreciate the story about Siegfried and the cat, but you will like it very much. It's a German story and Germans like German stories."

"The Germans like everything that is German," said Louise. "And Siegfried is the German people."

"And the cat, Louise? What is a cat? Can it also be a kind of Siegfried?"

"Siegfried is unique," replied Louise.

"You are right! Siegfried is unique and all other people are cats. Now listen to a story about Siegfried and the cat. I was in the village of Rita, close to Pančevo, in front of Belgrade, waiting to cross the Danube. A few rifle shots pierced the air of that white April morning stretching out like a linen screen between us and the blazing city. A squad of SS men were waiting for orders to force a crossing; they were all very young; they all had Gothic triangular faces, pointed chins, sharp profiles and Siegfried's pure, cruel look in their eyes. They sat silently on the bank of the Danube, their faces turned to the spires of Belgrade, their tommy guns rested between their knees. One of them was sitting close to where I was. He was a lad about eighteen years old, fair, with blue eyes and red lips lighted up by a cold innocent smile. We began talking, we spoke about the cruelty of war—its destruction, bereavements, slaughter. He told me that the recruits of the *Leibesstandart* of the SS were all trained to bear other people's pains unflinchingly. I must tell you again that his blue eyes were extraordinarily pure. He added that an SS recruit is not fit to belong to the *Leibesstandart* until he is able to get through the cat trial with flying colors. With his left hand, the recruit must grab a live cat by the skin of its back so as to allow it to use its claws to defend itself, and gouge out its eyes with a little knife held in the right hand. That is how one learns to kill Jews."

Louise clutched my sleeve and her nails hurt me through the material. I felt her hand trembling. "You have no right . . ." she said in a low voice, turning her pale face toward the two blind soldiers who ate in silence, their heads slightly thrown backward. The nurse was helping them with slow light gestures, correcting the uncertain movements of their arms and touching the backs of their hands with her fingertips whenever the knife or the fork wandered about the edge of the plate.

"Oh, Louise, forgive me!" I said. "Horrible stories give me the creeps too. But there are certain facts that you must know. You must know that, in a certain sense, cats also belong to the same species as Siegfried. Has it ever occurred to you that, perhaps, Jesus Christ is a kind of Siegfried—that Jesus Christ is a crucified cat? You must not think, as all Germans are taught to think, that Siegfried is unique and that all other people are cats. No, Louise, Siegfried also belongs to a species of cats. Do you know the origin of the word *kaputt?* It comes from the Semitic *kapparoth,* which means a 'victim.' The cat is a *kapparoth;* it is a victim as opposed to Siegfried. It is a sacrificed Siegfried, a Siegfried given as an offering. There is a time, a time that always recurs, when Siegfried, the unique, also becomes a cat, becomes *kapparoth,* a victim, becomes *kaputt.* It is the time when Siegfried is nearing death, when Hagen-Himmler gets ready to gouge his eyes as if he were a cat. It is the German people's doom to turn into a *kapparoth,* into a victim, to go *kaputt!* The secret meaning of its history is to be found in this metamorphosis from Siegfried into a cat. There are certain facts that you must know, Louise. You, too, must know that we are all Siegfrieds, that we are all destined to become *kapparoth* some day, victims, to go *kaputt;* that is why we are Christians, that is why Siegfried also is a Christian, and why Siegfried is also a cat. Emperors and the sons of emperors must know certain facts. You have been very badly educated, Louise."

"I am not a Siegfried any longer," said Louise. "I am much closer to a cat than to an Imperial princess."

"Yes, Louise, you are closer to a working woman than to a Hohenzollern princess."

"You think so?" asked Louise shyly.

"A working woman would take to you, if you were her friend in a factory."

"I should like to work in a factory. I should change my name and work like any other factory hand."

"Why change your name?"

"A Hohenzollern— Do you imagine that the other workers would respect me, if they knew my real name?"

"What good is the Hohenzollern name today?"

"Tell me the story of the glass eye," said Louise with sudden softness.

"It's a story like so many others, Louise. It's useless to tell it. It is a Christian story. You no doubt know some Christian stories, don't you? They are all alike."

"What do you mean by a Christian story?"

"Have you read Aldous Huxley's *Point Counterpoint?* The death of the child, of tiny Philip, in the last chapter is a Christian story. Aldous Huxley might have spared himself the useless cruelty of letting the child die. Huxley was once ordered to appear at Buckingham Palace. Queen Mary and King George V wanted to know him. Just then *Point Counterpoint* was enjoying its greatest success. The King and Queen welcomed Aldous Huxley most affably. They spoke to him about his books, asked him about his travels, the works he was planning, the trends of modern English literature. After the audience, when Huxley had already reached the threshold, His Majesty George V called him back in a kindly voice. The King seemed ill at ease; he apparently had something to say, but he hesitated. Finally the King said to Huxley in an uncertain voice, 'Mr. Huxley, the Queen and I would like to reproach you for something. It really was unnecessary to let the child die.'"

"Oh, what a lovely story!" exclaimed Louise.

"It is a Christian story, Louise."

"Tell me the story of the glass eye," said Louise blushing.

During the winter of 1941 I was in the Ukraine, near Poltava. The countryside was infested with partisans. It seemed as if the days of the Cossack uprisings of Chmielnicki, of Pugachev and Stienka Rasin had returned. Bands of partisans roamed about the woods and marshes along the Dnieper, rifle shots and bursts of machine-gun fire broke unexpectedly from the ruins of villages, out of the ditches and thickets. Then silence fell again, the fat, dull, dreary silence of the vast Russian plain.

One day a German officer was riding through a village at the head of an artillery column. Not a living soul was anywhere in the village; the houses looked as if they had been abandoned long ago. In the stables of the *kolkhoz* about a hundred starved horses were lying on the ground, still tied by their halters to the empty bins. The village had that sinister appearance that is characteristic of Russian villages after they had been swept by the fury of German reprisals. Sadly, vaguely ill at ease, almost with fear, the officer looked at the deserted houses, the straw on the thresholds, the wide-open windows and the empty silent rooms. In the orchards, above the fences, were the black, round, motionless eyes of the sunflowers, staring from within the frames of their long yellow lashes and following the passing column with their sad vacant stare.

The officer rode bending forward over the horse's mane, both hands resting on the pommel. He was about forty years old, with already graying hair. Now and again he lifted his eyes to the misty sky, then stood up in his stirrups and turned to watch the column. The soldiers walked in groups behind the gun carriages; the horses pressed their hooves into the muddy road; the whips hissed through the damp air; the men shouted *Ja! Ja!* to urge the horses on. It was a gray day and the village had a ghostly appearance in the ashen autumn air. A wind had risen; the bodies of several Jews were swinging from the branches of the trees. A constant whisper fled from house to house as if a crowd of children ran barefoot through the squalid rooms; there was a constant crackling as if an army of mice gamboled through the abandoned houses.

The column halted in the village and the soldiers were already scattering through the lanes between the orchards in search of water for their horses when the officer trotted up hurriedly. He was strangely pale and shouted, "*Weg, weg, Leute!*—Off, off, boys!" and, in rushing by, he touched with his whip the soldiers who had already plumped down on the steps of the houses. "*Weg, weg, Leute!*" he shouted. Then a rumor spread among the soldiers, *Fleck-typhus*—spot typhus—and the ghastly word crept along the column, down to the last gun that had stopped outside the village. All the men went back to their places, and the column moved on. "*Ja! Ja!*" The whips hissed through the gray air, and the artillerymen, in passing, cast frightened glances through the open windows into the houses where the corpses, bleak, colorless, livid and ghostly, were stretched out with wide-open eyes on the straw. The officer sat quietly on his horse in the center of the village square, close to Stalin's statue that lay tumbled into the mire. He watched the column moving past him and, now and again, he lifted his hand to his forehead and very slowly, with a gentle, tired movement, stroked his left eye.

Sunset was still far away, but the first evening shadows were gathering in the foliage of the woods that by degrees were growing darker, thicker, and of a deeper and duller blue. The officer's horse was restless, it pawed the muddy ground and threatened to rear or to gallop after the column that was already moving out of the village. The officer held the horse down to a walk, trailing the last gun carriage. He kept in the rear of the column and when he reached the last houses, he stood up in his stirrups and looked back. The road and the square were deserted, the houses were gloomy and empty. And yet there was that whisper, that crackling which the wind made running its rough tongue over the walls of mud and straw, that whisper and that crackling as if barefoot children and famished mice were following the column at a distance. The officer raised his hand to his forehead and with a bored, sad gesture touched his eye. Suddenly a shot rang out from the village and a bullet hissed by his ear.

"Halt!" shouted the officer. The column stopped and a machine gun belonging to the rear battery began firing at the houses in the village. Other shots had followed the first one, and gradually the firing of the partisans became livelier, more insistent and angry.

Two artillerymen were hit. The officer spurred his horse and gal‧
loped along the column shouting orders. Groups of soldiers, firing
on the run, moved off through the fields to surround the village.
"Man the guns!" shouted the officer. "Destroy everything!" The
partisans continued firing. Another artilleryman was hit. Then the
officer flew into a terrible rage; he galloped through the fields
urging the men on and placing the guns so they would bear on
the village from all sides. A few houses caught fire. A hail of in-
cendiary shells rained on the village, bursting open the walls,
piercing the roofs, rending the trees, raising clouds of smoke. Fear-
lessly the partisans kept up their fire, but very soon the violent
artillery fire turned the village into a pyre. And there, from amid the
smoke and flames, a group of partisans, their arms raised high, ran
out. Some were old, the majority young, and among them was a
woman. The officer leaned over the saddle and looked them over
one by one. Sweat was dripping from his brow and streaming
down his face. "Shoot them!" he said in a harsh voice, and pressed
his eye with his hand. His voice was bored, perhaps even the
gesture with which he pressed his eye expressed boredom.

"Feuer!" shouted the Feldwebel. After the rattle of the tommy
guns was over, the officer turned and looked at the fallen. He made
a sign with his riding whip. *"Jawohl,"* said the Feldwebel firing
his pistol into the pile of corpses. Then he raised his hand, the
gunners harnessed the horses to the guns and the column formed
and started off down the road.

The officer, bending over the horse's mane, his hands resting on
the pommel of the saddle, followed the column keeping about fifty
paces back of the last gun. The hoofbeats, dulled by the mud of the
plain, already sounded distant, when suddenly a rifle bullet hissed
by his ear. "Halt!" he shouted. The column stopped; the rear battery again opened fire on the village. All the battery's machine guns
rattled away at the blazing houses. But slowly and regularly a few
rifle shots pierced the cloud of smoke. "Four, five, six . . ." counted
the officer aloud. "It is only one rifle shooting, only one man." Suddenly a shadow with raised arms ran out through the cloud of
smoke.

The soldiers grabbed the partisan and pushed him in front of the
officer who, bending from his saddle, looked him over carefully.

Ein Kind!—A child!" he said softly. The boy was not more than ten years old, thin, squalid; his clothes were in rags, his face black, his hair singed, his hands scorched. *Ein Kind!* The boy looked at the officer calmly and blinked; now and again he raised his hand slowly and blew his nose with his fingers. The officer slipped from the saddle and winding the reins around his wrist, stood facing the boy. He looked tired and bored. *Ein Kind!* He had a son at home, in Berlin, at Witzleben Square, a boy about the same age. Maybe Rudolf was a year older. This boy really looks like a child, *ein Kind!* The officer struck his boot with the riding whip, and the horse pawed the ground with an impatient hoof and rubbed its muzzle against the officer's shoulder. Two steps away the interpreter was waiting at attention with an irritated expression. "He's only a child, *ein Kind!* I did not come to Russia to make war on children." Suddenly the officer bent over the boy and asked him whether any other partisans were left in the village. The officer's voice was so tired, so full of boredom that it almost leaned on the interpreter who angrily repeated the question in Russian.

"*Nièt,*" replied the boy.

"Why did you fire at my men?"

The boy looked at the officer with a surprised air; the interpreter repeated the question twice.

"You know already. Why do you ask?" replied the boy. His voice was calm and clear. There was no trace of fear, no indifference in his tone. He faced the officer squarely and, before answering, came to attention like a soldier.

"Do you know who the Germans are?" asked the officer in a low voice.

"Aren't you a German yourself, *tovarish* officer?" countered the boy.

The officer made a sign, and the Feldwebel grasping the boy by the arm, took his gun from his belt.

"Not here, farther away," said the officer turning his back.

The boy moved off, taking quick steps so as to keep up with the Feldwebel. Suddenly the officer turned, raised his riding whip and shouted, "*Ein Moment!*" The Feldwebel turned, looked perplexedly at the officer and came back pushing the boy with his outstretched arm.

"What time is it?" asked the officer. Without waiting for a reply, he began to pace up and down in front of the boy, striking his boots with the riding whip. The horse pulled at the reins and followed, snorting and shaking its head. Finally the officer stopped before the boy, stared at him for a long time in silence, then said in a slow tired voice full of boredom: "Listen, I don't want to hurt you. You are a child, and I am not waging war against children. You have fired at my men, but I am not waging war on children. *Lieber Gott,* I am not the one who invented war." The officer broke off, then went on in a strangely gentle voice: "Listen, I have one glass eye. It is difficult to tell which is the real one. If you can tell me at once, without thinking about it, which of the two is the glass eye, I will let you go free."

"The left eye," replied the boy promptly.

"How did you know?"

"Because it is the one that has something human in it."

Louise was breathing heavily, clutching my arm.

"And the boy? What happened to the boy?" she said in a low voice.

"The officer kissed him on both cheeks, clothed him in gold and silver and, having summoned a royal coach drawn by eight white horses and an escort of a hundred horse guards with shining breastplates, sent the boy to Berlin where Hitler welcomed him like a king's son amid a cheering crowd and married him to his daughter."

"Yes, I know," said Louise. "That's how it was bound to end."

"I met that officer again later at Soroca on the Dniester—a very serious man, a good father, but a true Prussian, a true *Piffke* as the Viennese say. He talked to me about his family, about his work. He was an electrical engineer. He also spoke about his son Rudolf, a boy ten years old. It was really difficult to tell the glass eye. He told me that the best glass eyes are made in Germany."

"Stop it!" said Louise.

"Every German has a glass eye," I said.

XII

A Basket of Oysters

WE WERE LEFT ALONE. The two blind soldiers, led by the nurse, had left. Ilse, who had not spoken until then, smiled and looked at me. "Glass eyes," she said, "are like glass birds. They cannot fly."

"Oh, Ilse, do you still believe that eyes fly? What a baby you are, Ilse!" said Louise.

"Eyes are caged birds," said Ilse. "The eyes of those two soldiers were empty cages."

"Blind people's eyes are dead birds," said Louise.

"Blind people cannot look outward," said Ilse.

"They are looking at themselves in a mirror," said Louise.

"Hitler's eyes," said Ilse, "are full of dead people's eyes. They are full of dead people's eyes. There are hundreds, thousands of them." She seemed like a baby, Ilse. She was a baby full of odd whims and strange fancies. Perhaps because her mother was English it occurred to me that Ilse was a picture of Innocence such as Gainsborough might have painted it. No, I was wrong. Gainsborough painted women as if they were landscapes, with all the candor, the proud sadness and the languishing decorum of the English landscape. There was something in Ilse, something whimsical, a sort of fanciful madness, that is lacking in the English landscape and in Gainsborough's paintings. Ilse was more like the portrait of Innocence as Goya might have painted it. That blond hair, short and curly, that milk spreading over the face amid the roses of dawn, those lively blue eyes with gray specks around the pupils, that graceful habit of tilting her head on her shoulder with mischievous yielding made her look like a portrait of Innocence painted in the Goya style of "The Caprices," against the background of a pink and gray horizon of a deserted Castilian landscape, parched, swept by a high invisible wind, stained here and there with the reflection of blood.

Ilse had been married three years and still looked like a girl. Her husband had left for the front two months before and was lying in a field hospital near Voronezh with a splinter in his shoulder. Ilse had written to him: "I'm going to have a baby. *Heil* Hitler!" Expecting a child was the only way to escape the decree about compulsory work. Ilse did not want to work in a factory, she did not want to be a factory hand. She preferred to have a baby. "The only way of making Hitler a cuckold," said Ilse, "is to expect a baby." Louise blushed and shyly reproached her, "Ilse!" And Ilse said, "Don't be so Potsdam, Louise!"

"Eyes are made of horrible stuff," I said, "of slimy, dead stuff. You cannot hold them in your fingers. They slip through your fingers like snails."

During April 1941, I was traveling from Belgrade to Zagreb. The war against Yugoslavia had been over for several days, the Free State of Croatia was just born; Ante Pavelič was ruling in Zagreb with his *ustashi* bands. In all the villages large portraits of Ante Pavelič, Poglavnik of Croatia, were pasted on the walls, along with the notices and decrees of the new national Croatian state. The first spring days were here and a transparent silvery mist rose from the Danube and the Drava. The Fruska hills were melted into slight green waves spread with vineyards and wheat fields. The light green of the vineyards and the darker green of the wheat followed one another, alternated and mingled in a play of light and shade below a silken blue sky. We were having the first clear days after weeks of rain, the roads looked like streams of mud. I was forced to stop for the night at Ilok, midway between Novy Sad and Vukovar. In the only inn in the area, supper was served on a large common dining table, around which sat armed peasants, policemen in Serbian uniforms with Croatian badges on their breasts, and refugees who had been ferried across the river between Palank and Ilok.

After supper we left the room and went out to the terrace. The Danube glistened in the moonlight and the lights of the trawlers and barges could be seen appearing and disappearing among the trees. A vast silvery peace sank into the green Fruska hills. It was curfew. Patrols of armed peasants knocked at the doors of Jewish homes for the evening checking, calling out names in monotones. These doors were marked with a red Star of David. The Jews came to the windows and said, "We are here, we are at home." The peasants shouted "*Dobro! Dobro!*" and banged the butts of their guns on the ground. The large three-colored posters of the *proglas* of the new Zagreb government pierced in vivid red, white and blue splotches the moonlight on the walls of the houses. I was dead tired and toward midnight I stretched out on my bed. I lay on my back watching through the open window the moon climbing gently over the trees and the roofs. A huge portrait of Ante Pavelič, the chief of the new Croatian state, was posted on the house across the street in which the Ilok *ustashis* were housed. The portrait was printed in black on thick paper faintly tinted with green: the Po-glavnik stared at me with his large black eyes, deep-sunk below a low, stern and obstinate brow. His mouth was wide, thick lipped, his nose straight and fleshy, his ears huge. I never would have thought that any man's ears could be so vast or so long. They came halfway down his cheeks, ludicrous and monstrous; they surely were drawn in the wrong perspective—a mistake of the artist who had drawn the portrait.

Toward dawn a company of Hungarian *Honved*, braced in their yellow uniforms, passed singing beneath my windows. The Hungarian soldiers have a fragmentary distracted way of singing. From time to time a single voice rose, began a song and fell silent. Twenty, thirty voices responded briefly, and also fell silent. For some minutes only the rhythmic steps and the bouncing of rifles on leather were heard. Then another voice took up the song again and broke off; twenty, thirty voices hinted at a response and fell suddenly silent. Again the hard and heavy cadence of steps, the bouncing of rifles on leather. It was a sad and cruel song; there was something lonely in those voices, in those responses and sudden silences. They were voices full of bitter blood, those sad, cruel, distant Hungarian voices that rise up from the deep, remote plains of men's sadness and cruelty.

Next morning in the streets of Vukovar patrols of Hungarian policemen armed with rifles stood on the corners—the square of

Vukovar near the bridge was crowded with people; groups of girls walked along the sidewalks and gazed at their own reflections in the shop windows; one girl dressed in green moved back and forth, slow and light, looking like a green leaf in a breeze; the portraits of Ante Pavelič stared at me from the walls with those eyes of his, deep-sunk under the low hard brow.

The Danube and the Drava breathed forth a sweetish smell of rotting grass into the rosy morning. All the way from Vukovar to Zagreb, across Slavonia, rich with pasture, green with woods, watered by rivers and brooks, the Poglavnik's portrait greeted me with its black glances. By then it had become a familiar face—that of Ante Pavelič; it seemed to me a friend's face. I felt as if I had known it for a long time; it was the face of a friend. The posters pasted on the walls announced that Ante Pavelič was the protector of the Croatian people, the father of Croatian peasants, the brother to all those who were fighting for the freedom and independence of the Croatian people. The peasants read the posters, shook their heads and turned their faces toward me with their thick hard protruding bones, gazing at me with the same black deep eyes of the Poglavnik's.

And so when I saw Ante Pavelič for the first time seated at his writing table in a palace in the Old City in Zagreb, I felt as if I were meeting an old friend, as if I had known him from time immemorial. I noticed his wide, flat face with its hard coarse features. His eyes shone with a deep black fire in his pale, earthen-colored face. An undefinable air of stupidity was stamped on his face, perhaps stemming from his huge ears, that seen closely, looked even more vast, ludicrous and monstrous than in his portraits. But little by little it occurred to me that maybe that air of stupidity was only shyness. The sensuous look that his fleshy lips lent to his countenance was practically obliterated by the odd shape and unwonted size of his ears, which, as compared with those all too fleshy lips, seemed two abstract things, two surrealistic shells drawn by Salvador Dali, two metaphysical objects. They aroused in me the same impression of deformity as is produced by listening to certain musical compositions by Darius Milhaud and Eric Satie—perhaps the association of ideas between music and ears was responsible for this.

When Ante Pavelič turned his face offering his profile to my eyes, those huge ears seemed to lift his head sideways, as if they were wings striving to soar into the air with that massive body. Then, a kind of delicacy, an almost graceful leanness, such as appears in some portraits by Modigliani, became delineated in the face of Ante Pavelič like a mask of suffering. I gathered that he was good-natured, that the fundamental trait of his character was a simple and generous humanity, resulting from shyness and Christian charity. He appeared to me a man who would be capable of bearing unflinchingly atrocious physical pain, terrible torture and toil, but who would be unable to stand the slightest moral pain. He appeared to me a good-natured man; his stupid air seemed to me shyness, goodness, simplicity and a peasant-like way of facing facts, people and things as if they were physical elements—material, not moral elements—belonging to his physical, not to his moral world.

His hands were broad, thick, hairy; and his knuckles knotty with muscles. One realized that his hands bothered him, that he did not know where to put them. First he placed them on the table, then he raised them to stroke the lobes of his huge ears, and then he stuck them into his trouser pockets, but most of the time he rested his wrists on the edge of the writing table and, crossing his thick hairy fingers, he kept stroking and rubbing them against each other with a coarse, shy gesture. His voice was deep, musical and very sweet. He spoke Italian slowly with a slight Tuscan accent. He spoke about Florence and Siena where he had spent many years in exile. While I listened to him I thought that he was the terrorist who was responsible for the murder of King Alexander of Yugoslavia, that he was the man on whose conscience was Barthou's death. I was inclined to believe that, perhaps, while unhesitatingly countenancing extreme methods for the defense of his people's freedom, he was horrified by bloodshed. He was a good-natured man, I mused, a simple and generous man. Ante Pavelič gazed at me with his deep black eyes and, setting his monstrous ears in motion, he said, "I shall rule my people through goodness and justice"—moving words in a mouth so oddly shaped.

One morning he asked me to go with him on a quick tour through Croatia, in the direction of Karlovac and the Slovene frontier. It was a fresh clear morning, a morning in May. Night had not yet disentangled its vast green mantle from the woods and thickets along the Sava; the green May night was still covering the forests, the hamlets, the castles, the fields and the misty banks of the river. The sun had not yet peeped out from the glistening edge of the skyline, sharp as a piece of glass. A multitude of birds swelled the foliage of the trees. Suddenly the sun lighted the wide sweet valley, a pinkish vapor arose from the fields and the woods, and Ante Pavelič ordered the car to stop, alighted on the road, and embracing the landscape with a wide gesture, said to me: "This is my fatherland."

The gesture of those hairy hands, their knuckles knotty with muscles, was perhaps too brutal for so gentle a landscape. That tall, massive, herculean man standing on the side of the road against the green of the valley and the dusty blue of the sky, that large head of his and those huge ears stood out from that gentle and sensitive landscape as roughly as the statues wrought by Mestrovič stand out against the backgrounds of the luminous squares in the cities of the Drava and the Danube. Then we climbed into the car again and drove all day through the gorgeous country stretching from Zagreb to Ljubljana. We climbed the slopes of the Zagrebska Gora, the woody heights above Zagreb, and ever so often the Poglavnik alighted, and lingered talking with the peasants. He spoke of the seasonable weather, the sowing, the crops which looked promising that year, the cattle, the days of peace and labor that the country's freedom would bring to the Croatian people.

I liked the simplicity of his manner, the kindness of his words, the humble way in which he approached the poor, and I listened with pleasure to his deep musical voice, that very sweet voice. We drove back through a damp evening, streaked with purple rivers spanned by airy bridges of crimson clouds, flecked with green lakes amid blue woods. The memory of that very sweet voice, those deep black eyes, those monstrous ears against the delicate Croatian landscape has lasted a long time.

A few months later, toward the end of the 1941 summer I was returning from Russia weary and ill, after spending long months in the dust and mud of the huge plain between the Dniester and the Dnieper. My uniform was worn, discolored by the sun and rain, soaked in that smell of blood and honey that is the odor of war in the Ukraine. I spent a few days at Bucharest to rest a little after the toil of the long journey through the Ukraine, Bessarabia and Moldavia, but, on the very evening of my arrival, a secretary of the President of the Council rang me up at the Athenée Palace to warn me that the Vice-President of the Council, Mihai Antonescu, wanted to speak to me.

Mihai Antonescu welcomed me kindly, gave me a cup of tea in his vast light study and began talking about himself in French, with a vainglorious air that reminded me of Count Galeazzo Ciano. He wore a morning coat with a starched collar and a gray silk tie. He had the appearance of director of a *maison de couture*. The rosy face of a woman, who resembled him like a sister, seemed to be painted on his round, fat face. I told him that he looked handsome and he thanked me with a smile of profound complacency.

He spoke, staring at me with his small black, glittering snake-like eyes. No other eyes in the world resemble a snake's eyes more than Mihai Antonescu's. A bunch of roses were blossoming in a vase on his desk. "I'm very fond of roses," he said. "I prefer them to laurels." I mentioned that his policy threatened to be as short-lived as the roses—the length of one morning. "The length of a morning!" he answered. "That's eternity!" Later, gazing fixedly at me, he advised me to start immediately for Italy. "You have been indiscreet," he said. "Your war reports from the Russian front have been the subject of much criticism. You are no longer eighteen. It is not consistent with your age to play the *enfant terrible*. How many years have you already spent in prison in Italy?"

"Five years," I replied.

"Isn't that enough for you? I advise you to be more careful in the future. I have great regard for you; everybody in Bucharest has read your *Technique du Coup d'Etat* and everybody likes you. Let me tell you that you have no right to maintain that Russia will win this war. Besides, you are wrong. Sooner or later Russia will collapse."

"She will collapse on your back," I replied.

He looked at me with his snakelike eyes, smiling. He offered me a rose and saw me to the door. "Good luck," he said.

I left Bucharest next morning without even having had time to call on my dear Parisian friend, Princess Martha Bibescu who lived the lonely life of an exile in her villa at Mogosoëa. I spent only a few hours at Budapest and journeyed on to Zagreb where I stopped to rest for a few days. On the evening of my arrival I was on the terrace of the Esplanade Café with my friend Pliverič and his daughter Neda. The vast terrace was crowded with people who seemed to be kneeling around the iron tables. I gazed at the handsome and languid Zagreb ladies, dressed with that provincial smartness in which all the grace of old imperial Vienna, the grace of 1910 and of 1914 still survives, and I thought about the peasant women of Croatia who are naked under their ample, starched linen skirts that resemble the shells of crustaceans or the hard wings of crickets. Beneath that hard, crackling linen crust the rosy, smooth, warm flesh of nakedness can be imagined.

The Esplanade orchestra was playing old Viennese waltzes; the gray-haired musicians were perhaps the same who had seen Archduke Ferdinand riding by in his black coach drawn by four white horses, and the violins were perhaps the same that had been played at the wedding of Empress Zita, the last Austrian Empress. The women and young ladies, including Neda Pliverič, were "*alte Wien.*" They also were "*Austria felix*"; they were also "Radetzky Marsch." The trees glistened in the warm night; the pink, green, and blue sherbets were slowly melting in the glasses, feather fans and those silken fans bespangled with glass beads and specks of mother-of-pearl swayed to the rhythm of the waltzes; thousands of languishing eyes, light or dark or moon-like, flashed in the night on the terrace of the Esplanade, flashed above the trees of the avenues, above the roofs, like birds in the green, silk sky slightly worn at the edge of the horizon.

After a time an officer approached our table. He was Major Makiedo, Count Makiedo, formerly a captain in the Imperial Austrian Army and now adjutant of Ante Pavelič, Poglavnik of Croatia. He walked swaying his hips between the tables and the iron chairs, and from time to time he raised his hand to his kepi, gracefully bowing right and left. Languishing feminine eyes glanced at his high, hard, ancient Hapsburg-style kepi. He approached our table with an ancient, faded, out-of-date smile that lighted his fat face with its small mouth shadowed by a clipped dark-blond mustache. It was the same smile with which he welcomed foreign diplomats, high civil servants and the chiefs of the *ustashis* in Ante Pavelič's waiting room, where he sat behind a typewriter, bending over the black keys, his hands covered with spotless white gloves, such as were once worn by the officers of the Imperial Austrian Guard, and, his lips tight, he hit the black keys with a single finger of his right hand—very slowly, with concentrated gravity, while his left hand rested on his hip as if he were dancing a quadrille. Count Makiedo bowed before Neda, raised his white-gloved hand to the shiny visor of his kepi and stood leaning forward and smiling silently. Then he straightened out with a sudden snap and turned to me, after expressing his pleasure at seeing me in Zagreb once again. In a tone of amiable reproach, scanning his words as if he were singing to the rhythm of the Viennese waltz that the orchestra was playing—"Why didn't you let me know at once that you had arrived in Zagreb? Come and see me tomorrow morning at eleven. I will add your name to the list of callers. The Poglavnik will be pleased to see you again." And in a low voice, bowing as if he were making a loving confidence, he added, "He will be very, very pleased."

Next morning at eleven I was seated in the waiting room of Ante Pavelič. Major Makiedo, bending over his typewriter, his left hand resting on his hip, was very slowly tapping the black keys with a single finger of his right hand faultlessly encased in a white kid glove.

Several months had passed since I had seen Ante Pavelič and when I entered his study, I noticed that he had changed the arrangement of the furniture. The last time I had called on him, a few months before, his desk was at the end of the room, in the corner farthest from the window. Now it stood directly in front of the door, with just enough room between the door and the desk to allow one man to get by. I went in and almost knocked my knees against the desk.

"It's a plan of my own devising," said Ante Pavelič, shaking my hand and laughing. "Anyone coming in here with criminal intentions, bumping into the desk and facing me suddenly, will lose his composure and betray himself. Hitler and Mussolini favor a different plan; they interpose the empty space of a very large room between themselves and their visitors."

I watched him while he spoke. He seemed to me greatly changed; tired, marked with fatigue and worry. His eyes were reddened by lack of sleep. But his voice as it had been before—deep, musical and very sweet—was the voice of a good-natured, simple and generous man. His huge ears had grown strangely thinner. They had grown transparent. Through the right ear that was turned toward the window, I could see the pink reflection of the roofs, the green light of the trees and the blue sky. The other ear that was turned toward one of the walls, was in the shadow and seemed to be made of a white, soft and fragile substance—an ear of wax. I studied Ante Pavelič, his thick hairy hands, his low, hard, obstinate brow, his monstrous ears, and I was overcome by a kind of pity toward that good-natured, simple and generous man, endowed with such a delicate sense of humanity. The political situation had become considerably worse during those few months. The rebellion of the partisans raged throughout Croatia from Zemun to Zagreb. The pale, almost ashen face of the Poglavnik was marked with a sorrow that was deep and sincere. How grievously this excellent heart must suffer, I thought.

After a while Major Makiedo came in to announce the Italian Minister, Raffaele Casertano. "Let him come in," said Ante Pavelič. "The Italian Minister must not be kept waiting."

Casertano came in and we spent a long time discussing simply and cordially the gravity of the situation. The partisan bands had pushed by night into the very suburbs of Zagreb, but the loyal *ustashis* of Pavelič would soon squash those tiresome guerrillas. "The Croatian people," said Ante Pavelič, "wish to be ruled with goodness and justice. And I am here to provide them."

While he spoke, I gazed at a wicker basket on the Poglavnik's desk. The lid was raised and the basket seemed to be filled with mussels, or shelled oysters—as they are occasionally displayed in the windows of Fortnum and Mason in Piccadilly in London. Casertano looked at me and winked, "Would you like a nice oyster stew?"

"Are they Dalmatian oysters?" I asked the Poglavnik.

Ante Pavelič removed the lid from the basket and revealed the mussels, that slimy and jelly-like mass, and he said smiling, with that tired good-natured smile of his, "It is a present from my loyal *ustashis*. Forty pounds of human eyes."

XIII

Of Their Sweet Deaths

LOUISE STARED AT ME, while a disgusted, pained look spread over her face.

"I feel ashamed of myself," she murmured with a deeply dejected smile. "We should all feel ashamed of ourselves."

"Why should I feel ashamed?" said Ilse. "I am not ashamed of myself. I feel as pure, innocent and virginal as the Mother of God. War has not touched me. It has no power over me. I carry a child in me. I am holy. My child. My child. Did it ever strike you that my child might be the Infant Jesus?"

"There's no need for another Infant Jesus," I said. "Any one of us might save the world. Any woman might beget another Saviour; any one of us might climb his Calvary and whistling and singing, let himself be nailed to the Cross. It's not very difficult to be a Christ today."

"It depends only on us, whether we feel as pure and innocent as the Holy Mother," said Ilse. "The war cannot defile me. It cannot defile the child in my womb."

"It isn't war that defiles us," said Louise. "It is we who defile every thought and every feeling within us. We are unclean. We defile our children in our wombs."

"To hell with war!" said Ilse.

"Oh, Ilse!" said Louise in a reproachful tone.

"Don't be so Potsdam, Louise. To hell with war!"

"Let me tell you the story of Tatiana Colonna's children," I said. "It is another Christian story."

"I'm afraid of your Christian stories," said Louise.

Listen to this story of Tatiana Colonna's children:—During the summer of 1940, when Mussolini declared war on Great Britain, the officials of the Royal Italian Legation at Cairo left Egypt and returned to Italy. The Secretary of the Royal Italian Legation at Cairo, Prince Guido Colonna, left Tatiana and her two children in Naples in his mother's house, and went on to Rome where he stayed for some time at the Foreign Office awaiting a new assignment. One night, in the early autumn, Tatiana was awakened by an alarm. A group of British bombers, flying inward from the sea, swooped low above the roofs of the city. It was the first bombing of Naples. There were many casualties and much serious damage, and the damage would have been still greater if the city were not protected by the blood of St. Gennaro, the only anti-aircraft defense which the unfortunate Neapolitans could trust. Both Tatiana's children were terrified. The youngest one fell ill and for weeks suffered with fever and delirium. As soon as the little one was better, Tatiana left to join her husband who, meanwhile, had been appointed Secretary at Stockholm.

Winter was nearly over when Tatiana reached Stockholm; swarms of sparrows were announcing the coming of spring. One morning, while her children slept, a sparrow flew into their room through an open window. The children awoke screaming with fear. "Mummy, Mummy, help!" Tatiana rushed to them. The children, pale with terror, shook with a frantic trembling; they shouted that a British plane had come through the window and was flying about the room.

The poor little twittering sparrow flitted from one piece of furniture to another, frightened by the screams of the children and by Tatiana's movements. It would have flown out of the window, but it was confused by the mirror on the wardrobe, against which it had knocked its beak two or three times already. At last it found the window and escaped.

The children were ill and lay in bed pale and exhausted, afraid lest a British plane should again fly through the open window. Neither doctors nor drugs could free them from that inordinate fear. Spring had faded, the pale glow of summer was already burning in the clear Stockholm sky. From the tops of the Karlaplan trees rose the twitter of the sparrows, and the two children, flat in their beds, their heads nestled under their sheets, trembled with fear, listening to the innocent twitter of the birds.

One day, Tatiana went into the nursery with a large box full of toys: small spring-propelled airplanes, stuffed birds, picture books with illustrations of birds and planes. The children started sitting up in their beds, playing with the cloth birds and the tin planes. They turned the propellers with their fingers and glanced through the pages of the picture books. Tatiana explained to them the difference between a plane and a bird, told them about the lives of sparrows, black caps and robins, about the deeds of famous airmen. Each day she placed stuffed birds on the furniture and hung small red-and-blue painted planes from the ceiling; she hung little wooden cages with merrily twittering golden canaries on the walls. When the two children were stronger, Tatiana took them every morning to play under the trees of the Skansen; sitting on the grass, they wound the springs making the propellers of the small tin planes hum and letting them hop about on the grass. Then Tatiana crumbled some bread on a rock and the birds flew down from all sides, twittering and pecking at the crumbs. Finally Tatiana took the children to the Bromma airport to let them see at close hand the large three-engined planes that take off every morning for Finland, Germany and England. Sparrows hopped briskly on the airport grass chattering among themselves, and they were not afraid of the huge aluminum birds that glided along the grass with a tremendous roar before they rose in flight or dropped down from a high and distant sky to land smoothly on the grass. And so Tatiana's children were cured. Now they are no longer frightened by birds; they know that sparrows will not bomb towns—not even British sparrows.

"How charming!" said Ilse clapping her hands.

"It's a very beautiful story," said Louise, "almost a fairy tale." She added that the story of Tatiana Colonna's children reminded her of certain drawings by Leonardo da Vinci in which children's and women's heads are entwined with birds, skeletons and flying machines.

"No doubt," she said, "Tatiana Colonna is as pure and gentle as one of Leonardo's women."

"Oh, yes!" said Ilse. "She is certainly as pure and gentle as a woman painted by Leonardo. No doubt Tatiana is like the birds and children; she believes in heaven. Could you ever imagine a bird or a child who did not believe in heaven?"

"There is no more heaven in Europe," said Louise.

"Tatiana is like the butterflies who invent wonderful fairy tales to whisper to the flowers," I said. "Before Tatiana told her children that birds will not bomb cities, it was certainly true that the birds had bombarded cities."

"Butterflies enjoy dying," said Ilse.

"It was a woman, a woman who is now dead, who told me one evening that there are two kinds of women, and two kinds of roses —the immortal ones living forever and those who enjoy dying."

"Even dead roses are immortal," said Ilse.

"Shakespeare loved the scent of dead roses," I said. *Of their sweet deaths are sweetest odours made.* . . . I was dining one evening at the villa of the Italian Embassy on the shore of the Wannsee. The night was clear and the last winter moon shone on the frozen lake. Although the young German ladies seated around the table were extraordinarily good-looking and refined, there was something rotten in their light eyes, in the sheen of their flesh and of their hair. They laughed with a cold indifferent laughter, and gazed at each other's faces with slightly clouded eyes. Their way of laughing and staring lent an unpleasant feeling of loneliness and complicity to their beauty. Sheaves of gorgeous roses, some white, some crimson, some milky pink as a girl's cheek, flowered proudly in the Nymphenburg and Meissen vases standing here and there on the furniture, and in the wide Murano shell cloudy as a morning lagoon that was placed in the center of the table. The roses had arrived by air from Venice that morning; they were still moist with Venetian air; the call of the gondoliers along the lonely canals was still trembling on their wide transparent petals. The light of the silver candlesticks was mirrored in the Saxony ware with the dull reflection of sleeping waters, and faded softly into the deep glow of the glasses scattered around the table, into their frosty glow of an Alpine glacier at dawn, and into the glistening surface of the large glass doors that separated the covered veranda on which we had gathered from the trees of the park and the shores of Wannsee —motionless in the cold moonlight.

A flickering flame occasionally lighted the faces of the guests;

perhaps the reflection of the rose-colored satin tablecloth through an ancient Burano lace of a faint ivory tint, perhaps it was the reflection of the roses—the secret breath of those sweetly scented roses wafted into the room the atmosphere of a Venetian loggia at the hour when the smell of the lagoon mud mixes with the breath of nocturnal gardens. A few canvases of a minor French school, resembling Watteau, hung on the walls; their original hues had been heightened by a coat of varnish in the process of a recent unskilled restoration; still-life roses flashed through a dark landscape of statues, black trees, silver amphorae and green fruit. The roses looked like shadows of roses, so that when the eyes rested on the Venetian roses, rising with youthful pride from the Saxony vases and the Murano shell, they encountered the memory of roses long dead—a living and vital recollection of ancient roses.

The guests, it seemed to me, sat in strange positions: their shoulders pressed stiffly against the backs of the chairs, their busts slightly sagging. They ate looking upward as if they were instinctively backing away from the food. The ladies spoke in unexpectedly soft and gentle voices; they seemed to me remote voices—unreal and weak. Their blue-ringed eyes had a weary look. Something at the same time careless and conventional was in their refined manners, their elegant dresses, coiffures and make-up. Their refined elegance appeared to be the result of an unconscious effort for which the only moral excuses were wealth, carelessness with money and the privileges of birth and social position. The gift that women possess to such a high degree—of enjoying the present, of the Faustian passing moment—seemed to be dimmed and betrayed in them by a secret fear of time, of fleeting youth, by an inner craving that was unable to overcome the sadness of the hour and of the events. Malicious envy, bitter regret and haughty proud dissatisfaction had mastered every part of their natures and had produced a kind of sensual pride of caste.

By contrast the men seated at the table had a detached, cheerful, I might say a rested, almost indifferent air. Among them were a few Italians, a Swede and the Brazilian Ambassador; all the others were Germans; all belonged to the diplomatic world; all by constant association with foreigners and because they had lived away from Germany, appeared to be men of almost another stock than the

Germans, almost free, though secretly afraid and lacking confidence because they differed from the other Germans. Unlike the women, the men had a calm appearance, they laughed freely without a shadow of suspicion or of pride, as if at that table in the villa of the Italian Embassy they felt miles away from the grim, dark and cruel Germany of that terrible winter.

"Eddi a soldier? A real soldier?" laughingly asked Count Dornberg, the Chief of Protocol at the Ministry of Foreign Affairs of the Reich. The gigantic Dornberg, almost seven feet tall, to whom the short pointed beard gave the look of a faun, leaned across the table and rested his large hairy hands on the satin cloth.

"A real soldier," I replied.

"Eddi will be very shy when he has to undress before the eyes of his comrades," said Veronica von Klem.

"Poor Eddi, he is so timid!" said Princess Agatha Ratibor.

Axel Munthe, in Capri, was the one who had told me a few days previously about Eddi Bismarck—that Eddi had left Capri to spend a few weeks in the small house owned by the Bismarcks in Switzerland, and that unexpectedly he had been called back to Germany by the military authorities. Eddi was now despairing in a Strasbourg barracks and, as Veronica put it, "very uncomfortable." In telling me about Eddi Bismarck's military vicissitudes, Axel Munthe had smiled, showing his sharp pointed teeth. Upright, leaning on a stick, his cloak thrown over thin shoulders, his head shook with laughter; the entire vast seascape of rocks and olive trees against which he leaned, as though it were a wall, seemed to have been shaken by a dry thunderstorm. We had stood on the top of his Materite tower; Axel Munthe's mischief spread like a solitary tree under the blue sky of Capri. Not a blade of grass grew around him in his parched and dusty shade. Only the soil all yawning with deep fissures surrounded him, and out of the cracks some lean lizards, green as despair, peeped occasionally.

The man, the soil, the trees, the lizards looked as if they had been painted by El Greco. Axel Munthe had taken Eddi Bismarck's letter from his pocket and had begun reading it aloud, purposely stumbling over the words and stopping at the end of each sentence to grin through his little gray beard, the color of worm-eaten wood. Now and then he became angry, repeated a word two or three times and pretended he could not pronounce it, with the air of an actor who loves to make fools of his audience.

"Eddi Bismarck a soldier!" shouted Axel Munthe raising his arm and waving the letter as if it were a flag—"Eddi Bismarck a soldier! Forward, march! *Für Gott und Vaterland!* Ha, ha, ha!"

"It is right and proper," said the Italian Ambassador, Dino Alfieri, in his silly, gentle voice, "that Germany should appeal to all her best children. It is fine that a Bismarck will fight as a plain soldier in the army of the Reich."

Everybody laughed and Dornberg, with deep seriousness, said, "Thanks to Eddi, Germany will win the war."

A few days previously, before leaving Capri to return to Finland, I had gone to the Grande Marina and, strolling through the narrow lanes shut in by high walls stained white with brine, I had passed in front of the Fortino, the villa of Mona Williams in which, during her absence in America, Eddi Bismarck played the jealous housekeeper. It was raining and the Fortino had a sad, sick look.

"The Count has gone to the war," said the Capri gardener as he saw me go by. The thought of the blond, delicate Eddi peeling potatoes in the Strasbourg barracks filled me with mischievous glee. "The Count has gone to the war. Forward, march! *Für Gott und Vaterland!*" shouted Axel Munthe, shaking with dry laughter as he brandished Eddi's letter with a gesture of spiteful joy.

"Eddi on the battlefield will certainly be a magnificent soldier, worthy of the name he bears," said Alfieri in his gentle fatuous voice, and everybody laughed.

"Eddi is a very nice boy, and I am very fond of him," said Anna Marie Bismarck. "Without him this war would be only a war of ruffians." Anna Marie is a Swede; she married Eddi's brother, Prince Otto von Bismarck, Councilor of the German Embassy in Rome.

"The name he bears is too fine for a battlefield," said Count Dornberg in an ironical tone.

"I cannot imagine anything more ridiculous than for a Bismarck to be killed in this war," said Anna Marie.

"Oh, yes, it would be truly ludicrous," said Princess Agatha Ratibor in a playful voice.

273

"Wouldn't it?" said Anna Marie casting a sweet and scornful glance at Agatha.

Something small, arrogant and evil had entered the conversation that Veronica and Agatha were leading with a dry grace which lacked brilliance. Listening to those handsome young women I thought of the women workers on the outskirts of Berlin. This was just the hour when they walk back to their homes or their *Lägers* after a long day's work in the war factories of Neuköln, Pankow and Spandau. They don't all belong to the working classes. Many belong to the upper middle class or are the wives of civil servants and officers, but they have been caught in the cogwheels of compulsory work. Many are "slaves" from Poland, the Ukraine, White Russia or Czechoslovakia, and *P* or *Ost* is embroidered on their shirtfronts. But one and all, workers, middle-class women and slaves procured from occupied territories respect, help and stand up for one another. They work ten, twelve hours a day under the eyes of SS men armed with tommy guns, each of them within a narrow space between lines chalked on the floor. At nightfall they go out tired, dirty, black with engine grease, their hair rusty with iron shavings, the skin of their hands and faces burned by acids, their eyes circled with livid signs of hardship, fear and anxiety. The same anxiety and fear, though defiled and abashed by an arrogant sensuousness, a shameless pride, a sad moral indifference, I saw again that evening in the young German women seated at the table of the Italian Ambassador. Their dresses had been smuggled from Paris and Rome, from Stockholm and Madrid in the dispatch cases of the diplomatic couriers, as had their perfumes, their powders, their gloves, shoes and lingerie. Not that they were proud of the privilege of their elegance. They were well brought up and took pride in those small things that belonged to them by right and were due them. But their elegance undoubtedly was a considerable part of their patriotic feeling. *Of their patriotic feeling*. They felt proud of the suffering, the want and the losses of the German people, of all the horrors of the war, that they—owing to an old or recent privilege—held it to be their right to share with the people. And this was *their patriotic feeling*—a heartless complacency in their own fear, in their own anxiety and in all the hardships of the German people.

In that warm room, thickly carpeted, lighted by the cold, honey-colored moon and the pink flames of candles, the words, gestures and smiles of those young women evoked with envy and regret, a happy, immoral, pleasure-loving world, servile and satisfied with its own sensuousness and vanity, a world called back to life with a macabre sense of rotting flesh by the scent of dead roses and the dull glow of the silver and the ancient china. Veronica von Klem, the wife of a German Embassy official in Rome, had returned from Italy only a few days before and was still bubbling over with the most recent gossip gathered in the Excelsior Bar, at the dinners of Princess Isabelle Colonna and at the Acquasanta Golf Club—gossip mostly concerning Count Galeazzo Ciano and his political and social affairs. The manner with which Veronica repeated the latest Roman scandal, and the way in which the other young German women—Princess Agatha Ratibor, Maria Teresa, Alice, Countess von W——, Baroness von B——, Princess von T——, commented on it—had a shade of contempt that the other ladies—Italian, American, Swedish and Hungarian—Virginia Casardi, Princess Anna Marie von Bismarck, Baroness Edelstam, Marquise Theodoli, Angela Lanza, Baroness Giuseppina von Stum—countered with a mischievous and ironical charity, both bitter and pointed.

"There is a lot of talk about Filippo Anfuso lately," said Agatha Ratibor, "it seems that the handsome Countess D—— has passed from the arms of Galeazzo Ciano into those of Anfuso."

"That shows," said Marquise Theodoli, "that at the moment Anfuso is in great favor with Ciano."

"Could one say the same about Blasco d'Ayeta?" asked Veronica. "He has inherited little Giorgina from Ciano and that gave rise to the rumor that he had fallen into disgrace."

"Blasco will never fall into disgrace," said Agatha. "His father, a court chamberlain, defends him from the King; Galeazzo Ciano, Mussolini's son-in-law, defends him from the Duce; his wife, a devout Catholic, defends him from the Pope. Blasco will always have some Giorgina within reason to protect him against Galeazzo."

"Roman politics," said Veronica, "are in the hands of four or five playboys who are busily engaged shifting among themselves the same thirty silliest women of Rome."

"When those thirty women are over forty," said Princess von T——, "there will be a revolution in Italy."

"Why not when those four or five perennial bachelors are over forty?" asked Anna Marie von Bismarck.

"Ah, it's not the same thing," said Count Dornberg. "It is much easier to get rid of politicians than of thirty old mistresses."

"From a political point of view," said Agatha, "Rome is nothing but a *garçonnière*—a love-nest."

"Why are you complaining, my dear?" asked Virginia Casardi with her American accent. "Rome is a holy city, the city God has chosen to keep a *pied à terre*."

"I have just heard a nice story about Count Ciano," said Veronica. "I don't know whether I should repeat it. It comes from the Vatican."

"You may repeat it," I put in. "There are back stairs, even in the Vatican."

" 'Count Ciano is engaged in making love,' they say in the Vatican, 'and thinks that he is engaged in politics.' "

"Von Ribbentrop told me," said Agatha, "that when they met in Milan to sign the Pact of Steel, Count Ciano looked at him in a way that made him feel uncomfortable."

"You sound," I said, "as though Minister von Ribbentrop has also been Ciano's mistress."

"By now," said Agatha, "he has passed into the arms of Filippo Anfuso."

Veronica mentioned that Countess Edda Ciano, for whom she had a sincere liking, lately had often expressed her intention of having her marriage to Ciano annulled so she could wed a young Florentine aristocrat, Marquis Emilio Pucci.

"Is Countess Edda Ciano one of those thirty women?" asked Princess von T——.

"Edda, politically, is the least successful one of those thirty," said Agatha.

"The Italian people worship her as a saint. They never forget that she is Mussolini's daughter," said Alfieri in his silly gentle voice.

Everybody laughed, and Baroness von B——, turning to Alfieri, said that the most handsome of ambassadors was also the courtliest of men. They laughed again and Alfieri, bowing graciously said, "I am the ambassador of the thirty best-looking women in Rome," —a remark that was greeted with hearty laughter by the guests.

Countess Edda Ciano's pretense of wanting to marry young Marquis Pucci was at the time only a trivial piece of gossip. But in Veronica's words, in the comments of those other young German women, in the fact that Alfieri, greedy for gossip and particularly for Roman gossip, sometimes preferred to be considered the ambassador of the thirty best-looking women in Rome, rather than Mussolini's Ambassador—the piece of gossip assumed the importance of a national event, of a fundamental event in Italian life; it implied an unspoken judgment of the entire Italian people. The talk revolved for a long time around Count and Countess Ciano; they described the young Minister of Foreign Affairs in the midst of the gilded band of beauties in the Colonna Palace and among the dandies of the Chigi Palace. They amiably poked fun at the rivalries, intrigues and jealousies of that elegant and servile court to which Veronica herself felt flattered to belong and to which Agatha Ratibor would have belonged if she were not an old maid, something Galeazzo Ciano, something of a spinster himself, abhorred above anything else in the world. They dwelt on the whole Roman smart-set, made it march in procession before our eyes with its interested servility, its greed for favor and pleasure and its moral indifference—the true mark of a deeply rotten society. The corruption of Italian life, the cynical and hopeless passivity of the entire Italian people toward the war were proudly and continuously compared with the "heroism" of German life. Veronica, Agatha, Princess von T——, Countess von W——, Baroness von B——, all seemed to say: Behold how I suffer, behold what hunger, hardship, toil and the cruelty of war have done to me; behold, and blush! And the other young women, feeling themselves foreigners in Germany, were actually blushing, as if they had no other means of concealing the smile which that worldly eulogy of the "heroism" of German life, the luster of those precious jewels, called forth to their lips, or as if deep down in their hearts they felt themselves on the same level with the others and equally guilty.

Opposite me, between Count Dornberg and Baron Edelstam, sat a lady no longer very young, who listened with a tired smile to the frivolous and mischievous words of Veronica and her friends. I knew nothing about her except that she was Italian and that her family name was Antinori, that she had married a high official in the Ministry of Foreign Affairs of the Reich, whose name often appeared in German political columns, Minister Baron Braun von Stum. Drawn by a common sadness my attention lingered on her tired, wan features that for fleeting moments could still be youthful; on her light eyes filled with a veiled sweetness and an almost secret shyness; on those thin lines on her temples and around her sad, bitter mouth. The Italian gracefulness of her face had not faded completely and that sweet fantasy Italian women have in their eyes that resembles a love glance had not been lost between half-raised eyelids. From time to time she looked at me and I felt her glance resting on me so confidently and yieldingly that I felt inwardly troubled. I realized after a while that she was the object of hostile attention on the part of Veronica and her friends who, with female irony, kept gazing at her simple dress, unpainted nails, eyebrows neither plucked nor painted and unreddened lips, as if they felt a malicious pleasure in discovering in the face and in all of Giuseppina von Stum signs of an anguish and fear different from theirs, of sadness that was not German, that lack of pride in other people's distress of which they seemed so blatantly proud. Little by little the hidden meaning of that look in which I discerned a mute appeal for my sympathy and help was revealed to me.

Through the misty windows, the frozen Wannsee looked like a huge slab of glistening marble on which the marks made by skates and iceboats had cut mysterious inscriptions. The high wall of the woods, black in the glow of the moon, surrounded the lake like a prison wall. Veronica was talking about the winter sunshine on Capri and the Capri days of Countess Edda Ciano and her frivolous court.

"It's unthinkable," said Dornberg, "the sort of people Countess Ciano gathers around herself. I never have seen anything like them even at Monte Carlo around the *vieilles dames à gigolos*—old girls with their gigolos."

"At heart Edda is a *vieille femme*," said Agatha.

"But she is only thirty!" exclaimed Princess von T——.

"Thirty years is a lot, if one has never been young," said Agatha, and added that Countess Ciano had never been young, that she was already old, that she had the wit, the temper and the capricious and despotic whims of an old woman. Like those old women who surround themselves with smiling servants, she tolerated around her only obliging friends, easy lovers and evasive people capable of amusing and distracting her. "She is a mortally sad woman," Agatha concluded. "Her worst enemy is boredom. She spends the nights playing dice like a Harlem Negress. She is a kind of Madame Bovary. Can you imagine what Madame Bovary would have been, if she were the daughter of Mussolini?"

"She often weeps. She spends entire days locked in her room, weeping," said Veronica.

"She always laughs," Agatha said in an evil voice. "She often spends the nights drinking in the beautiful company of lovers, crooks and spies."

"It would be much worse if she drank alone," said Dornberg. And he told us that in Adrianople he had met an unhappy British consul who was bored to death and who, in order not to drink alone, sat all evening in front of his mirror; he kept on drinking hour after hour, in silence, in his lonely room, until his reflection in the mirror began laughing. Then he rose and went to bed.

"Edda would have thrown her glass at the mirror within the first five minutes," said Agatha.

"She has weak lungs and she knows she has not long to live," said Veronica. "Her eccentricities and her capricious and willful temper are a result of her illness. At times I feel sorry for her."

"The Italians hate everybody whose most humble servants they are," said Countess W—— contemptuously.

"It may merely be a servants' hatred," said Agatha, "but they detest her!"

"The Capri people," said Alfieri, "are not fond of her, but they respect her and forgive her all her eccentricities. 'Poor Countess,' they say, 'it's no fault of hers that she is a madman's daughter.' The Capri people have an odd way of looking at history. After my illness last year I went for a few weeks of convalescing to Capri. The fishermen of Piccola Marina, watching me go by looking thin and pale, and thinking that I am a German, because I am Ambassador in Berlin, said to me, 'Don't take it too much to heart, sir. What do you care if Hitler loses the war? Think of your health.'"

"Ha, ha, ha!" laughed Dornberg. "'Think of your health!' That's not a bad policy."

"They say she hates her father," said Princess von T——.

"Actually, I think she abominates her father," said Veronica, "and her father worships her."

"And what about Galeazzo?" asked Baroness von B——. "She is supposed to despise him."

"She may despise him, but she is also very fond of him," said Veronica.

"At any rate she is very faithful to him," said Princess von T—— ironically.

Everybody laughed, and Alfieri, "the best-looking ambassador and most chivalrous of men" said, "Ah! Are you casting the first stone?"

"I was eighteen when I cast the first stone," replied Princess von T——.

"Had Edda received a better education," said Agatha, "she would have been a perfect nihilist."

"I don't know what form her nihilism is," I said, "but there certainly is something savage about her. At least that's what Isabelle Colonna believes. One evening at a dinner in a great Roman house the talk turned to the Princess of Piedmont. Countess Ciano said: 'The Mussolini dynasty is like the Savoys; it will not last long. I shall end like the Princess of Piedmont.' Everyone was aghast. The Princess of Piedmont was seated at the same table. Once, at a dance in the Colonna Palace, Countess Cianto said to Isabelle who was advancing to meet her, 'I'm wondering when my father will make up his mind to sweep away all this.' We were talking about suicide one day. She suddenly said to me, 'My father will never have the pluck to kill himself.' I said to her, 'Show him how to shoot himself.' Next morning a police inspector came to my house to request in the name of Countess Ciano that I avoid her in the future."

"And you have never seen her again?" asked Princess von T——.

"Yes, only once, a little while later. I was strolling toward Matromania through the wood at the back of my house when I met her on the path. I told her she should avoid entering my woods, if she had no desire to see me. She looked at me with an odd expression and replied that she wanted to talk to me. 'What have you to tell me?' I asked. She looked sad and downcast, 'Nothing! I wanted to tell you that I could ruin you, if I wanted.' She held out her hand, 'Let us be friends,' she said, 'shall we?' 'We have never been friends,' I replied. She moved off in silence. At the end of the path, she turned back and smiled. I felt very shaken. I have felt very sorry for her since that day. I should add that I feel a superstitious respect for her. She is a sort of Stavrogin."

"A sort of Stavrogin, did you say?" asked Baroness von T——. "Why do you think that she is a sort of Stavrogin?"

"She loves death," I replied. "Her face is extraordinary; on some days it is a mask of murder, on other days it is a mask of suicide. I would not be surprised if I were told some day that she had killed somebody or that she had committed suicide."

"Yes, she loves death," said Dornberg. "On Capri she often goes out alone at night; she scrambles over the cliffs that rise sheer above the sea. She balances herself on the edge of precipices. Peasants saw her one day sitting on the little wall of the Salto di Tiberio, her legs swinging in the void. She leans over the Migliara rock, above a precipice fifteen hundred feet deep, as if it were a balcony. One night, during a thunderstorm, I saw her with my own eyes walking about the roof of the Certosa, leaping from dome to dome like a bewitched cat. Yes, she loves death."

"Is it enough to love death," asked Countess von W——, "to become a murderer or a suicide?"

"It is enough," I replied. "That is Stavrogin's secret morality, the mysterious meaning of his awful confession. Mussolini is aware that his daughter is of the same cloth as Stavrogin. He is afraid of her; he has her watched; he wants to be informed about her every step, her every word, her every thought and vice. He went so far as to push a man belonging to the police into her arms, so he could spy, even through another man's eyes, to spy on his daughter in her moments of abandonment. He would like to draw from her Stavrogin's confession. His only enemy, his real rival is his daughter. She is his secret conscience. All the black blood of the Mussolinis is not in the father's veins; it runs in Edda's, too. Were Mussolini a legitimate sovereign and Edda a prince and his heir, he would have done away with her to safeguard his throne. At heart Mussolini rejoices in his daughter's disordered life and in the disease that is threatening her. He can rule in peace. But can he sleep in peace? Edda is merciless, she obsesses his nights. Some day there will be bloodshed between the father and the daughter."

"That's a very romantic story," said Princess von T——. "Isn't it the story of Oedipus?"

"Yes, perhaps," I replied, "in the sense that a shade of Oedipus can be found in Stavrogin."

"I think you are right," said Dornberg. "It is enough to love death. Captain Kifer, a doctor in a German military hospital in Anacapri, was summoned one day to the Quisisana Hotel to attend Countess Ciano who was suffering with a violent and persistent migraine. This was his first opportunity to observe Edda closely. Captain Kifer is an able physician who knows how to look at things; he knows that disease is mysterious. He felt very troubled after leaving Countess Ciano's room. He said later that he had noticed a discolored spot on her temple that resembled the scar of a pistol shot; he added that, no doubt it was the scar of a pistol shot that she would one day fire into her temple."

"Another romantic story!" exclaimed Princess von T——. "I admit that I am beginning to be fascinated by that woman. Do you really believe that she will shoot herself at thirty?"

"Don't be afraid; she'll kill herself when she is seventy," said Giuseppina von Stum suddenly.

We turned to look at her in amazement. Everybody laughed. I watched her in silence. She was very pale and she smiled. "She is not of the butterfly breed," said Giuseppina von Stum in a contemptuous voice.

Her words were followed by an uncomfortable silence.

"Last time that I came from Italy," finally said Virginia Casardi with her American accent, "I brought an Italian butterfly with me."

"A butterfly? What an idea!" exclaimed Agatha Ratibor. She looked angry, almost hurt.

"A Roman butterfly from the Appian Way," said Virginia. And she told us that the butterfly had dropped into her hair one evening, while she was having supper with some friends in that inn with the odd name near the tomb of Cecilia Metalla.

"What is the odd name of that inn?" asked Dornberg.

"It is called 'One Never Dies Here,'" replied Virginia.

Giuseppina von Stum began laughing, stared at me, then said softly, "Horrible!" and covered her mouth with her hand.

"A Roman butterfly is not a butterfly like any other," said Virginia. She had brought that butterfly from Rome to Berlin by air in a cardboard box and she had released it in her bedroom. The butterfly fluttered about the room a while, then it settled on the mirror, where it stayed motionless for a few days; now and then it only moved its very delicate pale blue antennae. "It looked at itself in the mirror," said Virginia. One morning, a few days later, she found it dead on the mirror.

"It had drowned itself in the mirror," said Marquise Theodoli. "That is the story of Narcissus."

"Do you believe that the butterfly drowned itself?" asked Veronica.

"Butterflies love to die," said Giuseppina von Stum softly.

Everybody laughed and I looked at Giuseppina, annoyed by that silly laughter.

"Its reflection killed it, its own reflection looking out of the mirror," said Countess Emo.

"I think that its reflection died first," said Virginia. "That's the way things always are."

"Its reflection stayed in the mirror," said Baroness Edelstam. "That butterfly did not die. It flew away."

"*Papillon.* It's a nice word, *papillon—*" said Alfieri in his silly and flirtatious voice. "Have you noticed that *papillon* in French is masculine, and *farfalla* in Italian is feminine? We are very gallant with the ladies in Italy."

"You mean with the butterflies," said Princess von T——.

"In German also," said Dornberg, "the name is masculine: *der Schmetterling*. We tend to exalt the masculine gender in Germany."

"*Der Krieg*—War," said Marquise Theodoli.

"Death, too, is masculine in Greek: the god *Thanatos*," said Dornberg.

"In German the sun is feminine *die Sonne*." I said: "You cannot understand the history of the German people, unless you keep in mind that it is the history of a people for whom the sun is feminine."

"Perhaps you are right," said Dornberg.

"What is Malaparte right about?" asked Angela in an ironical tone. "The word moon is masculine in German, *der Mond*. That is important, too, if you want to understand the history of the German people."

"Certainly," replied Dornberg. "That is very important!"

"All that is mysterious in the German character," I said, "all that is morbid in it springs from the feminine gender of the sun—*die Sonne.*"

"Yes, we are unfortunately a very feminine people," said Dornberg.

"Speaking of butterflies," said Alfieri turning to me, "didn't you write in one of your books that Hitler is a butterfly?"

"No, I said that Hitler is a woman."

They all looked at one another, surprised and a little embarrassed.

"Just so," said Alfieri, "to compare Hitler with a butterfly seemed to me absurd."

Everybody laughed and Virginia said, "It would never occur to me to press Hitler between the leaves of *Mein Kampf* like a butterfly. It's a very odd idea."

"It's a school girl's idea," said Dornberg smiling through the hair of his short faunlike beard.

It was the time of the *Verdunkel* and Alfieri, not to miss the view of the frozen Wannsee glittering under the moon, instead of having the curtains drawn to darken the windows, had the candles extinguished. By degrees the ghostly reflection of the moon like faraway music invaded the room and spread over the glassware, the china and the silver. We were left tense and silent in the silvery half light; the waiters in that lunar half light moved silently around the table, in that Proustian light that appeared to be the reflection "of an almost curdled sea, of the bluish color of milk." The night was clear, without a breath of wind—the trees stood motionless against the pale sky; the snow glittered in a bluish whiteness.

We sat a long time gazing at the lake. A proud fear was in that silence, the same anguish that I had noticed before in the laughter and the voices of those young German women. "It's too beautiful," all at once burst forth Veronica rising suddenly. "I don't like being sad." We all followed her into the drawing room flooded with light, and the pleasant conversation lasted far into the night. Giuseppina came to sit next to me in silence. At one moment I became aware that she was about to speak to me, but instead, she looked at me, rose and left the drawing room. I did not see her again that evening and I was under the impression that she had driven away because I thought I heard the crunch of wheels on snow and the fading hum of a motor. It was two in the morning when we left Alfieri and Wannsee. I drove back to Berlin with Veronica and Agatha. On the way I asked Veronica whether she knew Giuseppina von Stum well. "She is Italian," replied Veronica.

"She is rather crazy," added Agatha in her slightly squeaky voice.

I was in a subway car crowded with pale, sweating, dirty people with ashen faces, and suddenly I saw Giuseppina von Stum sitting in front of me with a large bag on her lap. She smiled at me and blushing said, "Good evening." Her clothes were simple, almost poor; her hands were bare, cracked by frost and creased by those short reddish cuts that bleach produces on a delicate skin. She seemed to be downcast and exhausted; she was pale and wan; her eyes had red circles and her lips were livid. As if apologizing she told me she had been out to buy something for supper and that she had had to wait in line outside a shop for four hours; now she was hurrying home, it was late and she was a little anxious about her two children who had been waiting for her at home alone. Then she added, "A hard life." She smiled as she spoke, but her voice shook, and now and then she blushed.

She asked me for news of Italy. She wanted to go back to Italy, even for a few days—to Rome or to Umbria, to her mother's house. She was badly in need of rest, but she could not go—her duty as a German woman, and she blushed when she said "German woman," made her stay in Germany to do her share for the war.

I said to her, "It's good to be an Italian up here, isn't it?" Dark sadness settled on her face, as though the night were settling on a sweet Italian landscape. She replied, "By now, Malaparte, I am no longer an Italian. I am a German woman," and something arose in her face, something humble and despairing. I had been told that

285

of her husband's three sons—Baron Braun von Stum had been a widower and had three sons by his first wife—one had died in Russia, the second had been seriously crippled, and the third was lying wounded in a Berlin hospital. Of the three children she had had with Baron Braun von Stum, the second, a ten-year-old boy, had tragically drowned a few months previously in the bathing pool of an hotel in the Tirol. Giuseppina had to look after the home, sweep, wash, cook, wait in line in front of the shops, take the girl to school and nurse the baby. "I have no milk left. I am worn out, Malaparte," she said blushing. She had descended little by little into the dark and lonely feminine world of Germany at war, into that gloomy world, filled with anguish and bereft of grace and hope.

Minister Baron Braun von Stum was proud that his wife shared the want, suffering and privations that war had inflicted on all German women. He had not wanted Giuseppina to enjoy the privileges granted to the wives of diplomats and of the high officials in the Ministry of Foreign Affairs of the Reich. "I want my wife to be an example, to share the common lot." The privations, the toil, the suffering and the dumb despair of his wife crowned his day as a loyal and faithful Prussian official. He was proud that Giuseppina worked and suffered like any other German woman. Minister Baron Braun von Stum was proud that his wife stood in line in front of the shops, that she carried home the sack with the monthly ration of coal, washed the floors and cooked the meals. He had his meals at the club connected with the Ministry of Foreign Affairs, unless he was attending one of the frequent and abundant banquets. In 1942 the chef of the Auslander Club was famous throughout Berlin. The cellar also enjoyed a justifiable reputation. He preferred red to white wine, Châteauneuf du'Pape to any brand of Moselle or Rhine wine. His favorite brandy was Courvoisier. In winter he preferred Hennessy. "I met Monsieur Hennessy in Paris in 1936." He drove home late in the evening in a luxurious government car, and he was proud to find his wife pale, worn out and filled with fear and anguish. Minister Baron Braun von Stum was an honest and faithful functionary of the Reich, a Prussian loyal to his duty, devoted above all to the German fatherland and the Reich. *Ja, ja! Heil* Hitler!

After a while she said to me, "I get off here. Good evening." It was not my station. I should have gone on to Kaiserhof, but I rose too, picked up the heavy suitcase, and said to her, "Allow me to see you home." We climbed up the stairs, went out of the subway station and walked along the streets which were already dark. The muddy snow crackled under our boots. We took an elevator to the third floor; in front of her door Giuseppina said, "Won't you come in?" But I knew that she had to cook supper for her little girl, feed the baby and set the house in order, and I replied, "Thanks, I must go. I have an important engagement. With your permission I will come some other time and then we can talk. . . ." I would have liked to say to her: We shall talk about Italy. But I was too sorry for her—it seemed too cruel to talk to her about Italy. And besides who knew whether Italy really existed? Perhaps Italy was a fairy tale, a dream; who knew whether Italy still existed; who knew? Nothing existed any longer except gloomy, cruel, proud, despairing Germany. Nothing existed any longer. Italy, indeed! And so I went down the stairs laughing, and at that moment I was no longer sure that Italy existed. I went down the stairs laughing and as soon as I reached the street, I said aloud, "Italy, indeed!"

A few months later on my way back from Finland I stopped for two days in Berlin. As usual I had only a transit visa; as usual I was not allowed to stay in Germany more than two days. In the evening, in his Wannsee villa, Alfieri, toward the end of dinner, told me in his silly, gentle voice that Giuseppina von Stum had jumped out of a window. I was neither shocked nor grieved. For me it was an old sorrow. I had known for many months that Giuseppina had jumped out of a window. I had known about it since that evening when I had gone down the stairs laughing, spat on the muddy snow and said aloud, "Italy, indeed!"

XIV

The Soroca Girls

"OH, HOW DIFFICULT it is to be a woman!" said Louise.

"Minister Baron Braun von Stum," said Ilse, "when he learned that his wife had committed suicide—"

"Did not bat an eye. He blushed a little. He said '*Heil* Hitler!' That very morning he presided as usual at the daily conference of the foreign press at the Ministry of Foreign Affairs. He looked perfectly calm. No German women went to the funeral of Giuseppina, not even the wives of the colleagues of the Minister Baron von Stum. Following the hearse were only a few Italian women living in Berlin, a group of Italian workmen of the *Todt* organization and a few officials of the Italian Embassy. Giuseppina was not worthy of the sympathy of the German women. The wives of German diplomats take pride in the suffering, the want and the hardships of the German people. The German wives of German diplomats do not jump out of windows, they do not kill themselves. *Heil* Hitler! Minister Baron von Stum followed the bier in the uniform worn by Hitler's diplomats; now and then he looked around suspiciously; from time to time he blushed. He felt ashamed that his wife—*Ach!* he had married an Italian woman—had not had the strength to withstand the suffering of the German people."

"Sometimes I am ashamed of being a woman," said Louise softly.

"Why, Louise? Let me tell you the story of the girls of Soroca," I said, "of Soroca in Bessarabia, on the Dneister. . . ."

They were poor Jewish girls who had fled into the fields and the woods to escape the hands of the Germans. The grain fields and the woods of Bessarabia, between Baltsiu and Soroca, were full of Jewish girls hiding in fear of the Germans, in fear of the hands of the Germans.

288

They were not afraid of their faces, their terrible raucous voices, their blue eyes, their broad and heavy feet, but they were afraid of their hands. They were not afraid of their fair hair or their tommy guns, but they were afraid of their hands. When a column of German soldiers appeared at the end of the road, the Jewish girls hiding in the wheat and among the trunks of acacias and birches shook with fear; if one of them began crying and screaming, her companions jammed their hands over her mouth, or filled her mouth with straw; but the girl would struggle and howl—she was afraid of the German hands; she already felt those hard smooth German hands under her dress. She already felt those iron fingers penetrating her secret flesh. They lived for days hidden in the fields amid the wheat, stretched out between the furrows among the tall golden ears as in a warm forest of golden trees; they moved very slowly lest the golden ears should sway. Whenever the Germans saw the ears swaying in the windless air, they called "Achtung! Partisans!" and fired volleys with their tommy guns into the forest of golden wheat.

They were Jewish girls, about eighteen to twenty years old; they were the youngest and best looking. The others, the ugly and crippled girls of Bessarabian ghettos, remained shut up in their houses, and peered from behind the curtains to watch the Germans go by and shook with fear. Maybe it was not only fear, maybe it was something else that made all these unfortunate women tremble: the hunch-backed, the lame, the halt, the scurvy-scarred, the pock-marked or those with their hair devoured by eczema. They shook with fear as they lifted the curtains to watch the German soldiers go by, and they drew back frightened by the casual glance, the involuntary gesture or the voice of some soldier; but they laughed, red in the face and sweating, within those darkened rooms, and they ran limping and bumping against each other to the window of the next room to watch the German soldiers rounding the bend in the road.

The girls hidden in the fields and in the woods grew pale when they heard the rumble of motors, the clatter of horses, the creaking of wheels on the roads leading to Baltsiu in Bessarabia, to Soroca on the Dniester, and to the Ukraine. They lived like wild beasts, feeding on what little they could beg from the peasants, a few slices of *mamaliga* bread, some scraps of salted *brenza*. There were days when at sunset the German soldiers went out to hunt for Jewish girls in the wheat. They spread out like the fingers of a huge hand, raking the wheatfields, and they hailed one another, "Kurt! Fritz! Karl!" They had youthful slightly hoarse voices. They looked like sportsmen beating a moor to raise the partridges, quails and pheasants.

The larks, surprised and frightened, fluttered in the dusty sunset air. The soldiers raised their faces following them with their eyes, and the hidden girls held their breath, watching the hands of the German soldiers clutching their tommy guns and appearing and disappearing amid the grain—those German hands covered with light glistening down, those hard, smooth German hands. By now the hunters were close, they stooped a little as they advanced. They could be heard breathing noisily with a slightly hoarse hiss. At last one of the girls let out a shriek, then another, and still another.

One day the Department of Sanitation of the Eleventh German Army decided to open a military brothel in Soroca. But there were only old and ugly women in Soroca. Most of the town had been wrecked by mines and by German and Russian shells. Almost the entire population had fled and the young men had followed the Soviet Army toward the Dnieper. Only the part around the public gardens remained standing and the old castle which was built by the Genoese on the western bank of the Dniester in the midst of a maze of squat hovels made of mud and wood where wretched crowds of Tartars, Romanians, Bulgarians and Turks lived. From the top of the cliff overhanging the river, the town can be seen hemmed in between the river and the steep wooded bank. In those days the houses looked crumbling and gutted; a few beyond the public gardens were still smoldering. Such was Soroca on the Dniester when the military brothel was opened in a house close to the wall of the Genoese castle—a city in ruins, its streets cluttered with columns of soldiers, with horses and cars.

The Department of Sanitation detailed special patrols to hunt for the Jewish girls hiding in the grain and in the woods around the town. And so, when the brothel was officially opened with an inspection, very military in style, by the commander of the Eleventh Army, some ten pale trembling girls, their eyes scorched with weeping, received General von Schobert and his suite. All were very young, a few were still children. They did not wear those long silken loose gowns, red, yellow and green, with wide sleeves that are the traditional uniform of eastern brothels. They just wore their best dresses, the simple and honest clothes of middle-class girls in the provinces, so that they looked like students—some of them were students—who had gathered in the house of a friend to prepare for an examination. Their appearance was humble, shy and frightened. I had seen them go by in the street a few days before the opening of the brothel, about ten of them. They walked in the middle of the street with bundles under their arms or else carrying a leather suitcase or a parcel tied with string. Two SS men armed with tommy guns followed them. Their hair was gray with dust, wheat ears clung to their skirts, their stockings were torn; one of them limped with one bare foot, carrying a shoe in her hand.

A month later, when I was passing through Soroca, Sonderführer Schenck asked me one evening to go with him to see the Jewish girls in the military brothel. I refused and Schenck laughed, looking mockingly at me. "They are not prostitutes. They are girls who belong to good families," said Schenck.

I replied, "I know that they are decent girls."

"It isn't worth while feeling very sorry for them. They are Jewish girls."

I replied, "I know that they are Jewish girls."

"Well then," said Schenck, "perhaps you fear that they might feel hurt if we pay them a visit?"

I replied, "You cannot understand some things, Schenck."

"What is there to understand?" he asked.

I replied, "These unfortunate Soroca girls are not prostitutes. They are not selling themselves of their own free will. They are compelled to prostitute themselves. They are entitled to respect from everyone. They are war prisoners whom you exploit in an ignoble way. What percentage of the earnings of these unfortunate girls goes to the German Command?"

"The love of these girls costs nothing," said Schenck. "It is a free service."

"You mean compulsory work?"

"No, a free service," replied Schenck. "In any case, it's not worth while paying them."

"Not worth while paying them? Why?"

The Sonderführer explained that when their turn was over, after a couple of weeks, they would be sent back to their homes and replaced by another team of girls.

"Home?" I asked. "Are you certain that they will be sent back to their homes?"

"Yes," replied Schenck with some embarrassment, blushing slightly, "home, maybe to a hospital; I don't know. Maybe to a concentration camp."

"Instead of those unfortunate Jewish girls, why don't you put Russian prisoners in that brothel?"

Schenck burst out laughing and kept laughing. He clapped me on the shoulder and laughed, "*Ach, so! Ach, so!*" But I was certain that he had not grasped what I had meant; he, no doubt, fancied that I had hinted at the story about a certain house in Baltsiu in which a *Leibesstandart* of SS men had a secret brothel for homosexuals. He had not fully grasped what I had meant, and he laughed open-mouthed, slapping me on the shoulder with his hand.

"If instead of those unfortunate Jewish girls," I said, "there were Russian soldiers, the fun would be greater, wouldn't it?"

At last Schenck thought he understood and began laughing louder. Then suddenly he asked in a serious tone, "Do you think that the Russians are homosexuals?"

"You'll find out at the end of the war," I replied.

"*Ja, ja, natürlich,* we'll find out at the end of the war!" said Schenck gurgling with laughter. . . .

One evening, very late, close to midnight, I set out for the Genoese castle. I went down to the river, turned into a lane of that miserable neighborhood, knocked at the door of that house and went in. In a large room lighted by an oil lamp hanging from the center of the ceiling, three girls were seated on the sofas placed along the walls. A wooden staircase led to the upper floor. From the rooms above came the squeakings of doors, light footsteps and a murmur of distant voices that seemed sunk in darkness.

The three girls raised their eyes and looked at me. They sat sedately on the low sofas covered with those ugly Romanian carpets of Cetacea Alba striped in yellow, red and green. One of them was reading a book that she put down on her knees to watch me as soon as I entered. It looked like a brothel interior painted by Pascin. They watched me in silence; one of them smoothed with her fingers her black crinkly hair that had gathered on her forehead like a child's. In a corner of the room, on a table covered with a yellow shawl, stood several bottles of beer, of *zuica,* and a double row of glasses.

"*Gute Nacht,*" said the girl after a while, as she smoothed her hair.

"*Buna seara,*" I replied in Romanian.

"*Buna seara,*" said the girl sadly attempting to smile.

At that moment I no longer remembered why I had gone to that house, although I was aware that without letting Schenck know, I had gone not out of curiosity or from a vague feeling of pity, but for something that my conscience now refused to accept.

"It's very late," I said.

"We are closing soon," said the girl.

Meanwhile one of her companions had risen from the settee, and covertly glancing at me, lazily approached the gramophone standing on a little table in a corner; she turned the handle and placed the needle on the record. A woman's voice singing a tango rhythm came from the gramophone. I went over and lifted the needle from the record.

"Why?" asked the girl who with arms raised was getting ready to dance with me. Without waiting for a reply, she turned her back on me and went back to sit on the sofa. She was short and quite plump. Her feet were clad in light green cloth slippers. I joined her on the sofa and, staring intently at me, she tucked her skirt under her leg to make room for me. She was smiling, and I cannot tell why the smile irritated me. Just then a door opened at the top of the stairs and a woman's voice called, "Susannah!"

Down the stairs came a pale, thin girl holding a lighted candle shielded by a funnel of yellow paper. Her hair hung loosely over her shoulders. She wore slippers, a towel draped over her bent arm, her hand held up her dressing-gown—a sort of bath wrap tied around her waist with a cord—as if it were monk's cloak. She descended half way down the stairs, and looked me over attentively, frowning, as if my presence annoyed her, then she looked around with more suspicion than anger. She looked at the gramophone on which the record was still turning idly with a slight rustle. She looked at the untouched glasses, the orderly array of bottles and, opening her mouth in a wide yawn, she said in a slightly hoarse voice in which there was something harsh and rude, "Let's go to bed, Susannah. It's late."

The girl whom the newcomer had called Susannah laughed, looking at her companion mockingly, "Are you tired already, Lublia?" she asked. "What have you been doing to make you so tired?"

Lublia did not reply. She sat on the sofa opposite ours and with a yawn she carefully examined my uniform. Then she asked: "You are not German. What are you?"

"Italian."

"Italian?" The girls were now looking at me with curiosity. The one who was reading closed her book and looked at me in a tired, absent-minded way.

"Italy is beautiful," said Susannah.

"I would rather it were an ugly country," I said. "It's no use, just being beautiful."

"I would like to be on the way to Italy," said Susannah. "To Venice. I would like to live in Venice."

"In Venice?" asked Lublia, and began to laugh.

"Wouldn't you go to Venice with me?" said Susannah. "I've never seen a gondola."

"If I weren't in love I would start right now."

Her companions laughed and one of them said, "We are all in love."

The others began laughing again and casting strange glances in my direction.

"We have many lovers," said Susannah in French, with the soft accent of Romanian Jews.

"They would not let us leave for Italy," said Lublia lighting a cigarette. "They are so jealous!" I noticed that she had a long, narrow face and a small sad mouth with thin lips. It looked like the mouth of a child. But her nose was bony, the color of wax, with red nostrils. She smoked raising her eyes to the ceiling now and then, blowing the smoke into the air with a studied indifference.

There was something resigned and at the same time despairing in her white glance.

The girl who had been sitting with the book in her lap rose and, clutching the book in her hands, said *"Nopte buna."*

"Nopte buna, Domnule Capitan," the girl said again bowing to me with a shy, clumsy grace. She turned and went up the stairs.

"Do you want the candle, Zoe?" asked Lublia following her with her eyes.

"Thanks, I am not afraid of the dark," replied Zoe without turning.

"Are you going to dream about me?" shouted Susannah after her.

"Certainly! I am going to sleep in Venice!" replied Zoe as she disappeared.

We were silent for a while. The distant roar of a truck broke gently against the windowpanes.

"Do you like the Germans?" Susannah suddenly asked me.

"Why shouldn't I?" I answered in a slightly suspicious tone that was not lost on the girl.

"They are very nice, aren't they?" she said.

"Some of them are very nice."

Susannah stared at me for a long time, then she said with inexpressible hatred. "They are very kind to women."

"Don't you believe her," said Lublia. "At heart she is very fond of them."

Susannah laughed and looked at me in a strange way. Something white and soft was lifting from the depths of her eyes; they seemed to be melting.

"Perhaps she has reasons to love them," I said.

"Certainly," said Susannah. "They are my last love."

I noticed that her eyes filled with tears, although she smiled. I gently stroked her hand and Susannah dropped her head on her chest, letting her silent tears stream down her face.

"What are you crying about?" said Lublia in a hoarse voice, as she threw away her cigarette. "We still have two more days of gay life. Do you want more? Haven't you had enough?" Then, raising her voice and her arms, shaking her hands above her head, as if she were calling for help, in a voice filled with hatred, revulsion and grief, she screamed, "Two days, two days more and then they will send us home! Only two days more and here you are crying! We'll be free, don't you understand? Free, free!" Dropping on the sofa, she buried her face in the cushions and began trembling, her teeth chattered violently and, now and again in that strange voice of fear, she repeated, "Two days, only two days!" One of her slippers dropped off her foot and hit the wooden floor; her bare foot as small as a child's was exposed reddish, wrinkled, seared by white scars. I thought that she must have walked miles and miles; who knows where she came from, who knows through how much space she had fled before she was caught and brought by force into that house.

Susannah was silent, her head lowered, her hand between my hands. She did not seem to breathe. Suddenly she asked softly, without looking at me, "Do you think they will send us home?"

"They cannot make you stay here all your life."

"Every twenty days they change the girls," said Susannah. "We have been here eighteen days already. Two days more and we shall be replaced. They have warned us already. But do you really think that they will let us go back to our homes?" I felt that she was afraid of something, but I could not understand of what. She told me that she had learned French in school in Kishinev, that her father was a Baltsiu merchant; that Lublia was a doctor's daughter; that three of her other companions were students, and she added that Lublia studied music, that she played the piano like an angel, and —she said—she would be a great musician.

"When she leaves this house," I said, "she will be able to resume her studies."

"Who knows? After all we went through! Besides, who knows where we shall end up?"

Meanwhile Lublia had raised herself on her elbows. Her face was tight as a closed fist; her eyes shone strangely in her waxen face. She shook as if she had a fever. "Yes, I shall certainly become a great musician," she said and began laughing as she searched through the pockets of her dressing-gown for a cigarette. She rose, went to the table, opened a bottle of beer, filled three glasses and offered them to us on a wooden tray. She moved lightly, without any noise.

"I'm thirsty," said Lublia drinking greedily with closed eyes.

The air was stiflingly hot; through the half-shut windows came the thick breath of the summer night. Lublia walked barefoot about the room, an empty glass in her hand, her eyes staring blindly. Her long, lean body swayed under the flabby bell of the loose red dressing-gown, her bare feet made a soft muffled noise on the wooden floor. The other girl, who all this time had not uttered a single word or given any sign of life—as if she had been gazing at us without seeing us—unaware of what was happening around her, had meanwhile fallen asleep; she lay on the sofa in her poor patched gown, one hand resting on her leg, the other clenched in a fist on her bosom. Now and then, from the public gardens, came the sharp crack of a rifle. From the opposite bank of the Dniester, down the river from Yambol, came a rumble of artillery that was stifled in the wooly folds of the sultry night. Lublia stood in front of her sleeping companion and gazed at her in silence. Then, turning to Susannah, she said, "We must put her to bed. She is tired."

"We have worked all day long," added Susannah, as if apologizing. "We are worn out. By day we have the soldiers; in the evenings from eight to eleven—the officers. We haven't a moment's rest." She talked in a detached way, as if she were discussing any ordinary sort of work. She did not even show any signs of disgust. While she spoke, she rose and helped Lublia to lift her friend who awoke as soon as her feet touched the floor; moaning, as if she were suffering from pain, she yielded and almost lay in the arms of her friends as they moved up the stairs, until her moans and the sound of their steps died away behind the closed door.

I was left alone. The oil lamp hanging from the ceiling was smoking. I rose to turn down the wick and the lamp continued to sway, rocking my shadow along the walls along with the shadows of the furniture, the bottles and other things. It would have been better if I had left at that moment. I was seated on the sofa looking at the door. I had a dim feeling that it was wrong for me to stay in that house. It would have been better if I had left before Lublia and Susannah came back.

"I was afraid we would not find you here," said Susannah's voice behind me. She had come noiselessly down the stairs; she moved slowly about the room as she arranged the bottles and glasses and then came over and sat next to me on the sofa. She had powdered her face and looked even paler than before. She asked me how long I would stay in Soroca.

"I don't know, not more than two or three days," I replied. "I have to leave for the Odessa front, but I shall be back soon."

"Do you think the Germans will take Odessa?"

"I care nothing about what the Germans do," I replied.

"I wish I could say the same," said Susannah.

"Oh, I am sorry, Susannah. I did not mean . . ." I said. After an uncomfortable pause, I added, "It does not matter what the Germans do. It takes more than that to win a war."

"Do you know who will win the war? Perhaps you imagine that the Germans or the British or the Russians will win the war? The war will be won by us, by Lublia, Zoe, Marica; by me and all those who are like us. It will be won by whores."

"Shut up," I said.

"It will be won by whores," repeated Susannah raising her voice. Then she broke into silent laughter and, finally, in a shaky voice, in the voice of a frightened child, asked, "Do you think that they will send us home?"

"Why shouldn't they send you home?" I replied. "Are you afraid that they will send you to another house like this?"

"Oh, no! After twenty days of this work we are not fit for anything. I saw them—I saw the other ones." She broke off and I noticed that her lips were trembling. That day she had had to submit to forty-three soldiers and six officers. She laughed. She could no longer bear life. The physical exhaustion was worse than the disgust. "Worse than the disgust," she repeated smiling. That smile hurt me; it seemed as if she meant to apologize, or maybe that there was something else in that ambiguous smile, something obscure. She added that the other ones, those who had been there before her, before Lublia, Zoe and Marica, when they had left that house had been reduced to a pitiful condition. They no longer appeared to be women. They were rags. She had seen them going out with their suitcases and with their bundles of rags under their arms. Two SS men armed with tommy guns had shoved them into a truck to take them no one knows where. "I would like to go back home," said Susannah. "I want to go back home."

The lamp was smoking again; a greasy smell of oil spread through the room. I gently held Susannah's hand between mine, and her hand trembled like a frightened bird. The night was breathing on the threshold like a sick beast; its warm breath penetrated the room together with the rustle of the leaves in the trees and the ripple of the river.

"I have seen them when they went out of here," said Susannah with a shudder. "They looked like ghosts."

We sat like that, in silence, in the twilight of the room, and I was filled with bitter sadness. I no longer trusted my own words. My words were false and evil. Our silence also seemed to me false and evil.

"See you soon, Susannah," I said softly.

"Don't you want to come upstairs?" she asked.

"It is late," I replied making for the door. "See you soon, Susannah."

"*Au revoir*," said Susannah smiling.

Her poor smile was shining on the threshold, and the sky was full of stars.

"Did you ever hear anything more about those poor girls?" asked Louise after a long silence.

"I learned that two days later they were taken away. Every twenty days the Germans provided a change of girls. Those who left the brothel were shoved into a truck and taken down to the river. Later Schenck told me that it was not worth while to feel so sorry for them. They were not fit for anything any more. They were reduced to rags, and besides, they were Jewish."

"Did they know that they would be shot?" asked Ilse.

"They knew it. They trembled with fear. Oh, they knew it! Everybody knew it in Soroca."

When we came out into the open, the sky was full of stars. They shone, cold and dead, like glass eyes. The raucous whistle of the train was heard from the station. A pale spring moon rose in the clear sky, the trees and the houses appeared to be made of a slimy, soft material. Over by the river a bird was singing. We walked along a deserted road to the bank and sat on the dam.

In the darkness, the river rustled like bare feet on grass. Then, in the branches of a tree that was already lighted by the pale flame of the moon, another began singing and others far and near replied. A large bird flew with silent wings through the trees, swooped down almost skimming the water and crossed the river in a slow and uncertain flight. There came back to my mind the summer night in the Roman prison, *Regina Coeli*, when a flight of birds settled on the roof of the prison and began singing. They certainly had come from the trees on the Gianicolo. They had nests in Tasso's oak, I thought. I thought that they had their nests in Tasso's oak and I began weeping. I felt ashamed of weeping, but after such a long imprisonment, a bird's song is stronger that a man's pride. "Oh, Louise," I said and without meaning to, I took her hand and held it gently in mine.

Just as gently, Louise withdrew her hand and gazed at me with wonder rather than reproach. She was surprised by my unexpected gesture. Perhaps she regretted that she had evaded my sorrowful caress and the things I wanted to tell her. There rose in my mind Susannah's hand resting between mine—the small, sweating hand of Susannah—down there in the Soroca brothel; there rose in my mind the hand of the Russian working woman that I had covertly pressed one evening in a coach of the Berlin U-Bahn—that broad, lined hand, cracked by acids. It seemed to me that I was sitting with Susannah, the unfortunate Jewish girl, on the sofa in the Soroca brothel. A deep feeling of pity swept over me for Louise, Louise von Preusse, for the Imperial Princess, Louise von Hohenzollern. The birds were singing around us in the dark light of the moon. The two girls were silent as they gazed at the dull glint of the river flowing past the bank in the darkness.

"*J'ai pitié d'être femme,*" said Louise softly in that Potsdam French of hers. "I'm sorry I am a woman."

PART FIVE

THE REINDEER

XV

Naked Men

THE GOVERNOR OF LAPLAND, Kaarlo Hillilä, raised his glass and said, "*Maljanne.*" We were dining in the Governor's palace at Rovaniemi, Lapland's capital built on the Arctic Polar Circle. "The Arctic Circle runs right under the table between our feet," said Kaarlo Hillilä. Count Augustin de Foxa, Spain's Minister to Finland looked under the table; there was a burst of laughter and de Foxa whispered softly through his teeth, "Damned drunks!" Everyone was drunk and pale, their brows sweaty, their eyes staring and glistening—those Finnish eyes that alcohol tinges with mother-of-pearl lights.

I said to de Foxa, "Augustin, you are drinking too much." Augustin replied, "Yes, you are right. I'm drinking too much, but this is my last glass." Then, on Olavi Koskinnen's raising his glass and saying, "*Maljanne,*" de Foxa replied. "Thanks, I'm not drinking any more." The Governor stared at him and said, "Are you refusing to drink our health?"

Softly, I whispered to de Foxa, "For God's sake, Augustin, don't be reckless! You must always say 'Yes,' always 'Yes,' for God's sake!" And de Foxa said, "Yes, always Yes." At intervals he raised his glass saying "*Maljanne,*" and his face grew redder, his brow glistened with sweat and his eyes wavered behind his misty spectacles. Heaven help us! I thought, looking at de Foxa.

It was close to midnight. The sun, wrapped in a thin veil of mist, shone on the horizon like an orange wrapped in tissue paper. The ghostly light of the North, penetrating in frozen gusts through the window illuminated the huge hall where we had been at the table for six hours. The ball was decorated in an ultra-modern Finnish style that has the blinding glare of an operating room—a low ceiling, white-painted walls and a floor of pinkish birch wood. The large windows, long and narrow, looked out on the wide valleys of the

Kemi and the Ounas, on the wooded horizon of the Ounasvaara. Ancient *ryyas,* those tapestries that Lapp herdsmen and Finnish peasants weave on their rustic looms, hung on the walls side by side with fine prints of the Swedes, Schjöldebrand and Aveelen, and of the French Viscount de Beaumont. Among the others was one *ryya* of great value: trees, reindeer, bows and arrows were woven in pink, gray, green and black; there was another extremely rare one in which the dominant colors were white, pink, green and brown. The prints showed landscapes of East Bothnia and Lapland, views along the Oulu, the Kemi and the Ounas rivers, seascapes of the Törne harbor and of the Tori of Rovaniemi. At the end of the eighteenth century, when Schjölderbrand, Aveleen and Viscount Beaumont made those beautiful etchings, Rovaniemi was only a large village of Finnish pioneers, reindeer-breeders and Lapp fishermen; a village of small cabins built of rough-hewn logs and with high stockades around them for protection; the entire village was herded around the Tori, the cemetery and the fine stained-wood church built by the Italian, Bassi, in a neoclassical style that despite its Swedish origin bears traces of the France of Louis XV and of Catherine's Russia—a wood that is found in the white lacquered furniture of the old houses of Finnish pioneers in northern East Bothnia and Lapland. Between the windows and above the doors hung panoplies of ancient *puukkos,* their blades hand wrought and their handles covered with soft, short-haired reindeer skin. Each of the guests had a *puukko* hanging from his belt.

The Governor sat at the head of the table on a chair covered with a white bear skin. For some unexplained reason I sat at the Governor's right, while the Minister of Spain, Count Augustin de Foxa, was at his left. De Foxa was furious. "Not for myself, don't you know?" he said to me, "but for Spain."

Titu Michailescu was drunk and said to him, "Ah, it's on behalf of Spain, isn't it? On behalf of *your* Spain?"

I tried to calm him down. "It isn't my fault," I said.

"You are not representing Italy, are you? Why then are you sitting on his right?" asked de Foxa.

"*He* represents Italy, doesn't he? Don't you represent *your* Italy, Malaparte?" said Michailescu.

"To hell with you!" said Augustin.

I am fascinated by the talk of drunks so I listened to Michailescu and de Foxa wrangling with the ceremonious rage of drunken people.

"Don't worry, the Governor is left-handed," said Michailescu.

"You're wrong; he is not left-handed. He squints," replied de Foxa.

"Ah, if he squints, it is a different matter, and you should not grumble," said Michailescu.

"Do you imagine he squints on purpose to make me sit on his left?" asked de Foxa.

"Most certainly. That's just why he squints," replied Michailescu.

Then Count Augustin de Foxa, the Minister of Spain, turned to Kaarlo Hillilä, the Governor of Lapland and said: "Sir, I am seated on your left. This is not my place."

Kaarlo Hillilä gazed at him with surprise. "Why isn't it your place?"

De Foxa made a slight bow. "Don't you think that I should be seated in Malaparte's place?"

Kaarlo Hillilä looked at him with growing surprise. "Why is that?" He said to me, "You wish to change places?"

Everyone looked at me in surprise.

"Not at all. This is my place," I replied.

"You see?" said the Governor triumphantly, turning to the Spanish Minister. "He is seated in his right place."

Then Titu Michailescu said to de Foxa, "Come, my dear Augustin, can't you see that the Governor is ambidextrous?"

De Foxa blushed, wiped his glasses with a napkin and said with an embarrassed air, "Yes, you're right. I had not noticed it."

I looked severely at Augustin, "You've had too much to drink," I said to him.

"I am sorry!" replied Augustin with a deep sigh.

We had been sitting at the table for six hours and after the *krapu,* the red Kemi prawns, after the Swedish hors d'oeuvre, after caviar, *siika,* and smoked reindeer tongue, after the huge Cunas salmon—pink as a girl's lips, after roast reindeer and baked bear's paws, after a cucumber salad dressed with sugar, on the misty horizon of the table between the empty bottles of schnapps, Moselle and Château Lafite, in its dawn-tinted sky the brandy finally appeared.

We all sat motionless, sunk in that deep silence of Finnish dinners when the brandy hour strikes and stared at each other fixedly, breaking that ritual silence only to say *"Maljanne."*

Though we had finished eating, the jaws of the Governor made a dull, continuous, almost menacing noise. Kaarlo Hillilä was a little over thirty, stocky, with a short neck sunk deeply between his shoulders. I studied his thick fingers, his athletic shoulders, his short muscular arms. His eyes were small, cut aslant beneath two heavy, red eyelids under his narrow brow. His hair was blond, curly, almost frizzy—and as short as a fingernail. His bluish lips were swollen and cracked. When he spoke he lowered his head, resting his chin on his chest and pursing his lips, and looked up only now and again. A wild and cunning look, quick and violent with something wrathful and cruel in it, glittered in his eyes.

"Himmler is a genius," said Kaarlo Hillilä banging his fist on the table. That very morning he had had a four-hour interview with Himmler and he was exceedingly proud of it.

"Heil Himmler," said de Foxa raising his glass.

"Heil Himmler," said Kaarlo Hillilä and, staring at me with a severe and reproachful glance, added, "and you would have us believe that you met him, spoke to him and did not recognize him?"

"I repeat it," I said. "I did not know it was Himmler."

A few nights before a group of German officers were standing in front of the elevator, in the hall of the Pohjanhovi Hotel. On the threshold of the elevator cage stood a medium-sized man in a Hitler uniform, who looked like Stravinsky. A man with Mongolian features, high cheekbones and near-sighted eyes that resembled fish eyes—white behind the thick lenses, as if seen through an aquarium glass. His odd face wore a cruel, absent-minded expression. He spoke in a loud voice and laughed. After a while he closed the sliding door of the elevator and was about to press the electric button, when I came up on the run, pushed my way through the group of officers and, after sliding open the door stepped inside before the officers could stop me. The personage in the Hitler uniform made a gesture as if to push me back; this amazed me so that I pushed him back in turn and, having shut the door, I pressed the button. Thus it happened that I found myself in a cage of iron alone with Himmler. He looked at me with surprise and perhaps with a trace of irritation. He was pale, and he seemed to me rather uneasy. He took refuge in a corner of the cage, where, with his hands stretched out as if ready to defend himself against a sudden assault, and panting a little, he stared at me with his fish's eyes. I was puzzled. Through the glass door of the elevator I saw the officers, followed by Gestapo men, bounding up the stairs at great speed and knocking against each other on the landings. I turned to Himmler and smilingly apologized for pressing the button before I had inquired what floor he wanted. "Third," he said smiling, and as I thought, he appeared reassured. "I also am on the third," I said.

The elevator stopped on the third floor. I opened the door and made way for him, but Himmler bowed, pointed to the door with a courtly gesture and I went first under the wondering eyes of the officers and Gestapo men.

I had no sooner stretched out between the sheets when an SS soldier knocked at my door. Himmler was inviting me to have a drink of punch with him in his apartment. "Himmler? *Perkele!*" I said to myself. *Perkele* means "Devil" and is a taboo word in Finnish. Himmler? What did he want with me? Where had I ever met him? It never entered my mind that he was the man in the elevator. Himmler? It was too much trouble to get up and, besides, it was an invitation, not an order. I sent a message to Himmler thanking him for his invitation and asking to be excused. I was dead tired and had already gone to bed. Shortly afterward somebody knocked again. This time it was a Gestapo agent. He brought me a bottle of brandy as a gift from Himmler. I put two glasses on the table and offered the Gestapo agent a drink. I said, *"Prosit."*

"Heil Hitler," replied the agent.

"Ein Liter—One liter," said I. The corridor was watched by Gestapo agents, the hotel was surrounded by SS men armed with tommy guns. I said, *"Prosit."*

"Heil Hitler," replied the Gestapo agent.

"Ein Liter," I said. Next morning the manager of the hotel politely requested me to give up my room, and moved me to a double room on the first floor, at the end of a hall. The second bed was occupied by a Gestapo agent.

"You did not recognize him on purpose " said my friend Jaakko Leppo, staring at me with hostile eyes.

"I had never seen him before. How could I recognize him?" I answered.

"Himmler is an extraordinary man, an extremely interesting man," said Jaakko Leppo. "You should have accepted his invitation."

"He is a person with whom I don't want to have anything to do," I answered.

"You're wrong," said the Governor. "Before I met him, I also thought that Himmler was a terrible character, with a pistol in his right hand and a whip in his left. After talking for four hours with him, I realized that Himmler is exceptionally well read, an artist, a real artist and a high-minded man who responds to everything human. I'll say even more: a sentimental man." The Governor said, "A sentimental man." He added that after having had personal visits with him, and having had the honor of conversing with him for four hours, if he were called upon to paint his portrait, he would have painted him with the Gospels in his right hand and the Prayer Book in his left. The Governor actually said, "with the Gospels in his right hand and the Prayer Book in his left," and he banged his fist on the table.

De Foxa, Michailescu and I were unable to repress a discreet smile, and de Foxa, turning to me, asked, "When you met him in the elevator, what did he have in his hands, a pistol and a whip, or the Gospels and the Prayer Book?"

"He had nothing in his hands," I replied.

"Then it wasn't Himmler, it was someone else," said de Foxa gravely.

"The Gospels and the Prayer Book! Precisely!" said the Governor banging his fist upon the table.

"You pretended not to recognize him on purpose," said my friend Jaakko Leppo. "You knew perfectly well that it was Himmler."

"You ran a great risk," said the Governor. "Anyone present might have thought it was a criminal attempt and shot you."

"You'll certainly get in trouble about it," said Jaakko Leppo.

"*Maljanne*," said de Foxa raising his glass.

"*Maljanne*," all the others replied in a chorus.

The guests sat stiffly, resting heavily against the backs of their chairs and shaking their heads slightly as if a violent wind were blowing. The dry and pungent odor of brandy was spreading through the room. Jaakko Leppo stared intently at de Foxa, Michailescu and me, with a peculiar hostile flash in his dull eyes. *"Maljanne,"* said Governor Kaarlo Hillilä from time to time, raising his glass. *"Maljanne"* echoed the others in a chorus. Through the large windows I gazed at the sad, deserted, hopeless landscape of the Kemi and the Ounas valleys, those stupendously transparent and deep perspectives of forest, water and sky. A limitless horizon, chalky with the violent and pure bleached light of the North, touched the end of the distant rolling *tunturit,* those wooded hills in whose soft folds are concealed marshes, lakes, forests and the winding course of the great Arctic rivers. I was gazing at that empty lofty sky, that squalid abyss of light hanging over the cold glow of leaves and water. All the secret, mysterious meaning of that ghostly country was revealed in the color of the sky, in that frozen loneliness aglow with a wonderful white light and a dead and frozen splendor of chalk. Beneath that sky, in which the pale disk of the nocturnal sun seemed to be painted on a smooth white wall, the trees, the rocks, the grass and the water dripped with a queer substance, soft and slimy; that chalky light was the ghostly, dazzling light of the North, and in that still, pure glow the human faces looked like masks of chalk, blind and dumb. Faces without eyes, without lips, without noses—shapeless and smooth masks of chalk, resembling the egg-shaped heads of the characters painted by de Chirico.

Turning with a smile to the Governor, I said that his features and the features of all his guests recalled to my mind the faces of the sleeping soldiers in the Tori on the night I had reached Rovaniemi. They had been asleep on the ground on beds of straw. Their faces seemed carved from chalk: eyeless, lipless, noseless, smooth and egg-shaped. The eyes of the sleepers were delicate and sensitive surfaces on which the white light rested with a light timid touch, forming a small warm nest—just a drop of a shadow, just a drop of blue. The only living thing in those faces was that drop of a shadow.

"An egg-shaped face? My face also egg-shaped?" asked the Governor gazing at me with uneasy surprise and touching his eyes, his nose and his mouth.

"Yes," I replied. "Just like an egg." And I told them what I had seen at Sodankylä, on the road to Petsamo. The night was clear, the sky white, the trees, the hills, the houses, everything seemed made of chalk. The night sun looked like a blind eye without eyelashes. After a while I saw an ambulance coming down Ivalo Road. It stopped in front of the post office by the small hotel that housed the hospital. A few white-clothed attendants—ah, the dazzling whiteness of those linen uniforms!—began lifting the stretchers out of the ambulance and ranging them on the grass. The grass was white, mellowed by a transparent bluish veil. On the stretchers in heavy, motionless frozen postures, lay statues of chalk, their heads oval and smooth, without eyes, without noses, without mouths. Their faces were egg-shaped.

"Statues?" asked the Governor. "Do you really mean statues? Chalk statues? And they were being carried to the hospital in an ambulance?"

"Yes, statues," I replied. "Chalk statues. Suddenly a gray cloud spread over the sky, and out of the sudden twilight around me, revealing their real shape, emerged the beings and things that before had been merged into that still white glow. The chalk statues on the stretchers were abruptly changed into human shapes by the sudden shadow from that cloud. Those chalk masks were turned into living human features. They were men, they were wounded soldiers. They followed me with their wondering and puzzled glances, for I, too, had suddenly turned before their eyes from a chalk statue into a man—a living man, made of flesh and shadow."

"*Maljanne*," gravely said the Governor gazing at me with an amazed and puzzled look.

"*Maljanne*," echoed the others in a chorus and raised their glasses filled to the brim with brandy.

"What's Jaakko doing? Has he gone mad?" said de Foxá clutching my arm.

Jaakko Leppo was sitting on his chair, his body motionless, his head thrust slightly forward. Without gesturing he spoke in a low voice, his face impassive, his eyes burning with a black flame. Very slowly his right hand had slipped along his side, unsheathed the bone-handled *puukko* hanging from his belt, and suddenly, he had raised his short thick arm and was holding the knife and staring into Titu Michailescu's face. Everyone followed his lead and unsheathed their *puukkos*.

"No, that's not the way it should be done," the Governor said. He also drew his *puukko* and imitated the movements of a bear hunter.

"I've got him, straight through the heart," said Titu Michailescu, turning slightly pale.

"Like this, straight through the heart," repeated the Governor, making a downward thrust with his knife.

"And the bear drops to the ground," said Michailescu.

"No, he does not drop at once," Jaakko Leppo said. "He moves a few steps forward, then sways and drops. It's a most wonderful moment."

"They are all dead drunk," de Foxa said softly clutching my arm. "I am beginning to be afraid."

I said to him, "For God's sake, don't show them that you are afraid. If they notice that you are frightened, they are apt to take offense. They are not bad, but when they are drunk they are like children."

"They are not bad, I know," de Foxa said. "They are like children. But I'm afraid of children."

"To show them that you are not frightened, you must say '*Maljanne*' in a loud voice and, looking straight at them, drain your glass in one gulp."

"I'm done for," de Foxa said. "Another glass and I am done for."

"For God's sake!" I said to him. "Don't get drunk! When a Spaniard is drunk, he is dangerous."

"*Señor Ministro*," said a Finnish officer, Major von Hartmann, in Spanish to de Foxa, "during the Civil War in Spain, I amused myself by teaching my friends of the Tercio how to play the *puukko* game. It's a very amusing game. Shall I teach it to you too, *Señor Ministro?*"

"I don't see the need of it," said de Foxa suspiciously.

Major von Hartmann, who had been at the Pinerolo Cavalry School and had fought in Spain as a volunteer in Franco's army, is a courteous and willful man; he likes to be obeyed.

"Don't you want me to teach you? Why? It's a game that you *must* learn, *Señor Ministro*. Look. The left hand with the fingers spread out is placed on the table, the *puukko* is grasped in the right, and with a sharp thrust the knife's blade is driven into the table between two fingers." While he spoke he raised his *puukko* and made a thrust between the fingers of his open hand. The point of the knife stuck into the table between his thumb and his forefinger.

"Did you see how it is done?" asked von Hartmann.

"*Valgame Dios!*—God help me!" said de Foxa growing pale.

"Won't you try, *Señor Ministro?*" asked von Hartmann offering his *puukko* to de Foxa.

"I would be glad to try it," said de Foxa, "but I cannot spread my fingers. My fingers are like those of a duck."

"Odd!" said the incredulous von Hartmann. "Let me see!"

"It isn't worth your trouble," de Foxa said hiding his hands behind his back. "It's a blemish, a simple fault of nature. I cannot spread my fingers."

"Let me see!" said von Hartmann.

They all bent over the table to see the Spanish Minister's fingers that were shaped like a duck's, and de Foxa tried to conceal his hands under the table, stuck them into his pockets, thrust them behind his back.

"Are you web-footed?" the Governor said grasping his *puukko.* "Show us your hands, sir!"

They brandished their knives as they leaned over the table.

"Web-footed?" said de Foxa, "I'm not web-footed. Not quite web-footed, if you please. There's only a little skin between my fingers."

"The skin must be cut," the Governor said raising his long *puukko.* "It isn't natural to have *les pattes d'oie*—goose feet."

"What? *Les pattes d'oie?*" said von Hartmann. "You already have crow's feet at your age, *Señor Ministro?* Show me your eyes!"

"His eyes?" asked the Governor. "Why his eyes?"

"You, too, have crow's feet," de Foxa said. "Show them your eyes."

"My eyes?" the Governor said in an uneasy voice.

They were leaning over the table, looking at the Governor's eyes.

"*Maljanne,*" said the Governor raising his glass.

"*Maljanne,*" they repeated in a chorus.

"You do not wish to drink with us, sir?" the Governor said reproachfully to de Foxa.

"Governor, gentlemen!" the Spanish Minister said seriously, getting to his feet, "I cannot drink any more. I am going to be sick."

"You are ill?" asked Kaarlo Hillilä. "Are you really ill? Have another drink! *Maljanne.*"

"*Maljanne,*" said de Foxá without raising his glass.

"Have another drink!" the Governor said. "When one is ill, one must drink."

"For God's sake, Augustin, drink!" I said to de Foxá. "If they notice that you are not drunk, you're lost! So they won't see that you are not drunk, Augustin, you must drink." In the company of Finns one must drink. If anyone does not drink with them, if anyone does not get drunk with them, if anyone falls two or three *Maljannes* or two or three glasses behind, he becomes a person to be looked on with distrust and suspicion. "For God's sake, Augustin, don't let them discover that you are not drunk!"

"*Maljanne,*" said De Foxá with a sigh and raised his glass.

"Drink, sir!" the Governor said.

"God help me!" exclaimed de Foxá shutting his eyes and draining his glass brimming with brandy.

The Governor again refilled the glasses and said "*Maljanne.*"

"*Maljanne,*" echoed de Foxá raising his glass.

"For God's sake, Augustin, don't get drunk!" I said. "A drunken Spaniard is fearful. Remember that you are the Minister of Spain."

"I don't give a damn!" said de Foxá. "*Maljanne.*"

"The Spaniards," von Hartmann said, "don't know how to drink. During the siege of Madrid I was with the Tercio in front of University City . . ."

"What?" de Foxá said. "We Spaniards don't know how to drink?"

"For God's sake, Augustin, remember that you are the Minister of Spain!"

"*Suomelle!*" de Foxá said raising his glass. *Suomelle!* means, "To Finland!"

"*Arriba España!*" said von Hartmann.

"For God's sake, don't get drunk, Augustin!"

"To hell with them! *Suomelle!*" de Foxá said.

"Long live America!" said the Governor.

"Long live America!" said de Foxá.

"Long live America!" the others echoed in a chorus raising their glasses.

"Long live Germany, long live Hitler!" said the Governor.

"To hell with them!" de Foxa said.

"Long live Mussolini!" the Governor said.

"To hell with him!" I said with a smile and raised my glass.

"To hell with him!" said the Governor.

"To hell with him!" all the others called in a chorus and raised their glasses.

"America is Finland's stanch friend," the Governor said. "There are many hundreds of thousands of Finns in the United States. America is our second fatherland."

"America," de Foxa said, "is the Finns' paradise. When Europeans die, they hope to go to heaven. When Finns die, they hope to go to America."

"When I die," the Governor said, "I shall not care to go to America. I shall stay in Finland."

"Naturally!" said Jaakko Leppo fixing a surly eye on de Foxa. "Dead or alive, we mean to stay in Finland."

"We certainly mean to stay in Finland when we die," the others said gazing with hostile eyes at de Foxa.

"I want some caviar," de Foxa said.

"You want some caviar?" asked the Governor.

"I'm very fond of caviar," de Foxa said.

"Is there much caviar in Spain?" asked Olavi Koskinnen, the Prefect of Rovaniemi.

"Once upon a time we had Russian caviar," replied de Foxa.

"Russian caviar?" said the Governor frowning.

"Russian caviar is excellent," de Foxa said. "It is very much liked in Madrid."

"Russian caviar is very bad," said the Governor.

"Colonel Merikallio," said de Foxa, "told me a very funny story about Russian caviar."

"Colonel Merikallio is dead," Jaakko Leppo said.

"We were on the Ladoga shore," went on de Foxa, "in the Raikkola forest. Some Finnish rangers had found a box full of dark grayish grease in a Russian trench. One day Colonel Merikallio entered a first line dugout in which some rangers were greasing their snow boots. He sniffed the air and said 'What a strange smell!' It was a fishy smell. 'It's this shoe grease that stinks of fish,' said a ranger showing the tin to the Colonel. It was a tin of caviar."

"Russian caviar is fit only for greasing boots," the Governor said with contempt.

Just then a waiter threw open the door and announced, "General Dietl!"

"Sir," the Governor said, rising and turning toward de Foxá, "the German General Dietl, the hero of Narvik, the supreme commander of the Northern Front, has done me the honor of accepting my invitation. I am glad and proud, sir, that you will meet General Dietl in my house!"

An unusual noise came from outside. It was a chorus of barks, meows and grunts, as if dogs, cats and wild pigs were fighting in the hall of the palace. We looked at each other in amazement. Suddenly the door opened and General Dietl appeared on the threshold. He crawled in on all fours followed by a group of officers also on all fours—one after the other. This strange procession, barking, grunting and meowing moved toward the center of the room, where General Dietl, getting to his feet and standing stiffly at attention, raised his hand to his cap and, stretching his arms out wide, in a thundering voice, shouted the customary Finnish wish to people after a sneeze: "*Nuha!*" I gazed at the extraordinary appearance of the man standing before us; tall, thin, or rather spare than thin, he was a piece of ancient wood roughly shaped by an old Bavarian carpenter. His features were Gothic, resembling wood carvings by an ancient German master. His eyes had a lively glitter that were wild and at the same time childish; his nostrils were extraordinarily hairy, his forehead and cheeks were cut by countless fine wrinkles, just like the cracks in an old, well-seasoned piece of wood. His dark smooth hair, cut short and drawn down over his brow like the fringes of Masaccio's pageboys gave his face both a monkish and youthful appearance that was unpleasantly accentuated by a twist of his mouth when he laughed. His movements were abrupt, restless and feverish, and revealed a morbid strain of character, a presence in, around and within him of something that he spurned, of something that he felt betrayed and threatened him. His right hand was maimed. Even the hampered and cut off motion of that stricken hand seemed to indicate a hidden suspicion of something that lay in ambush threatening him. He was still a youngish man of about fifty. But even he, just as his young Bavarian and Tirolean *Alpenjägers* scattered through the wild forests of Lapland in the marshes and the tundra of the Arctic region, along the huge front from Petsamo and from the Fishermen Peninsula, down along the banks of the Liza as far as Alakurti and Salla—even he showed in the greenish, yellowish color of his skin and in his humble, downcast looks the signs of that slow, fatal decay, not unlike leprosy, to which human beings fall easy prey in the extreme North—a senile decay that rots the hair, eats away teeth, cuts deep wrinkles in the face and wraps the still-living human frame in a greenish, yellowish shroud that envelops decomposing bodies. Suddenly he looked at me. His glance was the glance of a tame and resigned animal, he had something humble and despairing in his eyes that shocked me deeply. He gazed at me with the same wonderful and bestial eyes, with the same mysterious expression with which German soldiers, Dietl's young *Alpenjägers*—toothless, bald, wrinkled, with white thin noses like corpses—roamed sad and self-absorbed through the forests of Lapland.

"*Nuha!*" shouted Dietl. Then he added, "Where's Elsa?"

Elsa came in. Small, thin, gentle, dressed like a doll, Elsa Hillilä, the Governor's daughter who was eighteen but still looked like a child, entered through a door at the end of the huge room and carried a large silver tray lined with glasses of punch. She walked slowly across the pink birch floor, taking short, quick steps with her small feet. With a smile, she approached General Dietl and said with a graceful curtsy, "*Haivää päivää*—Good day."

"*Haivää päivää*," said Dietl with a bow. He took a glass of punch from the silver tray, raised it and shouted "*Nuha!*" The officers on his staff took their glasses of punch from the tray, raised them and shouted "*Nuha!*" Dietl tilted his head back, swallowed the drink down in one gulp, and his officers followed his example with a simultaneous jerk. The gamy wild smell of punch, sweetish and sticky, spread through the room. It was the same sweetish smell that reindeer have in the rain, the smell of reindeer's milk. I half closed my eyes and thought I was back in the Inari forest by the lake at the mouth of the Juutuanjoki.

It was raining, the sky was an eyeless face—a dead white face.

The rain murmured constantly in the leaves of the trees and the grass. An old Lapp woman, sitting by the shore of the lake, her pipe between her teeth, gazed at me impassively, never batting an eyelash. A flock of reindeer was grazing in the wood; they raised their eyes and looked at me. Their eyes were humble and despairing with the mysterious look of the dead. The smell of reindeer's milk spread through the rain. On the shore of the lake, beneath the trees, sat a group of German soldiers, their faces covered with masks of mosquito netting, their hands protected with thick gloves of reindeer leather. Their eyes were humble and despairing; in their eyes, too, was the mysterious look of the dead.

General Dietl grasped little Elsa around the waist and dragging her across the room danced to the waltz that the others were singing to, to the accompaniment of handclaps and the jingle of glasses struck with the handles of *puukkos* and *Alpenjägers'* knives. A group of young officers standing by a window were drinking silently and watching. One of them turned his face and looked at me without seeing me; I recognized Prince Frederick Windischgrätz, smiled at him from across the room and called him by his nickname, Friki; he turned the other way, searching for the voice that had called him. Who was hailing him out of the remote past?

The man who was standing before me was old. He was no longer the young Friki of Rome, Florence and Forte dei Marmi; yet something of his former gentleness remained, but his gentleness now had in it something corrupt. His brow was darkened by a white, almost ghostly shadow. I watched him raising his glass, moving his lips in order to say *"Nuha!"* and throw back his head to drink. The bones in his face appeared to be frail and close to the skin, his skull showed white through the thinning hair, and the dead skin of his forehead shone softly. He was losing his hair, his teeth were loose in his mouth. Behind his waxen ears the nape was as hollow, frail and tender as a sick child's—a frail nape of an aged man. His delicate hands shook when he put his glass on the table. Friki was twenty-five and he already had the mysterious look of the dead.

I went up to Frederick and said softly, "Friki." Slowly Friki turned and slowly he recognized me; he looked me over sadly, explored my own decomposing features, my weary mouth, my pale eyes. He pressed my hand in silence; we looked at each other and smiled for a moment, and during that long moment Frederick reappeared to me on the shore of Forte dei Marmi—the sun flowed like a river of honey over the sand, the fir trees around my house dripped a golden light as warm as honey; only by now Clara had married Prince von Fürstenberg and Suni was in love. We raised our eyes and gazed through the window at the white glow of the leaves, the water and the sky. Poor Friki, I thought.

Frederick was standing motionless in front of the window, and he scarcely breathed as he stared in silence at the huge Lapp forest, at those green and silvery perspectives of rivers, lakes and woody *tunturit* growing distant and spreading out beneath a white frozen sky. I passed my hand lightly over Frederick's arm, and— perhaps it was a caress. Frederick turned his face to me, his skin was yellow and wrinkled, his eyes were shining, humble and despairing. Suddenly I recognized his look.

I recognized his look and began to tremble. He had the look of a beast; I thought with horror that he had the mysterious look of a beast. He had the eye of a reindeer—the humble, despairing eyes of a reindeer. I wanted to say to him, "No, Friki, not you," but he looked at me in silence, like a reindeer, with humble and despairing eyes.

The other officers, Frederick's companions, were young too, per- haps twenty, twenty-five or thirty, and they all bore the same marks of age, decomposition and death on their yellow, wrinkled faces. All of them had the humble and despairing eyes of reindeer. In every face, in every eye was the beautiful, wonderful tameness, the sadness of wild beasts; each had that absorbed and melancholy madness of beasts, their mysterious innocence, their terrible sorrow —that fearful Christian pity that beasts have. It occurred to me that beasts were Christ, and my lips trembled and my hands shook. I looked at Frederick. I looked at his companions, and every one of them had the same withered, wrinkled face, the same bare brow, the same toothless smile, the same look of a reindeer. Even cruelty, even German cruelty had gone out of those faces. They had the look of Christ, the look of a beast. Suddenly I was reminded of what I had been told when I had first reached Lapland, of what everyone talked about in low voices, as if it were a mysterious thing, in fact it was mysterious, a forbidden subject; I was reminded of what I had been told since I had arrived in Lapland about those young German soldiers, those *Alpenjägers* of General Dietl's, who had hung themselves from trees in the depths of the forests, or who sat for days on the shores of a lake gazing at the skyline and then shot themselves through their heads, or else were driven by a wonderful madness, almost an amorous fantasy—roaming through the woods like wild beasts and threw themselves into the still waters of the lakes, or who stretched themselves on beds of lichen under the firs that roared in the wind and waited for death—letting themselves die slowly in the abstract, frozen loneliness of the forest.

No, Friki, not you, I wanted to say to him, but Frederick asked me, "Did you see my brother in Rome?" I replied, "Yes, I saw him one evening before I left, at the Excelsior Bar," and yet I knew that Hugo was dead, that Prince Hugo Windischgrätz, an officer in the Italian Flying Corps, had come down over Alexandria wrapped in flames. But I answered: "Yes, I saw him one evening at the Excelsior Bar. Marita Guglielmi was with him." Frederick asked, "How is he?" And I replied, "He is well. He inquired about you and sent you his greetings," and yet I knew that Hugo was dead.

"Didn't he give you a letter for me?" asked Frederick.

"I saw him only for a moment that evening, and he asked me to bring you his greetings," I answered; yet I knew that Hugo was dead.

Frederick said, "He is a nice fellow, Hugo is." And I said, "Yes, a really nice fellow. Everybody likes him and he sent you his love," and yet I knew that Hugo was dead. Frederick looked at me: "I wake up some nights and think that Hugo is dead," he said, and looked at me with the eyes of a wild beast, his reindeer eyes—with that mysterious wild beast look that is in the eyes of the dead.

"Why do you think that your brother is dead? I saw him at the Excelsior Bar, before I left Rome," I answered, and yet I knew that Hugo was dead.

"Is there any harm in being dead?" asked Frederick—"there is no harm in it; it is not forbidden. Do you think it is forbidden to be dead?"

Then I suddenly said to him, and my voice trembled, "Oh, Friki, Hugo is dead! I saw him at the Excelsior Bar the evening before

I left Rome. He was already dead. He asked me to bring you his greetings. He could not write you a letter because he was dead."

Frederick looked at me with his reindeer eyes, and he smiled. He said, "I knew that Hugo was dead. I knew long before he died. It is a wonderful thing to be dead." He filled my glass. I took the glass that Frederick offered me and my hand was shaking. *"Nuha!"* Frederick said.

I said *"Nuha!"*

"I would like to go back to Italy for a few days," Frederick said after a long minute of silence. "I would like to go back to Rome. Rome is such a young city." Then he added, "And Paula, what is she doing? Has it been long since you have seen her?"

"I met her on the links one morning, shortly before I left Rome. I'm very fond of Paula, Friki."

"I'm very fond of her, too," he said. Then he asked, "And Countess Ciano, what is she doing?"

"What do you expect her to do? She does what all the others do."

"Meaning . . ."

"Nothing, Friki."

He looked at me and smiled. Then he said, "And Alberta, what is she doing? And Luisa?"

"Oh Friki," I replied, "they all are whores. It is fashionable nowadays in Italy to be a whore. Everybody is a whore in Italy."

"It has always been so in Italy," said Frederick.

"It has always been so, it will always be so. For many years I, too, have been a whore, like all the others. Later I felt nauseated by that life. I rebelled and I ended in jail. But even to end in jail is a way of being a whore. Even being a hero, even fighting for King and for country is a way of being a whore in Italy. Even to say that this is a lie and an insult to all those who have died for freedom is a way of being a whore. There is no way out, Friki."

"It has always been so, in Italy," said Frederick. "It is always the same country, gaily beflagged down to the bottom of the same white belly:

> *Down where your belly is white*
> *my country is calling*
> *with all her flags unfurled.*

318

"Aren't those your lines?"

"Yes, they are mine. I wrote them in Lipari."

"It's a very sad poem. It is called 'Ex-voto,' I think. It is a despairing poem. One feels that it has been written in prison." He looked at me, raised his glass and said *"Nuha!"*

I said *"Nuha!"*

We kept silent a long time. Frederick was gazing at me and smiling, with that humble and despairing look of a wild beast. Savage howls came from the end of the room. I turned and saw General Dietl, Governor Kaarlo Hillilä and Count de Foxa standing in the center of a group of German officers. Now and then Dietl's voice broke through sudden and sharp and was followed by a deafening roar of voices and laughter. I could not make out what Dietl was saying; it seemed to me that he was repeating one word, over and over, in a very loud voice; it seemed to be the word *"traurig"* which means "sad." Frederick glanced around and said, "It's awful! Always carousing, day and night, while suicides among officers and men are increasing at a dizzy rate. Himmler in person has come this far north to try and put an end to this epidemic of suicides. He will place the dead under arrest. He will have them buried with tied hands. He thinks he can stop suicides by terror. He had three *Alpenjägers* shot yesterday because they had tried to hang themselves. Himmler does not know that to be dead is a wonderful thing." He looked at me with that look that the eyes of the dead have. "Many shoot themselves through the head. Many drown themselves in the rivers and lakes—they are the youngest among us. Others roam about the woods delirious."

"Trrraaauuurrriiig!" General Dietl was shouting in a very loud voice, imitating the horrible hiss of the Stuka, until Air General Mensch screamed "Boom!" imitating the terrible crash of an exploding bomb. Everyone joined in with howls, whistles and noises produced with lips, hands and feet, reproducing the crash of crumbling walls and the howling blast of shrapnel hurled against the sky by the force of explosion. *"Trrraaauuurrriiig!"* shouted Dietl. "Boom!" howled Mensch. And again everyone joined in the chorus of bestial sounds and noises. There was something savage and grotesque, something barbaric and childish in this scene. General Mensch was about fifty years old, short and thin; his face

was yellow and wrinkled, his mouth toothless, his hair thin and gray; his evil eyes were caught in a net of fine wrinkles. He howled "Boom!" as he started at de Foxa with a queer look, full of hatred and contempt.

"Halt!" suddenly shouted General Mensch raising a hand. Turning toward de Foxa he asked him rudely, "How do you say *traurig* in Spanish?"

"We say *triste,* I think," replied de Foxa.

"Let's try with *triste,*" Mensch said.

"*Trrriiisssteee!*" shouted General Dietl.

"Boom!" howled Mensch. Then he raised his hand and said, "No, *triste* is no good. Spanish is not a warlike language."

"Spanish is a Christian language," said de Foxa. "It is Christ's language."

"Ah, *Cristo!*" Mensch said. "Let's try *Cristo!*"

"*Crrriiissstoooo!*" shouted General Dietl.

"Boom!" General Mensch howled. Then he raised a hand, and said, "No, *Cristo* is no good."

"*Cristo* is not a German word," de Foxa said with a smile.

At that moment an officer approached General Dietl and whispered to him. Dietl turned toward us and loudly said, "Gentlemen, Himmler is back from Petsamo and is waiting for us at headquarters. As loyal German soldiers, let's go to pay our respects to Himmler!"

We drove at high speed through the deserted Rovaniemi streets that were sunk in a white sky. It could have been ten o'clock at night, or six in the morning. A pale sun was swaying above the roofs; the houses were the color of frosted glass, the river glimmered sadly through the trees.

Soon we came to a village of military barracks that were built on the edge of a silvery birch forest just beyond the town. Here were the general headquarters of the Northern Front. An officer approached Dietl, said something to him, and Dietl turned toward us and said, laughing, "Himmler is in the *sauna.* Let's go and see him naked." His words were greeted by a burst of laughter. Dietl went almost on the run toward a fir-log barrack a little way off in the wood. He pushed open a door and we went inside.

The interior of the *sauna,* the Finnish steambath, was occupied by a large grate and a boiler from which the water, raising a cloud of steam, dripped onto white-hot stones that were piled on the scented fire of birchwood. On the benches, ranged on shelves along the walls of the *sauna,* were seated or stretched out some ten naked men. They were so white, soft, flabby and defenseless, so extraordinarily naked that they seemed to have no skin. Their flesh looked like the flesh of lobsters, pale and rosy, exuding an acid crustacean smell. They had broad chests, their fat breasts were swollen and drooping. Their grim hard faces—those German faces —contrasted sharply with their white, flabby, naked limbs, and almost had the appearance of masks. Those naked men sat or lay on the benches like weary corpses. Now and then, laboriously and slowly, they raised their arms to wipe the sweat that dripped from their whitish limbs, sprinkled with yellow freckles that looked like shining scabs.

Naked Germans are wonderfully defenseless. They are bereft of secrecy. They are no longer frightening. The secret of their strength is not in their skin or in their bones, or in their blood; it is in their uniforms. Their real skin is their uniform. If the peoples of Europe were aware of the flabby, defenseless and dead nudity concealed by the *Feldgrau* of the German uniform, the German Army could not frighten even the weakest and most defenseless people. A mere boy would dare to face an entire German battalion. To see them naked is to grasp the secret meaning of their national life, of their national history. They stood naked in front of us, like shy and shameful corpses. General Dietl raised his arm and shouted in a loud voice, *"Heil* Hitler!"

"Heil Hitler!" replied the naked men laboriously lifting their hands that held birch switches. These switches are used for flogging, that is a traditional part of the *sauna,* its most sacred rite. But even the motion of those hands, holding the switches, was soft and defenseless.

I thought I recognized one of the naked men seated on the lowest shelf. Sweat was streaming down his high-cheekboned face, in which nearsighted eyes, stripped of their glasses, glittered with a whitish, soft light, that is seen in the eyes of fish. He carried his head high with an air of arrogant insolence; from time to time he threw his head back, at which sudden, brusque movement, sweat ran out of the hollows of his eyes and from his nostrils and ears, as if his head were filled with water. He sat with his hands resting on his knees like a punished schoolboy. Between his forearms protruded a little rosy swollen drooping belly, the navel strangely in relief, so that it stood out against that tender rosiness like a delicate rosebud—a child's navel in an old man's belly.

I had never seen such a naked and rosy belly; it was so tender that one was tempted to probe it with a fork. Large drops of sweat flowing down his chest glided over the skin of that soft belly and gathered in the hair like dew on a bush. The man seemed to be dissolving in water before our eyes; he sweated so much that I feared that in a short time there would be only a mass of empty flabby skin left of him, even his bones seemed to be softening, melting and becoming glutinous. The man looked like ice cream sitting in an oven. In a twinkling of an eye only a pool of perspiration on the floor would be left of him.

When Dietl raised his arm and said *"Heil* Hitler!" the man rose, and I recognized him. He was the man I had met in the elevator—it was Himmler. He stood before us, the big toes on his flat feet oddly thrust upward, his short arms dangling. Little streams of perspiration gushed like little fountains from the tips of his fingers. Around his flabby breasts grew two little circles of hair, two halos of blond hair; perspiration gushed like milk from his nipples.

He leaned against the wall so as not to slip on the wet, slimy floor and as he turned, he exposed protruding rotundities on which the grain of the wooden bench was imprinted like a tattoo. At last he succeeded in recovering his balance, turned, raised his arm and opened his mouth, but the sweat, streaming down his face and filling his mouth, prevented him from saying, *"Heil* Hitler!" And his gesture was mistaken for the signal for flogging. The other men raised their birch switches and began hitting each other first; then, by common consent, with ever-increasing energy, they applied their switches to Himmler's shoulders and back.

The birch twigs left the white imprints of their leaves on the tender flesh that turned red at once, and then disappeared. A fleeting forest of birch leaves appeared and disappeared on Himmler's skin. The naked men raised and lowered their switches with raging energy; their breath came in short hisses from their swollen lips.

At first Himmler tried to fend them off, shielding his face with his arms, and laughed, but it was forced laughter revealing rage and fear. Later, as the switches began biting his hips, he began twisting this way and that, covering his belly with his elbows, turning about on his toes and drawing his neck into his shoulders; he laughed with hysterical laughter while being whipped, as if he suffered more from tickling than from the birching. Finally Himmler saw the door of the *sauna* open behind us, stretched out his arms to push his way through and ran out the door, pursued by the naked men who never ceasing to hit him, fled toward the river into which he dived.

"Gentlemen," said Dietl, "while we wait for Himmler to return from his bath, I invite you to have a drink in my house."

We came out of the wood, crossed a meadow and, following Dietl, entered his little wooden house. It seemed like crossing the threshold of a dainty house in the Bavarian mountains. A nice fire of fir twigs crackled in the grate; a pleasant resinous smell spread in the warm air. We began drinking again, shouting *"Nuha!"* in a chorus whenever Dietl or Mensch, raising their glasses, gave the sign. After a time, while the others, gripping *puukkos* and *Alpenjägers'* knives, seated themselves around Mensch, and de Foxá pantomimed the last moments of a *corrida*—Mensch was the bull and de Foxá was the matador—General Dietl signaled to Frederick and me to follow him. We left the room and entered his study. An army cot stood against the wall in a corner. The floor was covered with skins of Arctic wolves; a magnificent white bear skin was spread on the cot. On the walls were tacked a number of photographs of mountains—the Towers of Vaiolet, the Marmolata, the Tofane, landscapes of the Tirol, Bavaria and Cadore. On the table next to the window in a leather frame was a photograph of a woman with three girls and a boy. The woman had a simple, pure and gentle air. From the next room came the shrill voice of General Mensch followed by outbursts of laughter, savage howls and the banging noise of hands and feet. The voice of Mensch made the windowpanes and pewter mugs on the mantel rattle.

"We'll let those boys amuse themselves for a while," said Dietl stretching out on his cot. He turned his eyes toward the window and he, too, had the humble and despairing eyes of a reindeer, he also had the mysterious animal look that the eyes of the dead have. A white sun aslant the trees lighted the *Alpenjägers'* barracks and the white houses of the officers ranged along the edge of the wood. From the river came the voices and laughter of the bathers—the laughter of Himmler of the pink belly. A bird called from the branches of a fir tree. Dietl had closed his eyes; he was asleep, one hand fallen by his side, the other on his chest—a child's hand, small and white. It is a wonderful thing to be dead. The distant roar of an engine dimmed the silvery green of the birch wood. A plane hummed through the lofty transparent sky. In the next room the orgy went on: the savage shouts, the noise of shattered glasses, hoarse voices outshouting one another, childish and violent laughter. I leaned over Dietl and scanned his yellow wrinkled face; Dietl, the conqueror of Narvik, was a German war hero, a hero of the German people. He was another Siegfried, he was Siegfried and a cat at the same time; he also was a *kapparoth*, a victim, a *kaputt*. It was a wonderful thing to be dead.

From the next room I heard the shrill voice of Mensch and de Foxa's deep tones, the noise of a quarrel. I went to the door. Mensch stood facing a pale and perspiring de Foxa. Each had a glass in his hand; the officers around them also were gripping their glasses.

General Mensch said, "Let us drink to the countries that are fighting for the freedom of Europe. Let us drink to Germany, Italy, Finland, Romania, Hungary . . ."

"To Croatia, Bulgaria, Slovakia!" others suggested.

"To Croatia, Bulgaria, Slovakia!" repeated Mensch.

"To Japan!"

"To Japan!" Mensch repeated.

"To Spain!" said Count de Foxa the Spanish Minister to Finland.

"No, not to Spain!" Mensch shouted.

De Foxa slowly lowered his glass, his brow was pale and covered with sweat.

"To Spain!" de Foxa repeated.

"Nein, nein, Spanien nicht!" General Mensch shouted.

"The Spanish Blue Division," de Foxa said, "is fighting alongside the German soldiers on the Leningrad front."

"Nein, Spanien nicht!" Mensch shouted.

All looked at de Foxa who, pale and firm, faced General Mensch and fixed him with a wrathful and proud glare.

"If you do not drink to Spain," said de Foxa, "I shall say *merde* to Germany."

"*Nein,*" shouted Mensch, "*Spanien nicht!*"

"*Merde* to Germany!" de Foxa shouted raising his glass, and he turned to me, a flash of triumph in his eyes.

"Good for you, de Foxa," I said. "You've won your bet."

"*Vive l'Espagne, merde à l'Allemagne!*" de Foxa shouted.

"*Ja, ja,*" Mensch shouted, raising his glass, "*Merde à l'Allemagne!*"

"*Merde à l'Allemagne!*" they all repeated in a chorus, raising their glasses.

They embraced each other and some fell to the ground. General Mensch was dragging himself on all fours, trying to catch a bottle that was slowly rolling across the wooden floor.

XVI

Siegfried and the Salmon

"ARMCHAIRS COVERED with human skin?" Kurt Franz asked incredulously.

"Yes, they were covered with human skin," I repeated.

Everybody laughed. Georg Beandasch said, "They should be very comfortable."

"The skin is very soft and thin," I said, "almost transparent."

"I have seen old books in Paris bound in human skin, but never armchairs."

"Those armchairs are in Italy," I said, "in the castle of the Counts of Conversano in Apulia. It was a Count Conversano who, toward the middle of the seventeenth century, had his enemies killed and skinned—priests, noblemen, outlaws, brigands—in order to cover the armchairs in the large hall of his castle. There is one, the back of which is covered with the skin taken from the belly and the breasts of a nun. One can still discern the shape of the breasts and the nipples polished and worn with use."

"With use?" queried Beandasch.

"Just think of the hundreds of people who have sat in that armchair during the course of three centuries," I said. "I fancy that is enough to wear out even a nun's breasts."

"Count Conversano," Victor Maurer said, "must have been a monster."

"I wonder how many hundreds of thousands of armchairs could be covered with the human skins of Jews whom you have killed during this war?" I asked.

"Millions!" Georg Beandasch said.

"A Jew's skin is no good for anything," Kurt Franz said.

"The German skins are no doubt of a better quality," I said. "Gorgeous upholstering can be made out of them."

"Nothing is as good as Hermes leather," said Victor Maurer whom General Dietl called "the Parisian." Victor Maurer was a cousin of Hans Mollier, the press secretary of the German Embassy in Rome, and he had spent many years in France. For him France meant Paris and Paris meant the Ritz Bar

"After the war," Kurt Franz said, "the German skins will be worth nothing."

Georg Beandasch laughed. He was stretched out on the grass, his face covered with mosquito netting. He was chewing a birch leaf and now and then he lifted the net to spit. He laughed and said:

"After the war? What war?"

We were sitting on a bank of the Juutuanjoki, near the lake. The river rushed violently by, twisting between the great boulders. Blue smoke rose over the Inari village where Lapp herdsmen were cooking their reindeer soup in copper pots hanging over the fires. The sun swayed on the horizon as if it were blown by the wind. The forest was warm, green and bluish, traversed by brooks of wind that rippled beautifully through the grass and the tree branches. A flock of reindeer was grazing on the opposite bank. Through the trees glittered the silvery lake veined with pink and green, like beautiful old Meissen ware. Those very green and pink tints, those shy and warm tints of Meissen china, those warm and shy greens, those warm pinks that here and there coagulated into little drops of glistening purple. It was beginning to rain—the everlasting summer rain of the Arctic lands. A slight and continuous buzzing was flowing through the forest. Suddenly a sunbeam struck the pink-green of the lake and a prolonged tinkle ran through the air, that sweet sorrowful tinkle of cracking china.

"The war is over for us," Kurt Franz said.

The war was far away from us. We were outside the war, in a remote continent, in abstract time, outside humanity. For over a month I had been roaming through the Lapland forests, through the tundra along the Liza, across the lonely, frozen and bare rockfields of the Petsamo fjord on the Arctic Sea, through the red pine woods and the white birch woods, along the shores of Lake Inari, over the *tunturit* of the Ivalo region; for over a month I had been living among a strange people: the young Bavarian and Tirolean *Alpen-jägers*, toothless and bald, with wrinkled yellow faces and the humble, despairing eyes of wild beasts. And I wondered what could have changed them so completely. They were still Germans, they were still the same Germans whom I had met before Belgrade, Kiev, Smolensk and Leningrad, with the same hoarse voices, the same hard brows, the same broad and heavy hands. But there was something wonderful, something pure and innocent about them that I had never before discovered in any German. Perhaps it was that bestial cruelty of theirs, that cruel innocence, like the innocence of children and beasts. They spoke about the war as if it were something past and distant, with an inward contempt, a grudge against violence, hunger, destruction and murder. They seemed to be content with the cruelty of nature, as if the lonely life in those limitless forests, the remoteness of civilization, the boredom of the everlasting winter night, the darkness of long months, ripped from time to time by the fire of the aurora borealis, the torture of everlasting summer daylight, the sun staring by day and by night through the window of the skyline—as if all this had driven them to a cruelty characteristic of mankind. They had acquired the despairing humility of wild beasts, that mysterious feeling for death. They had reindeer eyes, those dark, deep and glistening eyes; that mysterious animal-look that the eyes of the dead have. A few nights before, I had gone out into the woods. I could not sleep. It was past midnight; the white sky was wonderfully translucent, it looked like a sky made of tissue paper. There was not a sign of a cloud, or so it seemed to me; the sky was so clear and translucent that it looked like a vast, deep space, bare and void. Yet an invisible drizzle was falling from that clear sky and penetrated my bones and awakened a sweet murmur of music among the leaves of the trees, in the thicket and on the light carpet of lichen. I had walked through the forest for over a mile when a hoarse German voice summoned me to stop. An *Alpenjäger* patrol, their faces covered with masks of mosquito netting, approached me. It was one of the many patrols, specially trained for guerilla warfare in the Arctic forests, which searched the woods and the *tunturit* of the Ivalo and Inari regions for Russian and Norwegian partisans. We sat down in the lee of some boulders by a fire of twigs, and smoked and talked under the light drizzle that smelt of resin. They told me they had found the tracks of a wolf pack; they had been aware of its presence for some days, long before they discovered the tracks, because of the restlessness of the reindeer herds. Those soldiers were mountaineers from the Tirol and Bavaria. From time to time a branch crackled in the depths of the forest or a bird called. While we talked in low voices—one always speaks in a low voice in those climates where the human voice sounds alien to man, where it sounds false, artificial, unrelated to man and full of despair, where it really is the voice of an inner anguish that finds no way of expressing itself and exhausts itself in itself, in its own sound, in its own echo—we saw amid the trees, about a hundred paces away, some animals that looked like dogs, short-haired, grayish, the color of rusty iron.

"The wolves," the soldiers said.

They passed close to us and looked at us with their red glistening eyes. They seemed to have no fear, no suspicion of us. There was something in their confidence that was not only peaceful, but detached—a kind of sad and noble indifference. They ran noiselessly, fleet and light, with their long, nimble, soft gait. There was nothing of the beast in them, but a kind of noble shyness, a kind of proud and most cruel tameness. A soldier raised his gun, but one of his comrades pushed it down. The gesture was a renunciation of that cruelty characteristic of man. It was as if in those inhuman solitudes, even man found no other means of expressing his humanity, except by acknowledging a sad and tame wildness.

"For some days," Georg Beandasch said, "General von Heunert has been beside himself. He cannot catch a salmon. All the strategy of German generals is powerless against the salmon."

"The Germans," Kurt Franz said, "are poor fishermen."

"Fish are not fond of the Germans," said Victor Maurer.

Lieutenant Georg Beandasch, adjutant to Cavalry General von Heunert, was the first German I had met when I reached Inari. In civilian life Georg Beandasch was a judge in the Berlin courts. He was about thirty, tall, broad-shouldered, with a bony jaw. He stooped a little in walking and looked at people with a crooked glance. "A rather unsuitable glance for a judge," he said. From time to time, with a look of deep contempt on his dark face, he spat on the ground. His face was the color of leather. It was because of the leather color of his skin that we had begun talking that day about Count Conversano's armchairs covered with human skin. The habit of spitting on the ground—Georg Beandasch acknowledged—was rather unbecoming for an adjutant of a German cavalry general, "but I have my reasons for doing it." At times it seemed as if he were spitting on all the German generals. Although he was guarded in his speech, I never felt that he rated Hitler and his generals very highly. Given a choice between General von Heunert and the Lapland salmon, he preferred the salmon. But in the end, like all Germans, judges or whoever they are, he obeyed the generals. That is the tragedy of the salmon in Europe: although the Germans side with the salmon, they obey their generals.

As soon as I had reached Inari, I had gone through the village looking for a place to sleep. I was dead tired and knocked out by the lack of sleep. I had driven four hundred miles across Lapland to reach Inari, and I longed to stretch out on a bed. But beds were scarce there. There are only four or five hundred wooden houses in the village, all grouped around a country general store, the *sekatavara kauppa*, the owner of which, a Finn, Mr. Juho Nykänen, welcomed me with a cordial smile. He displayed before my eyes his best goods: celluloid combs, *puukkos* with handles of reindeer bone, saccharine tablets, dog-skin gloves, cream for mosquito bites.

"A bed? A bed to sleep in?" asked Juho Nykänen.

"What else would I want with it?"

"And you come to me for it? I am not selling beds. Once I had an army cot in my shop, but I sold it three years ago to the manager of the *Osaki Pankki* in Rovaniemi."

"Couldn't you direct me to someone," I said, "who might be willing to lend me a bed for a few hours?"

"Lend you a bed?" Juho Nykänen said. "You mean someone who will give up his turn to you? Uhm, I think it most unlikely. The Germans have taken our beds and we take turns in sleeping on the few beds that are left to us. You might try Mrs. Irjaa Palmunen Himanka. She may have a bed free in her hotel, or she may talk some German officer into allowing you to use his bed for a few hours. If so, while waiting for your turn to sleep, you might go fishing. I can provide you with everything that is needed for salmon fishing at a reasonable price."

"Are there many salmon in the river?"

"There were a great many before the Germans began building the bridge across the Juutuanjoki. The carpenters make a great deal of noise with saws, hammers and axes, and the noise disturbs the salmon. The Germans are building another bridge at Ivalo and the salmon have left the Ivalojoki. And that's not all! The Germans use hand grenades for fishing. That's slaughter! They not only destroy salmon, but every other kind of fish. Do they imagine that they can deal with salmon as they deal with Jews? We shall never allow it. I told General von Heunert the other day: If the Germans, instead of fighting the Russians, keep on fighting the salmon, we shall defend the salmon."

"It's simpler to fight salmon than the Russians."

"You're mistaken," Juho Nykänen said. "The salmon are very plucky, and it isn't easy to beat them. To my mind, the Germans have made a great blunder in waging war against the salmon. A day will come when the Germans will be afraid even of the salmon. That's how it will end. That's how the last war ended."

"Meanwhile the salmon are deserting your rivers," I said.

"Not because they are afraid," Juho Nykänen said with a tinge of resentment in his voice. "The salmon are not afraid of the Germans. They snub them. The Germans are unfair, particularly in the matter of fishing. They have no inkling of what fair play is. They slaughter the salmon with hand grenades. They think fishing is not a sport, but a form of *Blitzkrieg*. The salmon is the most noble animal in the world. It would rather die than break the laws of honor. Like the gentleman it is, it fights to the last breath and it faces death like a hero, but it will not demean itself to fight an unfair foe. It prefers exile to the dishonor of fighting an unworthy foe. The Germans are furious because they no longer find salmon in our rivers. And, do you know where the salmon are migrating?"

"To Norway?"

"What? Do you imagine the Norwegians are better off than the salmon? There are Germans in Norway too. They migrate to beyond Fishermen's Island, toward Archangel and Murmansk."

"Oh, so they are going to Russia?"

"Well, yes, they are going to Russia," Juho Nykänen said. His pale, Finnish, high cheekboned face crooked into a thousand little wrinkles like an earthenware mask in the sun. "They are going to Russia," he said, "and let's hope that they will not come back some day with red ideas."

"Are you sure that they will come back?"

"They will, and sooner than the people expect," Juho Nykänen said and, lowering his voice, added, "you may take it from me, sir, the Germans will lose the war."

"What?" I exclaimed. "Do you mean to say that the Germans will lose the war?"

"I mean the war against the salmon," said Juho Nykänen. "The people hereabout, the Lapps and Finns, all side with the salmon. The other day some German soldiers were found dead on the bank of the river. Probably, the salmon killed them, don't you think so?"

"Probably," I said. "I shall welcome with pleasure, my dear Mr. Juho Nykänen, the salmon's victory. Theirs is the cause of humanity and civilization. But meanwhile I would like a bed to sleep in."

"Are you very tired?"

"I'm dead tired with weariness and lack of sleep."

"I advise you to go to the hotel of Mrs. Irjaa Palmunen Himanka," Juho Nykänen said.

"Is it very far?"

"Not more than a mile. You'll have to make the best of the accommodations and probably sleep with a German officer."

"In the same bed?"

"Germans are fond of sleeping in other people's beds. If you tell him that the bed is not yours, he might make a little room for you."

"Thank you, Mr. Juho Nykänen, *kiitoksia pallion.*"

"*Haivää päivää.*"

"*Haivää päivää.*"

Mrs. Irjaa Palmunen Himanka gave me a kind welcome. She was a little over thirty years old, with a weary, sad face. She told me at once that she would ask Lieutenant Georg Beandasch, General von Heunert's adjutant, to give up one of his beds to me.

"In how many beds does this gentleman sleep?" I asked.

"There are two beds in his room," said Mrs. Irjaa Palmunen Himanka, "I hope that he will agree to give one of them to you. But you know, the Germans . . ."

"I don't give a damn about the Germans. I'm sleepy."

"Neither do I," said Mrs. Irjaa Palmunen Himanka. "But only up to a certain point. The Germans . . ."

"You must never ask a favor of a German," I said. "If you ask a favor of a German, you may rest assured of being refused. The entire superiority of the *Herrenvolk* depends on saying 'No.' With the Germans you must never ask or beg. Leave it to me, Mrs. Irjaa Palmunen Himanka. I've learned my lesson from the salmon."

The dull eyes of Mrs. Irjaa Palmunen Himanka lighted suddenly, "Oh, what a noble people the Italians are! You are the first Italian I have met in my life, and I did not know that the Italians also defend the salmon against the Germans. And yet you are allied to the Germans! You are a noble people!"

"The Italians are of the same breed as the salmon," I said. "All the peoples of Europe are salmon."

"What will happen to us," said Mrs. Irjaa Palmunen Himanka, "if the Germans destroy the salmon in our rivers or force them to migrate? In peacetime we make a living out of sporting fishermen; people come from England, from Canada and the United States to spend the summer in Lapland. Ah, this war . . ."

"Take it from me, Mrs. Irjaa Palmunen Himanka, this war will end like the last one—the salmon will drive the Germans out."

"Heaven make it so!" exclaimed Mrs. Irjaa Palmunen Himanka.

We went up to the first floor. The hotel in Inari is like an Alpine refuge; a wooden two-storied building, attached to a small inn where the Lapp herdsmen and fishermen gather on a Sunday after church to talk about reindeer, fire-water and salmon before going back to their huts and tents hidden in the depths of the boundless Arctic forest. Mrs. Irjaa Palmunen Himanka stopped in front of a door and knocked softly.

"Come in!" shouted a hoarse voice.

"I'd better go in alone," I said. "Trust me. You will see that all will be well."

I pushed the door open and went in. In the little room that was wainscoted with birchwood were two beds. On the one near the window Georg Beandasch was stretched out, his face covered with netting. Without bothering to say "Good evening," I threw my knapsack and my raincoat on the other bed. Georg Beandasch rose on his elbow, looked me over from head to foot, just as a judge looks at a criminal, smiled, and began to swear through his teeth with the greatest gentleness and courtesy. He was dead tired, he had been standing the entire day in the midst of an icy current in the Juutuanjoki next to General von Heunert, and he would like to sleep for another couple of hours.

"Sleep well," I said to him.

"Two in a single room cannot sleep well," said Georg Beandasch.

"Three sleep worse," I said dropping on the bed.

"I wonder what time it is?" asked Georg Beandasch.

"Ten o'clock."

"Ten in the morning or ten at night?"

"Ten at night."

"Why don't you go and walk in the forest for a couple of hours," Georg Beandasch said. "Give me at least a chance to sleep in peace for another two hours."

"I'm sleepy too. I will go walking tomorrow morning."

"Morning or night are the same here. The sun shines during the night in Lapland," Georg Beandasch said.

"I prefer the day sun."

"Have you come for those cursed salmon?" Georg Beandasch asked after a brief silence.

"Salmon? Are there still any salmon in this river?"

"There's only one, but the cursed fellow cannot be caught."

"Only one?"

"Only one," Georg Beandasch said. "But he is a huge beast, full of tricks and courage. General von Heunert has asked for reinforcements from Rovaniemi. He will not leave Inari until he has caught him."

"Reinforcements?"

"A general is always a general," said Georg Beandasch. "Even when he goes salmon fishing. We have been standing in the water up to our bellies for ten days. Tonight we were on the point of catching him. I mean to say that tonight he passed nearly between our legs. He came close, but he would not bite. The General is furious. He says that the salmon is making fun of us."

"Making fun of you?"

"Making fun of a German general!" Georg Beandasch said. "But tomorrow the reinforcements that the General has asked for from Rovaniemi will arrive at last."

"A battalion of *Alpenjäger?*"

"No, only a captain of the *Alpenjäger*, Captain Karl Springenschmid, a specialist in fishing mountain trout. Springenschmid comes from Salzburg. Have you read his book *Tirol am Atlantischen Ozean?* A Tirolean is always a Tirolean, even on the shores of the Arctic Ocean; if he is a trout specialist, he should at least be able to catch a salmon, don't you think?"

"A trout isn't a salmon," I said with a smile.

"Who knows? Captain Springenschmid says so, but General von Heunert denies it. We shall see who is right."

"It is not befitting for a German general to ask for reinforcements against a single salmon."

"A general is always a general," Georg Beandasch said. "Even if he is facing only a single salmon. In any case, Captain Springenschmid will be expected to confine himself to a little good advice. The General wants to catch the fish himself. Good night."

"Good night."

Georg Beandasch turned on his back and closed his eyes, but opened them again almost at once, sat up, asked me my name, parentage, date and place of birth, nationality, religion, race, just as if he were questioning a prisoner. Then he drew a bottle of brandy from under his pillow and filled two glasses.

"*Prosit.*"

"*Prosit.*"

He dropped again on his back, closed his eyes and gently went to sleep. The sun was streaming in on his face. A cloud of mosquitoes filled the room. I dropped off to sleep and had been slumbering a few hours when a distant rattle of castanets reached my ear. Beandasch was lost in a deep slumber, his face protected by a mask of mosquito netting, like a gladiator who had dropped dying on the sand of the arena. It was a gentle rattle of castanets, a rustling of grass and swishing of branches. An interminable procession seemed to be passing under my window. A procession of Spanish dancers, a nocturnal procession of Sevillian dancers on their way to the shrine of the Virgin of the Macarena, beating their castanets, their right arms curving softly above their heads, their left hands resting on their hips.

It really was the rattle of castanets, and little by little it grew louder, clearer and closer. All the sound lacked, however, was an echo of smells that usually accompany the rattle of castanets—the smell of withered flowers, of fritters and of incense. It was the sound of hundreds and hundreds of castanets. An interminable procession of Andalusian dancers marching within the glinting sheath of the frozen nocturnal sun. They were not followed by the shouts of crowds, by the bangs of firecrackers, or by the blare of distant bands. Only by that sharp and high pitched crackle of castanets that came always nearer.

I jumped out of bed and aroused my companion. Georg Beandasch rose on his elbow, listened and looked at me with a smile. He said in that peculiar precise and ironical manner of his, "Reindeer. The two toes that hang from their heels knock against each other when they run and sound like castanets." Then he added: "Did you mistake them for Spanish dancers? The first night General von Heunert thought that they were Andalusian ballet girls. I had to bring a reindeer into his room at two in the morning." He spat on the floor and smiling went to sleep. I looked out of the window. A herd of several hundred reindeer was galloping toward the river along the edge of the forest. In the Hyperborean forest they were the ghosts of the Mediterranean lands, of the warm lands of the South. The ghost of Andalusia anointed with olive oil and parched by the sun. And in the frozen thin air, I could sense an absurd, imaginary smell of human sweat.

The nocturnal sun slanted through the small islands scattered in the center of the lake and tinted them with the color of blood. A dog, far down in the Inari village, howled plaintively. The sky was covered with fish scales that glittered and trembled in the icy dazzling air. I was walking with Kurt Franz along the wooded slopes of the hill toward the lake. Among the hundred islets scattered in the middle of the lake I discerned Ukonsaari, the sacred island of the Lapps, the most famous heathen shrine in the entire Inari region. There, on that cone-shaped islet that the nocturnal sun reddens like a volcano, the ancient Lapps gathered in spring and autumn to sacrifice reindeer and dogs to their gods. Even today the Lapps stand in sacred awe of Ukonsaari and land on it only on certain days as if prompted by a subconscious recollection, by an obscure longing for their ancient heathen ceremonies.

We sat down to rest under a tree and gazed at the huge silvery lake stretched out naked in the icy flame of the nocturnal sun. The war was far away from us. I no longer smelled around me that sad odor of man, of perspiring man, of wounded man, of hungry man, of dead man that defiled the air in unhappy Europe. Only the smell of resin, that cold lean smell of Arctic lands, the smell of trees, water and earth, that smell of wild beasts. Kurt Franz was smoking his short Norwegian pipe, a Lille Hammer which he had purchased in Mr. Juho Nykänen's *sekatavara kauppa.* I watched him furtively and I smelled him. He was a man, perhaps a man like all other man, perhaps a man like myself. There was the odor of a wild beast about him—the odor of a squirrel, a fox, a reindeer. The odor of a wolf. The summer odor of wolves when hunger does not make them cruel. It was a primitive animal odor, the odor of wolves in the summer when the green grass, the warm wind and the waters free from ice, rippling and murmuring in a thousand rivulets toward the calm lake, dissolve their cruelty, their savagery, and quench their thirst for blood. He smelt like a sated wolf, a resting wolf, a wolf at peace. For the first time after three years of war, I felt untroubled beside a German. We were far from the war, outside war, outside humanity and outside time. He really smelt like a wolf in the summer, like a German when the war is over, and he is no longer athirst for blood.

We went down the hill and, just outside the forest, close to the Inari village, we passed by an inclosure surrounded by a high stockade of white birch logs.

"It's the reindeer Calvary," Kurt Franz said, "the autumn rite of slaughtering the reindeer is a kind of Easter for the Lapps that is reminiscent of the sacrifice of the Lamb. The reindeer is the Christ of the Lapps," Kurt Franz said. We entered the vast inclosure. Against the hard, cold light that cuts the grass, an extraordinary, wonderful forest spread before my eyes: thousands upon thousands of reindeer horns heaped haphazard in a fantastic entanglement, thin in some places, in other places standing like thickets of bones. The most ancient horns were clothed in a slight green-yellow, reddish mildew. Many horns were still fresh and tender, not yet encased in the hard, bony crust. Some of the others were broad and flat with many branches, still others were knife-shaped and looked like steel blades growing out of the ground. On one side of the inclosure were heaped thousands and thousands of reindeer skulls, shaped like Greek helmets, with empty triangular orbits in the hard frontal bones that were white and smooth. All those horns looked like the metal trophies of knights fallen on the battlefield—an animal Roncevaux. Yet there was no trace of a struggle anywhere. There was order, repose and a deep solemn quiet. A breath of wind passed over the meadow and made the blades of grass tremble between the motionless bony trees of that extraordinary forest.

During the autumn the herds of reindeer, prompted and guided by instinct, by an obscure call, cover immense distances to reach those savage Calvaries where they are expected by the Lapp herders who sit on their heels, their "four winds hats," the *nelyäntuulen lakki*, jammed on the nape of their necks, the short glinting *puukkos* clutched in their small hands. The smallness and delicacy of the Lapps' hands are a wonder. They are the smallest and most delicate hands in the world—a wonderful and most delicate contrivance made of the toughest steel. The thin, patient fingers are as accurate as the pincers of a *la Chaux-de-Fonds* watchmaker or of an Amsterdam diamond cutter. Tamely and docilely the reindeer offer their jugular veins to the deadly blades of the *puukkos;* they die without a sound, with a pathetic and despairing sweetness.

"Like Jesus Christ," Kurt Franz said. Within the inclosure the grass, fed by so much gore, is thick. But the small leaves of some of the bushes look as if they had been charred by a great fire; perhaps it is the heat and the very flame of blood that paints them red and sears them.

"No, it cannot be the blood," Kurt Franz said. "Blood does not burn."

"I've seen entire cities burned by a single drop of blood," I said.

"Blood disgusts me," Kurt Franz replied. "It's a dirty thing. It soils everything it touches. Vomit and blood are two things that disgust me the most."

He ran his hand over his forehead already gnawed by a scrofulous baldness. He gripped the mouthpiece of his Lille Hammer in his toothless mouth. Now and then he took the pipe out of his mouth and crossly spat on the ground, bending slightly forward. While we were crossing the village two old Lapp women, sitting on a doorstep, followed us with their half-closed eyes and slowly turned their yellow wrinkled faces. They were squatting on their heels, smoking short clay pipes, their elbows on their knees. A soft rain was falling. A large bird flew low over the branches of the firs and sent forth hoarse and monotonous cries.

In front of the hotel General von Heunert was getting ready to go fishing. He was wearing Lapp boots of reindeer leather that reached half way up his thighs. He had wrapped himself in a wide net cape against mosquitoes, and his arms were sunk up to the elbows in large gloves of dog's leather; he stood in front of the hotel waiting for his Lapp servant, Pekka, to finish packing the bag of food. General von Heunert was in full battle dress—his head was covered by a steel helmet, a heavy Mauser hung from his belt, and he was leaning on his long fishing rod like an ancient Teuton leaning on his long spear. From time to time he spoke to a short, thick-set, gray-haired *Alpenjäger* captain who stood beside him with the rosy, smiling face of a Tirolean. Behind the General, at a respectful distance, Georg Beandasch stood rigidly at attention. He was also shod, gloved, armed and wrapped in a net cape reaching down to his heels. He nodded to me and I gathered from the way his lips were moving that he was mumbling some amiable Berlin curses.

"This time," General von Heunert said to me, "I hold victory in the palm of my hand."

"You have not been very lucky these past few days," I said.

"That's what I think, too. I have had no luck," General von Heunert said. "But that's not what Captain Springenschmid thinks. To his mind, the fault is mine—the salmon are capricious and obstinate and I have overlooked their temperament. A most grievous error! Luckily, Captain Springenschmid has lectured me on the temperament of the trout, and now—"

"Of the trout?" I said.

"Of the trout. Why not?" General von Heunert said. "Captain

Springenschmid, who is well known throughout the Tirol as a specialist in trout fishing, maintains that the Tirolean trout has the same temperament as the Lapp salmon. Isn't it so, Captain Springenschmid?"

"*Jawohl*," Captain Springenschmid replied with a bow and, turning to me, said with that soft accent that the Tiroleans have when they speak Italian, "One must not seem to be in a hurry with trout. One needs patience—a monk's patience. When a trout perceives that a fisherman has patience and plenty of time on his hands, it becomes nervous and grows irritable and does something foolish. The fisherman must be quick to take advantage of that foolishness. Trout—"

"Yes, trout," I said. "But what about salmon?"

"Salmon are like trout," Captain Springenschmid said with a smile. "The trout is not a patient animal; it becomes tired of waiting and rushes into danger. As soon as it bites, it is lost. Gently, delicately it is reeled in by the fisherman. It is child's play. Trout—"

"Yes, trout," I said. "But what about salmon?"

"Salmon," Captain Springenschmid said, "is only a larger trout. Shortly before the war, at Landeck in the Tirol—"

"It looks," General von Heunert said, "as if my salmon were the finest specimen ever seen in these rivers. It's a huge beast, extraordinarily plucky. Just think, the other day it almost knocked its snout against my knees!"

"It's an insolent salmon!" I said. "It deserves to be punished."

"It's a damnable salmon," General von Heunert said. "The only salmon left in the Juutuanjoki. It probably thinks it can drive me by force out of the river and can remain master of the stream. We shall see who is more obstinate: a salmon or a German." He opened his mouth wide and began laughing, making the wide folds of the large mosquito net sway about him.

"Perhaps," I said, "it is irritated by your general's uniform. You should put on a civilian dress. It isn't fair to fish salmon in a general's uniform."

"*Was? Was sagen Sie, bitte?*—What? What were you saying?" General von Heunert said growing dark in the face.

"Your salmon," I said, "probably lacks a sense of humor. Perhaps

Captain Springenschmid can tell you how to behave with a salmon that has no sense of humor."

"You have to match wits with a trout," Captain Springenschmid said. "The General must pretend that he is in the middle of the river for quite another reason than the trout imagines. A trout has to be deceived."

"It won't escape me this time!" General von Heunert said firmly.

"You will teach the salmon to respect German generals," I said.

"*Ja, ja!*" exclaimed General von Heunert, but his face grew angry and he glanced at me with suspicion.

Just then Mrs. Irjaa Palmunen Himanka appeared on the threshold of the hotel, followed by Pekka who bore a tray with a bottle of brandy and several glasses. With a smile she approached the General, filled the glasses and offered them first to the General and then to each one of us.

"*Prosit,*" said General von Heunert raising his glass.

"*Prosit,*" we all repeated in a chorus.

"*Für Gott und Vaterland,*" I said.

"*Heil* Hitler," the General answered.

"*Heil* Hitler," the other repeated.

Meanwhile half a score of *Alpenjäger* turned up, each of them wrapped in a wide mosquito net and armed with a tommy gun. The patrol was detailed to escort the General to the river and to stand along the banks to guard him, while he was fishing, against a possible surprise attack by Russian or Norwegian partisans.

"Let's go!" the General said moving forward.

We walked in silence, preceded and followed at a distance by the escorts. An invisible drizzle murmured in the leaves. A bird screamed from the branches of a tree. A herd of reindeer passed us at a gallop with the rattle of castanets between the pines. In the cold light of the nocturnal sun the forest seemed made of silver. We walked along the bank of the river, sinking up to our knees in grass that dripped with rain. Georg Beandasch glanced at me quickly with the air of a whipped dog. Now and then General von Heunert turned and silently stared at Beandasch and Springenschmid. "*Jawohl!*" the two officers said in unison and raised their right hands to the brims of their steel helmets. At last after walking for about one hour, we reached the rapids.

The Juutuanjoki widens at that point into an ample stream, rapid but not deep, with scattered boulders of granite peeping through the foamy water. Pekka and the other Lapps who carried the fishing tackle and the sacks of food, stopped under the shelter of a rock. Some of the escorting soldiers spread along the shore, while others forded the stream and stood on the opposite bank with their backs to the river. General von Heunert carefully examined his rod, tested the reel, then, turning to Beandasch and Springenschmid said, "Let's go," and stepped into the water followed by the two officers. I was left on the bank sitting under a tree with Kurt Franz and Victor Maurer. The voice of the river was high, rich and throaty; at times it broke into a yell and then dropped to a deep, heavy sound. Standing in the middle of the stream up to his belly in icy water, the General wielded his fishing rod as if it were a rifle and gazed around as though pretending that he was there, in the middle of the river, for an entirely different reason than the salmon imagined. Beandasch and Springenschmid stood a few steps behind him, in an attitude of military respect. Pekka and the other Lapps sat together on the bank, smoked their pipes and looked at the General in silence. Birds shrieked in the branches of the firs.

About two hours went by, then suddenly the salmon attacked General von Heunert. The long rod jumped, bent, swayed and stretched out to its full length; the General wavered on his feet, took one or two steps forward; swayed on his knees, and bravely withstood the sudden attack. The battle was on. Scattered along the bank, the Lapps, the soldiers of the escort, Kurt Franz, Victor Maurer and I held our breath. Suddenly, taking long hard heavy steps, the General moved forward. He was following the stream, planting his boots heavily into the water, bracing his right foot first against one boulder, then against another, yielding ground step by step with careful deliberation. Such tactics were not new, even for a German general, because salmon fishing always requires one to give ground while advancing. From time to time the General stopped, consolidated the positions he had won at such heavy cost, and for a moment I thought that in the language of salmon fishing he had "lost"; but he persistently withstood the continuous furious jerks of his foe, and gently, slowly, cautiously maneuvering the steel rod, he began to wind the reel, pulling the plucky salmon toward him. The fish, in its turn, yielded ground slowly, with careful deliberation; one moment its shiny pink and silver back showed above the surface as it thrashed its strong tail and sent foamy splashes of water into the air; next moment, it came to the surface with its long muzzle, showing its half-open mouth and its round staring eyes. But no sooner did it find the support of two boulders between which it braced itself crosswise, or a more rapid current that gave support to its tail, than it made a sudden violent jerk and pulled its foe onward, drawing him downstream along the noisy steel hollow of the current. General von Heunert met these offensive thrusts by the salmon with a stubborn German tenacity, a Prussian pride, a feeling of superiority and a realization that, not only his personal prestige but also that of his uniform was at stake; now and again he let out a short hoarse cry, *"Achtung!"* He looked over his shoulder to scream at Beandasch and Springenschmid a few hoarse words that rose above the alternatingly deep and high-pitched chant of the river. But what assistance could poor Georg Beandasch render his general against such a salmon? What assistance could poor Springenschmid render him against such a trout? Every time the General stepped forward, Georg Beandasch and Captain Springenschmid could do no more than follow him; thus, step by step, the General and his two aides went almost a mile downstream, drawn onward by the jerks of the strong and courageous salmon.

The struggle had already lasted about three hours with varying success, when I perceived ironical smiles rising on the yellow wrinkled faces of Pekka and of the other Lapps who were huddled together, their clay pipes between their teeth. Then I looked at the General. There he was in the center of the river, in full battle dress, his big Mauser dangling from his belt, wrapped in the folds of a large mosquito net. The wide reddish stripes on his general's trousers glistened in the dead reflection of the nocturnal sun. Something was rising in him; I could feel it. I sensed it in his impatient gestures, in his hungry face, in the voice in which from time to time he shouted *"Achtung!"*—a voice with overtones of wounded pride, of a subtle and troubled fear. The General was angry and afraid. He feared that he was cutting a sorry figure. He had been struggling with the salmon for three hours already; it was below a

German general's dignity to be held in check by a fish for such a long time. He began to fear that he might be worsted. If only he were alone! But he was right before our eyes, before the ironic eyes of the Lapps, before the eyes of his escorts stationed along the banks of the river. And then there was the precedent of Soviet Russia. The struggle had to be brought to an end. His dignity, the dignity of a German general, of all German generals, of the entire German Army was at stake. And then, there was the precedent of Russia!

General von Heunert suddenly turned to Beandasch and shouted in a hoarse voice:

"*Genug! Erschiesst ihn!*"

"*Jawohl,*" replied Georg Beandasch, and he moved forward. He walked downstream with long, slow, hard steps; when he was close to the salmon that struggled in the foaming water pulling the General downstream, he stopped, drew his pistol from its holster, bent over the brave salmon and fired two shots point blank into its head.

PART SIX

THE FLIES

XVII

Golf Handicaps

"OH NO, THANK GOD!" said Sir Eric Drummond, First Lord Perth, His Britannic Majesty's Ambassador at the Quirinal, on an autumn day in 1935.

The sun split a rosy, green-edged cloud and a gold beam rebounded from the table making the glass and china tinkle. The vast expanse of the Campagna stretched out before our eyes with the deep perspectives of yellow grass, brown earth and green trees among which, in the October sunshine, the marble tombs and the red arches of the aqueducts stood out in their solitude. The tomb of Cecilia Metella flashed in the vivid autumn fire, the cypresses of the Appian Way scented with thyme and laurel swayed in the wind.

The luncheon was nearly over, the sun was reflected in the glasses, a subtle perfume of port permeated the warm, gentle, honey-colored air. Around the table half a dozen Roman princesses of American and British birth smiled at Bobby, Lord Percy's daughter who had recently married young Count Sandy Manassei. Bobby was telling us that Beppe, the one-eyed bath attendant at Forte dei Marmi, on the day when at the most critical moment in the diplomatic tension between Britain and Italy, the Home Fleet sailed into the Mediterranean in full fighting trim, had said to her, "Britain is like Mussolini: she is always right, especially when she is wrong."

"Do you really think that Britain is always right?" Princess Dora Ruspoli asked Lord Perth.

"Oh no, thank God!" Lord Perth replied with a blush.

"I wonder," said Princess Jane di San Faustino, "whether the story of the caddy and the Home Fleet is true?" A few days after the Home Fleet had made its appearance in the Mediterranean, Lord Perth had been playing golf. His ball had bounced into a pool of muddy water. "Will you fetch me the ball?" Lord Perth had said to the caddy. "Why don't you send the Home Fleet after it?" the Roman urchin had replied. The story most likely was not true, but it had delighted all of Rome.

"What a lovely story!" said Lord Perth.

The sun shining on his face, mischievously showed off the delicate, pink color of his forehead and lips and his clear blue eyes that had something childish and effeminate in them, so typical of every well-bred Englishman—a wonderful shyness, a color of innocence, a childish reticence that with the passing of years and with increasing responsibilities and honors instead of withering and dying out, finds new life and comes to marvelous bloom at a late age in a quality that in an Englishman, goes with white hair and blushing on the slightest provocation.

"Britannia may rule the waves, but she cannot waive the rules," I said with a smile.

Everybody around me laughed, and Dora Ruspoli, gesturing with her right hand and thrusting her sallow-skinned face toward Lord Perth, said in her hoarse, rushing voice, "It's a great privilege for a country to be unable to infringe on the laws of tradition, isn't it?"

"To rule the waves, to waive the rules. . . . It's a nice play on words," Jane di San Faustino said. "But I detest puns!"

"It's a joke of which Hammen Wafer is very proud," I said.

"Hammen Wafer is a gossip writer, isn't he?" Dora Ruspoli asked.

"Something on that order," I replied.

"Have you read *New York* by Cecil Beaton?" asked William Philips, the United States Ambassador who sat next to Cora Antinori.

"Cecil is a very attractive boy," said Beatrice, or "Bee" as her friends call the daughter of William Philips.

"It's a delicious book," Cora Antinori said.

"It's a pity," said Jane di San Faustino, "that Italy has no writer like Cecil Beaton. Italian writers are provincial and boring. They have no sense of humor."

"That is not entirely their fault," I said. "Italy is a province and Rome a provincial capital. Can you imagine a book written about Rome by Cecil Beaton?"

"Why not?" Dorothy di Frasso asked. "As far as gossip goes, New

York has nothing on Rome. What Rome lacks is not gossip, but a gossip writer like Cecil Beaton. Just think of the stories about the Pope and the Vatican. As far as I am concerned, I have never been responsible for as much gossip in New York as I am in Rome. And what about you, my dear?"

"Nobody has ever gossiped about me," Dora Ruspoli said with a hurt glance at Dorothy.

"They simply treat us like tarts," Jane di San Faustino said. "At least that keeps us young!"

Everybody laughed, and Cora Antinori said that provincial living was not the only reason why Italian writers were boring. "Even provincial writers can be entertaining!" she said.

"At heart," Dora said, "New York is also a provincial city."

"The idea!" exclaimed Jane looking at Dora with contempt.

"It depends partly on the nature of a language," Lord Perth said.

"The language is very important," I said. "Not only to writers, but to peoples and countries as well. In a certain sense, wars are only grammatical errors."

"Or merely errors of pronunciation," William Philips said.

"The time is over when the word 'Italy' and the word 'Britain' were spelled differently but pronounced the same way," I said.

"It may be only a matter of pronunciation," Lord Perth said. "That is precisely what I ask myself after leaving a talk with Mussolini."

I visualized Lord Perth during an audience with Mussolini in the huge room of the Palazzo Venezia:

"Announce the British Ambassador," Mussolini would say to Navarra, his chief usher.

At a discreet sign from Navarra the door would open obediently, Lord Perth would cross the threshold and move with slow steps across the marble patterned floor toward the massive walnut table standing before the great sixteenth-century fireplace. Mussolini would stand with his back against the table or the mantelpiece; he would be waiting with a smile and go to meet him; they would face each other; Mussolini self-conscious and, at the same time, strained from constantly trying to appear affable, would shake his huge, swollen, white, round, fat, bald head on which a large cyst just behind his ear protrudes from his neck to add a horrible massiveness; Lord Perth straight, smiling, cautious and shy, his forehead lighted by a faint childish blush. Mussolini, if he really believed in anything, believed in himself, but he never believed in the incompatibility of logic and luck, of will and fate. His voice was warm, deep and gentle—a voice that occasionally had strange, deep, feminine notes, something that was morbidly feminine. Lord Perth did not believe in himself. Oh no, thank God! He believed in the power, prestige, everlasting quality of the Fleet, the Bank of England, the Fleet's sense of humor, and in the fair play of the Bank of England. He believed in the close connection between the playing fields of Eton and the battlefield of Waterloo. Mussolini would stand there before him, completely alone: he was aware that he represented nothing and no one. He represented himself. Lord Perth was merely the representative of His Britannic Majesty.

Mussolini would say: "How do you do?" as if he meant, "I want to know how you are." Lord Perth would say, "How do you do?" as if he meant, "I don't want to know how you are." Mussolini spoke like a peasant from Romagna; he uttered the words: problem, Mediterranean Sea, Suez, Ethiopia—as if he were uttering the words: card game, Lambrusco wine, riot, Forli. Lord Perth had the accent of an Oxford undergraduate who is distantly related to someone in Scotland—the accent of Magdalen College of the Mitre Hotel, of the Mesopotamia Island and of Perthshire. He uttered the words: problem, Mediterranean Sea, Suez, Ethiopia—as if he were uttering the words: cricket, Serpentine, whisky, Edinburgh. His face was smiling but impassive, his lips moved slightly, caressing the words; his expression was deep and secretive, as if he were looking with closed eyes. Mussolini's face was pale and bloated, contracted into an amiable grimace of assumed calm and forced complacency; his thick lips moved as though sucking in each word, his eyes were staring and round, his gaze was both fixed and restless. He had the look of a man who knows how to play and how not to play poker. Lord Perth had the look of a man who knows what is and what is not cricket.

Mussolini would say: "I want!" Lord Perth would say: "I should like."

Mussolini would say: "I don't want." Lord Perth would say: "We can't."

Mussolini would say: "I think." Lord Perth would say: "I suppose, may I suggest, may I propose, may I believe."

Mussolini would say: "Unquestionably." Lord Perth would say: "Rather, maybe, perhaps, almost, probably."

Mussolini would say: "My opinion." Lord Perth would say: "The public opinion."

Mussolini would say: "The Fascist revolution." Lord Perth would say: "Italy."

Mussolini would say: "The King." Lord Perth would say: "His Majesty, the King."

Mussolini would say: "I." Lord Perth would say: "The British Empire."

"Eden, also, has had trouble in getting along with Mussolini," said Dorothy di Frasso. "They appear to pronounce the same words in different ways."

Dora Ruspoli began to tell about the amusing incidents that had aroused the morbid curiosity of Roman society during Anthony Eden's recent stay in Rome. Immediately after the luncheon given him by Lord Perth at the British Embassy, Eden went out for a walk. By six o'clock he still was not back. Lord Perth was beginning to worry. Shortly before closing time, a young secretary of the French Embassy, who only a few days before had arrived at the Farnese Palace straight from the Quai d'Orsay, was paying a novice's tribute to Rome by following in the footsteps of Chateaubriand and Stendahl and by roaming through the halls and passages of the Vatican Museums, perceived a fair young man with a small blond mustache, seated on the lid of an Etruscan sarcophagus, between the club of Hercules and the long, pale thigh of a Corinthian Diana; he was absorbed in reading a little leatherbound book that seemed to the young secretary of the French Embassy to be a copy of Horace. Remembering the photographs on the front pages of the Roman papers that day, the young Frenchman recognized the solitary reader as Anthony Eden who was relaxing over Horace's *Odes* in the twilight of the Vatican Galleries after the tedium of official dinners and receptions, diplomatic talks and discussions, and, perhaps, escaping the unconquerable boredom to which every well-born Englishman is prey when he thinks about himself.

This discovery, that the young secretary of the French Embassy innocently revealed to his colleagues and to two or three Roman princes whom he had met at the Hunting Club and at the Excelsior Bar, caused a great stir in Roman society, apathetic by nature, tradition and pose. That evening, at a dinner given by Princess Isabelle Colonna, it was the only topic of conversation. Isabelle was enraptured. That simple personal item, so meaningless in a certain sense, suddenly struck her as sublime. Eden and Horace! Isabelle could not recall a single line of Horace, but she felt certain that there was something in common between Eden and that dear old, amiable Latin poet. She felt secretly annoyed with herself that she had not guessed long before anyone told her what Horace had in common with Anthony Eden.

The next day, by ten in the morning, the entire Roman smart-set, as if by chance, turned up in the Vatican Museums, each member confidently carrying a copy of Horace under his arm or clutching one with jealous hands. But Anthony Eden failed to make an appearance and by noon, everybody left, feeling very disappointed. It was hot in the Vatican Galleries and Isabelle Colonna, pausing by a window to breathe a little fresh air with Dora Ruspoli and to let "all those people" get away, said to Dora when they were left alone, "Look at that statue, my dear! Doesn't it look like Eden? It's undoubtedly an Apollo. Oh, he looks like Apollo! He too is a wonderful, young Apollo!" Dora walked over to the statue, examined it with care through the rosy veil of her shortsightedness. "It's not an Apollo, my dear! Look at it more closely!" It was a statue of a woman, perhaps a Diana or a Venus. "Sex has no meaning in such matters! Don't you think it looks like him, anyway?"

Within a few hours, Horace became the fashion. On the tables of the Acquasanta Golf Club, on the red-and-white checked cotton tablecloths, next to a Parisian Hermes bag, a package of Camels or Gold Flakes and a Dunhill lighter, there was always a Schiaparelli Horace—that is, a copy of Horace wrapped in a silken handkerchief or cover, in accordance with Schiaparelli's latest advice in *Vogue* on how to protect books against the burning sands of the seaside and the humid dust of the golf links. One day an ancient Venetian copy of the *Odes* of Horace in a gorgeous cinquecento binding wrought in gold was found on a table; it could have been left there on purpose. The imprinted Colonna arms, although the gilt had slightly faded through the centuries, were shining on the binding; the Sursock arms were missing, but everyone guessed that it was Isabelle's bedside volume.

The following morning Eden had to go to Castel Fusano and, as soon as the news spread through Rome, there was a procession of luxurious cars on the road to Ostia. But Eden, after a brief swim and a sunning on the sand, left Castel Fusano an hour before anyone arrived there, and everyone went back to Rome disappointed and angry with one another. That evening in Dorothy di Frasso's house the "treasure hunt" was the only topic of conversation, and Dorothy spared no one except Isabelle who, according to Dorothy, had discovered that one of her ancestors, a Sursock who had lived many years in Constantinople during the days of Edward VII and in London during the reign of Abdul Hamid, had translated the *Odes* of Horace into Syriac. Consequently the Sursocks, Horace and, of course, Eden had something in common. This unexpected relationship with Anthony Eden filled Isabelle with legitimate pride. Later, when Eden suddenly left for London, everyone on the links of the Acquasanta looked at one another with suspicion like jealous lovers, or with sad reassurance like disappointed lovers. Isabelle, to whom someone returning from Forte dei Marmi had repeated Jane's innocent jest—it was an allusion to the ritual meal that follows after funerals in the East—had canceled a dinner at the last moment. Dora rushed to Forte dei Marmi to acquaint Jane with the latest events and gossip of that wonderful week of passion.

"You, too, my dear!" said Jane di San Faustino. "I saw you from a distance that day with such an expression on your face! I said immediately to myself: something has happened to her, she has struck her funny bone!"

"Rome is such an extraordinary city!" Lord Perth said. "Eternity can be felt in the very air. Everything turns into a legend, even society gossip. Behold Anthony Eden elevated to the world of legend. He has entered eternity by simply spending a week in the Eternal City!"

"Yes, but he left in a hurry, the wily fellow," Princess Jane said.

That had been the Golden Age for the Golf Club, the happy and haloed days for the Acquasanta. Later the war came, and the links became a sort of *paseo* where young Roman women marched under the eyes of Galeazzo Ciano and his court and balanced their golf clubs in their small white hands. Galeazzo's star, borne by the reddish vapors of war, had risen rapidly on the horizon, and a new Golden Age, new happy and haloed days seemed to return to the Golf Club though the names, manners, appearances and clothes had something too new and too colorful about them without arousing the often undeserved suspicion usually aroused by men and things too new in a world that is too old—a world in which newness and youth are never accepted as signs of realness. The excessively rapid rise of Galeazzo and his court was in itself an obvious sign of its illegitimacy, a sign that could not be mistaken.

The British had left. The French had left. Other foreign diplomats were preparing to leave Rome. German diplomats had replaced the British and the French, and there was a perceptible lowering of standards—a certain diffidence, an undefinable uneasiness had succeeded the old free graciousness, the old free ease. Princess Anne Marie von Bismarck—her clear Swedish features embroidered on the silken blue sky against a background of pines, cypresses and tombs of the Appian Way—and the other young women of the German Embassy had a shy and smiling grace that was rendered more gentle and reticent by a realization that they were foreigners in Rome where every other foreign woman feels Roman. There was sorrow in the air, a subtle and mellow regret.

Galeazzo Ciano's youthful court was rather easygoing and generous; it was the court of a vain and capricious prince to which entrance was gained through the favor of women and from which people were exiled because of the prince's sudden disfavor—a marketplace of smiles, honors, positions and sinecures. The court was rightfully presided over by a woman; not by one of Galeazzo's young and beautiful favorites, but by a woman who considered Galeazzo her favorite, and her colt. Roman society long since had finally accorded her the recognition after having offered hardy resistance to her in the beginning—a recognition of courtly predominance because of her name, rank, wealth and an angelic predisposition for intrigue, to which were added a natural gift of a vague sense of history and a class consciousness that obscured her already weak and uncertain political understanding.

Assisted equally by her long-undisputed position as "first lady of Rome," and by the dismay that had overtaken Roman society due to war dislocations and the uncertainty of the future—a sort of pagan despair that penetrates the weary veins of old Catholic aristocracies when some awful storm is approaching—and by the decay of moral principles and manners that is a harbinger of great revolutions, Princess Isabelle Colonna had in a short space of time succeeded in turning the palace of Piazza Santi Apostoli into a citadel of those principles of illegitimacy that were represented in the political, as well as the social field, with fresh and vivid glamour by Count Galeazzo Ciano and his court. This surprised only those who, being unfamiliar with the political vicissitudes of great Roman families during the last thirty or fifty years, or being ignorant of the "public secrets" of the smart-set, were not aware of the real position that Isabelle enjoyed in the Roman world.

The fact that for many years Isabelle had carried on the duties of a stern vestal of the most rigid principles of legitimacy, had not prevented the "little Sursock"—as Isabelle was called when, newly married, she had arrived in Rome by way of Cairo and Constantinople with her sister Matilda, the wife of Alberto Theodoli—from being considered by many people an upstart, an intruder who represented the Corinthian order in the Doric order of the Colonna house. Later, when confronted by an illegitimate Italy that Mussolini and his "revolution" had brought to the fore, Isabelle for several years, until the Concordat, assumed an honest and smiling reserve; she sat, so to speak, by the window. She adjusted her relations with the "revolution," as she saw it from the windows of the Colonna Palace, with the same minute etiquette and strict protocol that she provided for her notorious leases with the unfortunate Mrs. Kennedy who for a long time had been renting an apartment in the Colonna Palace. The "legitimate" Rome was not surprised the day when Isabelle had opened her doors to Italo Balbo, nor had this innovation caused any scandal. But then, one surmised the true and deeper reasons for Isabelle's changed attitude, and for Italo Balbo's presence in the drawing rooms of the palace of Piazza Santi Apostoli.

Not only to Isabelle and to Roman society, but to the entire

Italian people, the war became what the Spaniards, using a bull-fighting term, call *el momento de verdad*—the moment of truth—when a man, all alone, grasps the sword in his hand and faces the bull. In that moment the truth about the man and about the brute that faces him stands revealed. All vanities, human and animal, fall away. In that supreme moment the man stands naked and alone face to face with the brute who is also naked and alone. At the beginning of the war, in that moment of *verdad*, Isabelle also had found herself naked and alone; she publicly opened the great front gate of the Colonna Palace to Galeazzo Ciano and his court, making it clear that she had definitely made her choice between the principle of legitimacy and illegitimacy, and transformed the palace of Piazza Santi Apostoli into what the Paris Archbishop's palace had been in the days of Cardinal de Retz—herself becoming a Cardinal de Retz in a certain sense. Over that citadel of illegitimacy, over that palace where gathered everything equivocal and spurious that had risen to the surface in a new Rome and in a new Italy, Isabelle reigned as queen without for a moment renouncing an ancient, amiable and mischievous predisposition for tyranny. Within that world Galeazzo appeared more as a tool of tyranny than a tyrant.

Isabelle's table was no longer adorned with white and red roses and with winter strawberries—royal bounties, the gifts of Italo Balbo—sent daily by air from Libya, but with the smiling faces, rosy cheeks and strawberry lips of young women whom Isabelle offered as royal bounties to the insatiable vanity of Galeazzo.

By then Italo Balbo was dead, and dead were the roses and winter strawberries of Libya.

No young woman whom Galleazzo had noticed during a fleeting encounter, no foreigner of standing, no aspiring gallant, no dandy of the Chigi Palace who yearned for promotion or for a sinecure in some comfortable embassy, could escape the obligation that was sought through every conceivable art—to pay tribute with a convivial wreath of roses to Isabelle and Galeazzo. The chosen crossed the threshold of the Colonna Palace with an air of mysterious and yet open complicity, as if they were members of a publicly known conspiracy. An invitation from Isabelle was no longer of any real social value. Perhaps, it still had a political value, but many were mistaken even about the political value of an invitation to Piazza Santi Apostoli.

Isabelle was the first and, perhaps, the only one to perceive even before she opened the gates of the Colonna Palace to him, that Count Galeazzo Ciano, the young and dashing Minister of Foreign Affairs, the lucky son-in-law of Mussolini, was unimportant in Italian life and politics. Why then had Isabelle hoisted the colors of Galeazzo Ciano over the Colonna Palace? A number of people were simple-minded enough to accuse her of playing chaperon to Galeazzo merely out of social ambition—could a more ludicrous charge be imagined?—or out of a passion for intrigue, but they overlooked the fact that the "first lady of Rome" was not in any need of improving her social position and even less so of defending it; she had everything to lose and nothing to gain by her alliance with Galeazzo. Justice must be done to Isabelle's social genius and to her far-reaching, worldly policy; no one, not even Mussolini, could have reigned in Rome against Isabelle. In rising to power Isabelle had nothing to learn from anyone; she had carried out her own march on Rome and she had made a much earlier start, almost twenty years before Mussolini. Her efforts were crowned with much greater success.

The reasons for Isabelle's partiality to Galeazzo are much deeper and more complex. In a decadent social body approaching its final ruin, in a nation in which the principles of historical, political, and social legitimacy no longer held any authority, in a country in which the classes closely linked with the fate of social continuity had lost all prestige, in an Italy which, with her unfailing Sursock instinct Isabelle sensed, was about to become the greatest Levantine country of the West—from the standpoint of political morality Rome, no less than Naples, deserved Lord Rosebery's description: "The only Eastern city in the world that lacks a European quarter" —in such an Italy only the victory of the principles of illegitimacy could have insured a peaceful recovery from the terrible social crisis that was proclaimed and precipitated by the war, or could have attained the supreme and passionate aspirations of the conservative classes during days of serious social upheaval to save what can be saved.

Some people have been simple-minded enough to tax Isabelle

with abandoning the cause of legitimacy for illegitimacy, which, in the language of the smart-set, means having preferred Count Galeazzo Ciano to the Prince of Piedmont who, according to the conservative classes, embodied the principle of legitimacy, that is, of social order and continuity, and who appeared to be the only man capable of insuring a peaceful recovery from the upheaval within a constitutional framework. If there is any prince in Europe richly endowed with virtue, it is Humbert of Savoy. His grace, good looks and smiling simplicity of manner are the virtues the Italian people demand from their princes. However, he lacked some of the gifts that were indispensable for shouldering the task which the conservative classes assigned to him. The Prince of Piedmont thought that he had as much intelligence as he needed, but not so much as others thought that he needed. To say that he lacked a sense of personal honor would be unfair. He had a sense of honor, but not to a degree that conservatives expect from a prince in moments of danger. In the vocabulary of frightened conservatives the term "personal honor" in a prince means a particular kind of honor that is concerned with saving not only the monarchical principle, statutory institutions and dynastic interests, but also everything back of that principle—the institutions and interests that constitute the social order. Nor was there anyone in the Prince of Piedmont's entourage who could be expected to grasp what the term "sense of honor" means to conservatives during days of serious and dangerous social upheaval.

Many people pinned their hopes on the Princess of Piedmont, but she was not a woman with whom Isabelle could get along. During moments of serious social upheaval, when not only the Royal family and their dynastic interests, but everything is at stake and in danger, a Princess Isabelle Colonna, Sursock by birth, cannot conceive of coming to terms with a Princess of Piedmont except on equal terms. Isabelle called her "the Fleming" and, falling from Isabelle's thin lips, the word brought forth a vision out of a Flemish picture of one of those fleshy girls with red hair, wide hips and a lazy, greedy mouth. Isabelle was of the opinion that certain attitudes assumed by the Princess of Piedmont and certain strange, indeed rather foolhardy contacts maintained by her with opponents of the monarchy and even communists, justified the surmise that the

Princess of Piedmont was inclined to prefer the advice of men, even of foes, to the confidences of women, even of friends. "She has no friends, and she does not want any," was the inference Isabelle drew, and she was deeply concerned about it, not on her own behalf of course, but on behalf of the *pauvre Flamande.*

Between the Prince of Piedmont and Count Galeazzo Ciano Isabelle could only choose the latter. Yet among the many reasons that induced her to prefer Count Ciano to the Prince of Piedmont was one that was a grave error of judgment. Unquestionably, from a political and historical view Ciano was the most genuine representative of the principles of illegitimacy that among the conservative classes was known as "a tamed revolution," and a tamed revolution is always more advantageous for the object of social preservation than a raging, or merely a stupid and inept reaction. But Isabelle made a fatal mistake in permitting her choice to be influenced by an opinion she shared with many people that Ciano was the "Anti-Mussolini," that in fact as well as in the minds of the Italian people he embodied the only policy which could "save what can be saved," namely; a policy of friendship with Britain and America and finally, that, if not "the new man" sought for and awaited by everyone—Galeazzo at thirty-six was too young to be considered a new man in a country where men begin to be regarded as new only when they are past seventy—he was at least the man of tomorrow required by danger and the complexity of the situation. Later it became apparent how grievous was this mistake, and how pregnant with consequences. Some day it will be perceived that Isabelle was merely a tool of Providence—the very Providence with which Isabelle maintained such good relations through the Vatican —in speeding and evolving a style for the agony of a society that was fated to die.

Many people shared with Isabelle the delusion that Count Galeazzo Ciano was the "Anti-Mussolini," the man to whom London and Washington looked expectantly. Galeazzo himself, thanks to his vanity and smug optimism, was secretly convinced that he was viewed with favor by English and American public opinion; that in speculating about the future, London and Washington considered him the only man in Italy who could take over Mussolini's complex legacy and, after the inevitably disastrous ending of the war, accomplish a transition from the Mussolini order to a new order agreeable to the liberal, Anglo-Saxon civilization, without causing irreparable ruin, unnecessary bloodshed or a serious social upheaval; finally, he believed himself the one man who could guarantee to London and Washington a social order and, above all, a necessary continuity of social organization that had been badly shaken by Mussolini, and was now threatened with complete destruction by the war.

How could the unfortunate Isabelle avoid sharing this delusion? A Levantine by birth, an Egyptian in fact, she loved Britain through her nature, education, habits and moral and material interests. Consequently she was inclined, almost predestined to look for or imagine in others what she strongly and deeply felt herself and wanted other people to feel. Moreover, in observing Galeazzo's nature, character, manners, and external attitudes that easily could be mistaken for political convictions, she had discovered a number of traits that inspired her with confidence and opened her heart to great and lively hopes—traits that formed a kind of spiritual kinship between her and Count Ciano; the lower, so to speak, Levantine traits in the Italian character that never had been so conspicuous as when the crisis, the war, began to move toward its inevitable conclusion. Galeazzo had an abundance of such traits in a particularly sharp and apparent form. He was aware of them and was on occasion complacent about them, maybe because of the origin of his family that was more Magna Grecian than Tuscan. His ancestors, simple fishermen who owned a few wretched boats, hailed from Formia near Gaeta. However, he was born in Leghorn which of all Italian cities shows the most vivid and colorful traces and the greatest immediacy and reality of the Levant—or because of the unfortunate educational effects of his exceptional good luck, or because of his peculiar conception of wealth, power, glory and love—a conception strangely similar to that of a Pasha. Isabelle had good reason to sense instinctively another Sursock in Galeazzo.

Thus within a short time Isabelle became the arbiter of Roman political life in the strictly worldly meaning that the word "political" has in the smart-set. To an inexperienced observer who never looked beyond the various aspects of smiling arrogance, she might even have appeared happy. But her happiness as it always happens in a corrupt society when it comes on evil and calamitous days, through a subconscious force, gradually assumed the semblance of moral indifference and sad cynicism that were faithfully mirrored by the small court gathered around the table of the palace in Piazza Santi Apostoli.

Everything best and worst that Rome could offer in names, manners, reputations and behavior sat around that table. To be asked to the Colonna Palace became the supreme and fairly easily attainable ambition of young women who belonged to the Roman smart-set, of neglected beauties from the North who were beginning to cross the fateful threshold—scions of Lombard, Piedmontese and Venetian families who more than once had succeeded in mixing in their veins new and obscure blood of the Cianos with their own ancient and illustrious blood. There were also minor actresses of the Roman film colony who, during the later days, seemed to attract Count Ciano more and more through a kind of weariness, quite Proustian in character, the *Guermantes* way, or through his illusion of craving for sincerity.

Every day there was a greater number of "Galeazzo's widows," those simple-minded favorites who had fallen into disfavor with Count Ciano—who was always ready to seek out new loves and was as fickle in matters of love as he was in all others. They were in the habit of pouring their tears, their confessions and their jealous rages on Isabelle's bosom when she had a "widow's day" three times each week. On these days at designated hours between three and five in the afternoon, Isabelle was at home to the "widows." She welcomed them with open arms and a smiling face, as if to congratulate them on some danger that they had escaped or on an unexpected bit of good luck; she seemed to experience an extraordinary joy, a peculiar, almost physical pleasure, a morbid and sensual, gratification in mingling her shrill laughter and her irrepressible gay words with the tears and complaints of the unfortunate "widows," who instead of suffering with sincere grief and with deep pangs of a true love, were motivated by spite, humiliation and rage. Those were the moments when Isabelle's malignant genius, her genius for intrigue and delusion, rose to a height and nobility of pure art, of a free and voluntary game, of a disinterested immorality that was almost innocence. In that art, in that game of

Isabelle's *materiam superabat opus,* Isabelle's great secret, probed for so many years, spied upon and scrutinized in vain by the evil curiosity of all of Rome, would have been revealed to an indiscreet observer at such times if indiscreet observers had been allowed to witness the pathetic, malicious scenes of Isabelle's triumphs and of the humiliation of the "widows." To the shocked and troubled observer, Isabelle's queer joy was enough to cast a revealing, turbid and pathetic light upon her complex, mysterious and yet unhappy mind.

Around Galeazzo and his elegant and servile court the desert landscape of indifference, contempt or hatred, which was by then the moral landscape of unfortunate Italy, was daily closing in. There were moments when Isabelle felt the gloomy horizon closing in on her, but she had no eyes for anything she did not want to see; she was completely wrapped up in her hopes, and in the machinations of her unselfish intrigue that was intended to allow Italy to overcome the awful and unavoidable trial of defeat and to seek refuge like a new Andromeda in the loving arms of the British Perseus. The fact that everything was crumbling around her, that Count Ciano, with his fickle vanity, revealed more each day his severance from the realities of Italian life, confirming what she had known for a long time, what she had been the first one and, perhaps, the only one to discern: Galeazzo's complete lack of influence on Italian life, his purely formal and decorative value, his sole significance as a pretext—all this, instead of overwhelming her mind with bitterness and despair, instead of unsealing her eyes and making her aware of her fatal mistake, only strengthened her lofty and high-minded delusion and added new grounds for her pride. Galeazzo was the man of tomorrow. What if he were not the man of today? All alone Isabelle still believed in him. That young man loved by the gods, that young man whom the benevolent and envious gods had heaped with such extraordinary gifts and even more extraordinary favors, would some day save Italy, and carry her in his arms through the flames to the safe and generous bosom of Britain. There was the fervor of a Flora MacDonald about her mission as an apostle.

Isabelle conducted an able and tireless campaign through the Vatican, where Osborne, His British Majesty's Minister to the Holy

See, had taken refuge since the beginning of the war—to make London and Washington aware of the love and respect that the entire Italian people had for Count Ciano. Nothing could free her from the delusion that Galeazzo was the only man in Italy on whom British and American policy could depend, the only man whom London and Washington kept secretly ready for the day of reckoning, that is for the day which Englishmen describe as "the morning after the night before." Even the wisdom of the many and powerful friends she had at the Vatican, their persistent doubts, their advice of moderation and humility, their tightening of lips and shaking of heads, and the icy reserve of the British Minister Osborne could not shake Isabelle's faith. If anyone had told her, "Galeazzo is too much loved by the gods to be able to save himself"—if anyone had revealed to her the fate granted as a supreme favor by envious gods to those whom they love best and had said, "It is Galeazzo's fate to be Mussolini's lamb at the approaching and inevitable Easter and that is why he is being fattened by Mussolini," the halls of the Colonna Palace would have resounded with Isabelle's shrill laughter. "The very idea, my dear!" Isabelle, like Galeazzo, was too much loved by the gods.

During the years when war began to reveal its true, mysterious face, a kind of sinister complicity sprang up between Isabelle and Galeazzo, a complicity that gradually swept them, as if by an invisible force, toward an ever more flagrant moral indifference, to a doom that follows a long and habitual acceptance of laxity and mutual deception. The law that governed their relationship was the same that governed the dinners and gay parties in the Palazzo Colonna—not the Proustian code of Faubourg Saint-Germain, not that of Mayfair of recent years, not that of a still newer Park Avenue, but the easy and affluent social code of the fashionable, modern sections of Athens, Cairo and Constantinople. It was an indulgent code based on caprice and boredom, and it functioned without any scruples. In a corrupt court where Isabelle reigned as the servile queen, Galeazzo assumed the role of a Pasha. Fat, rosy, smiling and despotic, he needed only slippers and turban to be in harmony with the decadent, saccharine atmosphere of Palazzo Colonna.

After a long absence of more than a year on the Russian front, in the Ukraine, Poland and Finland, I finally returned one morning to the golf links of the Acquasanta. Sitting in a corner of the terrace I was overcome by a feeling of discomfort and unrest as I watched the players as slowly and uncertainly they moved along the distant brow of the rolling hills that slope gently toward the red arches of the aqueducts, against a background of pines and cypresses that surround the tombs of the Horatii and Curiatii. It was a November morning in 1942, the sun was warm and a damp wind brought a smell of seaweed and grass from the sea. An invisible plane was humming in the azure heavens and the sound rained down from the lofty sky like resonant pollen.

I had just returned to Italy a few days before after having lain long in a Helsinki hospital where I had undergone a serious operation that had exhausted my strength. I still walked with a cane and was pale and emaciated. Small groups of players were beginning to stroll back toward the clubhouse; the beauties of the Colonna Palace, the dandies of the Excelsior Bar, the cold and ironic young secretaries from the Chigi Palace, passed by and smiled greetings; some were surprised to see me: they did not know that I had returned to Italy, they thought I was still in Finland. Seeing me so white and worn they lingered a moment to inquire how I was, whether it was very cold in Finland, whether I would be staying in Rome for some time or whether I was preparing to return soon. My Martini shook in my hand, I was still so weak. I answered "Yes" or "No" and looked in their faces and laughed deep inside —until Paola came and we found a secluded table near a window.

"Nothing has changed in Italy, has it?" asked Paola.

"Oh, everything has changed," I said. "It's incredible how everything has changed."

"Strange," said Paola, "I had not noticed it."

She was looking at the door, and suddenly she exclaimed, "Here comes Galeazzo! Do you think he, too, has changed?"

I answered, "Galeazzo has changed. Everybody has changed. Everybody is awaiting with terror the great *Kapparoth*, the *Kaputt*, the great Cat."

"What?" Paola exclaimed opening her eyes wide.

Galeazzo came in. He lingered a moment on the threshold, and rubbing his hands he laughed pursing his lips. He raised his chin in acknowledging the greetings; opening his eyes wide with a broad cordial smile that did not unseal his lips, he carefully looked over the ladies and glanced swiftly at the men. Then, pushing out his chest and drawing in his stomach so as to try to conceal the fact that he had grown fat, he crossed the room. Still rubbing his hands and turning this way and that, he took a seat at a corner table where he was joined at once by Cyprienne and Marcello del Drago, and Blasco d'Ayeta. Voices that had dropped to soft whispers when Ciano had appeared in the door, rose again as everybody began talking loudly across the tables as if they were calling to each other from opposite banks of a river. Everybody addressed each other by name and hailed acquaintances across the room, glancing at Galeazzo to make sure that he had heard and noticed them; that was the sole purpose of the loud questions, the festive little shrieks, the smiles and fleeting glances. From time to time Galeazzo raised his face and took part in the general conversation. He spoke in a loud voice gazing intently now at this, and now at that girl. His eyes never rested on the men, as if there were only women in the room. He smiled, winked cunningly and made slight signs with an upraised eyebrow or with his fleshy, protruding lips. The women responded to his coquetry by laughing too loudly, bending over the tables with their heads tilted to one side so they could hear every word, all the time watching each other with jealous intensity.

At the table next to us sat Lavinia, Gianna, Georgette, Anne Marie von Bismarck, Prince Otto von Bismarck and two young secretaries from the Chigi Palace.

"Everybody looks happy this morning," Anne Marie von Bismarck said. "Has something happened?"

"How can anything new happen in Rome?" I replied.

"I'm new in Rome," said Filippo Anfuso, approaching the von Bismarcks' table. Filippo Anfuso had arrived that very morning from Budapest where he had recently been sent to replace Giuseppe Talamo, the Minister at the Royal Legation.

"Oh, Filippo!" Anne Marie exclaimed.

"Filippo! Filippo!" voices called from everywhere. Anfuso with his usual embarrassed air turned with a smile to greet this or that person; he moved his head as if he had a boil on his neck and, as usual, he did not know what to do with his hands that now were on his hips, then stuck in his pockets and then let hang limply by his sides. He looked wooden and newly varnished, and the blackness of his over-glossy hair seemed excessive even for a man like him, even for a Minister. He laughed; his eyes, those beautiful, almost mysterious eyes glittered, and as he laughed he flickered his eyelids in his usual languid and sentimental way. His knees, that were bent slightly inward and almost touched each other, were his weakness about which he secretly suffered. "Filippo! Filippo!" voices called from everywhere. I noticed that Galeazzo, his face darkening, had stopped in the middle of a sentence and, as his eyes fixed on Anfuso his face darkened. He was jealous of Anfuso. I was surprised that he was still jealous of Filippo. Ciano's knees were also his weak point, being slightly knock-kneed himself. The only thing that Galeazzo and Filippo had in common were knees that touched each other.

"Americans landed yesterday in Algiers," Anfuso said seating himself between Anne Marie and Lavinia at the von Bismarcks' table. "That's why everybody is so happy today."

"Shut up, Filippo! Don't be naughty!" Anne Marie said.

"In fairness, I should add that people were equally as happy the day Rommel reached El Alamein," Anfuso said.

In June four months earlier, when the Italian and German troops had rushed into El Alamein and seemed about to capture Alexandria and Cairo at any moment, Mussolini, in the uniform of a Marshal of the Empire, had hurriedly started by air for the Egyptian front, carrying in his luggage the famous "Sword of Islam" that Italo Balbo, the Governor of Libya, had solemnly presented to him a few years before. The Governor of Egypt whom the Duce was about to install in Cairo with such pomp was a member of Mussolini's suite. Serafino Mazzolini had been appointed Governor of Egypt. Formerly he had been Italian Minister to Cairo, and he, too, had started hurriedly by air for the El Alamein front accompanied by an army of secretaries, women typists, interpreters, experts in Arabian matters and a brilliant staff of officers many of whom were already quarreling and backbiting among themselves and filling the Libyan desert with their jealous and vainglorious complaints. They were lovers, husbands, brothers and cousins of Ciano's favorites along with some magnificent, proud, melancholy specimens from among Edda's discarded favorites. The Libyan war, said Anfuso, had not brought any luck to the favorites from Edda's and Galeazzo's harems. Whenever the British in the vicissitudes of the desert moved forward, some of those grand personages invariably fell into their hands. Meanwhile news had begun to filter back to Rome from the El Alamein front about Mussolini's impatience to make his triumphal entry into Alexandria and Cairo, and how Rommel was so furious with Mussolini that he refused to meet him.

"What has he come down here for?" Rommel had asked. "Who sent him here?"

Tired of waiting, Mussolini, silent and black, had passed up and down before the unfortunate, pale, silent Governor of Egypt. In Rome the wounds that the appointment of Serafino Mazzolini as Governor of Egypt had inflicted on the courtiers of the Chigi and Colonna palaces, had still been open and fresh; for many people the problem of the moment had been not how to conquer Egypt but how to prevent Serafino from reaching Cairo. Everybody put their trust in the British. Ciano, along with the others, although for different reasons, had not been satisfied with the way things were going and had made a show of ironic skepticism. "Oh, yes! In Cairo!" he had said, implying that Mussolini would never get there. Actually what had comforted Galeazzo during the many disappointments of the El Alamein victory days, had been—according to Anfuso's account—Mussolini's absence from Rome, even if it were only of a few days' duration. As Ciano had put it, "At last he was out of the way!"

"The relations between Ciano and Mussolini do not seem to be very good even today," I remarked. "At least that's what I have heard in Stockholm."

"Perhaps he would like to see his father-in-law suffer a minor defeat," Anfuso said in French, affecting a Marseille accent.

"You are not implying that the war to them is merely a family affair?" Anne Marie said.

"Alas!" Anfuso exclaimed, sighing loudly and raising his beautiful eyes to the ceiling.

"Cyprienne looks bored today," Georgette said.

"Cyprienne has too much sense of humor to find Galeazzo amusing," said Anfuso.

"That's very true! In the long run Galeazzo is boring," Anne Marie said.

"On the contrary, I find him very amusing and witty," said Prince Otto von Bismarck.

"He certainly is much more amusing than von Ribbentrop," said Filippo. "Have you heard what von Ribbentrop says about Galeazzo?"

"Of course I have," Otto von Bismarck replied uneasily.

"No, you haven't," Anne Marie said. "Tell us, Filippo!"

"Von Ribbentrop says that Galeazzo would be a great Foreign Minister if he would not meddle in foreign affairs."

"Considering that he is Minister of Foreign Affairs I must say that he meddles very little in them," I said. "His fault is meddling too much in domestic politics."

"Quite true," Anfuso said. "That's all he does from morning till night. His waiting room has become a branch office of the Home Office and of the Fascist party."

"He is more concerned about the appointment of a prefect or of a provincial party secretary," said one of the two young secretaries from the Chigi Palace, "than he is about the appointment of an Ambassador."

"Muti was one of his creatures," added the other secretary.

"But now they hate each other like poison," Anfuso said. "I believe the break came because of Count Magistrati's appointment as Minister to Sofia."

"What business was it of Muti's?" von Bismarck asked.

"Ciano directed the home politics and Muti the foreign policy," Anfuso replied.

"Galeazzo is a strange man," I said. "He is under the delusion that he is very popular in America and Britain."

"That's the least of his troubles," said Anfuso. "He even imagines that he is very popular in Italy!"

"What excellent imagination!" von Bismarck said.

"For my part, I'm very fond of him," Anne Marie said.

"That's because you believe that he will change the course of the war!" Anfuso said blushing with a strange air.

Anne Marie smiled and looked at Anfuso, "You're very fond of him? Aren't you, Filippo?"

"Of course I'm very fond of him," said Anfuso. "But what's the use? If I were his mother, I would be trembling for him."

"Why aren't you trembling for him, if you are so fond of him?" Anne Marie asked.

"I have no time. I'm too busy trembling for myself."

"What is the matter with all of you today?" Lavinia asked. "Is it the war that makes you so jittery?"

"The war?" said Anfuso. "What war? The people don't give a damn about the war. Haven't you seen the posters that Mussolini has had hung in every shop and pasted on all the street walls?" They were large posters in the national colors with only four words in large letters: WE ARE AT WAR. "He was right to remind us about it," Anfuso added, "because nobody remembers it."

"The state of mind of the Italian people during this war is extremely odd," Prince von Bismarck said.

"I wonder whom Mussolini would hold responsible," Anfuso said, "if the war should take a bad turn."

"The Italian people," I said.

"No. Mussolini never holds many heads responsible for anything. He needs only one head, a head that seems to be made for that special purpose. He would hold Galeazzo responsible. What other use could there be for Galeazzo? Mussolini keeps him there for that special purpose. Look at his head! Doesn't it seem to be made just for that?"

We all turned our eyes on Count Ciano. His head was round, a little swollen, and too large. "A little too big for his age," said Anfuso.

"You are unbearable, Filippo," Anne Marie said.

"I thought you were Galeazzo's friend," I said to Anfuso.

"Galeazzo needs no friends and does not want any. He does not know what to do with them. He despises them and treats them like menials," Anfuso said and added with a laugh, "He is satisfied with Mussolini's friendship."

"Mussolini is very fond of him, isn't he?" Georgette asked.

"Oh yes, very!" Anfuso said. "In February 1941, during that wretched campaign in Greece, Galeazzo sent for me at Bari to discuss matters concerning the Ministry of Foreign Affairs. For Ciano it was a very difficult moment. He was then a lieutenant colonel in a bomber squadron, at the Palese Air Field near Bari. He was very annoyed with Mussolini. He called him *il Testone*—the blockhead. Shortly before that a conference had taken place in Bordighera where Mussolini had met Franco and Serrano Suñer. Galeazzo, who had been ready to start, was left behind at the last moment. With a suitcase still in his hand, he said to me, 'Mussolini hates me.' That same evening Edda called to tell him that Fabrizio, their first born, was seriously ill. Galeazzo was very much upset by the news. He wept and said, 'He hates me! There's nothing I can do—he hates me!' Later he added, 'That man has always brought me bad luck.' "

"Bad luck?" Lavinia said with a laugh. "God in Heaven, men are so vain!"

"If I am not mistaken, Galeazzo was on the point of resigning," Gianna said.

"Galeazzo will never leave of his own accord," Anfuso said. "He is too fond of power. He fondles his ministerial seat as if it were a mistress. He trembles at the thought of being thrown out on a moment's notice."

"In those days in Bari," I said, "Galeazzo had another reason for being afraid. That was the time when Hitler, at one of their meetings at the Brenner Pass, handed Mussolini Himmler's report on Galeazzo."

"Wasn't it more of a report on Isabelle Colonna?" asked Anne Marie.

"How do you know about it?" Otto von Bismarck asked uneasily.

"All of Rome talked about it for months," Anne Marie said.

"It was a bad moment for Galeazzo," Anfuso said. "Even his most intimate friends turned their backs on him. Blasco d'Ayeta happened to tell me on that occasion that between Galeazzo and Isabelle, he would have sided with Isabelle."

I answered, "And between Hitler and Isabelle? Obviously it was clearly not a question of having to choose between Count Galeazzo Ciano and Princess Isabelle Colonna, though most people thought so. One morning Galeazzo asked me to come to his house. The hour was unusual, about eight o'clock. I found him in his bath. He got out of the tub, and while he was drying himself, said, 'Von Ribbentrop has stabbed me in the back. Himmler is behind von Ribbentrop. They have asked for my head in that report. If Mussolini presents my head to von Ribbentrop, he will reveal himself publicly as the coward that he is!' Then, pressing both his hands on his naked belly, he added: 'I must lose some weight.' When he dried himself, he dropped his bath towel and standing stark naked in front of a mirror, began to grease his hair with a bunch of grass he had sent to him from Shanghai that is used in China as brilliantine. 'A good thing that I am not the Foreign Minister of the Chinese Republic,' he said. 'You know China as well as I do. It is a delightful country, but think what would happen to me there if I were to fall into disfavor.' He began to describe to me Chinese tortures that he had witnessed in a Peking street. The victim, tied to a pole, was stripped with a penknife piece by piece of all his flesh, except for his nerves and his arteries and veins. The man became a kind of trellis made of bones, nerves and blood vessels through which the sun could shine and the flies could buzz. In that way the victim could live for several days. Galeazzo lingered with masochistic complacency on the most horrible details and laughed merrily. I felt the sensual pleasure he took in being cruel and also his fear and his powerless hatred. 'Things are not so different in Italy,' he said. 'Mussolini has devised a torture even more cruel than the Chinese— a kick in the behind.' As he said it, he touched his buttocks. 'It's not the kick that hurts,' he said. 'It's the waiting, the continuous, exasperating waiting from day to day, from hour to hour, from minute to minute.' In jest I remarked that he and I both had looked ahead and that luckily we were provided with fat buttocks. Galeazzo's face grew dark and, feeling himself he asked, 'Do you really think my behind is fat?' He was deeply concerned about it. Later, while he was dressing, he said, 'Mussolini will never present my head to anyone. He is afraid. He is perfectly well aware that all Italians are with me. The Italians know that I am the only man in Italy who dares to stand up to Mussolini.'

"It was a delusion, but it was not for me to disillusion him, and I kept quiet. Even as far back as that he was sincerely convinced that he was standing up to Mussolini. Actually, Galeazzo trembles from morning till night in fear of that kick in the behind. Face to face with Mussolini, Galeazzo is like everybody else, like all of us—a frightened menial. He always said 'Yes' to Mussolini. But behind Mussolini's back, he has the courage of a lion and is afraid of nothing. If Mussolini had his mouth in the back of his head, Galeazzo would not hesitate in placing his head between his fangs like a lion-tamer in a circus. Sometimes, when he is talking about the war, Mussolini and Hitler, he says the most amusing things. No one can deny that he has wit or intelligence. Sometimes he evaluates a political situation like a man who knows what he and others are about. Once I asked him how he thought the war would probably end."

"And what did he say?" Prince von Bismarck asked with an ironic smile.

"That it was still impossible to tell what country would win the war, but that it was clear what countries had already lost it."

"And what countries have already lost the war?" Prince von Bismarck asked.

"Poland and Italy."

"It's not very exciting to know who will lose it," Anne Marie said. "I would like to know who will win it."

"Don't be indiscreet," said Anfuso. "That is a state secret. Isn't it true?" he asked turning to von Bismarck.

"Naturally," said Prince von Bismarck.

"Occasionally, Galeazzo is unbelievably imprudent," Filippo Anfuso said. "If the walls of his study in the Chigi Palace and if Isabelle's table could talk, Mussolini and Hitler would hear some funny things."

"He ought to be more careful," Georgette said. "Isabelle's table is a talking table."

"That old chestnut again," von Bismarck said.

In the beginning of 1941, when Hitler at a meeting with Mussolini at the Brenner Pass had placed Himmler's report on Galeazzo in his hands, the news aroused first amazement in the Roman world, then fear and finally open and malicious pleasure. But at Isabelle's table people laughed about that report as if it were a bad joke by a faithless or indiscreet valet. "Hitler is a bungler!" Isabelle said. The report was aimed not as much at Count Ciano as at Princess Colonna, whom Himmler called "The Fifth Column." Day by day, and word for word, all the conversations that took place around that table were reported with scrupulous accuracy—not only the actual words of Galeazzo, Edda and Isabelle and the remarks of guests whose social rank or political and government positions made them important, not only the opinions about war of Ciano and of the foreign diplomats who visited the Colonna Palace, and Hitler's and Mussolini's mistakes of war policy, but even social gossip, women's backbiting and innocent words of minor figures such as Marcello del Drago or Mario Pansa were recorded. Edda's jokes about this or that, about Hitler, von Ribbentrop and von Mackensen; stories of her frequent trips to Budapest, Berlin and Vienna; Ciano's indiscretions about Mussolini, Franco, Horty, Pavelič, Pétain and Antonescu; Isabelle's cutting remarks about Mussolini's vulgar affairs and her bitter forecasts about the end of the war, along with Sandra Apaletti's amiable Florentine gossip and the scandalous little stories about young German and Italian actresses of the Roman movie colony and the love affairs of Goebbels and Pavolini—everything was recorded in that minute and detailed report, a large part of which was devoted to the amorous life of Galeazzo, his fickleness, the jealousy of his favorites and the corruption of his little court. What had saved Count Ciano from Mussolini's wrath was the tribute Himmler's report paid to Edda. If that report had not mentioned anything derogatory to Edda, her affairs, the *liaisons dangereuses* of her women friends, the scandals at Cortina d'Ampezzo and Capri, Galeazzo's fate would have been sealed. The charges against his daughter had forced Mussolini to defend his son-in-law. But Himmler's report had been successful in stirring suspicions in Ciano's and Isabelle's courts. Who had provided Himmler with the information for that report? The servants in the Colonna Palace? Isabelle's butler? Some of Ciano's or Isabelle's intimate friends? The names of this one and that were mentioned, and one young woman whose pride had been hurt by the recent success of a rival was suspected. Every "widow" was carefully questioned, scrutinized and investigated. "At any rate it cannot be you or I," Isabelle had said to Count Ciano. "Certainly, not I," Galeazzo had replied. "Oh, my dear!" Isabelle had answered raising her eyes to the ceiling, with its frescoes by Poussin. The only result of Himmler's report had been Count Ciano's temporary removal from Rome. Galeazzo left for Bari where he was assigned to a bomber squadron of the Palese Air Field, and for some time in the halls of the Colonna Palace and even in the Chigi Palace, he was not mentioned except in lowered tones or with affected indifference. But in her heart Isabelle, though deeply hurt by that "Certainly, not I," remained loyal to Galeazzo—a woman of her age simply could not be mistaken.

Turning toward Filippo Anfuso, Anne Marie graciously said, "I'll bet there wasn't a single word about you in Himmler's report."

"There was an entire page about my wife," Anfuso replied with a laugh. "That is more than enough."

"An entire page about Maria? Ah, poor Maria, what an honor!" Georgette said without a shade of malice.

"And what about me? Was there a whole page about me?" asked Anne Marie.

"Your question is the same kind of a question that General von Schobert once asked me. We were in the Ukraine during the first months of the Russian campaign and General von Schobert had asked me to supper at headquarters. There were about ten officers at the table. After we had been eating a while von Schobert asked me what I thought about the position of the German Army in Russia. 'It seems to me,' I answered remembering an Italian proverb, 'that the German Army in Russia is not like a chicken in the *stoppa*—flax chaff, but like a chicken in the steppe.'"

"Good heavens!" Anne Marie exclaimed.

"Very amusing," von Bismarck said with a smile.

"Are you certain," Filippo Anfuso said, "that General von Schobert understood what you meant?"

"I was hoping he would understand. General von Schobert had been in Italy and spoke a little Italian. But when Lieutenant Schiller, the interpreter, a Tirolese from Meran who had become a German national, translated my reply and tried to explain the meaning of the Italian proverb, General von Schobert asked me in a reproaching, severe and surprised voice, why were chickens raised on flax chaff in Italy. 'We never raise them on flax chaff!' I replied. 'It's just a popular saying that shows the difficulties with which a poor chicken struggles when he becomes entangled scratching in a pile of flax chaff.'

"'At home in Bavaria,' General von Schobert said, "the chickens are raised on sawdust or on straw.'

"'In Italy they are raised on sawdust or on straw also!' I replied.

" 'Then why did you mention flax chaff?' asked General von Schobert with a frown.

" 'It is merely a popular saying,' I replied. 'A simple manner of speech!'

" 'Hm, very odd!' General von Schobert said.

" 'At home in Bavaria,' General von Schobert said, 'the chickens are raised on sand; it's a cheap and practical way.'

" 'In certain parts of Italy, where the soil is sandy,' I said, 'chickens also are raised on sand.'

"I was beginning to sweat, and I softly begged the interpreter to help me—in God's name!—out of the mess. Schiller smiled and look out of the corner of an eye as if to say, 'A nice mess you have got yourself in, and now you expect me to get you out!'

" 'If that is so,' General von Schobert said, 'I cannot see what the flax chaff has to do with it. Granted that it is only a saying, but proverbs and sayings always have some connection with reality. This means, that no matter what you say to the contrary, there are parts of Italy where chickens are raised on flax chaff—an impractical and cruel way.' He stared at me with a stern expression that was tinged with suspicion and contempt.

"I wanted to answer, 'Yes, sir! I was afraid to admit it, but the truth is that in Italy chickens are raised on flax chaff. Not only in certain parts of Italy, but everywhere—in Piedmont, Lombardy, Tuscany, Umbria, Calabria, Sicily—everywhere, in all of Italy—and not only chickens, but children too are raised on flax chaff; have you ever noticed that all Italians have been raised on chaff? Watch them! Watch them carefully, and you'll see that all Italians have been raised on chaff!' Perhaps he would have understood me. Perhaps he would have believed me, without ever realizing how true my words were. But I sweated and I kept on repeating No, it was not true, nowhere in Italy were chickens raised on flax chaff, it was merely a proverb, a popular saying, *ein Volkssprichwort*. At that moment Major Hanberger, who for some time had been looking intently into my eyes with his glassy gray stare, said to me in a cold voice, 'Then explain to me what the steppe has to do with it. Never mind the flax chaff, you have completely cleared up the matter of flax chaff. But the steppe? What has the steppe to do with it? *Was hat die Steppe mit den Küken zu tun?*'

373

"I turned to the interpreter for help, beseeching him with my eyes to drag me, in the name of God, out of this new and more serious danger, but to my horror I noticed that Schiller was also beginning to sweat, that his brow was moist and his face quite pale. Then I became frightened. I looked around me. I noticed that everyone was glaring sternly at me. I felt lost, and I began repeating once, twice, three times, that it was only a proverb, a popular saying, a mere play on words.

"'Good!' said Major Hanberger. 'But I still cannot understand what the steppe has to do with the chickens.' Then I began to be irritated and replied in impatient tones that the German Army in Russia was like a chicken in the steppe, neither more nor less than a chicken in the steppe.

"'Good!' Major Hanberger said. 'But I cannot understand why the chickens of the steppe are so unusual. There are many hens in every Ukraine village, consequently there are many chickens, and they are not in any way unusual. They are like any other chickens.'

"'No,' I replied. 'They are not like any other chickens.'

"'They are not like any other chickens?' asked Major Hanberger, staring at me with an amazed expression.

"'In Germany,' General von Schobert said, 'chicken farming has reached a much higher scientific level than it has in Soviet Russia. Therefore, most likely the chickens of the steppe are far inferior in quality to the German chickens.'

"Colonel Stark drew on a scrap of paper a model chicken house that had been devised in East Prussia; Major Hanberger quoted statistics; thus, little by little, the conversation turned into a learned discussion of scientific chicken farming, to which the other officers contributed their share. I was silent and wiped away the perspiration that dripped from my brow. From time to time General von Schobert, Colonel Stark, and Major Hanberger broke off what they were saying to stare at me, and repeated that they were still unable to grasp what German soldiers and chickens had in common, while the other officers looked at me with deep sympathy. At last General von Schobert rose and said, '*Schluss!*' Then we all rose from the table, went out and scattered through the streets of the village in search of our beds.

"The moon shone round and yellow in the greenish sky, and the interpreter, Lieutenant Schiller, in wishing me good night, said, 'I trust that you have learned not to try your wit on Germans.'

"I answered, '*Ach, so!*' and completely baffled went to bed. I was unable to sleep; millions of crickets chirped in the clear night, and I imagined I heard millions of chickens chirping on the limitless steppe. At last when the cocks were beginning to crow I fell asleep."

"How adorable!" Anne Marie exclaimed clapping her hands. Everybody laughed, but Prince von Bismarck watched me with a strange expression: "You are very clever," he said, "at telling those funny stories. But I do not care for your chickens."

"I adore them!" said Anne Marie.

"I may as well confess the truth to you," I said turning to Otto von Bismarck. "In Italy the chickens are raised on strings. But this is a truth that cannot be told. We must remember that we are at war!"

Just then Marcello del Drago approached the von Bismarck's table. "The war?" he asked. "Are you still talking about the war? Couldn't you talk about something else? The war has gone out of fashion."

"Yes, as a matter of fact, it's a little out of date," said Georgette. "It is not being worn this year."

"Galeazzo wishes me to inquire," Marcello said turning to Anfuso, "whether he could see you for a moment today at the Ministry?"

"Why not?" Anfuso answered in an ironic and slightly hostile tone. "That's what I am paid for."

"About five, if it suits you?"

"Six would be better," Anfuso replied.

"Right, at six then," said Marcello del Drago and, pointing with his chin at a young woman who was sitting at a table not far from the von Bismarcks', he inquired who she was.

"Don't you know Brigitte?" asked Anne Marie. "She is a great friend of mine. Pretty, isn't she?"

"Enchanting," said Marcello del Drago and, on the way back to Galeazzo's table, he turned twice to look at Brigitte.

Meanwhile many people were beginning to leave and moved across the grass toward the links. We remained seated at our table, and a little later we saw Mario Pansa escorting Galeazzo to Brigitte's table. Anne Marie remarked that Galeazzo was growing fat.

"During the last war," Anfuso said, "everybody lost flesh; during this one everybody is growing fat. The world has truly gone awry. Who can make head or tail of it?"

Von Bismarck replied—and I cannot say whether there was irony in his words—that plumpness was a mark of moral health. "Europe," he said, "is certain of victory." I said that the people were thin and that all one had to do was to go through Europe to realize how thin the people were. "And yet," I added, "the people are certain of victory."

"What people?" von Bismarck asked.

"Every people," I replied. "The German people, too, of course."

"Did you say: of course?" said von Bismarck in an ironic voice.

"The workers are thinner than anywhere else," I said. "That includes German workers, of course, and yet, among all the workers, they are most certain of victory."

"Do you think so?" von Bismarck asked with amazement.

Count Ciano stood before Brigitte laughing and talking in his usual loud voice, and turning his head this way and that. Brigitte, seated with her elbows on the table, and her face raised between both hands, looked at him with her fine eyes filled with innocent mischief. Then she rose and went into the garden accompanied by Galeazzo; they strolled around the pool and talked listlessly. Count Ciano had a gallant air, and looked around with his proud, cordial scowl. Everyone watched them and winked at one another with a knowing air.

"That's that," Anne Marie said.

"Brigitte is really a charming woman," said von Bismarck.

"Galeazzo is irresistible to women," Georgette said.

"There's not a woman here who has not had an affair with Galeazzo," Anfuso said.

"I know several," Anne Marie said, "who were able to withstand him."

"Quite so, but they are not here," Anfuso said angrily.

"What do you know about it?" Anne Marie said in an easy, slightly provoking manner.

Just then Brigitte came in and walked over to Anne Marie. She was gay and she laughed her rather fat laugh.

"Take care, Brigitte," Anfuso said. "Count Ciano wins all the wars."

"Oh I know," Brigitte answered, "I have already been warned. I usually lose all my wars, but now I am tired of war and Galeazzo does not interest me."

"Really?" Anne Marie said with incredulity.

We went out into the garden together, and walking in the autumn sun that smelled of honey and withered flowers, made for the first tee. The golfers appeared and disappeared in the folds of the rolling ground, like swimmers in the hollows between the waves. We saw the clubs rise aloft and glitter in the sun; the golfers lifted their arms skyward, the joined hands poised for a second in an attitude of prayer and then the clubs swung describing a wide circle through the green, rosy air, disappeared and rose up glittering again. It looked like a ballet on a vast stage with the wind playing a sweet melody in the grass. The voices rebounded on the meadows, green, yellow, red and blue voices that acquired in the distance a resilient soft and faint sonority. A group of young women sat joking and laughing on the grass. They kept their faces toward Galeazzo who was strolling near by with Blasco d'Ayeta and passed that young mischievous inviting detachment on parade; it was a bouquet of the finest faces and finest names in Rome; along with them, but even gayer, with rosier complexions, more vivid eyes, redder lips and easier and more open manners, were some of the youngest and most lovely women from Florence, Venice and Lombardy. Some were dressed in red, and some in blue, some in dull green or old gold or ivory-pink, still others wore gray or a material the color of bare skin. One wore her hair short and curled, priding herself on her youthful brow and pure lips; another wore her hair plaited in the back, another brushed up her hair from her temples, and they all laughed and offered their warm faces to the sun and to the fresh air—Marita looked like Alcibiades, Paola like Fornarina, Lavinia like Amorrorisca, Bianca like Diana, Patricia like Selvaggia, Manuela like Fiammetta, Giorgina like Beatrice, Enrica like Laura. There was something of the courtesan that was also innocent about those foreheads, eyes and lips. A corrupt glory shone in those white, rosy faces and in those moist glances that the shadow of the eyelids clothed with a sensuous reticence.

Long shivers of wind ran through the warm air, a glorious sun gilded the trunks of the pines, the ruins of the tombs along the Appian Way and the stones and splinters of ancient marble scattered among the brambles at the edge of the meadow. Sitting around the pool, the young Anglomaniacs from the Chigi Palace spoke English in loud voices and some stray words that reached us had the smell of a Capstan and Craven Mixture. Along the fairway, faintly gilded by the weary flame of autumn, strolled old Roman princesses whose maiden names had been Smith, Brown and Samuel—solemn dowagers leaning with long, tapering fingers on silver-handled canes, old beauties of the D'Annunzio generation, slow of gait, their eyes ringed with black. A girl with her hair flying ran yelling after a fair young man in golf knickers. It was a lively scene, but it was already a little weary, slightly out of focus and rumpled at the edges like an old color print.

After a while Galeazzo saw me, left Blasco d'Ayeta, came over and put his hand on my shoulder. I had not spoken to him for over a year and did not know what to say.

"How long have you been back?" he asked me with a touch of reproach in his voice. "Why didn't you come to see me?" He spoke confidingly, with a kind of abandon that was unusual in him.

I explained that I had been very ill in Finland, that I still felt very weak. "I am very tired," I added.

"Tired? Perhaps you mean disgusted?" he said.

"Yes, disgusted with everything," I replied.

He looked at me and after a moment said, "You'll see that things will be better soon."

"Be better? Italy is a dead country," I answered. "What can you do with a corpse? You can only bury it."

"One never knows," he said.

"Perhaps you are right," I said. "One never knows."

I had known him since we had been children and of his own accord, he had always defended me against everyone. He had defended me in 1933 when I had been given a five-year sentence. He had defended me when I was arrested in 1938, in 1939 and in 1941; he had defended me against Mussolini, against Starace, against Muti, against Bocchini, against Senise and against Farinacci; and regardless of any political considerations I felt a deep and warm gratitude toward him. I also felt sorry for him. I wanted to be able to help him some day, but there was no longer anything that anyone could do. Nothing was left to do but bury him. I felt sure that, at least they would bury him. With so many friends at least they would bury him.

"Watch out for the old man," I said.

"I know. He hates me. He hates everybody. At times I wonder if he is mad. Do you think anything can still be done?"

"There is no longer anything that can be done now. It's too late! You should have done something in 1940 to prevent him from dragging Italy into this shameful war."

"In 1940?" he said, and laughed in a way that I did not like. Then he added, "The war could have turned out well."

I remained silent. He sensed the pained hostility in my silence and said, "It's not my fault. He wanted the war. What could I do?"

"Clear out."

"Clear out? And then?"

"Then? Nothing."

"It would not have done any good," he said.

"It would not have done any good. But you still should have cleared out."

"Cleared out, cleared out. Whenever we talk about these things, you never can say anything else. Clear out! And then?"

Galeazzo broke away suddenly and walked quickly toward the clubhouse. I saw him as he paused a moment on the threshold and then went in.

I lingered for a while in the meadow, then I went back to the clubhouse too. Galeazzo was sitting at the bar between Cyprienne and Brigitte, and around him were Anne Marie, Paola, Marita, Georgette, Filippo Anfuso, Marcello del Drago, Bonarelli, Blasco d'Ayeta and a very young girl whom I did not know. Galeazzo was telling how he had communicated the declaration of war to the French and British Ambassadors.

When the French Ambassador, François Poncet, had entered his study at the Chigi Palace, Count Ciano welcomed him cordially and said, "You certainly understand, sir, why I wished to speak with you?"

"I am not usually very quick," replied François Poncet, "but this time I understand."

Then Count Ciano, standing in front of his desk, read the official formula of the declaration of war. *"Au nom de Sa Majesté le Roi d'Italie, Empereur d'Ethiopie, etc."*

François Poncet grew uneasy. He said, "So, it is war?"

"Yes."

Count Ciano was wearing a uniform of lieutenant colonel in the Flying Corps. The French Ambassador said, "And you, what are you going to do? Will you be dropping bombs on Paris?"

"I believe so. I am an officer and I shall do my duty."

"At least try not to get killed," replied François Poncet. "It is not worth while."

After making that remark the French Ambassador had seemed deeply moved and said a few words that Galeazzo did not think he should repeat. Later Count Ciano and François Poncet had shaken hands and parted.

"What could the French Ambassador have said?" asked Anne Marie. "I am dying to know."

"A very interesting thing," answered Galeazzo, "but I cannot repeat it."

"I bet he said something rude," Marita said. "That's why you refuse to repeat it."

Everybody laughed and Galeazzo laughed louder than the others.

"He had a right to be insulting," Galeazzo replied, "but, as a matter of fact, he was not. He was deeply moved."

Then he told how the British Ambassador had received the declaration of war. Sir Percy Lorraine had entered, and asked at once why he had been called. Count Ciano read the official formula of the declaration of war: *Au nom de Sa Majesté le Roi d'Italie, Empereur d'Ethiopie, etc."*

Sir Percy Lorraine had listened attentively, as if intent on not missing a single syllable, then asked coldly, "Is this really the precise wording of a declaration of war?"

Count Ciano was unable to hide his surprise. "Yes, this is the precise wording."

"Ah!" exclaimed Sir Percy Lorraine, and asked, "May I have a pencil?"

"Yes, certainly." Count Ciano offered him a pencil and a piece of stationery of the Royal Ministry of Foreign Affairs.

The British Ambassador carefully tore off the letterhead with the assistance of a paper knife, neatly folded the sheet, examined the point of the pencil and said, "Would you mind dictating to me what you have read?"

"With pleasure," Count Ciano replied, and more than ever surprised, he read very slowly, word by word, the declaration of war. When he had finished dictating, Sir Percy Lorraine who had all the time shown no signs of emotion as he bent over the sheet of paper, rose, shook Count Ciano's hand and walked toward the door. He lingered for a moment on the threshold, then went out without looking back.

"You have omitted something in your account," Anne Marie von Bismarck said with her slight Swedish accent.

Galeazzo looked at Anne Marie with surprise and appeared a little uneasy, "I haven't omitted anything," he said.

"Ah yes, you have omitted something," Filippo Anfuso said.

"You have forgotten to tell us," I said, "that Sir Percy Lorraine, as he reached for the door, turned and said, 'You think that the war will be easy and short, but you are wrong. The war will be very long and very difficult. *Au revoir!*'"

"So you know about it, too?" said Anne Marie.

"How do you happen to know about it?" asked Galeazzo, obviously annoyed.

"I was told by Count de Foxa, the Spanish Minister in Helsinki. Everybody knows about it. It is a typical Italian secret!"

"I heard about it for the first time in Stockholm," Anne Marie said. "Everybody knows about it in Stockholm."

Galeazzo smiled and I don't know whether he was more annoyed or embarrassed. Everyone was smiling as they watched him, and Marita shouted, "Don't take it to heart, Galeazzo." The women laughed and playfully made fun of him. Galeazzo joined in the merriment but there was a false ring, a flaw in his laughter.

"François Poncet was right," Patricia said. "It isn't worth while."

"No, really, it isn't worth while to die," Georgette said.

"Nobody wants to die," said Patricia.

Galeazzo's face wore an angry and worried expression. The conversation was now gently tearing down some of Count Ciano's colleagues. The young women were making fun of a diplomat who on his return from South America had pitched his tent by the golf club, so he would be constantly under Galeazzo's eyes, and would not be overlooked or forgotten. "He even plays golf in the waiting room of the Chigi Palace," Cyprienne said. Patricia mentioned Alfieri, and all the women agreed that Italy was fortunate to have an Ambassador like Dino Alfieri. "He is so handsome!" they explained. Just then a story was making the rounds in Italy that later turned out to be the fabrication of some wit: it was said that a German Flying Corps officer who had surprised Alfieri with his wife had lashed his face a couple of times with a whip. "I hope to heaven he hasn't been disfigured!" said Patricia. Anne Marie asked Galeazzo whether the general belief were true, that he had sent Alfieri as Ambassador to Berlin because he was jealous of him. Everybody including Ciano laughed, but it was evident that he was annoyed. "I? Jealous!" he said. "That's what Goebbels is saying! He is the one who is jealous of Alfieri and would like to have him recalled."

"Oh, Galeazzo! Let him stay where he is," Marita said without any malice. "He is doing so well in Berlin!" Everybody laughed and began to talk about Filippo Anfuso and his Hungarian love affairs. "In Budapest," Filippo said, "the women will not have anything to do with me. Hungarian women are dark and they are crazy about blond men." Georgette turned to Galeazzo and asked him why he had not sent a blond Minister to Budapest. "Blond? Who are there blonds in our service?" replied Galeazzo and began counting them on his fingers.

"Renato Prunas," one woman suggested. "Guglielmo Rulli," suggested another. Galeazzo, who could not stand Rulli and never lost an opportunity to run him down frowned and said, "No, not Rulli." "I am blond," Blasco d'Ayeta said. "Yes, Blasco! Blasco! Send Blasco to Budapest," all the women shouted. "Why not?" Galeazzo said. But Anfuso, knowing how promotions and appointments were made at the Chigi Palace, could not see the joke; he turned to Blasco d'Ayeta with a smile and, alluding to the fact that Blasco had succeeded him as chief secretary to Count Ciano, sneeringly said, "You always seem very eager to step into my shoes!" Meanwhile the women were protesting because Alberto had not yet been promoted to Councillor, because Buby had not yet succeeded in obtaining a post in the Minister's office, because Ghigi had been transferred to Athens though he had been so successful in Bucharest, and because Galeazzo could not make up his mind to appoint Cesarino as Minister to Copenhagen to succeed Sapuppo, "who has been in Denmark long, and nobody knows why," Patricia said.

"I want to tell you," Galeazzo said, "how Minister Sapuppo learned the news about the German invasion of Denmark. Sapuppo swore by everything holy that the Germans would never be silly enough to invade Denmark. Virgilio Lilli swore by everything holy that they would. Minister Sapuppo said, 'No, no, my dear Lilli! Why would the Germans come to Denmark?' Lilli replied, 'What difference does it make to you why the Germans might come into Denmark? All you want to know is whether they will or will not come.' 'They will not come,' said Sapuppo. 'They will come,' Lilli said. 'My dear Lilli, are you under the impression that you are better informed than I?' asked Sapuppo.

"Virgilio Lilli lived at the Hotel Britannia. Every morning, exactly at eight, an old, white-haired waiter, his rosy face framed in long, old-fashioned, white side-whiskers, and wearing a blue livery with gold buttons, entered his room with a tea tray, placed it on a little table by the bed, and with a bow said: 'Here is your tea, as usual.'

"This ritual went on for twenty days every morning exactly at eight, and it always ended with the same sentence, 'Here is your tea, as usual.' One morning the old waiter came in, as usual, punctually at eight, and with the usual inflection in his voice bowed and said, 'Here is your tea, as usual. The Germans have come.' Virgilio Lilli bounced out of bed and called Minister Sapuppo to announce to him that during the night the Germans had occupied Copenhagen."

Everybody was very much amused by the story about Sapuppo and Lilli, and Galeazzo, who laughed with the others, seemed to recover from his uneasiness and embarrassment. From Sapuppo the conversation went on to the war and Marita said, "What a bore!" Her friends protested because no more American films were being shown at the Quirinetta and because not a drop of whisky or a single package of American or English cigarettes could be found anywhere in Rome. Patricia said that in this war the only thing the men could do was fight if they wanted to and if they had the time. "We want to," Marcello del Drago had said, "but we haven't the time." While the women could only wait for the arrival of the British and the Americans with their victorious battalions of Camels, Lucky Strikes and Gold Flakes. "I'd walk a mile for a Camel," Marita said using advertising slang she had picked up from *The New Yorker*. Everyone began talking in English using a peculiar mixture of Oxford and *Harper's Bazaar* expressions.

Suddenly a fly came in through the open window, then another, then ten more, twenty, a hundred, a thousand, and within a few minutes the bar was filled with clouds of flies. It was the hour of flies. Every day, at a certain hour that varies with the seasons, a buzzing swarm of flies attacks the golf club of the Acquasanta. The players swing their clubs to drive off that storm of black glistening wings, the caddies drop the bags on the grass and wave their hands before their faces, and the old Roman princesses nee Smith, Brown and Samuel, the solemn dowagers, the old D'Annunzio beauties strolling on the fairway, flee as they flail the air with their hands and silver-handled canes.

"The flies!" screamed Marita jumping to her feet. Everybody laughed and Marita said, "You can laugh, but I am afraid of flies!"

"Marita is right," Filippo Anfuso said, "flies bring bad luck."

Filippo's words were greeted by a burst of laughter, and Georgette remarked that each year a new scourge hits Rome; one year it is mice, next year—spiders, next year—beetles. "As soon as the war began the flies came," she said.

"The Acquasanta links are notorious for the flies," Blasco d'Ayeta said. "At Montorfano and at Ugolino they all laugh about it."

"It is not a laughing matter," Marita said. "If the war goes on, we will end up by being eaten by flies."

"That's an end we all deserve," Galeazzo said. He rose and, taking Cyprienne's arm, walked to the door followed by the others.

As he passed by me he looked at me and seemed to remember something. Freeing Cyprienne's arm he placed his hand on my shoulder and kept on walking beside me, as if he were pushing me. We went into the garden. We walked in silence, and suddenly

Galeazzo said to me, as if pursuing a disagreeable thought aloud: "Do you remember what you once said to me, talking about Edda? I lost my temper and would not let you finish. But you were right. My real enemy is Edda. She does not realize it, it's not her fault. I don't know and I don't even ask myself whether it is, but I feel that Edda is dangerous for me, that I must beware of her as if she were an enemy. If Edda were to leave me, if she had something else, something serious in her life, I would be lost. You know that her father worships her, that he never would do anything against me if he knew it would hurt her, but he is only biding his time. Everything depends on Edda. I have tried several times to make her understand how dangerous her behavior is for me. Perhaps there's nothing bad in what she does; I don't know. I don't want to know. But one cannot talk with Edda. She is a hard, strange woman. You never know what to expect from her. At times she frightens me." He spoke jerkily, in that hoarse toneless voice of his, and he drove off the flies with a monotonous gesture of his fat white hand. The flies, angry and persistent, buzzed around us; now and then from a distant tee came the soft crack of a driver against a ball. "I don't know who starts those silly rumors about Edda, about her plans to have our marriage annulled so she can marry someone else. Ah, these flies!" he exploded with an impatient gesture. After a moment he added, "Nonsense! Edda will never do anything of the sort. But meanwhile her father has already pricked up his ears. You will see that I will not stay long in the Cabinet. Do you know what I think? I think that I will always be Galeazzo Ciano, even if I cease to be a Minister. My moral and political position will only stand to benefit if Mussolini sends me away. You know what the Italians are; they will forget my mistakes and my sins, and they will see me only as a victim."

"A victim?" I said.

"Don't you think the Italian people know who is the only person responsible for everything? They know how to differentiate between me and Mussolini! They know that I was opposed to war, that I did everything in my power—"

"The Italian people," I interrupted, "know nothing, do not want to know anything, and believe in nothing any longer. You and the others should have done something in 1940 to prevent this war.

You should have done something, risked something! That was the time to sell your lives dearly. Now your lives are worth nothing. But you were too fond of power. That is the truth and the Italians know it."

"Do you think that if I cleared out today . . ."

"It is too late now. You will drown with him."

"Then what should I do?" Galeazzo said with shrill impatience in his voice. "What am I expected to do? Should I allow myself to be thrown away like a filthy rag when it suits his convenience? Should I resign myself to drowning with him? I do not want to die!"

"To die? It isn't worth while," I replied, repeating the words of the French Ambassador François Poncet.

"Quite so, it isn't worth while," Galeazzo said. "Why die? The Italians are a kind people. They do not want anyone's death."

"You are mistaken," I said. "The Italians are no longer what they once were. They would be pleased to see you die—him and you. Him and you, and all the others."

"And what would our deaths accomplish?" asked Galeazzo.

"Nothing. Nothing at all."

Galeazzo was silent. He was pale and his brow was damp with sweat. At that moment a girl crossed the meadow on the way to meet a group of golfers who were walking toward the clubhouse, swinging their putters in their hands.

"What a good-looking girl!" Galeazzo said. "Would you like to have her?" and he gave me a slight dig in the ribs with his elbow.

XVIII

Blood

As soon as I was released from the *Regina Coeli* prison in Rome I went straight to the railway station and boarded the Naples train. It was the seventh of August 1943. I was running away from the war, the slaughter, typhus and hunger; I was running away from the prison, from the stinking, dark, airless cell, the filthy straw mattress, the loathsome soup, bugs, lice and the pail full of excrement. I wanted to go home, I wanted to go to Capri, to my lonely house high above the sea.

By then I had reached the end of my long, cruel four-year journey through war, blood, hunger, burned villages and wrecked towns. I was tired, disillusioned and cowed. Jail after jail, always a jail in Italy. Nothing but jail, policemen and manacled men—that is Italy. Mario Alicata and Cesarini Sforza, as soon as they had been released from *Regina Coeli*, after the long months they had spent in their cells also had gone home. I went to the railway station and boarded the Naples train. I, too, wanted to go home. The train was packed with refugees, old people, women, children, officers, soldiers, priests and policemen; the roofs of the coaches swarmed with soldiers, some of them were armed, others not; some were in uniform, others in tatters, dirty and downcast; still others were half-naked, filthy and merry; they were deserters going home, or simply fleeing without knowing where, singing and laughing, as if overwhelmed and inspired by a great and wondrous fear.

They were fleeing from war, hunger and plague, from the wreckage, the terror and death; they were running toward war, hunger and plague, toward the wreckage, the terror and death. They were fleeing from the Germans, bombardments, want and fear. They were running toward Naples, toward war, the Germans, bombardments, want and fear; toward filthy air shelters polluted with the dung of famished, worn-out and stupefied people. They were fleeing from despair, from the miserable and wondrous despair of a lost war; they were running toward the hope of an end to their hunger, an end to their fear, an end to the war—toward the miserable and wondrous hope of a lost war. They were fleeing from Italy and running toward Italy.

The heat was stifling. I had not as yet had a chance to wash. I was just as I had been in my cell, Number 462 in the fourth block of *Regina Coeli*. I still had the sweet, greasy smell of bugs about me. I was unshaven, my hair was disheveled, nails cracked. We were twenty, thirty, forty, no one knows how many, in the compartment; we were pressed against each other, piled on each other; our lips were swollen with thirst. Our faces were purple and we stood on tiptoe, our necks stretched upward, our mouths wide open so we could breathe. We looked like people who had been hung and were swinging horribly with each jolt of the train. Every now and then a "toc, toc, toc" came from the sky, the train stopped with a jerk. Everybody leaped to the ground, crouched in the ditches and hollows along the railway embankment and gazed upward until that "toc, toc, toc" came to an end. At every station we met long German trains that were moving or waiting on sidings—trains loaded with soldiers and weapons. The Germans looked at us with their cruel, gray eyes. What weariness, what contempt, what hatred were in those eyes! My companions said, "Where are they going?" One of them asked me whether I was returning from the front. "What front?" a soldier asked. "There is no front any more. No war any more. No more unfailing victory. No more *long live the Duce!* No more anything. What front?"

I answered, "I am returning from *Regina Coeli*." The soldier looked at me with suspicion, "What is *Regina Coeli*? A convent?" he asked. "It is a prison," I replied. "What prison?" the soldier challenged. "There is no longer any prison. No more policemen, no more jailers, no more jail. No more anything. There is no longer any prison in Italy. Prison is ended, Italy is ended. No more anything!"

Everybody laughed as they listened to the soldier. It was a coarse, evil, painful laughter, a despairing laughter. They laughed in his face, and I also laughed, "There is no longer any prison in Italy!"

they said. "No longer any prison! Ha, ha, ha!" Everybody laughed in our compartment, in the corridor, in the other compartments, in the other corridors, in the other coaches, everybody laughed. The train itself laughed, from one end to the other, as it jolted and twisted on the rails, and laughing coarsely the train whistled, slowed down and came to a stop before a huge pile of debris and bloody rags. This was Naples.

Through a black, glistening cloud of flies the sun beat down on the roofs and asphalt paving; gusts of heat rose from the debris piled around the disemboweled buildings, a mist of dry dust rose like a cloud of sand from beneath the feet of pedestrians. At first, the city looked deserted. Then, little by little, one distinguished a hum coming from the lanes and courtyards, a stifled chatter of voices, a faint and distant noise. Penetrating the secret of the *bassi* —the windowless ground-floors, probing the depth of the narrow clefts between the towering houses that are the noble streets of ancient Naples, one saw a restless swarm of people who stood, moved about and gesticulated; groups of people were squatting on their haunches and around little fires that burned between two stones and watching the water boil in old gasoline cans, kettles, pans or coffeepots; men, women and children slept piled upon each other, on mattresses, straw beds and bedding of any and all kinds, stretched out before the gates, in the courtyards, among the debris, in the shade of crumbling walls or by the entrances to the caves hewn in the damp, brackish *tufa,* a limestone that penetrates to the bowels of the earth in every part of Naples. Inside the *bassi* people were standing, sitting or resting on the high, baroque, iron or brass beds decorated with landscapes, saints and Madonnas. Many crouched silently on the thresholds with that melancholy air of the Neapolitans who, not knowing what to do, simply wait. At first the city seemed silent as well as deserted, but little by little, it seemed to me a confused rumble came into being in the dusty air. It acquired form and consistency in my ears until it resounded all around me with the steady, continuous, solid roar of a raging river.

I was walking toward the harbor, along a straight, long road, walking as in a dream, stunned by that infernal din, blinded by the dust swept up by the sea breeze from the debris of the wrecked houses. The sun struck with its large, golden hammer the terraces and fronts of houses, stirring up swarms of buzzing black flies; when I lifted my eyes, I saw the wide-open windows, balconies and the women combing their hair and looking from the windows at the sky as if it were a mirror. Singing voices fell from somewhere above and were taken up at once by a thousand lips that sent them humming from mouth to mouth, from window to window, from street to street, as if they were bounced by jugglers. Groups of sweaty, barefoot boys dressed in rags and tattered shirts—the youngest ones stark naked—chased screaming up and down the streets; yet there was something distant, cautious, and wily about them; they were not playing any adventurous and fanciful game. Watching them carefully, one soon discovered that they were busy trading: one was carrying a basket of lettuce, another a handful of charcoal, another a can of nondescript dish-water, another an armful of wood, while others, like little ants hauling a grain of wheat, were struggling with a charred beam or a cask or old ramshackle pieces of furniture unearthed from the piles of debris. The stench of corpses rose from under the mountains of stones and plaster. Entire families of lazy fat flies with gold wings buzzed over the debris. At last I came to the sea.

The sight of the sea moved me and I began to weep. A river, a plain, a mountain, not even a tree or a cloud—nothing has in it the feeling of freedom like the sea. A prisoner in jail stares hour after hour, day after day, month after month, year after year at the walls of his cell. They are always the same white smooth walls, and when he gazes at those walls, at the sea, he cannot imagine it blue; he can only imagine the sea's being white, smooth, bare, without waves, without storms—a squalid sea illuminated by the flat light penetrating through the bars of his window. That is his sea, that is his freedom—a white, smooth bare sea, a squalid and cold freedom.

But there, before me, was the warm and delicate sea, the Neapolitan sea, the free blue sea of Naples—all crumpled into little waves that rippled after one another with a gentle sound under the caress of a wind scented with brine and rosemary. There, before me, was the blue sea, the free and limitless sea rippling in the wind; not the white, cold, smooth bare sea of the prison but the warm, deep blue sea. There, before me, was the sea, there was freedom, and I wept gazing at it from a distance, from the road that descended to the sea across a large square. I did not dare to come any closer. I even did not dare to stretch out my hand toward it lest it flee, lest it disappear beyond the skyline, lest it retreat in disgust from my dirty, greasy hand with its cracked nails.

Gazing at the distant sea I stood motionless in the middle of the street and wept. And I did not even hear the humming of bees high up in the remote sky. I did not notice the people fleeing to the caves hewn into the hill. Finally a boy approached me, touched my arm and said in a gentle voice: "*Signo' stanno venenno*—Sir, they are coming!" Then I realized that I was surrounded by a mob that ran screaming down the wide road sloping toward the shimmering sea. I was not sure where I was, but seeing the columns of a church, I thought I recognized Santa Lucia Street. The mob rushed through a large gate and disappeared as though it had been swallowed into some secret cave. I was about to follow them and seek shelter within the dark bowels of the earth when I raised my eyes and became paralyzed with fear.

A silent crowd was moving toward me along the lanes and down the steps that lead from Santa Lucia Street to Pizzofalcone and Monte di Dio. It was a mysterious crowd of ghosts and monsters that have their lairs in the grottos in the courtyards and in the *bassi* of that quarter of Naples that lies at the far end of the hundred dark alleys and constitutes the maze of the Pallonetto. They moved toward me in a body, like an army about to attack a fortified castle. They walked slowly and silently, in that lonely silence that comes before the crash of the first bombs, in that terrified loneliness draped around them by the sacred character of their horrible deformities. They were the cripples: the halt, the twisted, the lame, the hunchbacked, the maimed, the legless—those "monsters" who, in Turin, are sheltered from human sight within the merciful solitude of the *Cottolengo*. The war had driven them out of the religious seclusion in the innermost part of the houses, where pity, horror, superstition and family shame, had hidden them all their lives and kept them in darkness and silence. The "monsters" moved slowly, helping each other, half-naked, clothed in rags, their faces distorted, not by fear, but by hatred and glory. Maybe because of the dazzling light and the ghostly glow of that moment, or because of the terror of the impending downpour of steel and fire, the expression on those faces was satanic—an evil leer with nothing but spite for all creation—a strange light shone in their eyes that burned with fever or were flooded with tears. A horrible grin twisted their drooling mouths. They all had in common: fear, a helpless rage, and foaming saliva at their mouths.

There were women covered all over with hair and clothed in filthy rags, their breasts dangling from under tattered slips. One woman, covered with stiff bristles, led a young man of about thirty, who could have been her husband or her brother; his eyes were wide open and staring, his legs were shrunk and twisted by some disease of the bones; she walked with her breasts bare—one small and withered, eaten away by decay or gnawed by cancer, a black, almost carbonized breast, while the other one, flabby and shriveled, hung down to her belly. Some were skeletons clothed in rags, their heads covered with yellow skin stretched tightly over their skulls, their teeth bared by an atrocious grin; some were old men, bald and toothless, with dog faces. There were young girls with monstrously large and swollen heads attached to tiny, fleshless bodies; there were old hags huge, fat, swollen, with enormous bellies and small shriveled birdlike heads on which the hair stood hard and bristly, like feathers. There were crippled children with apelike faces; some of them dragged themselves on all fours; others limped, leaning on makeshift crutches; still others huddled in small, primitive carts that were pushed along by their companions. They were the "monsters" preserved with a sacred timidity in the inner bosom of the Neapolitan alleys, the objects of religious idolatry as intercessors in that worship of magic that is the secret cult of the people. For the first time in their consecrated existence the war had driven them from their lairs into the sunlight; their silent march toward the caves hewn in the hill was like a procession of sacred idols, like an array of Plutonic deities who, having emerged to the surface because of some subterranean cataclysm, were again seeking shelter within the mysterious bowels of the earth.

Suddenly I saw the god among them. I saw the secret god on whom the worship of the "monsters" centered. I saw the king of that "court of miracles." *It* moved forward slowly, assisted by a mob of horrible dwarfs. I did not know whether the creature was a man or a beast; *It* was hidden from head to foot by a large cloth covering and looked thin and small in stature. Thrown over Its head, as if to shelter *It* from profane eyes, was one of those silken coverlets that in Naples adorn even the poorest beds; it was yellow and very large; the coverlet hung from the shoulders, reached the feet and dragged along the ground as it fluttered in the breeze that blew from the sea. Some of the dwarfs, who formed a circle around *It*, supported *It*, because *It* was blinded by the coverlet and could not walk without assistance. Others with stifled shrieks that sounded like grunts, made way for *It* by shoving the crippled, the lame and the blind who had straggled on the dusty way. With their fingers they quickly cleared a path of pebbles, bricks and plaster so *It* would not stumble. Others grasped the edges of the coverlet so the god would not slip or so the wind, by lifting the coverlet, would not reveal Its horrible secret to profane eyes. Their efforts did not prevent me from catching, beneath an edge lifted by the wind, a glimpse of a leg that seemed to be as hairy as a beast's.

It walked slowly, with Its hands beneath the coverlet outstretched in the attitude of the blind; Its knees seemed burdened and weighted down by a mysterious load *It* carried on Its head. Beneath the coverlet, where the head should have been, was something shapeless and huge that swayed slowly and hung first on one shoulder, and then on the other; what made me shudder was that the monster made no effort to keep the load from dropping. *It* made none of those instinctive gestures that help to balance a large, heavy object on the head. With a chill I thought that the horrible monster, the secret god of Naples could be a man or a woman with an animal's head; a goat's, or a dog's, or judging by its size, most likely a calf's head; or maybe there were two heads. This seemed even nearer to the truth, judging by the strange movements beneath the coverlet, as if both heads moved independently of each other. The lane along which *It* descended was piled with debris and filth; almost every house had been bombed and wrecked. Against that background of ruin and death the god proceeded as if across a desert. *It* had fled from Its secret temple; now *It* was on the way to descend into the bowels of the earth, into the subterranean kingdom of Plutonic Naples. I do not know whether I screamed, or whether I merely drew back with fear; the god surrounded by Its court of dwarfs was approaching me, and Its two monstrous heads were swaying beneath the yellow coverlet. Brought back from my horror by the guttural shouts of the dwarfs who were very near, I turned in search of an escape and found myself at the mouth of a cavern toward which, in a sinister silence broken only by the solitary scream of a child or by a woman's prayer, the consecrated mob of monsters was moving, followed by their terrible god. They walked dragging their feet through the dust and plaster; their arms were held to their breasts, their hooked hands twisted outward, their lips protruding; they were ready to scratch, bite, tear and rend flesh to open for themselves a path into the stinking darkness of the cavern. The silence was charged with wrath and menace.

Driven by that mob of monsters, I entered the cavern; it was a dark and deep grotto, one of those subterranean galleries through which pass the Angevin aqueducts that form a huge unexplored maze underneath Naples. Here and there a shaft of light penetrated through a pit that opened on a street above; some of those pits were mentioned by Boccaccio in the story of Andreuccio da Perugia. In those gloomy dens, in those thousands of caverns cut in the *tufa* had lived for three years this queer, ragged population that had found shelter and safety from the bombs in that subterranean maze. They lived in frightful promiscuity, wallowing in their own excrement, sleeping on bedding brought from the ruined houses, trafficking, trading, celebrating weddings and funerals, going on with their small tasks, their commerce and their sinister activities. As soon as I had taken a few steps through that subterranean city, I turned my head and through the mouth of the cavern I saw the shimmering sea. Thick clouds of smoke and dust were rising above the harbor. The crash of bombs seemed faint in that Plutonic country; the walls of the cavern shook and rivulets of dust cascaded through the cracks in the *tufa*. Instead of weeping, of teeth-grinding or sobs, I was met by a din of shouts, songs and voices hailing and answering above the noise of the crowd. I recognized the age-long, joyous real voice of Naples. I felt as if I were looking on a marketplace, on a square filled with a festive crowd aroused by the tunes of Piedigrotta or by the liturgical chants of a procession. It was the real, the living Naples that had survived three years of bombardment, hunger and plague; it was the Naples of people, of the alleys, of *bassi*, of hovels, of the quarters without light, sun or bread. The electric lights hanging from the vault of the cavern showed many thousands of faces, and the constant motion that kept the crowd on the go produced an illusion of a large square in a crowded quarter of Naples on the night of a great and popular festival.

I had never felt so close to the people—I—who until then had always felt like a stranger in Naples; I had never felt so close to that crowd which until that day had seemed so different and alien. I was covered with dust and sweat, my uniform was torn, my face unshaven, my hands and face greasy and soiled. I had come out of prison only a few hours before and found in that crowd a human warmth, a human affection, a human companionship, distress of the same kind as my own, suffering of the same human kind as my own, but only greater, deeper and perhaps more real and ancient than mine. A suffering rendered sacred by its age, its fatalism, its mysterious nature, compared with which my own suffering was only human, new and without any deep roots in my own age. A suffering bereft of despair and lighted by a great, beautiful hope, compared with which my own poor and small despair was merely a puny feeling that made me feel ashamed.

Bright fires were burning along the walls of the cavern where the *tufa,* cut by the chisel, forms so many rustic niches and where the lateral conduits of the Angevin aqueduct branch off from the main stream of the subterranean rivers that run under the hill. Pots of soup were boiling over the fires. They seemed to me the very community kitchens which Mussolini had forbidden in Naples and which the people, left on their own by the flight of the princes and the wealthy, were organizing with their own means, by their own initiative, in an effort to avoid starvation, by mutual assistance. The smell of potato and bean soup rose from the pots along with the familiar cry *"Doie lire! doie lire! 'na ministra 'e verdura, doie lire! doie lire!*—Two liras! two liras for vegetable soup, two liras, two liras!" Earthenware dishes, cups, tins and containers of all sorts were hoisted by hundreds of hands; they strode over the sea of heads, floated above the crowd and glistened white with the reflection of the electric lights. Through the red glow of the fires came the sucking of lips, the rude, brutal crackling of jaws and the tinkle of plates, miserable pewter and tinware. Now and then the chewing slowed down, the jaws stopped, the shouting and the voices died down, the cries of water vendors and cooks were stifled in their throats. Everybody stood and listened in fearful silence, broken only by the hiss of breathing that replaced the din and clamor of voices. The wave of the bomb crash ran through the cavern with the swish of an ebbing sea, it ran from niche to niche, deep into the gloomy bowels of the hill. The silence was devotional, a pause that came not from fear, but from pity and sorrow. "Those poor things!" somebody near me shouted, thinking of the anguish in the hit houses, of the people buried alive beneath the debris, in the cellars, in the puny shelters of the harbor district. Little by little a song rose from the end of the cavern as crowds of women joined the chanting litanies for the dead; queer, ragged priests, bearded, incredibly filthy, their black cassocks whitened by the plaster dust, blended their voices with the women's choir; they stopped from time to time to bless the crowd and to grant everybody absolution from their sins in a barbarous mixture of Latin and Neapolitan. The crowd shouted the names of their dead, of their relatives who were in danger, of their kinsmen living in the harbor districts hammered by the bombings, of those who were away at sea or at war. The people shouted "Micheee! Rafiliii! Carmiliiii! Guncittiii! Mariii! Gennariii! Pascaaa! Peppiii! Maculatiii!" and they stretched their hands toward the priests with fists closed, as if they were clutching relics of their dead in their fingers—a lock of hair, a piece of cloth or leather, a splinter of bone. For a few minutes the huge crowd wept, dropped on their knees and raised their arms toward Heaven and shouted pleas to the Carmine Madonna—to San Gennaro and to Santa Lucia, while the crashes of the bombs came closer, shook the earth, echoed through the hollow hill and penetrated the foul, gloomy dens with their hot blasts. Then, suddenly, as the explosions became more distant, the melodious cries of cooks and peddlers, of potato fritters and of water, *"Acqua fresca! Acqua fresca!"* broke through the lamentations of women and the deep chanting of priests. Coins tinkled in the alms boxes that filthy lean monks and worn-out nuns shook among the crowds, and here and there laughter was heard, a shrill outburst of laughter, a song, a gay voice, the name of a woman echoing, rebounding and singing through the cavern. The ancient noise of Naples, the loud ancient voice of

Naples rose and was heard again and again, like the voice of the sea.

At that moment a woman was taken with labor pains. She screamed, prayed, moaned and howled like a dog at night. Instantly, a hundred volunteer midwives, wooly-haired grandmothers, their eyes glistening with joy, made their way through the crowd and closed in around the woman in labor, who suddenly sent forth a piercing scream. The midwives fought for the infant and one of them, a fat and shapeless old hag with touseled hair, quicker and more daring than the others, clutched it, fingered it, lifted it high to protect it from the crowd, dried it with her skirt, and washed it by licking it and spitting in its face, just as a priest came up to christen it. "A little water!" he called. Everybody offered bottles, coffeepots and jars. The crowd shouted, "Name him Benedetto! Name him Benvenuto! Name him Gennaro! Gennaro! Gennaro!" These cries, these names faded into the vast subterranean noise, into songs, the laughter and the long melodious cries of cooks and peddlers; they blended like separate parts of one song, of one life, with the neighing of horses that the cabmen had led into the safety of the shelter. The huge cavern seemed like a great square on the night of Piedigrotta, when the noise of the feast is dying down in the city, and the crowd, returning from Fuorigrotta, alights from carriages and lingers in the square to breathe a little fresh air before going to bed and drinks another lemonade, eats another pastry while everywhere people are saying good night and bidding farewells and loud good-bys to godfathers, godmothers, friends and relatives.

Crowds of boys at the entrance to the cavern were already announcing that the danger was over and shouting news about houses that had been hit, about the dead, the wounded, the buried and the damage. The crowd was stirring and getting ready to leave, when from above, from a kind of castle of furniture erected in a deep niche, as though from a high balcony, a tall old lout with a thick black beard raised his arms and towering with his imposing build above the crowd, began to shout in a fierce, terrible, rousing voice: *Ih bone femmene, ih figli 'e bone femmene, ih che bordello! jatevenne! jatevenne! jatavenne!*—Hi, good women, hi, sons of good women, what an uproar! Away! Away! Away!" and he gestured with his hands as if he were driving intruders from his castle. He yawned and rubbed his eyes, not as if he merely had been roused from his bed and slumber, but as if the great crowd of strangers were annoying him, as if it were a threat to his prerogatives, as if it had invaded the subterranean kingdom of which he was king and master.

So complete was the illusion that I was in the neighborhood of Rua Catalana, of Dogana del Sale, of Spezieria Vecchia, near the harbor, that I lifted my eyes to the ceiling of black *tufa* and expected to see Vesuvius looking down from the horizon with its short clay pipe between its teeth, and a pink scarf of clouds around its neck like an old sailor looking out of a window at the sea. Gradually the crowd laughing and chattering, calling out names, as if leaving a show, flowed out of the mouth of the cavern. As the people took the first steps in the open air they stumbled and lifted their eyes in anguish to the dense cloud of dust and smoke enveloping the entire city.

The sky was dull blue and the sea a glistening green. I walked hemmed in by a crowd, climbed toward Toledo, and in the meanwhile looked around in the hope to find a face I knew, a friend who would take me in for the night, until the little steamer that was to take me home arrived in the harbor from Capri. For two days the Capri steamer had avoided the landing at Santa Lucia; nobody knew how much longer I would have to wait before being able to reach home. Little by little, as the sunset approached, the heat became damp and heavy; I seemed to be walking wrapped in a woolen blanket. Here and there the streets were flanked with huge mounds of debris that under the delicious sky of blue silk seemed to me more cruel and funereal than the debris of Warsaw, Belgrade, Kiev, Hamburg and Berlin under their own misty, cold, uneasy skies. A feeling of loneliness froze my heart and I searched around me hoping to recognize a face of a friend among the crowds of ragged people who had a wonderful light of dignity and courage in their eyes, white with hunger, lack of sleep and anguish.

Groups of boys were encamped among the debris of the houses; they had furnished their caves, dug in the mountains of plaster and their miserable huts built between crumbling walls with pitiful furniture, mattresses, straw bottomed chairs, pots and broken crockery of all sorts which they had unearthed from under the piles of stones, beams and twisted iron. The girls busied themselves around the exposed fireplaces and cooked supper in tin pots for the boys, the youngest of whom played naked amid the refuse, thinking only about glass marbles, little colored stones and fragments of mirrors, while the older ones roamed about from morning till night, looking for something to eat, for any kind of work, carrying bags and parcels from one end of town to the other and helping the homeless to drag their belongings to the station or to the docks. They belonged to that wild family of forsaken children, the *besprizornii,* whom I had already seen in Kiev, Moscow, Leningrad and in Nizhnii Novgorod during the years following the civil war and the great famine in Russia. Beneath the debris, in which they had dug their caves and built their miserable huts of tin cans and charred boards, some number of people were buried alive, perhaps, still breathing—beneath the debris on which during three years of war destruction and slaughter, the foundations of a new Naples were being laid—of a more ragged, hungrier and bloodier, but of a purer, more noble and truer Naples. The aristocracy, the wealthy and the powerful had fled from the wrecked city. Only an immense army of ragged people remained, their eyes filled with an age-long, insatiable hope, and of *besprizornii* with hard mouths and brows on which the loneliness of hunger had chiseled lines of awful and mysterious words. I tread on a carpet of splintered glass, piles of plaster, the last wreckage of a terrible havoc, and an age-old hope welled up within me.

Now and again I was stopped by a dismal cry: *"Mo' vene! mo' vene! mo' vene!*—It's coming! It's coming! It's coming!" I saw flocks of boys and dogs backing away with faces turned upward or else fleeing for shelter, while others remained seated on the ground as they looked upward at the unsteady wall of a house that suddenly crumbled raising a huge cloud of dust. The dull crash was followed by joyful shouts; the boys and the dogs again were running amid the debris, repairing the damage which the falling wall had caused to their hovels. As I walked toward Market Square I saw more ruins. Some houses were still blazing. Crowds of ragged men and women tried to put out the fires by various means; some shoveled the debris and threw it on the flames in an attempt to smother them;

some passed from hand to hand pails of sea water which the last links of the human chain drew from the harbor; others dragged beams, pieces of wood and furniture from the debris so they would not feed the flames. Everywhere in town people were running back and forth, helping one another and hauling furniture from the wrecked houses to the entrances of the caves hewn in the *tufa*, while grocery wagons were constantly driven to the places where the people sought shelter and safety. Above the shouting and noise rose the simple, indifferent, melodious cry of the water vendors: "*Acqua fresca!*—Fresh water!"

In the central section of town squads of policemen were covering Mussolini's portraits and the words, "Long live the Duce!" with posters bearing portraits of the King and of Badoglio with the words, "Long live the King! Long live Badoglio!" Other policemen went about writing on walls, with brushes they dipped into pails of black paint, "Long live loyal Naples! Long live royal Naples!" That was all the assistance the new government, following in the footsteps of the old one, gave to the tortured city. Lines of carts traveled along Via Chiaia and the Piazza dei Martiri carrying to the sea the debris that hampered the movements of the German military columns. They dumped them on the rock dike in Caracciolo Street, in the small opening by the Dogali Column. Mixed with the debris were already decomposing arms, heads, fragments of human bodies. The stench was so overwhelming that the people blanched as the carts went by. The cart drivers, livid with lack of sleep, fatigue, fear and disgust—pitiable makeshift undertakers—were mostly draymen from the Vesuvian villages who used the same carts in the mornings to bring vegetables and fruit to the market in the thickly settled quarters.

Everybody was intent on helping others; pale, worn faces roamed among the ruins with bottles and jars full of water or with pots full of soup, distributing their meager sustenance among the poorest, the oldest and the sick who were stretched out amid the wreckage in the shadow of unsteady walls. The streets were studded with cars, trucks, streetcars abandoned on the twisted rails, carriages, and horses that lay dead between the shafts. Clouds of flies were buzzing in the dusty air. A silent crowd that had gathered in the square near the San Carlo Theater, as if just awakened from a deep slumber by livid, cold flashes dazzling their eyes, with fear and amazement imprinted on the faces, lingered before the closed shops and the shutters riddled by fragments of bombs; now and then carts drawn by exhausted, small donkeys and laden with pitiable furniture, appeared in the square and were followed by groups of miserable, ghastly-looking people, who ambled along, dragging their feet through dust and plaster, and looking upward, scrutinized the sky and wailed in a continuous chorus: *"Mo' veneno! mo' veneno! 'e bi'! 'e bi'! 'e bi' 'lloco!*—There they are! there they are! see them! see them! see them down there!"* The monotonous wail made the ecstatic crowd raise their eyes, the cry *"Mo' veneno! 'e bi'! 'e bi'!"* traveled from one group to another, from street to street, but no one moved or fled, as if the now familiar cry, the customary terror and danger no longer frightened anyone now, or as if utter weariness deprived the people of the strength and the will to flee and seek safety. Only when a distant humming of bees from the lofty sky was heard, did the crowd retreat into the courtyards and disappear as if by magic into the caverns. A few old men remained roaming about the deserted streets along with a few boys and a wretched woman dazed by hunger, but even they were grasped by friendly hands and dragged into the shelter by people crawling out of caves hidden under the debris.

Something triumphant hovered over the wrecked houses, the buildings still miraculously untouched; something, the nature of which I was at first unable to grasp: the clearness, the most beautiful, cruel clearness of the Neapolitan sky which, contrasted with the dazzling whiteness of the debris in the summer sunlight, of the piles of chalk-white plaster, of the clean and clear-cut outline of the immaculate walls, seemed black—that dark-blue color of the sky on a moonless, starry night. There were moments when the sky seemed to be made of something hard, like black stone. The city with its white-washed walls and burned-out pyres stretched gloomy and funereal beneath that thick, dark, most cruel and wonderful blueness.

The royal princes, the noblemen, the wealthy, the middle class, the powerful—everybody had fled from Naples; only the poor remained in the city, the countless masses of the poor—only the vast, unexplored, mysterious "Neapolitan continent" remained. I spent the night in the house of a friend on Calascione; it was an old house standing high above the roofs of Chiatamone and the Riviera di Chiaia, and next morning, from the edge of Pizzofalcone, I saw the little Capri steamer moored to the Santa Lucia dock. My heart leaped and I rushed down the hill toward the port.

But as soon as I left Monte di Dio and entered the maze of the Pallonetto, I heard a word whispered all around me, whispered in secret voice and mysterious tones. It came down from the windows and balconies, it emerged from the black caves, the squalid *bassi* and the far end of courtyards and the alleys. At first it seemed to me like a new word that I had never heard before or that had remained forgotten in the depths of my consciousness for no one knows how long. I did not understand its meaning. I was unable to grasp it. To me, who was returning from a four-year journey through war, slaughter, hunger, burned villages, and wrecked towns, it was an incomprehensible word; to my ear it sounded like a word in a foreign tongue.

Suddenly I heard it distinctly, clean and transparent like a piece of glass, as it came out of the door of a *basso*. I went to the threshold and looked inside. It was a poor room, almost completely occupied by a large iron bed and a chest of drawers on which I saw one of those glass bells under which are kept the wax images of the Holy Family. In a corner, a pot was steaming on a lighted stove. An old woman grasping a corner of her skirt in her two hands was poised over the stove as if she were fanning the burning charcoal, but she was motionless; she turned her face toward the door to listen. The raised skirt revealed her yellow, bony shins and her pointed, shiny knees. A cat was curled up on the red silken coverlet on the bed. A baby was asleep on a cot in front of the chest of drawers. Two young women were kneeling on the floor, their hands clasped, their eyes turned upward in an ecstatic attitude of prayer. Between the bed and the wall an old man sat wrapped in a green shawl decorated with red and yellow flowers, his eyes were open and staring, his right hand dangled by his side, his index and little fingers outstretched in an exorcising symbol which resembled an image on an Etruscan sarcophagus. The old man looked at me intently. Suddenly his lips moved and a word came clearly out of his toothless mouth: "'O sangue—The blood!"

I drew back in amazement and fear. The word disgusted me. For four years—a terrible, cruel, disgusting word, the German word: *Blut, Blut, Blut*—had been hitting my ears like the gurgle of water dripping out of a pipe. The Italian word, *sangue* also aroused fear and disgust in me. It nauseated me. But something about that voice, about that intonation, seemed wonderful to me. "*'O sangue!*" sounded gentle on the lips of the old man. The word was wonderfully ancient, and at the same time new. It seemed to me that I heard it for the first time and yet it sounded familiar and indescribably sweet. But the sound of that voice terrified the two young women; they suddenly rose, screamed: "*'O sangue! 'O sangue!,*" rushed through the door, took a few uncertain steps down the alley, and screamed the word as they tore their hair and rent their cheeks with their nails. Then, screaming, "*'O sangue! 'O sangue!*" they ran after a crowd of people who were walking toward Santa Maria Egiziaca.

I, also followed that screaming crowd and near Chiaia bridge we came to Santa Teresella degli Spagnuoli. Down all the alleys that descend like rivulets to Toledo from the high hills, people were running, their faces convulsed by anguish, despair and inexpressible love. From the top of the hill I could see still another rumbling crowd, walking northward along the Toledo, raising a confused noise out of which I could distinguish only one cry, "*'O sangue! 'O sangue!*"

For the first time during the four years of war, for the first time in the course of my cruel journey through slaughter, hunger and devastated towns, I heard the word "blood" spoken with sacred and mysterious reverence. In every part of Europe—in Serbia, Croatia, Romania, Poland, Russia and Finland—that word had spelled hatred, fear, contempt, joy, horror, cruel barbarous complacency and sensuous pleasure; it had always filled me with horror and disgust. To me the word "blood" had become more horrible than blood itself. I was less shocked touching blood, bathing my hands in that poor blood that was shed in every country in Europe, than I was when I heard the word "blood." But in Naples, in commonplace Naples, in the unhappiest, hungriest, most humbled, forsaken and tortured city in Europe, I heard the word "blood" uttered with religious awe, with sacred respect, with a deep feeling of charity, in that high, pure, gentle, innocent tone in which Neapolitan people say: mother, child, Heaven, Madonna, bread, Jesus—with the same innocence, purity and gentle simplicity. Those toothless mouths, those pale, worn lips, cried "*'O sangue! 'O sangue!*" as if it were an appeal, a prayer, a sacred name. Long centuries of hunger and slavery, of robed, canonized, crowned and annointed barbarism, long centuries of want, cholera, corruption and shame had not succeeded in smothering the sacred reverence for blood in that miserable and noble people. Screaming, weeping, stretching their hands to Heaven, the crowd ran toward the Duomo; they invoked blood with stupendous rage. They wept for wasted blood, the blood shed in vain, the soil bathed in blood, the bloody rags, the precious blood of man mingled with the dust of the roads, the clots of blood on the walls of prisons. A pity, a kind of sacred fear was reflected in the feverish eyes of the crowd and in the hands lifted to Heaven and shaken by a violent tremor. "*'O sangue! 'O sangue! 'O sangue!*" For the first time during four years of a ferocious, merciless, cruel war, I heard that word spoken with religious awe, with sacred respect, and I heard it on the lips of a famished multitude—betrayed, forsaken without bread, without homes and without graves. After four long years, once again that word had a divine sound. A sense of hope, rest and peace came over me at the sound of that word, "*'O sangue!*" At last I had reached the end of my long journey, that word was my port, my last station, my platform, my dock, and I could touch once more the earth of men, the country of civilized people.

The sky was clear, the green sea shone on the skyline like a vast meadow. The honey of the sun dripped down the fronts of houses bedecked with clotheslines strung between balconies, down the gutters of roofs, down the ragged edges of gaps cut in the walls by bombs and the wounds gaping in the sides of the houses, and as it did so the sky embroidered a gentle blue design. The northwest wind carried with it a smell and taste of the sea, a youthful sound of waves beating against the rocks, a lonely, mournful call of sailors. The sky flowed like a blue river over that city of ruins full of unburied dead, over the holy city of Europe in which blood was still sacred, over a good and merciful people who still felt respect, shame, love and reverence for the blood of men, over a people for whom the word "blood" was still a word of hope and security. When the crowd reached the closed gates of the Duomo, the people dropped to their knees, begged loudly for the gates to open, and raised the cry "*'O sangue! 'O sangue! 'O sangue!*" that shook the walls of the houses and was full of sacred wrath and merciful rage.

I asked a man beside me what had happened. A rumor had spread through town that a bomb had hit the Duomo and wrecked the crypt in which the two caskets containing the miraculous blood of San Gennaro are preserved. It was only a rumor, but it had spread like a fire through the town and reached the darkest alleys and the deepest caves. Until that moment during the four years of war, it seemed as if not a single drop of blood had been shed. Despite the millions of dead scattered over all of Europe, it seemed as if not a single drop of blood had moistened the earth. But as soon as the news spread that those two precious caskets had been shattered, that those few drops of clotted blood had been lost, it seemed as if the entire world were soaked in blood, as if the veins of humanity were severed to quench the unsatiable earth. Then a priest came out on the steps of the Duomo, raised his arms asking for silence and announced that the precious blood was safe. *'O sangue! 'O sangue! 'O sangue!* The kneeling people wept invoking the blood, and everybody was smiling; tears of joy ran down the faces hollowed by hunger; high hope filled everyone's heart, as if no single drop of blood would ever drip again on the thirsting earth.

To get down to the dock, I had to walk through debris-filled alleys behind Piazza Francese. The stench of unburied corpses polluted the air. Black swarms of flies buzzed between the walls. A thick cloud of smoke rose above the harbor. I was atrociously thirsty, my lips were swollen and black with flies. All the fountains were dry; there was not a drop of water in the entire town. I turned at the Two Lions and went back toward the Mercadante Theater. A dead boy was lying on the sidewalk. He seemed asleep. A halo of flies swarmed around his forehead furrowed with horrible wrinkles. I turned into Medina Street. A house behind the Mercadante statue was ablaze. Boys were chasing each other, playing and screaming in shrill voices. My footsteps aroused swarms of flies that rose buzzing, settled on my face stained with sweat and dust and filled the hollows of my eyes. A fearful stench rose from the piles of debris. The acid smell of the sea was penetrating. At the end of Medina Street I saw a small bar. I ran and stopped panting at the door.

The counter with a marble top strewn with fragments of glass was empty. A fat, flabby man, wearing a cotton undershirt with short sleeves was sitting at an iron table. His hairy, drooping breasts protruded from his undershirt that was glued to his skin with sweat. The man was fanning himself with a folded newspaper, and now and then he wiped his brow with a dirty handkerchief. A cloud of flies wheeled in the air. Thousands and thousands of flies were clinging to the ceiling, the walls and the broken mirrors. On the wall behind the counter black with flies hung portraits of the King and Queen, and the Prince and Princess of Piedmont.

"Can you give me a glass of water?" I asked.

The man looked at me, continued fanning himself and said, "A glass of water?"

"I am terribly thirsty. I can't stand it any longer."

"You are thirsty, and you want a glass of water?"

"Yes," I said. "A glass of water. The thirst is killing me!"

"A glass of water!" said the man raising his eyebrows. "Don't you know that water is rare? There is not a drop of water in Naples. First we shall die of hunger, then we shall die of thirst, and if we still are alive, we shall die of fear. A glass of water, indeed!"

"All right," I said and sat down at another table. "I will wait until the war is over before I have a drink."

"There is nothing to do but be patient," the man said. "Do you know that I have not budged from Naples? For three years I have been waiting here for the end of the war. When bombs are dropping, I close my eyes. I will not budge even if they wreck this house. It is only a matter of patience. We shall see who is more patient: the war or Naples. Do you really want a glass of water? You will find a bottle behind the counter. There should still be a little water in it. The glasses are over there."

"Thanks," I said.

Behind the counter I found a bottle with a little water. The shelves were lined with fragments of glasses. Not a single whole glass was there. I drank out of the bottle, driving away the flies from my face with my hand.

"Damn the flies!" I said.

"Quite so; damn the flies!" the man said fanning himself with the newspaper. "Damn the flies!"

"Why don't you fight the flies in Naples? At home, in northern Italy—in Milan, Turin, Florence, even in Rome—the city governments have organized campaigns against the flies. You never see a fly in our towns."

"There isn't a single fly left in Milan?"

"No, not a one. We have killed them all. It is a preventive measure to avoid epidemics and diseases."

"In Naples we also have struggled against the flies. We have actually waged war against flies. We have been fighting the flies for the past three years."

"Then why are there still so many flies in Naples?"

"Well, you know how it is! The flies have won!"

European Classics

Honoré de Balzac
The Bureaucrats

Heinrich Böll
Absent without Leave
And Never Said a Word
And Where Were You, Adam?
The Bread of Those Early Years
End of a Mission
Irish Journal
Missing Persons and Other Essays
The Safety Net
A Soldier's Legacy
The Stories of Heinrich Böll
The Train Was on Time
Women in a River Landscape

Madeleine Bourdouxhe
La Femme de Gilles

Lydia Chukovskaya
Sofia Petrovna

Grazia Deledda
After the Divorce
Elias Portolu

Yury Dombrovsky
The Keeper of Antiquities

Aleksandr Druzhinin
Polinka Saks • The Story of Aleksei Dmitrich

Venedikt Erofeev
Moscow to the End of the Line

Konstantin Fedin
Cities and Years

Fyodor Vasilievich Gladkov
Cement

I. Grekova
The Ship of Widows

Marek Hlasko
The Eighth Day of the Week

Bohumil Hrabal
Closely Watched Trains

Erich Kästner
Fabian: The Story of a Moralist

Valentine Kataev
Time, Forward!

Ignacy Krasicki
The Adventures of Mr. Nicholas Wisdom

Miroslav Krleza
The Return of Philip Latinowicz

Curzio Malaparte
Kaputt

Karin Michaëlis
The Dangerous Age

Andrey Platonov
The Foundation Pit

Valentin Rasputin
Farewell to Matyora

Alain Robbe-Grillet
Snapshots

Arthur Schnitzler
The Road to the Open

Ludvík Vaculík
The Axe

Vladimir Voinovich
The Life and Extraordinary Adventures of Private Ivan Chonkin
Pretender to the Throne

Stefan Zweig
Beware of Pity